My Thakur

MY THAKUR

Sri Sri Thakur Anukul Chandra:
His Life and Message

Nrusingha Tripathy
and
Akshay Mishra

BLACK EAGLE BOOKS
DUBLIN, USA | BBSR, INDIA

BLACK EAGLE BOOKS

USA address:
7464 Wisdom Lane
Dublin, OH 43016

India address:
E/312, Trident Galaxy, Kalinga Nagar,
Bhubaneswar-751003, Odisha, India

E-mail: info@blackeaglebooks.org
Website: www.blackeaglebooks.org

First International Edition Published by
BLACK EAGLE BOOKS, 2022

MY THAKUR
by **Nrusingha Tripathy and Akshay Mishra**

Copyright © **Nrusingha Tripathy**

All rights reserved. No part of this publication may be reproduced, stored in a retrieval system, or transmitted, in any form or by any means, electronic, mechanical, photocopying, recording or otherwise without the prior permission of the publisher.

Cover & Interior Design: Ezy's Publication

ISBN- 978-1-64560-319-1 (Paperback)

Printed in the United States of America

Charachare vidita tu hi gyanam
Pranamami Saraswati dehi padam

Adored by all,
as knowledge pure;
My obeisance to Saraswati,
Grant me thy feet's shelter.

— Sri Sri Thakur Anukulchandra

Dedicated to
MOST REVERED SRI SRI DADA

Contents

Preface

PART ONE
Life of Sri Sri Thakur Anukul Chandra : At A Glance
The socio-political scenario of Bengal in the last quarter of the 19th century; Sri Sri Thakur's advent; His education and starting of medical practice, The period of Kirtan and Trance, His visit to Puri, Odisha; Initiation of Krishna Prasanna and C. R. Das; Mahatma Gandhi's visit to Hemayetpur Ashram; Physicist Fritjoff Capra's experience of cosmic dance; Registration of Satsang under the Societies Registration Act; Lao-Tzu's forecast on the advent of a sage with specific characteristics which compare well with that of Sri Sri Thakur; Sri Sri Thakur's messages in Bengali and English; Indication about himself; Shifting of Satsang Ashram from Hemayetpur to Deoghar; His first address to workers; Objectives of Satsang; Clue to world peace; Declaration of Sri Sri Borda as his legal heir; Emphasis on mass initiation to save humanity from future calamities; His last sermon; Departure to eternity; Sri Sri Borda's masterpiece poetry remembering the Master; Sri Sri Thakur in the words of his kith and kin. (15-100)

PART TWO
Belongingness to the Environment, Love and Compassion for plants and animals, and service to man (101-112)

Thus Spake Sri Sri Thakur: On His previous birth, His advent in this world, Sri Jagannath Swami, Purshottam Sri Ram & Bhakta Hanuman, Sri Krishna, The Bhagavad Gita, Jesus Christ, Hazrat Mohammad, Episodes from His early life, the Future of Bharat. (113-126)

Sri Sri Thakur's group of prominent devotees: Anantanath, Nafar Chandra, Satish Chandra, Sushil Chandra, Krishna Prasanna, Prafulla Kumar and Pyari Mohan.(127-137)

Some prominent foreign devotees of Sri Sri Thakur: Spencer, Hauserman, Michael, Exman, Padlisak, Bob and Julie.(138-145)

PART THREE

Creation, Stato-dynamic urge, Vibration, Evolution, Brahma, Animate and Inanimate, Being and Becoming of man, Spiritualism, God, Ideal, Sadguru, Prophet, Tapasya, Siddhi, Dharma, etc.(146-186)

Yoga, libido, fixing of libido, Nam and Nami, Raasaleela, Pranayama, Rise of Kundalini, Tantric pursuits, Mayavada.(187-210)

Nietzsche forecasts the advent of the Superman, the Prophet; Bhakti, Jnana and Karma yoga.(211-238)

Education, Elevated intellectualism, Development of Personality, Nurturing the Environment, Nationalism, Tradition and Varnashrama (human, animal and bird), International scenario, militarization and war, auto-excretion, Universal Varnashrama and Language, and the Concept of One-world village (Vasudhaiba Kutumbakam). (239-274)

Women, Women's rights and liberation, Man-woman relationship, Marriage, Conjugal relationship, Chastity, Family, Child care, Divorce, Widow remarriage.(275-293)

Rebirth, Life after death, Communication between the living and the dead, Astral body, Ghost clan, Obsequial rites (Sraddha) and Libation (Tarpan), Memory consciousness, Past-life recollection and regression-Vipassana, Intuition and Clairvoyance.(294-315)

Miracles, Scientific Analysis, and the Cosmos.(316-323)

PART FOUR

Some of His Divine Tidings - Hemayetpur Ashram.(324-381)
Some of His Divine Tidings - Deoghar Ashram.(382-409)

Appendix

Initiation (Diksha) and the practices of Jajan, Jaajan, Istavriti, Swastyayani and Sadachar.(410-437)

Bibliography(438)

PREFACE

In April 2012, I travelled to Guwahati to attend the All India Satsang Ritwik Conference. When I met the Most Revered Acharyadev Sri Sri Dada, he said to me, "Tripathy-da, please write a book on Sri Sri Thakur, okay?" I could only nod in affirmation. The matter rested there.

A long time has since come to pass. I was uncertain about how to begin and the range of subjects to deal with. Sri Sri Thakur's literature is vast; it covers over 80,000 pages in print. I thought if I wrote it in English, it would be convenient for Sri Sri Dada. So I wrote two chapters with the help of the first volume of The Message, such as the origin of creation, Ideal, Providence, Sadguru, God, etc., and handed it to Reverend Binkida in the presence of Sri Sri Dada. Subsequently, when I asked how to proceed further, all Binkida had to say was: "Just go on."

In 2000, due to my personal involvement, and with the permission of Acharyadev Sri Sri Dada, Sri Sri Borda Eye Hospital came up in Bhubaneswar. I retired from government service in 2005, and the idea of upgrading the fledgling institution into a multi-specialty hospital preoccupied me more than ever. In those days, there wasn't even a single multi-specialty hospital worth its name in Bhubaneswar, as is the case now. As a matter of coincidence, Sri Sri Dada graciously donated the land on behalf of the Satsang for construction. Since 2008, Sri Sri Borda Hospital and Community Health Centre has been thriving through many ups and downs.

In 2003, I was implicated in a false case, and the respite came only after thirteen years in 2016. Due to this, I had to visit Chennai 10 to 12 times a year. My efforts to proceed with the book as promised to Sri Sri Dada went into the cold storage. During those days whenever I visited Deoghar whether to attend a Ritwik Conference or for some other reason, I spent all my leisure hours in the Computer Room in the company of Shivanand Prasad (Assistant Secretary and Editor of Satwati, a Hindi monthly journal published by Satsang). His colleague, Akshay Mishra was always on a desktop, next to him. The Hindi translation of some of my Odia articles had been published in that journal. Shivanand-da took utmost interest to publish as many anecdotes about Sri Sri Thakur as he could lay his hands on, in the journal. During our discussions, we thought a compilation of all these anecdotes between covers of a book would attract a wider readership and in close collaboration with Akshay-da I started working on it in the right earnest, beginning with translating the anecdotes first into Odia from Hindi and Bengali. After we were done with our compilation, the idea of incorporating a sketch of Sri Sri Thakur's life for a better understanding of the incidents and anecdotes dawned on us. In July 2019, when I was in Deoghar, Revered Sri Sri Dada was informed about the book by Revered Sri Sri Babaida, and he then blessed us with the name of the book: "Mo Thakur" (My Thakur).

That year, my son, my only child, began to suffer from acute stomach pain. At forty-six, he was already a renowned professor of Maxillofacial Surgery, specializing in Cleft Lip Surgery at the University of Medical Sciences, Bhubaneswar. Since 2000, he had been having serious problems in his bile duct and had miraculously managed without surgery. However, this time around, his pancreas was affected. Despite the best treatment in several superspecialty hospitals in Bhubaneswar and Delhi, he could not be saved. He left us in 2020, leaving behind a wife, a doctor herself, and ten-year-old twin children. To cope with the tragedy, a big blow to our family, we decided to visit the Deoghar Ashram soon afterward. A friend who always ridiculed my involvement with Satsang asked satirically: "Planning to go somewhere?" I replied,

"Yes, to the ashram in Deoghar." He quipped, "For thanksgiving?" What he was hinting at was loud and clear, so I said, "Tell me, should I accuse the Father of losing my son, or should I cling to Him as the only source of consolation?" " Is he your father?" he asked, and I replied, "Not only mine, but the Father of my son, of my father, of my grandson, and the Father of all." With disdain curling his lips, he rose to leave: "Madcap, you're incorrigible."

Clutching the words of consolation of Sri Sri Dada, and of other members of the Thakur family, I came back to Bhubaneswar. While completing the Odia manuscript of "Mo Thakur" we had an inspiration: why not include a glimpse of the Philosophy of Life by Sri Sri Thakur and make the book much more complete? We started work almost immediately. The otherwise horrific arrival of Covid came as a blessing in disguise. We had to stay indoors, and our work progressed well. We also thought this was a good opportunity to incorporate bits and pieces from the works of different philosophers and spiritual masters from around the world while detailing Sri Sri Thakur's views on various subjects. To make the narration precise and accurate, we had to adapt the questionnaire format. Ever ready and receptive throughout, Akshayda worked relentlessly with me. The book was finally published in July 2021. Although this was around the time of the second Covid wave, with severe restrictions on physical movements, we could somehow reach the book to Sri Sri Dada. He blessed the book with his own hands during the first week of August, expressing his elation at the sight of it, and asked for one more copy. His affectionate gesture was our reward for our labour of love, carefully crafted over two years, attained a sense of fulfillment. The book sold well and was reprinted three times in nine months. It was extremely unfortunate because soon afterward, Sri Sri Dada's health began to deteriorate alarmingly; he was admitted to the Mission Hospital, Durgapur, and left us on 16 December 2021. It was a great loss to the world.

The present Acharyadev went through the contents of the Odia book, and kindly expressed his desire for an English translation. We have tried our best to do it well. He had been kind enough to name this English transcreation as "My Thakur" subsequently.

Sri Sri Thakur had cherished only one wish that He should be presented in front of the world just as He is, undistorted. In the Odia book, as well as in this English version, we have taken utmost care to see that His recorded words in various books and compilations in Bengali and English are reproduced almost verbatim. In addition to theoretical discussions, we have tried to mention in short the practice part -Initiation(Diksha), Jajan, Jaajan, Istavriti, Swastyayani and Sadachar.

We always felt the presence of an unknown force inspiring and guiding us, providing us with the appropriate words and references. We pay our humble ovations to Him.

Sri Sri Acharyadev has taken keen interest in the publication of the book and has encouraged us from time to time. Rev Sepaida's kind words have inspired us. Pujaniya Binkida has read some portions of this book with appreciation and helped us in finalising the cover page. We are sincerely grateful to them.

Dr. Bairagi Charan Dwivedy, Principal of a Kendriya Vidyalay in Chhattisgarh has timely translated Part One/1 of this volume to the best of his ability. Surya Prakash Mohapatra, General Manager, WIPRO, Bangalore, has attempted translating Part Three/9. The hymns, verses in Bengali and other languages have been translated to English to our best ability. Abhishek Parija, a youngman aspiring for a career in the film industry has helped in our endeavour. Jeevan Nair has edited the volume. K.K Mohapatra, a very dear friend has been a constant guide from the beginning. We are indebted to them all. Bande Purushottamam.

16.9.2022   Nrusingha Tripathy

Do not die,
nor cause death,
resist death to death.

— Sri Sri Thakur Anukulchandra

PART ONE

1

Life of Sri Sri Thakur Anukul Chandra at a Glance

Sri Sri Thakur once said, "I am not keen on my biography, but it is essential to illustrate my mission and ideology. To the extent that it is authentic, and matter-of-fact, so far so good. The more genuine and realistic, the better."

In deference to Sri Sri Thakur's desire, we have tried to make this biography genuine, precise, and informative. Many facts, situations, and personalities not relevant to His Mission have been ignored.

Sri Sri Thakur Anukul Chandra (born 1888) hailed from Hemayetpur, a tiny hamlet of the Pabna district in East Bengal (now Bangladesh).

Bengal, during the nineteenth century, was a large province of British-occupied India. The western part had a Hindu majority, and the eastern had a moderate Muslim majority. The areas of Madaripur, Vikrampur, and Kishanganj had a Hindu majority, whereas the districts of Pabna, Dhaka, and Mymensingh, had a Muslim majority. Calcutta was the capital of India and later was shifted to Delhi. By 1900, the population of Bengal was around seventy million. There was communal amity, Muslims participated in Durga Puja, and Hindus did likewise in Eid and other Muslim festivals. The British policy of Divide and Rule slowly destroyed their communal unity by poisoning the mind of one community against the other. Viceroy Lord Curzon launched many such anti-India and anti-people policies that were implemented by the British Government. One such foolish step was to divide Bengal (Act of Partition of Bengal, 1905); it was intended to separate the Hindus and Muslims by carving out a region of the Muslim majority. Though the Act was revoked in 1911, the damage had been done.

Historians point out that at the beginning of the nineteenth century, the people of India were so demoralized that they had no confidence in their own culture and civilization. Though India was self-dependent in almost all spheres of life, after its occupation by the British and its exploitation, it was economically crippled. The peasantry, the working class, and the lower middle classes suffered the most.

Bengal was ravaged by famines, one in 1896-97, and the next was the Great Bengal Famine of 1943. During the monsoon every year, low-lying areas of the province would be heavily flooded. The British Government did little to avert such natural calamities; in fact, it ignored them altogether. On top of this, the tyranny of landlords, and the avarice of cunning moneylenders made the lives of people in rural Bengal extremely difficult. Unemployment was more acute in rural Bengal than in its cities.

The English-educated upper middle class, or the so-called elites of society, with their aversion to industry or trade, and preference for white-collar jobs and government service, found their ideal model in the middle class of Europe. The traditional Bengali youth was eager to adopt English culture. During the 20 years from 1885 to 1905, India, and especially Bengal, was in such a devastated state that Lala Lajpat Rai said, "Indians have got stones, instead of bread."

During this period, a current of national awakening called the Renaissance was taking shape in several Asian countries. The aim was a revival of culture and awareness about the greatness of their respective nations. In Bengal, Raja Rammohan Roy (1774-1833) founded the Brahmo Samaj in 1828. He aspired to revolutionize Hinduism against orthodoxy, excessive ritualism, blind faith, child marriage, and Sati (the practice of burning widows on their husband's pyres). Apart from the Brahmo Samaj, the Tattwa Bodhini of Debendranath Tagore and the Sangat Sabha of Keshav Chandra Sen were also aimed at socio-religious reform. Surendra Nath Banerjee tried to build a political movement and propagate it all over the country. Bijoy Krishna Goswami revived Vaishnavism. Sri Ramakrishna Dev experimented by following many religions and swept the world off its feet with the idea that God is One. It was an attempt to bring amity among different sects and communities. Swami Vivekananda started his mission 'To love and serve all' by establishing the Ramakrishna Mission. Syed Ahmed Khan started a movement to remove illiteracy and backwardness among Muslims. In Bombay, Swami Dayanand Saraswati established the Arya Samaj in order to revitalize the Hindus. These movements were not against the British administration. The positive effects of these movements were short-lived, and by the end of the 19th century, the state of the country, including Bengal, was as precarious as before. It is important to mention here that the village of Hemayetpur in Pabna was particularly notorious for crimes like robbery, eve-teasing, rape, and even murder for settling land disputes.

In the midst of such turbulent circumstances in Bengal, Anukul Chandra Chakravarty, later known as Sri Sri Thakur, was born to Shiva Chandra Chakravarty and Manmohini Devi on 14 September 1888. Ramendra Narayan, Shiva Chandra's father-in-law, passed away early. Land-grabbers forcibly occupied his landed properties. There was nobody in his family to retrieve the properties from the hooligans. Shiva Chandra had to take this arduous responsibility upon himself. He could recover only a portion of the grabbed land. Preoccupied thus, he could not take up any other work and the income from the land was the only source of livelihood for the two families. The physical and mental strain impaired his health. Anukul Chandra grew up at a time when his parents were facing acute financial hardship.

Anukul Chandra was extremely devoted to his parents and particularly fond of his mother. She wanted to shape her son for the service of the weak and downtrodden. This is evident from a Bengali quatrain she wrote, elaborating on the significance of his name. Each line in the Bengali verse begins with the syllables present in Sri Sri Thakur's name, 'A-nu-ku-la', in this order:

In English, the name contains six alphabets of Sri Sri Thakur's name. Adopting Manmohini Devi's style, we have tried our best to translate this small poem, in conjunction with the spirit and potency of the Bengali original:

Attend to the shoreless, afflicted and sad
Nourish them with humility
Uttering words of consolation
Keen in heart and soul
Until you ameliorate them
Let it be your aim to help all who suffer.

In her early days, Manmohini Devi had received, in a dream, the *Satnam* from Sri Huzur Maharaj, the second Guru of the Radhasoami spiritual order. Later on, she was formally initiated in person. His mother's devotion and faith in Sri Huzur Maharaj influenced Anukul Chandra from childhood to such an extent that he also regarded him as his Guru.

The first guru of the Radhasoami order was Sri Shiv Dayal Singhji Maharaj (1818-1878), later known as Swamiji Maharaj. He hailed from Agra and was married to Narayani Devi, later called Radhaji. He taught everyone the path of devotion, *Surat Shabd Yoga* by which a person can follow the sound (Shabd) that emanated from the Supreme Being at various levels of consciousness. By following it, a practitioner can reach the point of its origin, the abode of eternal peace and the ultimate. He had a number of disciples. Shaligram Singh, later known as Huzur Maharaj, was the most prominent.

Sri Huzur Maharaj (1829) was well-educated in Persian and English. He retired as the first Indian Postmaster-General in the north-western provinces, and succeeded Swamiji Maharaj as the second Guru of the Agra Radhasoami order and remained so until his death in 1898. He was succeeded by Pt. Brahma Shankar Mishra, a Bengali Brahmin, who worked as a professor at the Bareilly College, and in the Indian Postal department. He was reverentially known as Sri Maharaj Saheb (1861-1907). He introduced a new system of administration by establishing the Radhasoami Trust and initiated thousands of people into the Radhasoami faith. Sri Sarkar Saheb (1817-1913) was the fourth Guru of the Order, followed by Sahebji Maharaj (1913-1937), and so on.

The Radhasoami spiritual Order believed that Creation consisted of three descending spheres: pure spiritual, spiritual-material, and material-spiritual. The Supreme Being dwells in the first sphere, and Man in the last. Man can find his way to higher levels through his love for Sadguru, who is endowed with the qualities of the Supreme Being. The initiate has to follow the techniques and procedures as enunciated by the Paramguru of the time. Radhasoami taught its disciples a form of *Grihastha Ashram*, a spiritual path for householders, and discouraged people from leaving their families for spiritual ends. They disliked the idea of sadhus begging from door to door and asked them to settle down in Satsang centres, in order to proceed in the path of their *sadhana*. *(Socio-religious Reform Movements in British India)*

It is reported that Sri Maharaj Saheb had once told one of his devotees, "The Santh-Sadguru of the coming age has already taken birth in a Brahmin family, and is now young. When he wills, he shall reveal himself." When Sri Maharaj Saheb breathed his last in October 1907, Thakur Anukul Chandra had turned 19.

Due to the persistent bad health of his father for six years, the family income dwindled, and they were forced to live on practically a hand-to-mouth existence. During a discussion at a later period, Sri Sri Thakur honestly narrated the abject poverty of his early family days. "In those days, our family's financial condition was precarious. Sri Huzur Maharaj would send money to us at times; He used to call my mother Sister Manmohini." Biographers mention this incident:

One day, there was not even a single paisa in the house. Mother Manmohini Devi was grappling with grief, wondering what to do. How to manage the expenses of an ailing husband and such a large family? Reading her mind, Anukul Chandra approached her with a brave face, "Ma, why do you worry? Prepare puffed rice, I will sell it in the market. You will see how much money we shall get!" When he was six, he walked alone for over five kilometres, crossing a rivulet to Pabna town to fetch medicines for his ailing father.

Such incidents of loving concern and care towards his parents were many.

We come to know through his biographers that he had a post-mature birth in the twelfth month. A saint who came to the Chakravarty family saw the newborn and was overwhelmed with joy. He predicted he would go on to become Superman and that countless people would follow him. Sri Sri Thakur once said that he was aware of *Satnam*, even in his mother's womb. In due time, on the instructions of Sri Sarkar Saheb, his mother got him initiated.

In primary school, his class teacher once related an English maxim to the students and told them to memorize it, and practice it in their lives. The maxim was: "Do unto others as you wish to be done to you." Anukul Chandra was greatly influenced by this maxim and applied it even to the smallest acts of his life. He always did good for others, without expectation of any return whatsoever. He never talked about it and even refused any appreciation for it. He learned from an incident that feelings are created after the occurrence of the incident. The incident goes like this:

"One day, I climbed up a date palm tree to catch the tiny birds on its branches. Instead, I put my hands on a big, black snake. I twisted its body and put it back in the nest, slowly climbed down, and ran away in fear. After running for a while, my limbs become stiff, making movement difficult. Before this, I had never felt fear; now, after this incident, I saw a snake again by the roadside raising its hood. I jumped over it, and ran for some distance; I made an observation about my feelings. Fear only struck me after I had come down from the tree, and jumped over the snake. Due to several such incidents, I attained the perception that feelings only surface after the occurrence of an event. Therefore, I give so much emphasis on action. If we coordinate our wishes and our thoughts, we can act upon them. We mould ourselves to become better human beings. Needless to mention, our birth factor is the basis for the extent to which we can carry out necessary actions."

On another occasion, while telling his disciples how to overcome weakness, he shared a childhood experience as follows:

"I had a big weakness for rasgullas in my childhood. My mother could not afford any pocket money, so I bought it on credit. In time, the credit grew. One day, the shopkeeper warned me: 'You are from a good family; settle the backlog first and then come to eat rasgullas here. if you don't do so, I know how to collect.' When the shopkeeper cautioned me in front of other customers, I felt insulted, but my desire for rasgullas did not recede. The following day, when I headed towards the shop, there emerged a feeble objection within me, 'Don't go there.' I stood still, a force was dragging me towards the sweet shop, and another was prohibiting me from proceeding. It was beyond my control. As a last resort, I entered a pigeon-pea field, caught hold of a plant, and lay there for a while. There were terrible convulsions in me. A compromising voice from within was goading me, 'Never mind. The credit will be settled somehow, but why should you stop eating sweets? It's good for your health.' Another voice would protest and restrain me from going to the sweet shop. This duel, the push and pull, went on for about an hour. I eventually felt my drive to eat rasgullas had weakened, so I returned home. The next day, at that same time, my mother beat me badly and confined me to the house. The next day, after, at the same time, I picked up a quarrel with my friend, Hemant Chaudhury, for no reason, and avoided my rasgulla trip again. Ultimately, I realised that when a particular time arrived, my desire for devouring rasgullas grew manifold, so it is better to engage myself in other activities then. As the days passed by, I was successfully able to control my weakness for rasgullas, and did so continuously for the next three years. I made it a point to never look at the sweet shop again. Of course, in due time I was able to pay my dues to the shopkeeper.

Anukul Chandra's matriculation exams were due. His mother, Manmohini, managed somehow to arrange for the examination fees. While going to deposit it, he saw a classmate weeping below a tree in the school compound. He knew the poverty of his family and was deeply moved to see him in such a state. He held his hand out lovingly and said, "Why am I your friend? Come along. I will deposit your fees." He deposited the money in his friend's name. He came home with a complacent heart and was punished with a severe scolding for his stupidity. As his family could not arrange money again for the fees, he lost his chance to appear for the exam that year.

His parents' dream to send him to the National Medical School of Calcutta was shattered. What would he do now? A family acquaintance suggested approaching the Medical School authorities and appraising them of the circumstances for his failure to write the exam. With a letter of recommendation from a person well-known to the school authorities, Anukul Chandra met them. He could convince them to conduct a special entrance examination equivalent to matriculation, and admit him based on his performance. This was an event in the annals of the medical school to admit someone without a Matriculation certificate. It became a legend.

Anukul Chandra's life as a medical student in Calcutta began, but his family was not financially stable enough to send him his monthly expenses regularly. In his affluent days, Shiva Chandra had lent some money to an acquaintance, who ran a coal depot in Calcutta. He agreed to give Anukul Chandra a place to stay in his depot and ten rupees for his monthly expenses. It was an adjustment towards repayment of the loan. The amount was meagre, and often irregular. As a result, there was no money for Anukul Chandra to buy books, or even purchase soap to wash his clothes. He had to walk a distance of 12 kilometres to college every day. He had somehow arranged to have his meals in a small hotel on credit. However, after a few months, the hotelier refused to oblige him any further as the credit had piled up. Sri Sri Thakur, while remembering those awful days, said, "It was such a difficult time; I was living with the porters of the coal depot. When I came out on the road, I looked terrible as if someone had come out of a train engine. A friend commented, 'Why are you always so dirty?' I smiled at his insulting remark. When I was reading my lessons under the streetlight, it also became my sleeping spot. Luckily, no vehicle ran over me! For several days, I slept on newspapers on the Sealdah Railway station platform. In winter, I would just use another newspaper to cover myself. I clearly remember the newspapers were either called *Basumati* or *The Hitavadi*, or something similar. As I couldn't go to the hotel, I filled my stomach with water from the roadside municipality hand pump. I did this for two days. On the third day, it was unbearable, I lost consciousness. I narrated my sordid story to a fifth-year student in Medical school. He pitied me and gave me some money. I rushed to buy a sodium bicarbonate tablet to soothe the pain in my famished stomach. I went to Naihati and established a rapport with someone in the Lahiri Company. I did not know what came over him; he presented me with a book on Homoeopathy. Within a few days, I read the whole book and started treating the porters of the coal depot. Thus, my practice started with Homoeopathy. I could manage my needs with the fees and even save a little with which I helped out my porter patients."

One day, a few wicked classmates with the ostensible proposal of going for a stroll took him to a prostitute's house. There, a woman with an enticing outfit and seductive eyes stood before Anukul Chandra. He was aghast and said with tearful eyes, "Mother, what sort of appearance is this? You are my mother! How could you come in front of me in this attire?" Hearing herself affectionately addressed as mother, she began weeping and fell at Anukul Chandra's feet, 'Forgive me. Forgive me.' Later, he heard that the poor lady had donated all her property to some religious institutions and proceeded to Vrindavan.

While at medical school, Anukul Chandra married Sorashibala Devi on 13 August 1906. Soon, she took over the reins of the family and guided it through all the vicissitudes of life. Many years later, when Anukul Chandra came to be known as Sri Sri Thakur with a considerable number of followers, he observed, "If your Thakur had come in a feminine form, she would have shared a resemblance with your Borma, in her appearance, character, and way of life." She was reverentially called Sri Sri Borma by the devotees.

One day, Anukul Chandra went to the Kali temple at Dakshineswar. He was hungry and standing in front of Mother Kali's idol, he prayed for something to eat, but nothing came forth. He came out of the temple despondent and upset, and went to the adjacent Panchavati (tree garden), in the shade of a tree, and dozed off. As if in a dream, he felt that Mother Kali was near him with sweets and water. He complained, "Why didn't you give me food when I asked you? I won't eat it now." The Mother pleaded, "How can I give you the things you want in public, my darling? Take it now." She fed Anukul Chandra and a sudden wave of happiness rushed through him. Was it a dream or real? Sri Sri Thakur said later, that he was full and the taste was memorable.

In time, Anukul Chandra completed the medical course and returned to Hemayetpur to practice both Allopathy and Homoeopathy. He successfully cured many chronic patients with minimum medicines. Gradually, he gained money and fame. Seeing a patient from afar, he could diagnose and prescribe the required medicines. He attributed this quality to the repetition of the Holy Name.

Once, a Vaishnav saint came to Hemayetpur. Anukul Chandra told him how he prayed, "Oh Father the Supreme, thou art my father, I am your son, and I am exalted by your power. No weakness can ever touch me." The saint bit his tongue in disapproval, "No, no, you should never pray like that; it amounts to arrogance. You should be meek before God, and pray thus: 'O Lord! I am low and feeble, helpless and impious, I am a sinner, be merciful to me, prevent me from sin.' The Lord will be pleased by your humility." Anukul Chandra prayed as advised. Soon, he was overpowered by a sense of diffidence and inferiority, he looked small in his own eyes. He felt shrunk and suffocated from within, he could no longer tolerate it. One night, he ran to the desolate river bank of the Padma, looked at the sky, and cried out aloud, "O Father the Supreme, I am thy son, spotless and pious. I am not a sinner. I am ever evolving in thy blazing might. I surrender to thee. Accept me, O my loving Father." He felt relieved of the burden of inferiority.

Such an affirmation finds resonance in the booklet, *Satyanusaran* written by Thakur himself, 'Say not you are timid, say not you are evil-minded! Look towards the Father! Speak fervently, 'Oh, I am your son. Within me, there is no more dullness, no more weakness.'

Contextually, we must speak a little bit here about '*Satyanusaran*' (The Pursuit of Truth). It is a small booklet of 90 pages. Atul Chandra Bhattacharyya was one of the closest devotees of Sri Sri Thakur Anukul Chandra, the Supreme Love. He was going to Bajitpur Ghat steam station, far from Pabna, to join as station master. On the eve of impending painful separation from his beloved, he felt extremely distressed and prayed with tears of love that Thakur, with his own hands, wrote messages to guide him, and keep him ever-inspired with 'divine thought current.' This was during the Bengali year 1316 (1910) when Thakur was only 22 years old. Eventually, one night, in a spontaneous outpouring, Sri Sri Thakur wrote unfolding everlasting life and light. The prayer of the devotee has ushered into the world, the benign flow of the celestial stream that would enliven him along with every other human soul through the ages. *(excerpts from the Preface, 13th edition, 2015).*

A few messages from the *Satyanusaran:*

Oh, you who devotees are with hope for name and riches, don't make me your Lord and Master. Beware! If mastery within awakens not, Master Centre—none you have, and deceiving you shall be deceived.

First of all, we must wage war on weakness. We must be bold and brave, for weakness is sin incarnate! Drive it away at once— this depressing, blood-sucking vampire! Say you are bold, the offspring of Might, believe you are a son of Father, the Supreme! Before all else, be daring, be sincere, then it is clear you have the right to enter the kingdom of heaven.

Contraction is dejection. Expansion is a delight. There is a lack of happiness in that which brings weakness and fear in the heart, and that is grief.

Desire unfulfiled is misery. Don't expect anything. Be prepared for every situation. What can grief do to you?

Years passed by. Thakur's joy and love for life grew, and everyone in his presence felt enlightened. He would intimately mingle among thieves and drunkards, he made sure that his touch of love would reform them, and help them take to new ways of life. It was immaterial whether they were drug addicts, prostitutes, lechers, or living in filth and degradation, Thakur's conviction and sincerity worked miracles. People would bow at his feet, and call him Lord, but he would laugh in his quintessential childlike manner, and start talking about other things.

In those days, very few houses in villages had service latrines in their backyard. Most people went to the village pond, or to a nearby riverbed to ease themselves and bathe, morning and evening. As the Padma River was merely a stone's throw away from Hemayetpur, most men and women used to go there. A few young ruffians would misbehave and abuse the young women defecating behind the hedges, or while bathing. These ruffians wielded a lot of influence, the villagers were afraid of them. They tolerated them meekly. Over time, Doctor Anukul Chandra came to know about this undesired state of affairs. He frantically searched for a strategy to stop this menace. He discussed it with some of his friends and village elders. They suggested a discussion with the ruffians, but Anukul Chandra was not convinced. Unless the erring youths were engaged in any constructive work, mere discussion and advice would fall on deaf ears. He thought *kirtan* (group dancing and singing devotional songs with music) was the only way to distract them from evil. He composed lyrics and music, formed different youth *kirtan* groups, and organized *kirtans* every day. In this uncommon reformative movement, several of his earnest followers, Anantanath Roy, Kishori Mohan Das, Satish Chandra Goswami, Nafar Chandra Ghosh, and many others participated. The fever of *kirtan* spread to other towns such as Kushtia, Khoksa, Faridpur, Jessore, etc. His medical practice gradually dwindled. He looked more handsome and his eyes shone with an elixir of divinity. Sushil Chandra Basu, a sincere devotee and Sri Sri Thakur's biographer, has given a vivid in-person account of Anukul Chandra during kirtans:

"It was not conventional *kirtan* as we commonly understand, with mridangam and small cymbals. Two or three big drums would roar, many conches would excite the atmosphere, and big cymbals would accompany the rhythm of the drums. The participants danced in elation, repeating a few lines from a devotional song. When the kirtan is at its peak, Anukul Chandra would emerge, dancing with his hands in the air. Now the group was more stimulated and infused with energy. The dancing group would move slowly along the main village path. It was so captivating that cows grazing nearby would start to moo, and two or three stray dogs would rise, and follow the group for some time. Many men would come out of their houses, and join for some time. The ladies would come to their house verandas, and start ululating. I have heard Mahaprabhu Sri Chaitanya was also conducting *kirtans* with a similar force and exaltation. Invariably, during this time Sri Sri Thakur's face would be radiating with an exceptional glow. While dancing, Sri Sri Thakur would lose consciousness, and abruptly drop to the ground as if lifeless, with only his right toe shivering. In this condition, if somebody touched him, he would shout in unbearable pain. One day, he remained in this condition for about 40 minutes. On regaining his senses, he would yearn for water, and Anant Maharaj would fetch him some water in a copper bowl. I have heard that Sri Ramakrishna Paramhansa, while descending from the state of trance to normalcy, would clamour for water or tobacco, a mundane desire to come back to the normal plane.

"The episode of Lord Krishna in the *Mahabharata* comes to my mind. Lord Krishna uttered the *Gita* when He was totally anointed with the Supreme Father during the Kurukshetra war. After the war was over, when Arjuna asked Him to narrate the *Gita* once again, Sri Krishna said, "Whatever I told you in a state of trance, I cannot repeat it again." Nonetheless, the brief gist of the *Gita* He explained to Arjuna and thereafter it is known as the *Anugeeta*."

"I once managed to ask Sri Sri Thakur on a chance occasion, 'Please clarify, when you are at the peak of *kirtan*, and your body loses total consciousness in a state of trance, how you utter so many things, is it the final stage of sadhana, and all the utterances sacrosanct?; Sri Sri Thakur answered, 'I don't really know how I slip into that condition of losing consciousness. Whatever I have uttered in that state, I do not have any knowledge. I cannot own them. I only take responsibility for things I say in my conscious state.'

"I then asked, 'Did you ever practice your spiritual sadhana in solitude?' He said, 'No, I did not.' This sadhana was innately present within him. From the time of his birth, the incessant repetition of the Holy Name was a spontaneous and inseparable part of him. He thought every other individual was also endowed with such power. When he grew older, he realised his misconceptions. He said that from childhood, Mother Kali, Lord Krishna, and many other gods and goddesses would appear before him in their illuminated forms, and talk to him. Many times, the effulgence of a glorious light would manifest, and the uninterrupted supernatural sound (*Anahata Naada*) would resound in the back of his ears, which would make him lose his senses. At times, due to continuous repetition of the Holy Name, his body temperature would rise to such an extent that when someone sprinkled water on his face, it would evaporate at once. Such events were so otherworldly and rare that an ordinary person would not believe any of them unless he saw it for himself.

"Listening to all such unusual experiences which have occurred ever since his childhood, I was taken aback, and could not utter a word. After taking a moment for myself, I whispered in the silence, 'It is becoming difficult for me to believe your words, and I must express them to you.' The early part of Sri Chaitanya's life had no indication of any future in divine glory. He went to Gayadham to perform his father's post-death rites, and from there the sojourn of spiritual revelation began. Lord Buddha renounced his home at the age of 29 and went into austerities and deep meditation for a long period to realise the Supreme knowledge. The details of the life of Jesus Christ between the ages of 12 to 30 are unknown.

Some people say, he came to India for sadhana during this period, and thereafter his divine life started. The early part of Hazrat Rasul's life has no extraordinary indications about his subsequent divinity. In our time, Sri Ramakrishna Paramahansa did not attend his studies at the school, his parents were unhappy, and he had to leave home to join as a temple priest at Dakshineswar; it was there he became famous for his spiritual attainment. But you say that you have been doing the repetition of the Holy Name, since the time you have been in your mother's womb. Such repetition was so innate, and natural that the Holy Name did not leave you at any time. Due to your inborn knowledge, you could get a glance at illuminated supernatural forms, and you could communicate with them. I fail to understand how all this happened to you without any known rigorous spiritual practice?"

Sri Sri Thakur replied, "I never considered myself as any incarnation or some avatar. There is no comparison between those great men and a foolish, insignificant man like me. I am what I am. Whatever has happened to me, I have told you the truth. If my life experience does not coincide with that of others, what can I do about it?" *(Manas Tirtha Parikrama)*

It has been mentioned in several Bengali biographies that when his consciousness ascended to a higher plane, he felt that the whole of Creation was full of superconsciousness (Brahma). While eating, he would get up halfway and say, "I am Brahma, this food is also Brahma, all are one. How can I eat it?" As mentioned earlier, while dancing in kirtans with ecstasy he would fall unconscious and make various yogic postures; his body, hands, and legs would shrink and appear lifeless, with only the right toe shivering uncontrollably. He would remain in this state for hours together and would talk in a way that nobody can understand. After several days of remaining in a trance, a devotee could decipher the important messages that were being uttered. Those of the last 72 days of his trance would be recorded by devotees as far as possible. All have been compiled in the *Punya Punthi* (the Holy Book). Later, when the devotees wanted clarifications about what he had said, he would reply, "At that time, I was not in a conscious state, so don't ask me about it."

Nonetheless, below are some lessons from his trance-induced maxims:

Mere trust in God cannot give eternal throne.

The sound of your call must reach Me, because I am sound. Be   quick to get rid of these matters of the world!

At first, shake your heart, then you will shake the world. The world will shake then!

Yes, you perhaps absent yourselves from the world, and the world absences itself from you, (both) are equal.

Yes, when the mind is warm, external cold is insufficient to cool the body.

You, mind the master of all deities. Check your mind and move your mind all day towards God.

You say, fire burns and water can cool everything, (and tell me) it is supernatural.

Trust his name. He will give you everything.

Trust, I am not alone for this world. World is me—all these I, all these creatures, all the matters, the world—this I. (12)

The era of kirtans went for a period of five years, from 1914 to 1919. Doctor Anukul Chandra gave up his medical practice and immersed himself in kirtan. When income dwindled, his mother found it difficult to manage the family. She could not understand his obsession with kirtans. The Radha Soami spiritual order did not give much importance to kirtans.

Sushil Chandra Basu gives an account of how Sri Sri Thakur's father did not appreciate his son giving up the lucrative medical practice to organize kirtan groups"

"One day after lunch, while I was coming out of Thakur's residence, his father Shiva Chandra called me to his room for a chat. He asked me what vegetables were used in the curry, and if

I liked them. He also inquired if my stay was comfortable in their house. I replied, there had been no problems whatsoever; my stay here has been more comfortable than in my own house.

Now after a little bit of caressing, he came to the point and said: 'You all come from good families, hence you won't really talk about the inconveniences in food and stay you face here. I tell Anukul, so many important people are visiting your house; does it happen to anyone else in this village? It is your sheer luck. I tell him, you continue your medical practice, earn good money, and treat those who come to you. But look, how he has left all of that and is running after the mad rush of kirtans. What can kirtan really give him? Where are the means to take care of others through it? To me, service to man is the essence of religion.'

"He looked straight at my face, and asked point blank: What greatness do you find in him that you keep lying around here in spite of all odds? As if God didn't find any other place in this world, and arrived at Shiva Chakravarty's house! His mother (Manmohini Devi) also supports him. Had there been even an ounce of wisdom left in her, we would not have been in this state of affairs."

I humbly replied, "To you, Anukul Chandra is merely your son, it is quite natural for you to feel like this; but think about it, Sir, unless your son has some special qualities, why would people from far and near rush to flock around him? God is there in every being, that is right, but if we find divine attributes in a man amongst us, we call him God. This is why people call your son a God. What is wrong with it? Similarly, Sri Krishna came into Mother Devaki's lap, and Mother Sachi gave birth to Sri Chaitanya, and through Mother Chandramani came Sri Ramakrishna Paramhansa. If in your house, God has arrived in the same manner, what is so unusual about it?" (*Manas Tirtha Parikrama*)

From the beginning, Sri Sri Thakur was averse to charging fees from his patients. He was never willing to go for any salaried job. Once Sri Sri Thakur described, "Generally, people apply for jobs, so even I one day submitted an application to Sealdah Thakur Estate for the position of a doctor. I had not expected any intimation, but after some days came the cryptic appointment letter: salary Rs. 50 per month, free quarters, and private practice allowed. I had a reeling sensation in my head: If by any chance, my father came to know about it, I was done for. I tore it up at once, and threw it away, only then was I able to breathe."

Anukul Chandra had the least inclination for self-publicity and self-propaganda, rather, he preferred to stay in the background, and encourage people along the path of life and growth. Thakur Haranath, hailing from Sonamukhi, Bankura, was a realised saint. Due to his other-worldliness, people called him mad, but Sri Sri Thakur liked him very much. Though he composed the hymns for kirtans, he attributed them to Thakur Haranath. He also sent some of his disciples to him in order to learn. Once, Thakur Haranath confided in Kishori Mohan, a close childhood friend of Anukul Chandra, "Look, you will receive all that you want for your spiritual development from him who has sent you here, be certain, he is the Sadguru, soon he shall manifest himself, and will be worshipped all around." Thakur Haranath's remarks strengthened the belief of Anukul Chandra's followers in his divine powers. Gradually, they started calling him Thakur Anukul Chandra. He was not very happy about it. However, when people insisted, he conceded, and said, "In Bengal, a Brahmin cook is also addressed as *Thakur*."

Anukul Chandra's kirtans attracted many people. They came in large numbers and were initiated into Sri Sri Thakur's Faith. Satish Chandra Goswami, a descendant of Advaita Acharya, a staunch follower of Sri Chaitanya, was initiated into the spiritual discipline of Sri Sri Thakur. Initially, mother Manmohini Devi, Satish Chandra Goswami, and Anant Maharaj (a friend-turned-devotee) were assigned the power and responsibility to initiate. More people were initiated in Hemayetpur and adjacent areas. The followers of Sri Goswami, about 3,000, were also re-initiated into Thakur's Faith. Subsequently, Trailokyanath Chakravarty went to Burma (now Myanmar), and initiated a large number of people there.

Sri Sri Thakur once said that the *Satnaam* was the primordial name (*Adinaam*). It is the primary source of Creation, and sustainer of existence. Invisible cosmic rays are received by our brain, and nourish every part of our body; as a result, we are active and agile. This is our life force. The rhythmic repetition of *Satnaam* inwardly with concentration is known as *Ajapa Japa*. It consolidates the cosmic energy in our brains. When somebody is suffering from a disease, if the *Ajapa Japa* is done by holding onto him, cosmic energy is transmitted to his body, improving the body's overall metabolism. Experiments were done to use this technique to cure patients in the last stages of chronic diseases. The name of this medical research centre based in Kushtia was Life Research Society.

Apart from Hemayetpur, the adjacent town of Kushtia was vibrant with spiritual activity on the directions of Sri Sri Thakur. He inspired his followers in Kushtia town to organize celebrations on birthdays of various divine incarnations and spiritual leaders like Sri Ram, Sri Krishna, Sri Chaitanya, Sri Ramakrishna, Lord Jesus, Hazrat Muhammad, etc. The objective was to build a congregation of followers from different faiths and sects to bring about communal harmony. These celebrations were successfully organized by the Satsangis of Kushtia. It is natural that service to others expands one's heart; so volunteers would escort guests with respect, wash their feet, and feed them with care and affection. Discussions and meetings were held by exponents of various religions, where they talked about the universal love of their Masters.

Many of Thakur's disciples decided to celebrate the birthday of their Master in a similar manner. As Sri Sri Thakur was born in September, the dates of the function were fixed for 14 and 15 September 1918. They wanted to declare this as *Advent Day of the World Teacher*. Large-scale preparations started a few months earlier. It was decided to send invitations to various spiritual and religious organizations in Bengal. The gathering was estimated to host around 50,000 people. A list of eminent persons who would address the function was prepared. Arrangements for their stay were made. Residents were requested to spare one or two rooms of their houses for the purpose. Tents were to be erected a day before the celebration. A vast vacant land adjacent to Kushtia Railway Station was chosen as the venue. Rails were laid in a large portion of the ground for the movement of food-carrying trolleys, facilitating smooth distribution. Dynamos and generators were booked in advance from Calcutta to keep the whole area lit. Invitation cards, pamphlets, and posters were sent to various places.

The date of the celebration was approaching, there were only a few days left. Suddenly, it struck the organizers, "Aah! we are doing everything on our own, but Sri Sri Thakur has not been intimated about anything so far!" They probably thought that intimation was merely a formality and there was no reason why Thakur would refuse. After all, the purpose of this function was to establish the Guru as a world teacher. A group was dispatched to Hemayetpur to inform Sri Sri Thakur about the celebrations. He refused to attend and asked, "Have I ever told you that I am an incarnation? Why should there be such propaganda? How does it benefit the people to know if I am a Prophet or not?" The group was stunned and miserable. All their persuasion was turned down affectionately. When they left Sri Sri Thakur's presence, one of them suggested, "Let's fall at the feet of Mother Manmohini Devi, and appeal to her kindness; if she asks Sri Sri Thakur to come, he simply cannot refuse." The plan worked. Sri Sri Thakur with Manmohini Devi reached the Kushtia steamer station the previous night. There was a huge gathering of people near the bank of the Padma. Descending from the steamer, Sri Sri Thakur at once prostrated before the huge gathering. This gesture averted a probable stampede, as people were struggling with each other to go near him and pay their obeisance. With his mother, he then came to the venue of the function and went around the whole area once. He eventually left and did not come back again. Some of the guests met Thakur where he was staying. Due to incessant rains, the celebrations turned into a fiasco, and from that year on, such programs were not held in Kushtia.

Sushil Chandra Basu mentions in Sri Sri Thakur's biography that a few of those organizers, namely, Biru Roy, Aswini Kumar Biswas and others were of the view that Sri Sri Thakur, along with his staunch devotees, should move from place to place so that his message can spread faster among the masses. What is the use of sitting here in Hemayetpur? Sri Sri Thakur turned down the proposal. They alleged that Thakur would send his followers from one place to the other to propagate his message, but he would relax in his mother's lap! Sri Sri Thakur told them, "You have accepted me as your master, identifying some superiority in me." Hence, it is clear that I know things better than you. I am your guide, and you are to be guided. I know what is to be done and when."

Narrator: Sri Sri Thakur once remarked: "A Sufi Guru was praying to the Almighty, 'O, Supreme Father! Provide me with an articulator', and thereafter came Jalal-ud-Din Rumi, who went on to put forth all about his mentor before the public. I had found such a soul in Das-da (C. R. Das), but he died prematurely, and I am yet to find another person who can match his abilities. To undertake any monumental project, we need competent people. Now those who are with me do their best, but it is often not enough. One has to be committed by sacrificing his ego and whims, tolerating criticism and humiliation, and maintaining his cool to sustain himself against all odds; only then will he acquire the ability to shoulder and tackle the work of the Supreme Father. It is not a trivial job, one needs more than luck. His work needs pure souls."

As a result of the oppressive policies of the British, with economic discontentment and large-scale unemployment, the spirit of nationalism awakened among the masses. Though the All India National Congress was established as early as 1885, its aim was to only find decent representation for Indians in government service and recommend other administrative changes for better governance. It was only in 1906 that the Congress changed its goal with the demand for *Swaraj* (independence). The leaders of the Congress were completely influenced by English education and culture. Some of them did not share the view of the National Congress that *Swaraj* could be obtained through non-violent methods, hence they took to militant nationalism. They were called nationalist revolutionaries. Bengal was the epicentre of these revolutionary movements. A newspaper called *Jugantar* was published to preach revolution to the masses. It was founded by Barindranath Ghosh (Sri Aurobindo's younger brother), and Bhupendranath Dutta (Swami Vivekananda's younger brother) among others. Other such revolutionary publications included *Sandhya* and *Navashakti*. A revolutionary committee was established with 500 branches all over the country to inspire people with a revolutionary spirit and sacrifice their lives for the country's freedom. In 1907, a train on which the Governor of Bengal was travelling was set ablaze with explosives. In December of that year, a magistrate from Dhaka was shot dead at the Faridpur railway station. The revolutionaries also tried to kill the British monarch, King George V. Subsequently, the police seized a weapons factory in the Maniktala locality of Calcutta. In 1911, sixteen bombings took place in Bengal. The government then took stern steps and imprisoned several people for treason. The situation was such that the British had to shift its capital from Calcutta to Delhi. Such violent, revolutionary uprisings were also seen in other parts of the country, but due to the government's unabashed suppression, militant nationalism had almost died by 1919.

In 1920, Barindranath Ghosh visited the ashram at Hemayetpur and spent a few days with Sri Sri Thakur. He was highly impressed, and greatly moved by the affectionate care of the ashramites. When he came back to Calcutta, he published an article titled *Pabna Satsang's Madhuchakra* in a popular Bengali journal called *Narayan*. The narration of his discussion with Sri Sri Thakur, and about the loving atmosphere of the ashram created an uproar among the intelligentsia of Calcutta. From then on, the stream of visitors to Hemayetpur increased manifold; barristers, doctors, professors, and respectable persons from Calcutta's civil society started visiting the Hemayetpur Ashram. Some of them took Initiation to Sri Sri Thakur's Faith, and the number of his followers in Calcutta swelled. At their behest, Sri Sri Thakur's visits to Calcutta began. During his early visits, Sri Sri Thakur resided at Chandrasekhar Sen's (Barrister, Calcutta High Court) house. Later, a house was taken on rent. At Mr. Sen's residence, Barrister J. N. Dutta and his wife (subsequently known as Dutta Ma) came to see Sri Sri Thakur. Mrs. Dutta worshipped *Bal Gopal* (the divine childhood form of Sri Krishna, worshipped widely). As soon as Dutta Ma glanced at Sri Sri Thakur, she became emotional, and with tearful eyes said, "In my puja room, when I was in a deep, pensive meditation, you appeared in my inner vision as Bal Gopal, and called out to me with your childlike affection, when I came to take your blessings, you kindly told me, 'Don't prostrate before me, you are my mother.' I didn't know who you were at that time, but now I realise it."

We come across so many reports of uncommon experiences. By that time, Sri Sri Thakur had migrated to Deoghar. A Muslim from Dhaka, while offering 'Monazat' (love offer), after his namaz every day, would see in his inner vision, a handsome person clad in white cloth, black shoes, and a sacred thread on his body receiving his offerings. He had never seen him before. He observed this every day, but could not recognise the person. One day, in the market, he saw in a shop a portrait of the man resembling that brilliant person of his dreams. He was surprised. He came to know from the shop owner about Sri Sri Thakur. He wrote a letter to him and narrated his experience. This letter was read out to Sri Sri Thakur. He smiled and said sometimes this happens. (*Naba Veda Vidhata*)

One evening in 1920, Sri Sri Thakur was discussing various contemporary issues with an elite group when he suddenly blurted out in Bengali:
A day will come
In villages and cities of the entire world
This Holy Name (Satnam) would be known.

A few of the devotees could not understand this, so one of them asked, "In the entire world, really? Do you know how big this world is? Is it so easy?" Sri Sri Thakur gave a short reply, "When the Supreme Father has made me burst out with the statement, He will fulfil it."

By this time, the flow of devotees to Hemayetpur had swelled, and some of them started living there permanently. Several bamboo-mud huts were constructed around Sri Sri Thakur's paternal residence. This setup went on expanding according to the needs, and it came to be known as the Satsang Ashram.

One day in April 1921, Sri Sri Thakur gathered all the devotees of Satsang, and took them for a bath to the Padma River. He massaged the body of each devotee with a little oil, and when they had bathed, he wiped them dry. He dressed them, polished their shoes, and brought them to his house for lunch. After feeding them, he carried each, one by one, on his shoulders, and moved around outside. In Vaishnavism, this relationship between master and disciple is called *Sakhya Bhava* (feeling of camaraderie)

Sri Sri Thakur had a fever the next day. Every afternoon, his temperature would rise, and continue throughout the night. The doctors of Hemayetpur and Kushtia tried their best, but nothing worked. He was taken to Calcutta where several eminent doctors attended to Him. As the saying goes: Doctors differ. He was administered different types of powerful medicines. The adverse effects of overdosage by many different doctors made his body weaker every day. Everybody was scared and concerned about Sri Sri Thakur. In one of his trances after an intense kirtan performance, he said, "The Medium cannot last long, don't you know Ananta?

Not more than five years." His illness coincided with the fifth year of his forecast. Under the advice of a physician, he was shifted to Kurseong, a hill station, for a change of climate.

It was during this period that a devotee thought up a treacherous plot. Krishna Chandra Das was born into a traditional blacksmith family in Kashipur, a nearby village. He sat twice for Bachelor of Arts in the local Sanskrit college, but failed. Sri Sri Thakur used to provide him with financial support as and when required. After his failure, he came to Sri Sri Thakur and stayed in the ashram. Sri Sri Thakur encouraged Krishna Chandra to read a number of treatises in Sanskrit, and over a course of time made him an authority on religious scriptures. Now a B.A.-failed Krishna Chandra was giving discourses on religious topics. Thakur used to send some money to his disciples. Those who were interested in studying Hindu scriptures he now sent to Krishna Chandra for guidance. He allowed him to sit beside him, to the displeasure of other devotees. Krishna Chandra's arrogance irked many, but they kept quiet as he was a darling of the Master. He had mentioned many times to Sri Sri Thakur the necessity of a printing press. In response, Sri Sri Thakur arranged for a hand press and treadle machine. Krishna Chandra named the press Saraswati Press, rejecting Satsang Press as suggested by the devotees.

Two journals—*Shashwat Sambad* and *Supath Sanket*—were published from Saraswati Press. Later, Krishna Chandra shifted the press to his residence. Prof. Panchanan Mitra of Calcutta University took initiation and settled permanently in the Satsang Ashram. He became a good friend and follower of Krishna Chandra. As Sri Sri Thakur was ill in Kurseong and showing no signs of improvement, they concluded that he would soon breathe his last. They hatched an evil plan; after Sri Sri Thakur's death, Krishna Chandra would take over the ashram. Panchananda and he spread the news that Sri Sri Thakur himself had pronounced that he would be no more. While Thakur was ill, Krishna Chandra had gone to Gauhati, and before returning prefixed *Satyashrayi* to his name. Thus, he was called Satyashrayi Krishna Chandra Das.

Sri Sri Thakur returned from Kurseong to Hemayetpur still ailing. All treatments had failed. Devotees close to him believed that Thakur alone could cure himself under this circumstance. They prayed earnestly before him to save himself. Long sessions of chanting the Holy Name took place before him for his survival. This went on for some days. One night, Sri Sri Thakur called Anantanath (a close devotee), and asked, "Do you want me to live?" Anantanath prostrated with folded hands, and prayed, "You have to live for us." Thereafter, Sri Sri Thakur told him to fetch a homeopathic medicine and after using it, he was on the road to a speedy recovery.

The news of his recovery spread like wildfire. There was elation, kirtans, and the distribution of sweets. However, the recovery of Sri Sri Thakur came as a jolt to Krishna Chandra. His aspirations to become the owner, administrator, and master of the Satsang Ashram were shattered. Krishna Chandra and Panchanan now fabricated a new story that according to his own prediction, Sri Sri Thakur's soul had left the body. Now only the body remained but looked alive with the soul of Satan residing within. The Satanic form in the body of Sri Sri Thakur should be excreted as soon as possible; only then would the truth be re-established. They brainwashed his Brahmin cook and a Kshatriya attendant that only murdering Sri Sri Thakur was the solution.

To avoid disturbance, Sri Sri Thakur was kept in a garden house a little distance from his residence. Right before the attack on Thakur, the cook and the attendant were caught. Under heavy pressure, they admitted in writing the plan to assassinate Sri Sri Thakur and disclosed the identity of the perpetrators—Krishna Chandra and Panchanan Mitra. When Thakur was informed, he urged the devotees to suppress the matter. The next day, Krishna Chandra was noticed loitering in the ashram with a rope in his hand, saying, "There is no penance other than death for the sin I was going to commit. Thus, I am searching for a way to my death." Sri Sri Thakur sent for him and convinced him about his goodness and purity of knowledge. However, Krishna Chandra was so ashamed and full of guilt. He went to Pabna, and never returned to Hemayetpur. It was reported shortly thereafter that he had been afflicted by an incurable disease and had died a miserable death.

Towards the end of 1922, the parents of Subhash Chandra Bose (Janakinath Bose and Prabhabati Devi) came to Hemayetpur Ashram, and stayed for a few days. They were staunch devotees of Sri Sri Thakur and were concerned about his health. Janakinath Babu was a renowned advocate of the High Court in Cuttack. He had a big mansion, 'Haranath Lodge', at Puri, They requested the Master to visit Puri for a change. The climate of Puri is temperate and suitable for regaining health. Sri Sri Thakur, along with his family, went to Puri in January 1923. Around 250 people had gathered there with him and stayed for over a month. The Bose couple took all possible care for his comfort. A photograph of Sri Sri Thakur taken then standing with the sea in the background is deeply adored by the devotees. The news of Thakur being in Puri drew many disciples and social elites. Biographers have mentioned many incidents during his stay at Puri. We narrate two of them here:

A local Brahmin was engaged as a cook in Haranath Lodge. He pilfered rice habitually and stored it in a pit under a mango tree in the premises. One day, he was caught red-handed. When the inmates were about to punish him, Sri Sri Thakur reached there and asked the Brahmin," Why do you steal?" He replied, "I am very poor. The wages do not suffice to feed my family. What can I do?" Sri Sri Thakur graciously gave him all the rice he had hidden and some more from the store. He also arranged a goodly sum of money as a gift. The cook was overwhelmed, and with tearful eyes promised never to steal again. He was with Sri Sri Thakur's family until the end of their stay in Puri.

The second incident: One day, Sri Sri Thakur with his wooden footwear went alone for a stroll towards the beach of Puri. He came across the road to Sakshigopal, and walked nearly 11 to 12 kilometres to reach there. Sakshigopal is famous for the temple of Sri Gopala. It was dusk, and Sri Sri Thakur was missing in Puri. Searches all over proved futile. Ultimately, in the evening he returned to Haranath Lodge. Why he went alone to Sakshigopal without telling anyone still remains a mystery.

Sri Sri Thakur once remarked on Puri and the Jagannath Temple thus: Since when has the Jagannath Temple at Puri been a centre of culture; there is no account. It might be before Sri Chaitanya Dev's visit. The Jagannath temple of Puri, the Lingaraj Temple of Bhubaneswar, and the Sun Temple of Konark are witnesses to the cultural heritage of Odisha. The place for eating *prasad* (offerings) in Jagannath temple is called 'Anand Bazar.' Mother Manmohini Devi liked this name. Since then, the common kitchen and dining place in the ashram at Hemayetpur, and subsequently at Deoghar was also called 'Anand Bazar.'

Krishna Prasanna Bhattacharyya was a research scholar in Physics at Calcutta. In 1922, he heard about Sri Sri Thakur. Out of curiosity, he visited the Hemayetpur Ashram. One evening, during a stroll along the banks of the Padma with him, he talked about the subject of his research; the existence and behaviour of atoms, electrons, protons, etc., while he wondered what Sri Sri Thakur would understand about the intricacies of Physics. Sri Sri Thakur listened to him silently and started discussing the most contentious issues of Physics. Krishna Prasanna was astounded, and questioned him, "Were you ever a student of Physics? How could you know such details?" Sri Sri Thakur simply replied, "Since my childhood, I have been observing the entire universe in the form of light particles, and those light particles in turn are condensed into matter in our surroundings."

Narrator: There is a great resonance between what Thakur had said, and the analysis of an eminent physicist of the last century,

Fritjof Capra, the author of a bestseller '*The Tao of Physics.*' There he made a comparative analysis of the laws of Physics, and Oriental spiritual science. An excerpt from the preface:

"Five years ago, I had a beautiful experience that set me on a road that has led me to the writing of this book. I was sitting by the ocean one late summer afternoon, watching the waves rolling in and feeling the rhythm of my breathing when I suddenly became aware of my whole environment as being engaged in a gigantic cosmic dance. Being a physicist, I knew that the sand, rocks, water, and air around me were made of vibrating molecules and atoms, and those consisted of particles that interacted with one another by creating and destroying other particles. I also knew that the Earth's atmosphere was continually bombarded by showers of 'cosmic rays', particles of high energy undergoing multiple collisions as they penetrated the air. All this was familiar to me from my research in high-energy Physics, but until that moment I had only experienced it through graphs, diagrams, and mathematical theories. As I sat on that beach, my former theoretical experiences came to life; I 'saw' cascades of energy coming down from outer space, in which particles were created and destroyed in rhythmic pulses; I 'saw' the atoms of the elements, and those of my body participating in this cosmic dance of energy; I felt its rhythm, and I 'heard' its sound, and at that moment I knew that this was the Dance of Shiva, the Lord of Dancers worshipped by the Hindus."

Krishna Prasanna took initiation shortly thereafter, discontinued his research, and from 1923 lived in the Hemayetpur Ashram with his family. On the initiative of Sri Sri Thakur, he started the World Science Centre in the ashram dedicated to scientific research on various matters. Experiments were done to extract electricity from the atmosphere. It was met with some success, but could not proceed further due to paucity of funds. Sri Sri Thakur liked intelligent and inquisitive individuals around him so that they could read books on science, philosophy, eugenics, etc., ask relevant questions and obtain his views. His views can thus be compared with that of authorities on those subjects. Despite the tight financial status of the ashram, Sri Sri Thakur never shirked away from arranging funds for books. Over course of time, Krishna Prasanna became the Chief of the Satsang Ritwik Association and was bestowed the title of *Ritwik Acharya*.

As biographers tell us, to a question as to who could best write his biography, Sri Sri Thakur declared, "My eldest son, *Baro khoka* (Sri Sri Borda), or Kestoda (Krishna Prasanna) can do it." Sri Sri Borda's discourses on *Satyanusaran* have now been compiled in several volumes of *Ishta Prasange*, and are greatly admired by the devotees. However, he did not attempt to write a biography of his father. In his turn, Krishna Prasanna very humbly remarked, "How can one express in words the love in his eyes, the expression on his face, the agility in his walk, the magic of his voice, the style of his talks, the elegance of his sitting, the grandeur of his personality? A biographer can only report some incidents of his life. At every moment he looks different, the lustre and brightness of his body change so frequently, how can we describe them in words? Whatever we write about him, it can only be a drop in the ocean."

Regardless, Kestoda still managed to write a brief biography titled *'Sri Sri Thakur Anukul Chandra and Satsang.'* He wrote, "Sri Sri Thakur started doing his work without having any resources, and was successful in developing many projects that were helpful in the life and growth of people. Love, life, and service are the basic factors of his life. Hindus have accepted him as the living ideal of Aryan culture, Muslims have realised Hazrat Muhammad in their lives more clearly and correctly after coming in contact with him; Christians cannot help but love him, and have got inspired to realise Christ more deeply in his company."

A Christian preacher from Australia said after meeting Sri Sri Thakur, "If Christ had come during the present times according to the need of the day, he would have done as Sri Sri Thakur is doing in the service to mankind."

In 1920, the leadership of the national movement passed into the hands of Mahatma Gandhi, and he transformed it into a mass movement. Gandhiji had no faith in bloodshed or violence, and he led the movement completely on the basis of non-violence, encouraging people to follow, through non-violent means, the five fundamental principles-to spin the *charkha*, to remove untouchability, to prohibit taking intoxicating drugs, to maintain unity among Hindus and Muslims, and to maintain the principles of equality towards women. Subsequently, he launched the Non-cooperation Movement in 1920. In November 1921, when the Prince of Wales visited India, Indians showed him black flags, and a countrywide strike was organized. By December 1921, more than 60,000 people were arrested. Shortly afterwards, an encounter took place in the Chauri Chaura region of Bihar in which the police opened fire on several satyagrahis, killing a few of them. The mob set fire to the police station, which resulted in two British constables dying. This was against Gandhi's principles, and after hearing about it, he called off the Non-cooperation movement.

On the other hand, the Muslim League was founded in 1906 as a rival to the Indian National Congress and was considered to be the chief representative of the Muslim voice in British India. When Gandhiji noticed that Muslims had become staunch enemies of the British Government and had started the Khilafat movement, he wanted their support in the Non-cooperation Movement.

In 1923-24, Chittaranjan Das was a renowned barrister of the Calcutta High Court, and a prominent member of the Indian National Congress, and its president in 1922. He had been part of the freedom movement for a long time and was a popular leader in Bengal. He learned about Sri Sri Thakur from the article, 'Pabna Satsang Madhuchakra', by Barin Ghosh in the Bengali journal, *Narayan*. He knew the author personally and had long discussions with him regarding Thakur. He thought of meeting Sri Sri Thakur at the earliest opportunity. Sri Sri Thakur was staying in Calcutta at that time. One evening, he came to Thakur and discussed many issues including the freedom struggle spearheaded by Mahatma Gandhi. Chittaranjan Babu was a great admirer of Gandhiji but did not think that independence could be achieved by merely implementing the five disciplines. Because of this difference of opinion, he formed the Swaraj Party. Chittaranjan Babu informed Sri Sri Thakur that he was not finding a suitable person who could manage it. He asked, "What should we do to unite the people of India to fight for freedom?" Sri Sri Thakur replied, "You are telling me that you are not getting a dependable person to manage your party, and to take it forward for the freedom movement. So the first and foremost factor is to get men with good character. If there are no good human beings, how can they be united with the family, in society, or in the country? We have to work out how good human beings can be born. Those who have already taken birth can be improved to some extent, but if the hereditary and genetic characteristics are not rich, it would be like varnishing inferior wood; it would not glaze that much. So, to create good human beings, the primary requirement is marriage reform, by which good human beings shall come into existence. For the time being, I feel the integrated development of an individual depends on how they accept and follow the Ideal. Unless a man is disciplined by the anchor of the Ideal, it is difficult to build a homogenous character in him. Subsequently, Chittaranjanda was initiated by Mother Manmohini Devi. Thereafter, in 1925, he visited the Satsang Ashram. He was so deeply influenced by the simplicity of Sri Sri Thakur, and the homely demeanour and affection of the ashramites that he wrote a letter to Mahatma Gandhi to visit the Satsang Ashram and Sri Sri Thakur during his Bengal tour. His letter was published in *Young India* on 16 July 1925. An excerpt from the letter.

"I have learned from my Guru, the value of truth in all our dealings. I want you to live with him for a few days at least. Your need is not the same as mine. But he has given me the strength I did not possess before. I see things clearly which I saw dimly before."

However, Chittaranjan Babu fell ill and was taken to Darjeeling for recuperation, but unfortunately, he breathed his last there in June 1925.

Mahatma Gandhi visited the Hemayetpur Satsang Ashram on 23 May 1925. He was taken around the Viswa Vigyan Kendra, Carpentry Workshops, Charitable Hospital, Kala Kendra, and a number of cottage industries. He was very impressed with the bearing of Manmohini Devi, and remarked that he had never seen such a 'masterful lady.' Due to his busy schedule, he could not spend time with Sri Sri Thakur on that day. However, later on, along with Dr. Rajendra Prasad, Gandhiji met Sri Sri Thakur at Calcutta and discussed the burning issues of the time.

Hemayetpur Satsang Ashram was registered under the Societies Registration Act, and Manmohini Devi became the first President and Sushil Chandra Basu, the Secretary. The expeditious growth of Satsang Hemayetpur became an eyesore to the landlords and the rich in the area. The Satsang Bank advanced loans at a lower rate of interest to agriculturists and encouraged small entrepreneurs of cottage industries. This affected the exploitation by landlords and moneylenders. They went against the social upliftment activities of Satsang. They employed some youngsters from the locality and violently attacked the ashramites, They were arrested soon after. Their parents and guardians came to Sri Sri Thakur and prayed for their release. He promised to do the needful. By coincidence, the next day there was an evening function at Satsang Kala Kendra on the occasion of Sri Sri Thakur's birth anniversary. The Judicial Magistrate, Pabna, was the chief guest. When the function was over, while coming out of the hall, the magistrate saw Sri Sri Thakur standing in a corner outside the gate. He was aware of his kindness and could guess the purpose. On seeing him, the magistrate bowed his head with folded hands. Sri Sri Thakur held onto his hands, and fervently pleaded, "Please do something to release those boys. They are all my children." The magistrate retorted, "If they are released today, they will repeat their menace tomorrow. Let them be punished." Sri Sri Thakur vehemently pleaded, "If children commit mistakes, will the father approach the law and order authority to punish them?" The magistrate was stunned and said, "Okay. Leave it to me. I will try to do something." The next day, when the matter came up in his court, he told the guardians to submit security bonds upon which the wayward youngsters were released on bail.

A weekly Bengali journal, *Shanibarer Chithi,* was published in Calcutta in those days. To increase its readership, it indulged in yellow journalism; publishing concocted stories about eminent persons of the time. The editor, Sajanikanta Das, continuously went on writing false, fictitious, and slanderous articles against Sri Sri Thakur and Satsang. The Satsangis met him and requested him to visit the ashram, meet Sri Sri Thakur and know the truth about the Master and his organization. He did not agree. The scandal-mongering was brought to the notice of the Police Commissioner, Calcutta. The Satsangis requested him to investigate the allegations in the journal. On a detailed police inquiry, it was found that the journal had acted wantonly to tarnish the image of Sri Sri Thakur and Satsang. The editor was punished and the publication came to an abrupt end thereafter.

At this time, Subhash Chandra Bose was undergoing ICS training at London. He came back to India midway through to serve his country. As mentioned earlier, his parents were devoted followers of Sri Sri Thakur. He came to meet the Master to know from what point he should start his service for the country. Sri Sri Thakur wanted to know how the British could subjugate India. He went on to explain it himself and said, "The British came as merchants and traders, took advantage of the mutual jealousy of the kings and rulers of the time, and the other weaknesses of the splintered kingdoms. So the basic criteria required today to fight them are men of good character and commitment to the motherland. Good men are born, not made." He emphasized marriage reformation as the most important step in nation-building. Subhash Chandra realised the truth in Thakur's argument, and said, "Swami Vivekananda has mentioned the need for men of good character for nation-building as well; he had given the emphasis on reforms in the education system. But now after listening to you, I understand if men of good character are not born out of compatible marriages, then how much can education do in their character-building? I think it cannot do much since a tree is born from a seed. How could there be a good tree without a good seed? I now realise this, but it is a time-taking process." Sri Sri Thakur replied, "Yes, it would take a long time, since we have done very little, almost nothing, in this regard, for our society, and for the country. A lot of rubbish has piled up. It will take time to clean it. I can't find any other permanent solution." It appears Subhash Chandra came to Sri Sri Thakur before his incognito departure from India in 1939. He had a house in Elgin Road, Calcutta, and in his room, he kept a photograph of Sri Sri Thakur on the wall, which has been preserved to date.

Sri Sri Thakur lost his father, Shiva Chandra Chakravarty in 1926. In 1927, his eldest son, Amarendra Nath (Sri Sri Borda) discontinued his studies at Edward College, Pabna, to devote all his time to Sri Sri Thakur and Satsang. He was married to Anandamayee Devi in 1929 and was blessed with a son, Asoke Chakravarty (Sri Sri Dada) in 1933. Anant Maharaj, a staunch devotee and close companion of Sri Sri Thakur, despite Thakur's wishes, went to attend the ceremonial bath (Ardhodaya Mela) in the Ganges at Calcutta and contracted smallpox. He had a painful death in the ashram in 1934. Sri Sri Thakur broke down completely on his demise and remained outside the ashram to assuage the sorrow for over a month.

In 1928, Sharat Chandra Chatterjee, a renowned Bengali novelist, visited the Hemayetpur Ashram. He came to attend an important function at Tapovan Vidyalaya. He was very happy to meet Sri Sri Thakur, and asked him a lot of questions. Sri Sri Thakur did not particularly like the tragedy in literature, whereas most of Sharat Chandra's compositions were catastrophic and tragic in nature, mostly ending with death. While talking to him about his literary career, Sharat Chandra said many people had written letters of confession to him: "I have known what goes on in our society through my experience, there is no limit to it. I have tried to express it in my literature." Sri Sri Thakur replied, "Many people have come to me as well, and confessed the worst of their sins to me. How shattering, horrid, and naked all this is! I have never disclosed the details to anybody. Do you know the reason why? There is no doubt that our society is on a course of decay. But those of us who are aware of these realities, if we choose to depict the perversions of this world in our creative expressions, I don't think we will be doing any good to anyone. It is the responsibility of Literature to serve people with meaningful and constructive depictions of human beings so that people are able to look for hope in the midst of hopelessness, and peace in the face of distress. We have to strike a balance between realism and idealism. If Literature is unable to create a sense of reliability in its readers if it cannot show the path of well-being, what kind of literature is it?" Sharat Chandra was attentively listening to Sri Sri Thakur's brilliant counsel with a sense of awe and bewilderment. He spoke in a distressed voice, "Until this point I thought by highlighting the negative aspects of society, I could attract the attention of reformers who would act on these ills and vices. You have truly changed my point of view. However, at this age, in the dusk of life, do you really think I can change my literary form of expression?" Sri Sri Thakur in a motivating tone declared, "Of course, you can. You must begin at once." It is said that after meeting Thakur, Sharat Chandra found the inspiration to write his famous novel *Bipradasa*.

As good work creates enemies, the Satsang movement became the target of some intolerant and envious people from the nearby areas. Devotee-biographer Sushil Chandra Basu writes, "It is simply astounding that at every step there were huge waves of hurdles that Sri Sri Thakur had to surmount. Even mountain-like impediments could not deter him from his determination to proceed. Probably, he was as calm and unperturbed as he could be; perhaps, as a seer, he could envisage the future. Sri Sri Thakur said once in a lighter vein, , 'True, my name is Anukul (meaning favourable), but adversity never leaves me.' Ever ready to forgive any assault on him, including his life, he said, 'There is a way to deal with the egoist, the arrogant, and the envious. He is a part of society, he is a part of us. We have to co-exist with him. We have to learn the skill to deal with him, mend him and bring him to our side; finding faults is of no use. There was a time when I was mingling with everybody in my village; I was going to every house, keeping account of everybody's welfare. Everybody was pleased with me. But subsequently, as the ashram grew, people came in numbers, so I became busy solving their problems. I did not get the time and opportunity to go and visit the people as earlier. I expected you people to take over from me, and continue good public relations with people around, but you did not do that, and I was disconnected from their lives. You must learn to deal with people, know their minds, put forth your cause, and attract them to things that are ultimately beneficial for them. Your aloofness will create an impression of misplaced superiority. So even if you do good for them, you will not win over their hearts. They would think that you are only showing kindness for the sake of formality, that you are not one of them. Man is seldom free from faults. We have to understand him, and put our best sight, skill, good conduct, and preparedness to accept him as our own, only then can you regulate him, and prepare him to rectify his misdeeds.

"Sri Sri Thakur continued, 'I have faced much treachery and betrayal in this life. There are people, whatever good you do to them, they will always harm you in return. Many times, I have thought I won't do anything for them, so that I will not be harmed by them any more, but when I see somebody in trouble, I forget his betrayal, his treachery, and jump up to relieve him from it.

Unless I do it, I feel suffocated. What can I say about myself, even a girl's mind is stronger than mine. I do not possess the capacity to preserve or protect myself; it is in your hands, in your court.'

Narrator: About 2500 years ago, Lao Tzu, the Chinese philosopher, and soothsayer, in his famous book, T*ao Te Ching* (Tao, the King) indicated the arrival of the sage with the following basic qualities. Here sage is used to mean the Prophet (Purushottam). It will not be out of place to mention that the indications absolutely befit the personality and nature of Sri Sri Thakur.

> "Who knows his manhood's strength,
> Yet still, his female feebleness maintains;
> As to one channel flow the many drains,
> All come to him, yea, all beneath the sky,
> Thus, he the constant excellence retains;
> The simple child again, free from all stains.
> Who knows how white attracts,
> Yet always keeps himself within a black shade.
> The pattern of humility displayed,
> Displayed in view of all beneath the sky;
> He in the unchanging excellence arrayed,
> Endless returns to man's first state has made.
> Who knows how glory shines,
> Yet he loves disgrace, nor e'er for it is pale;
> Behold his presence in a spacious vale,
> To which men come from all beneath the sky.
> The unchanging excellence completes its tail;
> The simple infant man in him, we hail."
>
> —*Tao Te Ching* by Lao Tzu. Translated by James Legge

It is important to emphasize, from the above-mentioned indications of a Prophet by Lao Tzu, the five qualities that were the fundamental traits of Sri Sri Thakur's personality, such as the possession of a soft and feeble heart like a woman's, dressed with white dhoti with black border, his footwear in black, the vast humility contained in his heart, despite the knowledge of his glory, his glad acceptance of disgrace, and finally, that he remains as a simple, infant man all his life. When Sri Sri Thakur was asked about the attributes of the Ideal (Sadguru), he gave a short reply, "He is endowed with total adherence to the Supreme Being, he is gorgeously simple, abnormally normal, and wisely foolish."

Sri Sri Thakur was always in search of committed disciples to carry his message far and wide. The twelve fishermen disciples of Jesus Christ overwhelmed the world with his message of love and compassion. Hazrat Muhammad's message was spread across the world by the committed effort of the first four disciples (Ali Bin Abu Talib, Abu Bakr, Omar, and Uthman). Swami Vivekananda brought Sri Ramakrishna Paramhansa and his teachings into the limelight. Sri Sri Thakur said, "An unmarried saintly type of disciple is best suited for the job. Let two such disciples come, they will multiply to ten, and the ten will multiply to many." After migrating to Deoghar, Sri Sri Thakur kept mentioning the need to prepare 40 totally committed disciples through whom his ideology could be propagated within and outside India to save the world from great disasters. In 1948, he put down in writing the conduct of these 40 committed disciples:

1. *Tendency of sincere, relentless adherence.*

2. *Presence of mind with common sense.*

3. *Intelligent and active acquisitive habits with a good sense of time.*

4. *Inquisitive responsive bent of mind, with educated adaptability.*

5. *Maintaining monastic tendency.*

6. *Forbearing perseverance, and a pain-staking attitude.*

7. *Absence of inferiority, and selfish serving attitude.*

Over and above these traits in their normal tenor, they should have sufficient general education along with good oratory skills, writing ability, and charming exposition. People with M.Sc. or M.A. degrees in Philosophy or Literature with an artistic bent or mind are preferable. If they are unmarried and saintly, even better.

Overcoming continuous adversities, Satsang expanded very well. People in large numbers thronged to the Satsang Ashram to be initiated. Sri Sri Thakur assigned Krishna Prasanna to select *Ritwiks* from among the deserving disciples. From now onwards, the initiation programme started.

The famous magician of the time, P. C. Sarkar, once visited the Hemayetpur Ashram. During his discourse with Sri Sri Thakur, he mentioned *Tratak Yoga;* Sri Sri Thakur then sketched a 16-petal-wheel on a piece of paper and called it the *Mahalaxmi Yantra*. Since 1935, this *Yantra* has been used as a part of the *Namdhyaan* (meditation), and is known as *Chakra Sadhana*. He added that after meditation, *Savasana*, as mentioned in the Yogic texts, should be invariably followed. In 1938, the quarterly Ritwik conference commenced. A booklet, *Ritwik* (containing guidelines for Initiation), was introduced in 1939, and subsequently, the multilingual *Ritwik Manual* was published. Two monthly journals, *Satsangi* and *Ritwik,* were also published by the ashram.

Sri Sri Thakur always encouraged his close disciples to ask questions on various subjects, both spiritual and mundane. Aswini Kumar Biswas, a follower of Sri Sri Thakur from the time of the kirtans began, asked questions about the aims and objectives of human life, the necessity of following the Ideal, the Ideal's responsibility towards a devotee in his present/afterlife, and so on. A book, *Amiya Vani,* was compiled containing Sri Sri Thakur answers. This book, published in 1921-22, was the first compilation of Sri Sri Thakur's message in a question-answer format. He encouraged discussions and research on eternal memory consciousness, and how some people take forward the memory of their previous birth to the next one. In 1938, He sent his devotee, Sushil Chandra Basu, to Delhi and Rajasthan to conduct a case study on people with memories of their previous life. Sushil Babu made an extensive study of various persons and submitted a detailed report to Thakur in 1939. He also compiled the reports and published a book titled *Jatismara Katha* (Bengali).

Krishna Prasanna used to ask questions on various subjects such as the existence of the soul after death, the difference between life and death, man-woman relationships, marriages, and so on. He compiled the answers in *Nana Prasange* in two volumes. Similarly, questions and answers regarding the ways of women, their relations with men, their instincts and activity as recorded by Panchanan Sarkar were incorporated in *Nareer Neeti* (Women's Code), and discourses regarding society, country, religion, politics, economics, man's joys, and sorrows were published in *Chalaar Sathi* in 1934. Disciples consult this book to solve problems of everyday life. Thakur spoke these discourses in his mother tongue, Bengali. An interpreter was necessary when the audience did not know Bengali, especially foreigners.

Krishna Prasanna had been constantly persuading Sri Sri Thakur to give messages in English. Sri Sri Thakur used to laugh it off, "Why are you making fun of an illiterate man?" However, one fine morning in 1935, Krishna Prasanna was urgently called by Sri Sri Thakur. Thakur looked at him and started speaking in English. Once the stream of messages started, it kept on flowing. After that, whenever Krishna Prasanna came to Sri Sri Thakur at any time, he carried a notebook and pencil with him to take down any important messages. Sri Sri Thakur dictated them spontaneously; there was no fixed time when he would call Krishna Prasanna to write them down. The so-called illiterate gave messages on the titbits of our existence. These messages have now been compiled in nine volumes with the title, *The Message*. The then Vice-Chancellor of Calcutta University, Rev. Dr. Arkuhart, went through them and remarked that they resembled the Gospels of the Bible. The first utterance was:

> *"The booming commotion of Existence*
> *that rolls in the bosom of the Beyond*
> *evolves into a thrilling rhyme*
> *and upheaval*
> *into a shooting becoming*

of the Being,
with echoes
that float
with an embodiment of Energy-
that is Logos,
the word,
The Beginning."

The devotees and followers of Sri Sri Thakur asked how he could frame the messages with such apt and accurate words. From where did he obtain such a vocabulary? Sri Sri Thakur replied, "When Kestoda (Krishna Prasanna) pestered me to speak in English, I never agreed. How could I speak in a language I know so little? But Kestoda would not give up. So I thought, whatever nonsense comes to my mind, let me blurt it out, only then he will understand the futility of his efforts, and leave me alone. But once I started talking, he jotted down my words, and it made sense. He was elated, and would not spare me any longer. Whatever came from Providence, I uttered only that. If you ask me now the meaning of those words, I would not be able to explain. That time is over. Believe me, I rely completely on the mercy of the ever-benevolent God to make possible what appears impossible to our intellect."

Similar to *The Message, Magnadicta* contains 246 stanzas of poetic expressions on various subjects in English. It was published in 1949. Sri Sri Thakur gave messages on various subjects, sometimes in prose and sometimes in poetry. They have been compiled subject-wise: *Acharacharjyaa, Charjyasukta, Devisukta, Vivaha Vidhayana, Shikhya Vidhayana, Tapo Vidhayana, Darshan Vidhyana, Swasthya O Sadachar, Sutra, Shashwati, Sambiti,* and *Sangya Samiksha*. All these Bengali messages have been published in a series of 23 volumes of *Aryya Pratimokshya*, and his messages in couplets have been published in seven volumes of *Anushruti*.

Maulavi Muhammad Khalilur Rahman was a staunch devotee of Sri Sri Thakur. He urged Thakur to share his views on Hazrat Muhammad, Islam, and its religious practices. Thakur discussed them from the Holy Quran in detail. We can know everything about Islam from the book *Islam Prasange*.

Guru Vandana (adoration of the Guru) is part of the morning and evening prayers. It consists of nine hymns; seven of them have been taken from the *Skanda Purana*, and one (*sthavaram jangamam vyaptam*) was included by Sri Sri Thakur. He felt awkward when the *Guru Vandana* was recited in his presence. He abhorred any praise for him in any manner.

Vigyan Bibhuti is a compilation of Sri Sri Thakur's utterances on scientific subjects including Physics and Astronomy. The recent discovery of the *God Particle* was indicated over a hundred years ago by Sri Sri Thakur as *Chid-Anu* (Particle of superconsciousness). This has been discussed in detail in Part Three of this book. Sushil Chandra Basu, like Krishna Prasanna, was also motivated to record Sri Sri Thakur's spiritual realisation and views on many other subjects. Three volumes of *Katha Prasange* came out of his efforts. Prafulla Kumar Das was private secretary to Sri Sri Thakur and was present with him most of the time. He used the rare opportunity to note down the discussions that took place in the presence of Thakur every day. They are available in the 22 volumes of *Alochana Prasange*. The cumulative total of all this literature by Sri Sri Thakur; the messages, views, discussions, discourses, etc., have run into more than 80,000 printed pages. Sri Sri Thakur once remarked, "Ramakrishna Paramhansa did not disclose everything, but this time, I am giving you the key to the entire knowledge of Being and Becoming."

In 1948, during a discussion, Sri Sri Thakur said, "I have given elaborate literature on spiritual *sadhana* in complete detail and about all the aspects of life. A superficial reading or listening in conferences, or in Satsang congregations is of no use. They are to be taken seriously in heart and soul, you have to ponder over them, and translate them into action. That is the only way you can realise the depth of my teachings." Sri Sri Thakur felt that to eradicate poverty and disease, coordination was necessary between the motor and sensory nerves of the human system. He introduced, in 1937, *Swastyayani,* to ensure a proper adjustment of motor-sensory activity. He said, "I can swear that in order to remove all types of poverty, grief, and diseases, and to establish peace and prosperity in society, *Swastyayani* is the only way."

With regard to the repetition of the Name and Meditation, Sri Sri Thakur shared his experience thus: "At one point, I kept myself engrossed in meditation and repetition of the Name, without doing any other work. I thought I might proceed on the spiritual path faster, but after a few days, lethargy took over; the tremor of life slowly disappeared. I was not able to discern between good and bad, pleasure and pain. In short, my sensations and feelings became numb; life became hard and motionless. I suffered hell and realised my folly. I started working alongside my spiritual practices, and gradually I returned to normalcy. Children who do not engage in household work, for example, are not involved in any motor activity; their brain's receptivity declines. Children who are eager to give something to their parents develop an integrated personality. Those who are not faithful to their parents and family, but are restless to serve neighbours, you can be sure about their improper mental growth."

He added, "Do you know how the wrathful king Ashoka became the peace-loving Ashoka? The powerful theme of a song of Upagupta redeemed him. Similarly, Jajan, Jaajan, Istavriti, and Swastyayani are the basics of our existence. Everything evolves out of them. The first is the individual, then comes society, and from there the country. When an individual is reconstructed with an integrated personality, society is homogeneous and the progress of the country is in safe hands. For achieving coherence in one's personality, one has to follow the most coherent and desegregated man; He is the Ideal. The Ideal gives the clue to prosperity. He teaches us that giving to others contributes to our own prosperity. This may sound weird, but it's true; the urge to give opens the gates of achievement."

Regarding his formal Initiation, Sri Sri Thakur said, "On the directions of Sarkar Saheb, my mother initiated me; she was my everything, the foundation of my formal spiritual journey. Whatever I did, it was to get a little appreciation from her." She would often recite this couplet:

Even when you see a pile of ash, with care blow it all,
Who knows, you may find a spectacular pearl.

This means that there are so many forms of existence in our world. A lot happens during the journey of our life, we do not observe them. So much mystery remains, yet to be revealed. Many people see the falling of an apple from a tree as normal and commonplace, but it struck Newton. He started thinking about it, he inquired why the apple did not go up, and hence discovered the Theory of gravity. You can also see and communicate with the ectoplasmic body. Ananta and many others are regularly coming to me after their death, and I communicate with them. What I see, you cannot. Science can develop instruments for us to know what happens to man after death, in what form does he exist, what are his activities, etc. I am not satisfied with only seeing it. I want all of you to know about life after death."

A child does not have lust, anger, greed, ego, and infatuation; Sri Sri Thakur was above all this throughout his life. For a child, the mother is everything; nobody can take her place. But we see that in ordinary day-to-day life the attachment with the mother is diminishing, and has been tilting in the favour of one's wife and children. One who remains a child forever will be oriented towards the mother throughout his life. Once, during Thakur's childhood days, his mother Manmohini Devi punished him. Anukul Chandra ran a little distance and then stood still. Mother caught up with him, and beat him black and blue. His younger brother observed this with glee from a distance. After her departure, he came to his elder brother and said, "Dada, you are a fool. Why did you stop? Mother would never have been able to catch you." Anukul Chandra replied, "I know that but running a long distance in the scorching sun would have exhausted her, and she had to gasp for breath. I never want my mother to be forlorn. Better to bear the thrashing."

On another occasion, Sri Sri Thakur said, "I had a great desire to be appreciated by my mother, but she was very hard on me, a strict disciplinarian. All I received was a lot of scolding and beatings, but never a word of recognition, no matter how badly I yearned for it. Be that what it may, without her I am undone; in spite of her annoyance, I seek an opportunity to please her. This was the sole purpose of all my activities."

He continued, "Unfavourable circumstances could never deter me from my efforts; rather, I would be stubborn to bring the situation under my control. During my childhood, many elderly neighbours were my self-appointed guardians. They would complain against me to my mother on flimsy matters, and then she would punish me. Without any reason, they would twist my ears, and slap me, and I would have to tolerate all of it. Yet, I was never desperate or disheartened. I always thought this situation is temporary and in time better days will come. You will laugh at how the neighbours were after me when I used to come home on holidays from Medical School. They would pass comments like 'The boy is not interested in studies, keeps running back home to his newly-wedded wife, and prolongs his stay.' Mother, on hearing it, would send me back to Calcutta long before my vacation ended."

As mentioned earlier, Sri Sri Thakur had a number of disciples in Calcutta and started visiting the city once in a while with his mother. In February 1938, when he decided to go to Calcutta, his mother was preparing to accompany him. Sri Sri Thakur suggested, "Ma, this time you are not coming with me. I know you will not be happy about it, but listen, I am making a short visit on important work, and as soon as it's over I will be back. So stay at home." Manmohini Devi agreed but was very sad. After a few days, she went to Calcutta with a disciple. Seeing her, Sri Sri Thakur was aghast. He was puzzled and asked her, "I beseech you not to come but, lo and behold, you have flouted my request. It's all over. What can I do now?" Manmohini Devi could not understand what was so unusual about her arrival that had rattled Sri Sri Thakur. The next day, she had a burning sensation in her stomach and was running a high fever. The best doctors of Calcutta failed in their attempts to treat her ailment. Sri Sri Thakur brought her back to Hemayetpur. Despite best efforts, she passed away on 20 March 1938. Sri Sri Thakur's grief was inexplicable; he was shattered. After her demise, he expressed in a short letter his mental agony:

"Ma, with all my enthusiasm, love, and labour I built this house for you. I took a lot of care in arranging every corner of this house as per your requirements, so you could be comfortable here. All I wished was for you to live here, use this place, and fulfil all your desires. But now you have left your mortal body, and moved on to the next world. All these dreams lie far behind. Look at the pangs of time, and how they have defeated me. The irony of my fate is to live this life like the walking dead. Learned people have said that after leaving this body, the soul exists as it is, before it finds a mortal body. It may take rebirth, with the previous life memories intact. Ma, O my mother! If the Merciful grants it, in case you come back to this Earth with your memory consciousness, if to my good fortune you remember your Anukul, if your compassionate heart searches for a waif, grace me with your presence. Live here, and use whatever little I have with me.

-Your unfortunate and poor son, Anukul."

We are distracted from the meaning of life when we lose our near and dear ones. What can alleviate our sorrow? What can we do for the peaceful existence of the soul that has departed from its body? All of us ask these questions when we encounter such turmoil of personal grief. Sri Sri Thakur said, "When our mind is fixed with the Ideal, and we think of the departed, they find peace." He further added, "It is natural that the death of our loved ones will torment us, and tear us apart into pieces, but still we have to keep searching for peace and solace with a sense of infinity within ourselves. Always think you are an actor, performing the role allotted to you in this world, and be ever conscious of your adherence to the Ideal. Everything happens as per the wishes of the Supreme Father; there is nothing you can do about it. The crux of the matter is that those who do not leave the shelter of the Sadguru till their last breath acquire the essence of spiritualism." During his discussions, Sri Sri Thakur liked to repeat a small dictum, "Do never die, nor cause death, but resist death to death—what is more potent than this?" He continued, "If we have the memory consciousness of our previous birth, we can understand the cause-and-effect relationship between birth and death, after which the fear of death vanishes. The absence of the fear of death is in effect to conquer death itself. To my mind, the foundation is the uncompromising adherence to the Ideal. If one's Ideal-centric presence of mind gets enhanced, the desire for work grows, tolerance and his capacity to absorb pain increases, and ultimately one develops the ability to earn what he desires in life."

Everyone is born with a particular instinct exclusive to their being, it varies in each individual. Thus we find people with innumerable instincts. The Ideal (Sadguru) can decipher the instinctive trait of a particular person; he nourishes it, and as a result, the person achieves what he desires in life. This achievement is optimum. That is why the Ideal is called *The nourisher of instincts and fulfiler of the best*. Since the Ideal is adorned with unlimited wisdom and attributes, he has no inferiority complex, no ego, and a focused mind. As he is above all passions, he resolves all the problems of those who approach him.

In our so-called religious world, many disintegrated, unregulated, passion-tainted individuals claim to be the Guru or Master. The ordinary man, out of simplicity, follows them and falls into their schemes of deception. Therefore, if one does not have the fortune to find a true master (*Sadguru*), it is better to be devoted to his parents, instead of falling into any trap.

Sri Sri Thakur was able to know the past and future of a person at first sight. He said, "There is nothing extraordinary about it. If you can elevate your mind above the causal plane by the repetition of the Holy Name, you can see everything, because, in creation, all things are entwined with each other perfectly with accuracy, and when your mind travels above this level, you can transcend your soul beyond the existing body, and enter another body without any difficulty. Once I had the desire to taste the flesh of a dead cow and I entered the body of a vulture. It tasted well in the mouth of a vulture. Suddenly it occurred to me, what if the vulture dies? So I immediately came out of its body and entered on my own. Another time, I became a fox and acted like an animal, all this is very fresh in my memory. Man gets his appearance in accordance with the predominance of his inherent animal nature: bird-man, horse-man, frog-man, etc."

Sri Sri Thakur once told a close disciple (Bijaykali Bhattacharyya), "At times, my mind rises so high that I cannot sleep. I was always instigating people around me to quarrel with each other; listening to their quarrels would bind my mind earthwards, so I could sleep for a while." His personal physician, Dr. Pyari Nandi, reported an incident: "One night, when I came to Sri Sri Thakur with the last dose of medicine for the day, I found him uncomfortable on the bed; after taking the medicines, he lay down, trying to sleep. I knew that patting his body induced him to sleep. So, with his permission, I started doing it; I continued for a while, but he still would not sleep, constantly changing sides. So I asked, "What's the matter? Why don't you sleep?" Sri Sri Thakur replied, "To whom should I give what responsibility after five hundred years, that exercise is ongoing with the Supreme Father, not allowing me to sleep." Dr. Nandi was astonished, "What are you saying? After 500 hundred years!" Sri Sri Thakur replied, "Yes. I am in constant touch with the Supreme Father and receive His messages just like telegrams. You are all children of the Supreme Father, and I am bound to take everyone's responsibility. There lies my duty and delight."

In 1940, a devotee from Barisal stayed in the Hemayetpur Ashram for a few days. He was an advocate and thought himself to be quite smart. He was minutely observing all the ashramites and their activities. One morning, when Sri Sri Thakur was alone, he came up to him and started talking about the activities of the ashram, as if reporting, "Probably you may not have noticed, no doubt there are some sincere workers here, but there are many others, who are either lazy or wicked. These parasites with free food and lodging are whiling away their time. Why do you not throw them out?"

He thought Sri Sri Thakur would be extremely pleased with his assessment and would ask him to share more details. However, on hearing him, Sri Sri Thakur looked downcast and askance. He asked in a sad tone, "What can I do, my dear brother? I am a foolish father of many fallen sons. Suppose you are here with me and suffer from a fever, what should I do? Shouldn't I take steps to cure you, or throw you out of this place? If my son is crippled, should I not make all efforts for his treatment or should I send him away? Doesn't the father take extra care of the disabled son?"

On another occasion, during a discussion, Sri Sri Thakur summed up his feelings of oneness with all living beings, "I find myself in every being, as if I'm a replica. I can't think of anybody, outside of my being. Man stoops to theft due to his wants, stealing is not his nature. My duty is to make him get rid of it. This is the place for reform and reorientation. We take so much care to remove dirt from our bodies every day, this work must also be done with the same keenness. To reconstruct an individual, I am ready to forgo even a kingdom, if need be."

In 1939-40, communal harmony was at its lowest ebb; intolerance and violence were on the rise. It came as a great shock to Sri Sri Thakur. Giving expression to his cherished idea of one united nation, he wrote a beautiful patriotic song, *Arya Bharat Barsha Amar.* The founder of the Hindu Mahasabha, Shyama Prasad Mukhopadhyay, a senior advocate at the Calcutta High

Court, once came to see Sri Sri Thakur. Thakur suggested to rename his organization to Arya Mahasabha instead of Hindu Mahasabha, so that Muslims too could join. He also requested to arrange for the habitation of Hindus in Muslim-majority areas, and vice versa, in order to control communal riots. Shyama Prasad did take some steps in this regard, but could not reach the target set forth by Thakur. After the country's partition, Shyama Prasad came to the Deoghar Ashram again and admitted with remorse that Sri Sri Thakur's suggestion was indeed correct.

The first prime minister of undivided Bengal, Moulvi A. K. Fazlul Haque, also visited the Hemayetpur Ashram several times. Sri Sri Thakur's high regard for Prophet Mohammad and the rigorous workflow and discipline at the ashram influenced him a lot. He once expressed his opinion that the ideology of Satsang was somewhere similar to the ideology of Islam. Thus, it would not be an exaggeration to say that the Muslim community should build its character in accordance with Satsang's ideology.

At this time, Sri Sri Thakur was once walking with his wooden clogs when he slipped and a soft bone on his toe was fractured. He did not agree to surgery and somehow managed to tolerate the pain for two long years. One fine day, he simply pressed the swollen area and the broken piece of bone came out. The pain subsided thereafter. However, the joy of this unique miracle was lost in the sorrow induced by the sad demise of one of his closest disciples, Shyama Charan Mukhopadhyay (Gopalda), the then Secretary of Satsang, in a train accident.

By 1941, the fog of war had engulfed the nations of the world. Japan had now joined the war. Sri Sri Thakur wrote letters to all Satsangis to leave Burma at the earliest, and come back to India. Japan bombarded Rangoon soon after. In response to Sri Sri Thakur's caution, a large number of Indians staying in Burma had migrated to India and their lives were saved. There were many reports as to how miraculously devotees in Rangoon could hear the voice of Sri Sri Thakur to vacate the city immediately. Some of these incidents have been narrated in Part Four of this book.

The refugees who came to India narrated the trials and tribulations inflicted upon them by the English. As a result, tensions began to mount between Indians and the English back home. At that time, there was a reign of fear and terror in Bengal as the British government had occupied the lands of Indian farmers for military purposes. Their houses were set ablaze, their crops were destroyed without any compensation. Consequently, a tide of dissatisfaction and disappointment among the peasants was at its height. Then, Mahatma Gandhi started the Quit India Movement.

In 1942, the Quit India Movement took off. The government banned it as illegal. This caused a lot of violence and rioting. At that time, Medinipur district and its adjacent areas were severely damaged by a cyclone and the famine in its aftermath. An estimated 2.1 to 3.8 million Bengalis out of a population of 60.3 million died of starvation, malaria, and other diseases aggravated by malnutrition. Millions were impoverished as the crisis overwhelmed large segments of the Bengal economy and catastrophically disrupted the social fabric. There was no relief anywhere. The Satsangis collected cash and food grains to fund the relief of the suffering masses. Sri Sri Thakur instructed a staunch devotee, Kishori Mohan, to lead the volunteers. He worked day and night relentlessly. The exhaustion caused by heavy and continuous work led to him developing a fever and in fact, his health deteriorated fast. In May 1944, he breathed his last at the age of 63. Sri Sri Thakur was greatly distressed and heartbroken. That year, his eldest daughter, Sadhana, also lost her life. To add to the grief, soon after, a former teacher of His in medical school, Dr. Sashi Bhushan Mitra, a staunch devotee, also passed away. All this had a significant bearing on Sri Sri Thakur's health.

By 1945, the world war came to an end. The world was returning to normalcy, and international peace was being restored by the formation of the UN. By 1943-44, because of excessive mental stress, Sri Sri Thakur's blood pressure remained unstable; no improvement could be seen despite the best efforts of several eminent doctors. The causes of his distress were many; he had lost three of his close disciples and aides, namely, Ananta Nath, Kishori Mohan, and Shyama Charan. His eldest daughter also passed away much before her time. There were many incidents of treachery; even attempts to murder him. The growth of Satsang created animosity among the landlords and the rich money-lending community. The loss of life in the Bengal famine was heavy, and the government remained callous. The landlords and moneylenders created much trouble from time to time. Communal ill-feeling and hatred were on the rise, and Satsang was unduly dragged into it. The suggestions of Sri Sri Thakur to the public leaders to bring an alternative settlement to avoid riots were not taken seriously. Thakur felt forlorn and dejected. To save his health from further degeneration, doctors advised a change of climate and place. It was decided in August 1946 that Sri Sri Thakur would be shifted to Deoghar (now in Jharkhand). On the first day of September that year, Sri Sri Thakur travelled to Deoghar with his family and a few devotees. As his biographers had estimated, the value of the ashram property at that time currency was crores of rupees. After the partition of India, the Pabna district, including Hemayetpur, went to East Pakistan. The Pakistani government took over the ashram property and established a mental hospital there. No compensation was paid to Satsang for this forcible acquisition.

On the eve of partition, bad blood between the two communities was at its height. Hindus were attacked and murdered in broad daylight, and their houses were set on fire. Noakhali had a higher percentage of Muslims. This led to a mass massacre, with a fear psychosis unprecedented among the Hindus. They abandoned their villages with what little they could carry with them to save themselves. The exodus was in lakhs. It was estimated that one-and-a-half lakh people lost their lives in the riots. Aware of Sri Sri Thakur's presence at Deoghar, thousands of people rushed there hoping for safe shelter. They knew that they would not be turned away by Sri Sri Thakur. At Deoghar, for the accommodation of Sri Sri Thakur, his family, and accompanying devotees, a large house called the Boral Bungalow was taken on rent, and subsequently, a number of other houses were also rented. To take care of the fear-stricken daily arrivals from different parts of Bengal, the most important problem was to provide the homeless with a handful of rice and a place to sleep. The ashramites did not leave any stone unturned to help them. They begged for funds and food, from house to house in Deoghar town and the nearby villages, but even then the situation became unmanageable. Sri Sri Thakur was not in favour of buying provisions on credit. To improve the poor financial condition of the ashram, he entrusted its management and administration to his eldest son, Sri Sri Borda. Borda had to strive hard and gradually, through his sincere efforts, the financial position of the ashram began improving. To the homeless and desperate, Sri Sri Thakur was the destination of hope and consolation. He said:

"Becoming homeless is awful, but losing efficiency is still more dreadful. In order to make your efficiency grow in all its facets, you have to be actively Ideal-centric, with eagerness and inclination for the Ideal to bring meaning into your life, an all-embracing attitude brings an integration within the self. As far as possible, try not to be a parasite to others. Whatever little you have, try to take it as your capital for growth. Go on trying to regain what you have lost within a short period of time. Try to mould your life in an Ideal-centric manner from this moment on."

In August 1947, India and Pakistan became two separate nations. Referring to the devastation caused by partition, Sri Sri Thakur said, "I can say fervently, dividing one country into two halves is not good for either of them. The development of both shall be hampered, and both Hindus and Muslims will suffer great losses. And taking undue advantage of the mutual animosity between the two countries, external forces will try to exert their influence in the region. In the long run, it will harm both nations."

On 30 January 1948, Mahatma Gandhi was shot dead during a mass prayer. Sri Sri Thakur was deeply shocked and upset when he heard about it. He jotted down a few lines as his tribute to the Father of the Nation:

> *"To shoot the Mahatma*
> *Is to shoot the hearts of*
> *Lovers of existence.*
> *Oh, Thou Great Tapas!*
> *Bestow thy bliss*
> *With every shooting of*
> *The evils that obsess;*
> *Father the Supreme!*
> *Pour thy grace*
> *On this dumb appeal of the human heart."*

The country was devastated by the manner in which the Father of the Nation had been murdered. Sri Sri Thakur told his disciples and workers, "If we can create an army of five crores of welfare workers (Swasti Vahini), and train them to serve society in all aspects, only then can things be managed, otherwise everything will go for a toss in the country. By the grace of the Supreme Father, Satsang is the only forum where people from all communities confluence; all discord and disharmony vanish in favour of unity and fellow feeling. They do not in any way discard their sectarian identity, but under one roof of the Ideal, they help each other for common growth. I think householders with the Ideal at the centre can enhance their being, and take care of their surroundings. However, the progress of the country will be faster if a good number of people come forward, and abandon their individual interests and family life in the larger interest of society."

In 1948, Sri Sri Thakur urged six of his ardent devotees to undergo the strict discipline of a renunciator (Yati). They were required to maintain abstinence from family life, and practice the abnegation of comfort to follow a rigorous path to the attainment of wisdom. During those days Thakur used to spend most of his time with them and guided their sadhana, He gave instructions in the form of *Vani* (in poetry). All this has been compiled now into the volume, *Yati Abhidharma*. This Yati Ashram ran its course for three years.

Sri Sri Thakur's health continued to be fragile. Once, in a lonesome moment, he soliloquized: "I am a lone bird; in the corner of a tree I sit desolate, and warble my native wood notes; I am in the grip of old age, and do not know how long I can go on, or how much I can contribute to my country and others. In my country, none came forward to understand my agony and extend their shoulder to me. If it had happened, the picture of this country would have changed enormously."

A devotee had once asked a very pertinent question, "So many Incarnations, Prophets, and Saints have come to this Earth at different times but in spite of their advent, the world has not changed for the better. The selfishness of man, hatred for each other, violence, and war, have always been there. What then is the benefit of their coming?" Sri Sri Thakur replied, "When Prophets and pathfinders come, people accept them, they worship them, but do not follow and act on what they say. That is due to the bondage of passion. Nonetheless, they have created a flood of higher consciousness across the globe, so in spite of passion-oriented living, there are thousands of families slowly rebuilding their lives, and trying to make sense of the Prophet's teachings in their daily life." He further said, "Man's life is like a wave. There are ups and downs in it. A lot of rubbish has gathered in society. What is needed is to follow the Prophet ardently, and act according to his teachings and discipline. Unless the public leaders, the intelligentsia, and the powerful accept and follow the Ideal, the lower sections of society will not realise its importance."

On 2 January 1950, the All India Workers Conference of Satsang was held at Deoghar Ashram. Sri Sri Thakur addressed the workers. It was his first public address. An excerpt from his speech:

"I have spoken to you about what Dharma is, what life is, and how you should act in life. You have to be very sincere to understand the true nature of Dharma, the aim of your life, and the path of your activities. First and foremost is our adherence to the Ideal. The number of initiates is fast increasing, but in comparison, the number of workers is low. It is not possible to manage the affairs of the organization with the present strength of workers. There is a necessity of 40 to 50 completely dedicated individuals who can take the lead and responsibility of management. Only then can we develop into a force for the benefit of society.

Whatever I have asked you to do, do it with utmost sincerity, lest ravage and deterioration of human values come. You have to see that everybody in your surroundings is initiated, and adopts the path of truth, fellow feeling, and co-existence, so that man's character can shine. His existence becomes colourful and pleasant. It is of no use to merely talk about the principles of life and growth, you must exhibit them in your own character, otherwise, all that you say will go to waste. Whatever may be my blessings, they will not be manifested in the life, unless you act accordingly.

Those amongst us who are initiated, and are always working with an endeavour to follow principles actively, they are far more superior and developed than the common folk. If they are led properly, their achievements will be beyond comparison. I am always optimistic, and glad to see them. Their eagerness speaks of their inner strength; by nature, they are sympathetic, accommodative, serviceable, and sincere. By and large, they have been bestowed with the nature to sacrifice for others. This is why I say, they are at a higher level than the common man. As you know, the ground is vast, but farmers are few. Men who can lead are required; they are the future leaders. Each one of you has to become a leader.

The fundamental thing is initiation. I wish everyone in this country would be initiated. But we must not forget that nothing much can be achieved by mere initiation. Those who are initiated have to be properly led, and only then there will come power, ability, and integration.

Unless you work of your own volition, your efficiency will go down. Volition has to be materialised by action so that your potential is brought forth into the world.

Householders have to be educated to adjust themselves to a higher spiritual purpose. They should be encouraged to lead a life of truth and austerity. In Buddhism, this is called *Shramana* (to leave everything that was your own, and embrace people as your sole asset). If your narrow selfishness pulls you back, you cannot become a *Shramana*, and you cannot participate in making this society wholesome. The confined perspective of people can be widened through Initiation. Householders will develop efficiency and a sense of sacrifice for the overall growth of society.

I wanted to prepare a group of three thousand able men (Krishti Bandhav), who will act like soldiers to promote welfare and safeguard the interests of society. It has not been done so far due to our own lethargy. You have to attract people to your path by pleasant behaviour, you must speak words that are soothing to their ears for the sake of their existence, in short, the nectar of Being and Becoming.

This is not a very difficult task, you can do it if you want to. When we move with the best interests of others in our hearts, only then will we be successful.

Success does not come unless you are attached to the Ideal, do a regular repetition of the Name, and meditate. Mankind looks for such a person by seeing whom they are delighted, and encouraged for righteous living, keeping the Ideal at the centre.

Everything veers around the three basic principles, *Jajan* (self-upliftment), *Jaajan* (nurturing the environment), and *Istavriti* (daily oblation). We want to grow, we want to become big with the attributes of divinity like our ancestors. We do not want anybody to suffer from any kind of poverty. Let everyone be affluent and majestic.

I have great faith in the dignity of women. They should try to be efficient within their jurisdiction. They have to be taught etiquette, good hygiene, and amity in an effective manner. That is real *Jaajan*, to bring everyone to the Ideal's path, which shall make them virtuous and honest."

In the same month, Sri Sri Thakur dictated a long verse underlining the aims and objectives of Satsang. The translated verse in English is as follows:

*"Satsang wants man
in the name of the One Supreme Creator
of all beings, God, Khuda or Existence,
whatever you call Him.
Satsang does not think in terms of
Hindu, Christian, Muslim, Buddhist,
and regards each and every one
as a child of Him alone.
Satsang wants to make all
submissive to that One.
Satsang does not think in terms of
Pakistan, Hindustan, Russia, China, Europe,
or America either—
Satsang wants man, every individual of mankind,
whether Hindu, Muslim, Christian or Buddhist or whatever
in pursuit, nurture and fulfilment,
in elevating offering, in mutual compassionate co-operation
and in an uplifting, efficient, and industrious way of life
so that everybody, by proper work
earning their food and clothing can survive,
maintaining the distinctiveness of being
and moving in the way of becoming.
So that everyone can understand*

that everyone belongs to him,
So that no one can think
that he is helpless, penniless, shelterless,
so that every single person can say courageously
with active cooperative zeal of love
I am everyone's
and everyone is mine.
Satsang wants the greatest cooperation between states
so that there is not the least flaw
in anyone's existential becoming
and so that each and every one
can move on freely
in this world
in one accord
with self-elevating, efficient and active,
progressive service,
growing in integration
that is mutually fulfiling—
being illuminated with the inspiration
that cultivates the good.
with an eye to fulfiling that Ideal man
being meaningful in that unparalleled One."

Pandit Jawaharlal Nehru became the Prime Minister of the interim government of independent India and continued to work as the PM till his death in 1964.

On 12 February 1950, Sri Sri Thakur was sitting under a teak tree in the front yard of Yati Ashram. The morning congregational prayer was over. He asked for a microphone and delivered an enlightening speech *extempore* (in Bengali). Here we have tried to translate it to the best of our ability.

"Why do we pray? The essence of prayer is to undertake a resolve to achieve something. To materialise the resolve we have to take recourse to do a particular thing, and then contemplate the ways in which it can be done.

Prayer is to draw out the talent that lies within you by the pursuit of praise to your Love-Lord in a conscious plane. By doing it, you invigorate your heart and accelerate your ability with an illuminating hope. When there is no enthusiastic admiration for your Lord (Ideal), when there is no feeling, and no eagerness for him, the resolve seldom fructifies. Unless the determination is firm and the feeling is deep, success remains at the shore. The purpose of prayer is to make the resolve firm and steadfast and to do the needful at any cost.

Today our problems are manifold. I have said much earlier that the country may undergo a very difficult period in the future, we have to be prepared to save people from misery, distress, and sorrow. I have talked about *Swasti Vahini:* this group is to be trained properly, so they can come to the rescue at the time of suffering of any human being, whether a Hindu, Muslim, or Christian.

One more thing. Our existence (Satsang) is yet to achieve its desired stability. Wherever our lands have been acquired, we have to build a sound organization in those places without any delay so that even the poorest of the poor, the people living in huts should get someplace to stay according to their status. We have to create employment opportunities for the livelihood of everybody. We should not sit idle expecting government assistance. We have to do it ourselves.

The project of *Kristi Vandhab* should have progressed very well by this time. Had we been able to circulate our message among the people at large, they should have comprehended, and acted accordingly. Due to our negligence, we have put the people and also ourselves at a big loss.

We have to go for an endearing way of life. That means the manner of living, which delights others, charms them, and enchants them to contentment and happiness. Our behaviour should make others healthy, enlightened, cheerful, and serviceable. The basic factor is unwavering adherence to the Ideal. Without such an inclination to the Ideal, if you try to live an endearing life for the benefit of others, you will end up in pretence. When you fail to integrate these values within yourself, solidarity with others debilitates. Every man wants to know and wants to grow; no one wants to remain stuck in one place. The Ritwiks are the messengers, the representatives to show people the path of life, the light of progress, and to guide them to their proper destination. So they are first and foremost. They have to come up to that level. Man cannot teach himself, he needs an efficient teacher. When he finds the teacher (Ritwik) to be graceful and promising, learning becomes easy and automatic.

Just as a government requires a minister and an officer, in the same way a family also requires someone to act as an integrating and crystallizing agent. In addition to this structure lies the responsibility of Ritwik, the ministering agent. Both put together will not allow any family to deteriorate. By rendering genuine advice, actual acumen, bonafide service, and real assistance, each family will be guided towards enhancement, making decline impossible. A tellurian family will enjoy the bliss of heaven if the parents support each other with thoughtful service and exuberant love. Such a couple gives birth to godly children with a fine genetic equilibrium. Because of this genetic excellence since birth, they embrace the avenue of nobility and walk in that direction. The fabric of society transmutes to divinity.

Girls are to be trained in such a way that their minds do not move from the decent and ethical to the disgraceful and dishonourable. Let not your daughter marry a man from an inferior family. The natures of the bride and the groom, and the hereditary culture of both families should be compatible. If either family is Ideal-centric, then their lives too will be ideal.

In the case of students, it is almost the same. When they come into the shelter of the Ideal and adore and serve their teachers, knowledge is entwined with their being. Education is seldom condensed and meaningfully adjusted. In this case, it is barely any better than a gramophone record going on repeating itself.

Cottage industries should be introduced in every family. Man becomes self-reliant, and the children in the family are motivated by it. They learn not to become dependent and not be parasites. It is not only their finances that make them independent, their creativity also expands. So, over the course of time, the younger generation can produce things more efficiently, and of better quality.

For increasing work efficiency, peaceful coexistence in the family is very much necessary. The more the misunderstanding between man and woman, the greater the family turmoil. The wife should be completely inclined towards her husband, and the husband must keep the Ideal at the centre of their lives. He should always take proper care of his wife. Everything lies in the mind. The couple should be attached to each other mentally. The outward expression of marital love is not enough. Similarly, all members of the family caring for each other bring forth camaraderie within. One more important thing, while serving any member of the family, you have to maintain a respectable distance. Too much proximity and closeness should be avoided. In essence, one should talk, act, and behave as per the situation. Never should we cross the limit. This should be kept in mind while serving family, relations, friends, and others.

Now almost all nations are talking about world peace. For this, various proposals and negotiations are being contemplated, but without a solid foundation, they are bound to fail. When the sentiment of belonging is condensed, centripetal consolidation comes forth; peace marches in. In other words, when all the countries are actively concentric towards the Ideal (Prophet of the age), they develop a feeling of sympathetic coexistence. The principle remains the same for the individual as well as the nation. One should always be actively interested in their surroundings; only then peace becomes spontaneous.

With the support of a torch-bearing organization, severing the barriers of narrow sectarianism is possible to bring peace nationally and internationally. If we can do it sincerely, we will achieve it. We have to be fast, deep-rooted, and elegant in our approach. We have done nothing so far. We have only listened a lot, but done very little. Long ago, I discussed the urgent need for a *Swasti Vahini*. The proper organization of these volunteers into an army should have by now brought forth positive results for the society and the country at large. It is still not too late.

We require ascetic leaders who have the zeal to fulfil the Ideal, and can serve the people wholeheartedly. Some initiates should come forward to offer daily oblations *(Istavriti)* of at least three rupees a day. We require *Shramana*, whole-time dedicated workers who can carry our message from door to door. If you sincerely do what I say, success will be a never-ending story.

Unless we organize ourselves to be capable and coherent, what can the government do? If we do not implement the plans and projects of the government sincerely and honestly, can it deliver? We want integrity and unity in society, among all the countries, between communities, and between all individuals."

Sri Sri Thakur had thought of a university with standards and calibre that of the great institutions of our past like Nalanda, Taxila, and Ujjaini, which were renowned throughout the world as great centres of learning. In this ideal university, all subjects should be taught with practical applications. It should implement the age-old Indian notion of a strong, personal relationship between the student and the teacher (*Guru-shishya parampara*). Sri Sri Thakur felt that mere bookish education cannot bring out the latent talent in a student. Therefore, a syllabus for each discipline should be prepared, keeping this vital aspect in mind. Sri Sri Thakur named it Shandilya University. He also thought of establishing micro-level universities in a cluster of villages. He felt the large universities in the city and their smaller counterparts in the village should impart not only theoretical education, but also practical training, so that students do not run after salaried jobs but can produce resources to earn their livelihood.

Eighty years ago, Sri Sri Thakur had thought of joining all the rivers of the country for proper distribution of water to augment agricultural and industrial production by uninterrupted water supply. It would have also controlled the havoc of floods that endangers the lives and property of millions of people during the rainy season every year. For the first venture, he desired a confluence of the Darwa river flowing adjacent to Deoghar with the Ganges flowing through Bengal. That project is yet to be taken up by the government.

Sri Sri Thakur was free from any kind of imperfection. He wanted his disciples to take him as an example to mould their own characters. Sometime in 1952, he was putting a clove in his mouth when it slipped and fell under his bedstead. He immediately stood up, and dusted his clothes, but found no trace of it. He sat down and continued to look for the clove, ultimately finding it behind a leg of the cot. He looked bright as if he had regained a lost diamond. One of the devotees who stood near him asked, "Why were you so anxious for a tiny clove? There is plenty in stock with you." Sri Sri Thakur laughingly replied, "A small careless event paves the way for a number of undisciplined mishaps. Its immediate rectification should never be avoided. If such lapses persist, it creates holes in your willingness to surrender, to concentrate, take the right decisions, and mental health." He added, "A blessed person can only realise the three tenets of our existence here, i) Human birth is a rare possibility, ii) One should get rid of passions, and iii) If you find a Sadguru, you should surrender to Him." During a conversation, Sri Sri Thakur opined that a time may come when life can be created out of a living cell of a recently dead human being, just as a plant is generated from a leaf.

Sri Sri Thakur did not really appreciate moralists much. He believed their assertion that they are the custodians of morality creates an inflated ego, and paralyzes their minds.

In October 1953, he turned 66; it was the seventh year of his arrival at Deoghar. His birth anniversary celebrations and the 62nd

Ritwik Conference were organized together for nine consecutive days in a big way in the ashram. The then Deputy Speaker of the Lok Sabha, Anantshayanam Iyengar, many political leaders, High Court judges, poets, and litterateurs had been invited.

Under the leadership of Sri Sri Borda, and the hard labour of many ashramites, many institutions like the printing press, publishing house, Tapovan Vidyalaya, chemical laboratories, hospitals, and guest houses were established within a very short period of time. The rapid progress of Satsang was an eyesore to many in the surroundings. Envious persons concocted stories to defame Sri Sri Thakur and the ashram. The ashramites were not spared from their wrath; there were several attacks on them both from inside, and outside the ashram. Sri Sri Thakur's health was passing through many ups and downs. He would fall ill abruptly, his blood pressure would rise, and within a few days, he would be absolutely normal. There was a large rush of people coming with their problems, patients who have been sent back by doctors and suffering from intractable diseases. Sri Sri Thakur would give them a patient hearing and then provide solutions. For the afflicted, he would take special care to soothe them with hope; would also console them saying that he would pray to the Supreme Father for their recovery. He would see to it that while leaving him, the hopeless patient had a smile on his face. Miraculously, most of the patients would be cured. It is believed that Thakur would *suo moto* assimilate the diseases of others in his own body, and suffer from them himself.

In May 1956, Sri Sri Thakur's blood pressure rose high in spite of heavy medication. He had a mild stroke and the right side of his body, his face and his hand were partially paralyzed. A few days before this, a patient with severe paralysis was brought to Sri Sri Thakur by his relatives. He beseeched Thakur: "Baba, look at me. I can no longer bear this torment. Please take my disease away. You are the giver, you are also the taker." Sri Sri Thakur said, "I cannot take anything nor can I give." However, after this incident, he suffered from a stroke. With the treatment of super specialists in Calcutta, and the vigilant care by Sri Sri Borma, and Sri Sri Borda, Sri Sri Thakur recovered. During his treatment, he was advised not to take long walks; he simply would sit near the sawmill in the shade of a tree for long hours. If anyone asked, "Are you not fed up with the bizarre sounds from the mill?" He would reply, "The sounds from the machine accelerate my thought process, I enjoy it." By December of that year, Sri Sri Thakur had completely regained his health.

Throughout 1957, Sri Sri Thakur's health was more or less stable. By that time, the number of initiates was over four lakh. The ashram was vibrant with activity. Thousands of people thronged there for solutions to their problems, and the number of enemies also rose. At the back of Sri Sri Thakur's mind, a thought kept recurring, "Who can manage Satsang and take care of the growing number of initiates?" He decided that his eldest son, Amarendranath (Sri Sri Borda) would be the right choice. He alone could shoulder such a heavy responsibility. For the last several years, Sri Sri Thakur used to send persons approaching him with their multifarious problems to Sri Sri Borda to solve. He was satisfied with his competence and deftness, his extraordinary ability to get things done, and his compassionate heart with an awe-inspiring personality. Sri Sri Borda knew how to deal with the trouble-mongers and the wicked, and put them to productive and purposeful employment to enable them to earn so that there is no time for evil thoughts. One of the primary aims of Sri Sri Thakur was to transform the evil-minded to be good. Sri Sri Borda was a perfect master for the job. Therefore, on 2 June of the same year, he declared Sri Sri Borda as His heir-apparent of Satsang. The declaration was made through a legal document. That year, Sri Sri Thakur's birth anniversary function and the Ritwik conference were celebrated with jubilation.

In 1958, Sri Sri Thakur's health was moderate. Once Kestoda asked him, "Many are getting initiated, but do not follow the discipline later. What is the solution?" Sri Sri Thakur replied, "The fault is on our part. Suppose I am a Ritwik, but I never go to my oblates (the people initiated through me), and do not pay any attention to them. How can I blame the starters when the veterans are not doing their job properly; we have to infuse in our disciples an inclination to understand and love life. Remember, they are your living wealth; to ignore them is to ignore your very purpose."

In June that year, a cook, Jajneswar Jha, died after a prolonged illness. The adversaries of Sri Sri Thakur, who were hostile to the progress of Satsang, alleged murder, and filed an FIR at the local police station. The police during their frequent visits to the ashram interrogated many and arrested a few of the ashramites. It took quite some time to obtain bail for them. In those days, Sri Sri Borda was away at Calcutta to attend the marriage of a close relative and had taken ill. The opponents could manage a non-bailable warrant against him. After his recovery from illness, Sri Sri Borda returned to Deoghar and surrendered before the court. He was arrested, and in due course was released on bail. The criminal case went on for over a year. It was proved that the allegations were baseless, and the criminal case against Sri Sri Borda was dismissed. The miscreants approached Sri Sri Thakur for forgiveness. As usual, he embraced them and gave them new clothes and sweets.

But this incident broke Thakur's heart. Since the beginning of his mission, he had been constantly facing opposition, envy, and false allegations. Now he was so upset that he thought of closing the ashram at Deoghar and shifting to some other place. However, sensing it, a few gentries headed by the chief priest of the Baidyanath Temple approached Sri Sri Thakur. A long meeting was held and they begged him to revoke his decision. Sri Sri Thakur chuckled and said, "Oh, the crown priest! Every day is miserable here, our safety is at stake, and our image has been tarnished. How can you ask us to continue here?" The chief priest and the others supplicated, "From today onwards, the safety of the ashram is ours, leave it to us, and stay assured." Sri Sri Thakur gave an affirmative nod. The Satsang Ashram continued in Deoghar.

To make the workers action-enthusiastic, Sri Sri Thakur wrote a long verse titled, *Tapo-Arunima*, which is now available in a compiled form in *Arya Pratimoksha*.

In July 1958, on the eve of the workers' conference, Sri Sri Thakur hinted about the forthcoming difficult days for India and the world at large in a verse excerpted below:

> *What I said—you failed to carry out,*
> *on what I especially emphasized,*
> *you ignored them with utter inertia;*
>
> x x x
>
> *This goes on creating for you,*
> *for the country, for the world, deadly fissures.*
>
> x x x
>
> *It is doubtful whether you will survive or not—*
> *your capricious, ungodly way of life*
> *derogates life,*
> *society, surroundings, the governance, all treading the nasty path*
> *goaded by Satan in day-to-day life;*
> *so I say, at least from now come, be firm,*
> *start doing at least from now, take the stride in the glorious*
>   *path,*
> *which is effulgent in your heart,*
> *towards enlivening progress,*
> *live and let others live,*
> *lest the gloom becomes denser*
> *the depths of hell will not spare you,*
> *be sure enough. (Charyasukta, 157)*

By 1959, Sri Sri Thakur's health was fine. Sectarian antagonism flared to unexpected heights causing the mass massacre of innocent lives, burning of houses in the suburbs and villages, and looting of property in broad daylight. In the Satsang Ashram, it was a routine affair for Kestoda (Krishna Prasanna) to read out the daily newspaper to Sri Sri Thakur in the mornings. The reports made him sad and restless. Kestoda asked, "All these gratuitous and unwarranted sectarian hatred culminating in huge loss of life and property; can't it be stopped? What is the way out?" Sri Sri Thakur dejectedly replied, "What can you do about that? Where are those, whom we can call human beings? I always ponder over it. That is why, I always tell all of you to increase the initiation process rapidly. But you did not pay any heed to me. Not only our country, but the whole world is also badly infected and polluted with this sort of cynicism and pessimism. The day when three-fourths of the world's population perishes may not be too far away. Even the roads will be filled with dead bodies, and men may have to trudge over them; such horrible days await us in the near future when a man will not get a handful of rice in lieu of a handful of gold. Prepare yourselves from now on to provide shelter to the destitute, to open a free food centre (Annashram), so that people don't have to starve, and we can keep their candle of life burning."

It was during this time that Sri Sri Thakur one day remarked, "This evening while offering *Pronam*, I had a vision similar to the ones I would regularly have during my Hemayetpur days, starting from the Rishis, Vyasadeva, and Vashistha, up to Sri Ramakrishna Dev. Everyone was present there and all of them were singing a hymn. The bits of it that I remember would be something as follows:

Bharga, Vibhuti, Sabita, Souri, Sundarashree
Viswadruk Paalanadhruti Paramapurusha Namaste.
O thou destroyer of all sins! Eternal benefactor,
and handsome like the sunshine,
Onlooker and Protector of the universe
O Supreme Being, salutations to Thee.

Sri Sri Thakur, continuing the conversation, said, "Maybe after thousands of years, mankind will remember Anukul Chandra, the son of Shiva Chandra Chakravarty, and his message. You can disclose my vision only to the deserving after my departure, never before, lest it may be construed as self-boasting or a display of ego." On another day, in a lonesome mood, he uttered again, "My arrival here is fortuitous and sudden; none like me has come before, nor shall come in the future."

He then talked about Bharat saying, "It is certain, this country is going to be the World Guru one day."

By 1961, even though the number of initiations was growing, Sri Sri Thakur was not happy. He wanted 10 to 12 crore people to be initiated by then. While this was going on, an American psychiatrist, Dr. Carl Pantal, stayed for several days in the ashram. In a discussion with him, Sri Sri Thakur said, "Unless man changes his lifestyle, the entire world would become a mental asylum, so take care." This was at the back of his desire to increase the number of Initiations as rapidly as possible.

Sri Sri Thakur gave a formula for the preparation of Ayurvedic drugs for the treatment of cancer. Two doctors of the ashram, Dr. Nani Gopal Mondal and Dr. Dhirendra Bhattacharyya, were in charge of the medicine preparation. Many patients during the initial stage of the disease were cured. The medicines were given free.

The belligerent attitude of China towards India and its attack on our borders perturbed Sri Sri Thakur greatly. He instructed all the Satsangis to contribute as much as they could to the National Defence Fund. His close devotee, Satish Chandra Goswami, passed away that year. It was a great loss for him, and the pain lasted for many days. Once, Sri Sri Thakur said, "A device can be invented which can defuse the atom bomb." (details are given in Part Three of this book).

In 1963, Kestoda (Krishna Prasanna), the inquisitive intellectual, breathed his last. The loss of his close associates one after another had an adverse effect on Sri Sri Thakur's health. Not only did his blood pressure fluctuate, but diabetes also set in. He looked tired and worn out. The doctors advised him physical exercise, and morning and evening walk. Sri Sri Borda was also suffering from rheumatism. So, in 1964, a one-month-long *Namsankirtan* (chanting of Hare Krishna Hare Ram 24 hours a day) was arranged in the ashram. In September, an *Ayurdha Yajna* was also performed in Varanasi for three consecutive months for the early recovery of Sri Sri Thakur and Sri Sri Borda.

In 1964, the Prime Minister of India, Jawaharlal Nehru passed away, and he was succeeded by Lal Bahadur Shastri. When he was the Central Railway Minister, Shastriji was invited as the guest of honour to the 70th birth anniversary of Sri Sri Thakur at Deoghar in October 1957. He came and discussed various contemporary national and international issues with Sri Sri Thakur and was blessed with a *Danda* (staff).

In 1965, during a discussion, Sri Sri Thakur laid down four indispensable principles for the Being and Becoming of mankind:

Adherence to Ideal in speech, action, and every walk of life.

Compassionate attitude towards the surroundings.

Performing the right task in the right manner with the right consideration, without worrying about the perversion of the mind.

There would be hindrances of two kinds to achieve this—the first one is a go-between, and the other is a distortion of the libido, but do not be upset over it and go ahead.

In 1967, for most of the time, Sri Sri Thakur was in a state of trance. In ecstasy, he would enquire, "Where am I now? Who are all of you before me? What is this all about?" It appeared as if he no longer belonged to this mundane world. After a while, he would be normal again. This frequent other-worldliness was a cause of worry to Sri Sri Borda and other close disciples. Many renowned physicians from Calcutta examined Thakur and found nothing abnormal in him. However, Sri Sri Borda arranged for a *Maha Mrutyunjaya Shanti Yajna* for the long life of Sri Sri Thakur. During these days, Sri Sri Thakur uttered a Sanskrit hymn:

'*Anukula sadabibhu padmanabha manah prabhu.*'

In 1968, a 50-bed charitable hospital was started on the ashram premises. In the same year, delegates from the University Grants Commission came to discuss Shandilya University. It was also during this time that his first great-grandson, the Rev. Sri Sri Babaida (the present Acharyadev of Satsang), was born. Sri Sri Thakur was ostensibly happy with the arrival of his fourth generation. In December, He delivered his last sermon, "Let your inner self be enlightened and graceful by the practice of simple Sadhana."

It was during this period that he suddenly enquired about his parents one day. On another occasion, he told Sri Sri Borma, "You are my mother, and the mother of mankind as well." After a while, when Sri Sri Borda was with him, He looked at some of his portraits on the wall, and told him, "Look, they are all your photographs." He then insisted that Sri Sri Borda sit beside him. He was hesitant at first, but to honour Sri Sri Thakur, he sat at the edge of the bed for a while and then shifted to a chair next to the bed.

The year was 1969. The January Ritwik conference had ended. On 9 January, a picnic was arranged at Manikpur in an idyllic atmosphere, 10 kilometres away. Sri Sri Thakur went with Sri Sri Borma, other family members, and the ashramites. Although his health was not very good, he looked extraordinarily cheerful and moved around the place with enthusiasm.

Again, on 26 January 1969, Sri Sri Borda took Thakur and Sri Sri Borma for a drive to Manikpur. Sri Sri Thakur appeared joyous and exuberant. In the evening, he had an early dinner of his favourite dishes and retired early. At 3.30 a.m., Sri Sri Thakur woke up and sat still on his bed. He complained of unbearable chest pain to Sudhapanima (a devotee attendant), and lay down. Extremely nervous, Sudhapanima woke up Thakur's sister (Rev. Guruprasadi Devi), who was nearby. After a while, she noticed in the dim light that her brother's face looked unnaturally pale. She saw no sign of breathing and began calling out to everyone frantically. It was too late. Within a few moments, Thakur's youngest son, Rev. Dr. Kajalda, arrived on the scene and gave a life-saving injection directly to his heart but to no avail. There was no pulse. By this time, Sri Sri Borda had also arrived. Quickly, the room filled with people. At the age of 81, Sri Sri Thakur, the sole inspiring source of millions, had left his body quietly, simply, and peacefully. The news spread like wildfire. Weeping masses streamed in. Sri Sri Borda, who was sitting at Thakur's feet, was consoling everybody, including his mother, Sri Sri Borma.

That winter was severe. The air was filled with a thick fog, hindering visibility. At dawn, a cluster of black clouds on the eastern horizon obstructed the sun's rays. They looked lacklustre and pale while they escorted the son of God who was on Earth, back to the bosom of the sun for his onward journey to a destination unknown to science.

Subsequently, after about two years, the most Rev. Sri Sri Borma breathed her last on 9 May 1971.

On the departure of Sri Sri Thakur, Sri Sri Borda wrote a great elegy in Bengali. Its translation in English follows:

> *Your colour (of love) has coloured my heart wholly.*
> *How can I ever bid you farewell?*
> *The universe is throbbing with your music,*
> *And my mind too is filled with that song.*
> *My vision is entranced with your beauty;*
> *Your joy blows in the breeze and fills the heavens;*
> *Your fragrance goes in ripples through the world;*
> *And my body is thrilling at your touch.*
> *It's for your sake I wake through night and day,*
> *For everything I want in you I find.*
> *Without you, every wish is empty, void.*
> *My heart keeps crying, crying only for you.*
> *You alone are my wish to go on living.*
> *It's you I am looking for in all I am doing.*
> *There is no want or sorrow, no dejection.*
> *For Master, you completely fill my heart.*
>
> (*Discourses on the Ideal*, vol. II, 7.12.1975)

Will there be a second advent of Sri Sri Thakur on this Earth? Sri Sri Borda said, "During his discussions at Yati Ashram, Sri Sri Thakur had expressed many times that he would not come to Earth for the next ten thousand years."

(*Discourses on the Ideal*, vol. I, 27.9.1974)

Sri Sri Thakur's Daily Routine

Sri Sri Thakur would get up at 4 a.m., and after a quick wash, would meditate on the bed inside the mosquito net wrapped with a white sheet of cloth. He would offer *Istavriti*, and on the completion of 30 days every month, send it to Sri Sarkar Saheb of Agra Satsang. As an oblation to his Ritwik, he would deposit Rs 7 to the credit of Mother Manmohini Devi in the Philanthropy Office.

He did not drink tea. His favourite dishes were, Dal Phelani (pulses boiled with a number of vegetables), Dhokar dalna, curries of banana flowers and jackfruit, banana kofta. On winter nights, he would like soft puris, samosa, cheese (paneer) in thick gravy, and thick chana dal. He did not like thin or watery curries. He sat on the floor to eat and was served in brass plates and bowls. His usual breakfast was cheese with salt and pepper, and at times puffed rice. Sometimes, sweet lime juice with an equal amount of barley. For evening refreshments, he liked fried rice flakes, cucumber, pumpkin seeds, groundnuts, and roasted makhna (fux nuts). The roasted (makhna) fux nuts, or lotus seeds, were his very favourite. His intake was very little, but he liked several recipes. He would change his diet according to the seasons. For example, during summer, he preferred watered rice with lemon leaves. He liked dry rasgullas. More than eating, his satisfaction was in feeding others. When he was ill, Sri Sri Borma or Sri Sri Borda fed him.

Sri Sri Thakur had betel leaves sometime in the day. The betel wrap contained black cardamom, dried peel of an orange, mace, betel nuts (soaked in water), cloves, etc. He liked to smoke a hookah. The tobacco came from Gaya. When he smoked, a pleasant aroma pervaded the air. When he received good news, or was in a pleasant mood, he would ask for more fillings of the hookah. He liked soda and ice cream from Spencer's, in the latter period of his life. After an early dinner, he would retire at around 10 p.m. Someone had to rub his back softly, and he would soon fall asleep.

In case of urgency, or to solve somebody's problem, he broke his routine.

He wore a sacred thread of nine rounds, a white dhoti with a black border, a collarless white half-shirt, a collarless half-cotton jacket, and a white vest. His umbrella was black and large in circumference. Most of the time during the day, except in the winters, he preferred to keep his upper body bare. In winter, he covered himself with a very thin and weightless quilt. At times, he put on the white *Ritwik chuddar* sheet which was six feet long, three feet wide, with no coloured borders. He wore back open half-shoes, or black chappals, and at times, wooden clogs. He had his own staff. He could not tolerate severe winters and preferred the summer season.

He used Forhan's toothpaste, Rexona, and Imperial Leather soaps every day. After shaving, he applied alum water to his face. First, he or an attendant would massage his body with mustard oil. Then, he would dip himself in a neck-deep water tank and complete his bath. His secretary, Prafulla Kumar Das, would read out important items from the daily newspaper. Sometimes, he listened to All India Radio, Calcutta, and liked to listen to patriotic songs.

Those days, people used pocket watches, but Sri Sri Thakur used it once in a while. For writing, he had a Waterman fountain pen. He always maintained a lot of cleanliness around him, but was very simple and pomp free in his attire, as well as in all other belongings. As everything was spotless white, his dress and surroundings looked gorgeous. In short, his standard of living was of a middle-class Bengali family. At Deoghar, at dusk, he used to go with the devotees to a ground adjacent to Rohini Road and was pleased to see the Mughal Sarai Passenger pass on the railway line. Elsewhere, Sri Sri Thakur has said that he likes passenger trains because they halt at all stations, and carry all types of passengers.

His Likes and Dislikes

Likes: His dhoti, shirt, jacket, vest, bed sheets, towels, and napkins were all white. He would always keep his shoes tiptop, and close to each other.

Favourite flower: the night queen.

Favourite place: Open spaces and looking at the sky, especially the Hemayetpur shore of the Padma River. In Deoghar, he liked the following places, *Bada Dalan* (the large building, now known as Memoria), *Goltasu Ghar* (a round-tent-roofed big-sized room, now extinct), *Tasur Ghar* (now the Parlour), *Nirala Nivesh, Jamtala Sriangan, Nivrit Ketan,* and *Khader Ghar* (Thatched House).

Favourite songs: Poet and playwright Dwijendra Lal Ray's *Oi mahasindhur opar theke, Dhana Dhanye Puspe bhara, Banga amar janani amar, Je din sunil jaladhi haite,* Devotee-poet Rajanikant Sen's *Ora chahite Janena Dayamay,* and poet Kazi Nazrul Islam's, *Khelichha E Vishwa laye.* In his good moods, he would hum one or two lines of these songs. He liked the two lines of the song *Bhalobasar Nidane Paliye Jabar Bidhan, Bandhu Achhe konkhane.* (In the care home of love/where do you get my friend the rule to retreat?). In his younger days, Sri Sri Thakur had heard this song in a play at the Pabna Institute. He was so impressed that he repeated it in all appropriate situations.

Favourite poetry: Rabindranath Tagore's *Balaka;* He recited very often the first few lines of the long poem *Chanchala.* In good humour, he liked singing, *Tirer sanchay tor pade thak tire/takas ne phire, sammukher bani nik tore tani/mahasrote paschater kolahal hote atal andhare akul aloke* (All your collections at the shore/will remain only there/don't look back, let the message in front of you carry you along/in the eternal tide of unlimited light/lest the noise pull you back to darkness).

Favourite quotations:
- *Do unto others as you wish to be done by.*
- *There are more things between heaven and earth, Horatio, than are dreamt of in your philosophy.*
- *But for the want of a nail, a battle was lost.*

- *When the giver of punishment and the punished suffer the same, that is the judgement best.*
  —Rabindranath Tagore
- *Be you calm, you be awake like a lamp leaving lethargy/ in the middle of the night if you sleep you will miss the star.*
  —Rabindranath Tagore
- *If nobody comes when you call—go ahead along.*
  — Rabindranath Tagore
- *Mukam Karoti Vachalam Pangum Langhayate Girim Yatkripa Tamaham vande Paramananda Madhavam.*

Meaning: Remember with devotion the divine grace of Krishna, who can make the dumb speak with eloquence, and the lame cross high mountains; Remember and extol that grace which flows from the Supreme Bliss manifestation of Madhava.

Dislikes:
- Formal (oral) education without practice
- To be a slave of money
- Uncleanness and untidiness
- Go-Between: Not to keep your word and promises, non-punctuality
- Failure to observe the five principles of *Swastyayani*
- Treachery
- Ingratitude
- To sleep at the time of sunrise and sunset
- Gluttony
- Backbiting
- Eating out
- Free mingling of boys and girls
- Air travel
- Incompatible marriage
- Partition of India
- Indignity towards the holy scriptures, *Srimad Bhagavad Gita, Ramayana, Holy Quran, Bible, Guru Granth Sahib,* etc.

- Disrespect and dishonour of past Prophets
- Ridiculing a Brahmin's sacred thread and pigtail
- Employment of women in other than educational and medical services

Sri Sri Thakur in the words of his Family, a few anecdotes

Sri Sri Borma

This incident happened at the Hemayetpur Ashram on 2 October 1953. There was a fellow Satsangi named Adinath Majumdar, who was a *Moktar* (legal practitioner) by profession and drafted legal documents for Satsang sometimes. He had a registered Power of Attorney on behalf of Satsang in the name of a certain Enayat Biswas of Pabna on the directions of Kshepuda (Prabhas Chandra Chakravarty, Thakur's younger brother). He did this without consulting Sri Sri Thakur. Getting a hint of this, a devotee inquired, "How could you take such an important decision on behalf of Satsang without the knowledge of Sri Sri Thakur?" Adityanath's ego was hurt, and he responded, "If not him, I have done this in consultation with his younger brother. I treat them equally. Is there a difference? I don't think so." Sri Sri Borma was passing by just then and overheard this. She was deeply hurt and confronted Adinath immediately. She said, "Just by virtue of belonging to Thakur's bloodline, is everyone equal to him? If that is so, why are you all coming to him? You should rather visit all the other family members, and call them Thakur as well, isn't it? Can Thakur ever be compared to us ordinary human beings? I was married into this family at the age of 12, and now I am 60. In over 50 years of my life here, I cannot match Thakur in even one of the great attributes he bears. I do not know anything about your property matters, but your nonchalance and disregard towards Thakur's authority are very disrespectful." Adinath could now realise his mistake and apologised to Sri Sri Borma. Sri Sri Thakur played down the seriousness of the matter, and excused Adinath by saying, "He is indeed a simpleton. Had he not been so naive, would he have done such a thing without my permission? Let's drop this matter here, and not tire ourselves." *(Parama Uddhata Sri Sri Thakur Anukul Chandra)*

Sri Sri Borda

It was 7 December 1975. During a discourse after the morning prayer, in a certain context, Sri Sri Borda recollected a childhood incident of a dog bite. He laughingly remembered it, and said, "It was a pleasant incident. I was 17 then and bathed three times a day—morning, midday, and evening. One morning, I came home after bathing when a red dog approached from behind and bit me. Everyone said it was mad. When I reached home, my grandmother was very worried about it. At that time, Sri Sri Thakur was sitting in grandma's cottage, surrounded by devotees. As soon as he saw me, he asked, "A dog has bitten you? Show me where." I showed him the marks of the animal's teeth and the blood dripping from the wound. Grandma said, "Go to Calcutta at once with Brajagopal." Brajagopal, the teacher, was prepared to leave at once. Meanwhile, some people in the village chased the dog and killed it. Thakur told me, "If your grandma is asking you to go, you better leave for Calcutta at the earliest." After arriving at Ishwardi station, we got a Calcutta-bound train at 8 a.m. and started the journey. After getting off at Sealdah, we went directly to the Tropical Hospital. After listening to the teacher, the doctor swept his hand across my belly and said, "This particular spot has to be injected for 17 consecutive days, one injection every day. Listening to this, I got off the bed, and slowly walked to the door. Then, I ran for my life. Brajagopalda and the doctor kept calling out to me from behind, but I didn't listen to them. The very thought of 17 injections scared me. I reached the station somehow and got on a train to Pabna at once. When I reached the ashram, I saw Thakur sitting on the western side of Grandma's cottage. As soon as Grandma saw me, she ran after me, shouting aloud, "This naughty chap has got no brains, and has come back home." I cried and said, "I don't want to stay there for 17 days without Thakur, that too taking injections every day." Grandma was aghast, "A mad dog has bitten you, and you don't want to take injections. No one in our family has ever died of a dog bite. Do you want to die?" Sri Sri Thakur took Borda in his arms, and said, "Nothing will happen to him. Don't worry."

Once during a discourse, Sri Sri Borda said, "I have to build myself according to the gospels that Sri Sri Thakur has given. This understanding should be consolidated in each one of us. We read *Satyanusaran* every day, but these sayings need to be characterized by us. Thakur has given me the maxims to prepare me, to build my character."

Panditda, who was present, asked, "People say, is it really possible to characterize whatever Sri Sri Thakur has said about family, society, and the nation?"

Sri Sri Borda replied, "Thakur had to hear such comments many times over and over." Those days, Prafulla Das and Devi Mukherjee were sitting near Thakur, and noting down whatever He uttered. Many others were also there. Almost all the time, Thakur would utter gospels; even during his bath and toilet. Aunt Maya asked, "You are uttering so many gospels day and night, who will execute them? How will they be used? For whom are you imparting all this?" Thakur felt very uneasy about this, but did not say anything. Afterwards, having heard her, Sri Sri Thakur asked everyone present there, "For whom am I uttering these maxims?" Everyone replied, "It is all for us." He then looked at me, and asked the same question, to which I replied, "It is all for me." He then told Aunt Maya, "I have given all the gospels for him, and he shall obey them all." After a while, Sri Sri Borda said, "Thakur has already indicated, that whatever he has to give, he has given it, it shall remain in print forever. Even if there is only one person who follows his way, he shall execute all this in action; if there is no one, it will all still remain in history, waiting for someone in the future." (*Ishta Prasange*, Vol. 2, 19.04.1975)

Sri Sri Dada

It was 9 September 1999, 7 in the morning. Sri Sri Dada was sitting in the Natmandap after prayer. In a certain context, he said, "There is no limit to Thakur's mercy." Dr. Biswanath Mukherjee's uncle, Rabin Banerjee, was a renowned homeopathic doctor of Calcutta, and he usually came to visit Sri Sri Thakur. Once he had come to meet Thakur after giving medicines to a chronically ill patient. He had to return in three days to see the patient and administer the second dose. He sought permission from Sri Sri Thakur to go back on the fixed date. Thakur told him, "You will go home when I say so." He again approached Sri Sri Thakur after a day, and requested, "I have to give medicines to a serious patient." Thakur asked him about the patient and his medicines. After the conversation, he said, "Don't worry, stay here, she will be alright."

Even after Thakur's reassurance, Rabin Babu was worried about the patient. Monday and Tuesday passed off. On Wednesday, finally, Sri Sri Thakur allowed him to return. Arriving in Calcutta, Rabinda took a taxi and went directly to the patient. The patient's mother opened the door, and was taken aback on seeing Rabinda. She asked, "Why have you come here again?" Asked about her daughter's condition, she said, "She is all right; she is completely fine after taking the medicines you had given her on Monday morning. She is not running a fever any more."

Rabinda examined the patient and discovered that the mother was indeed telling the truth. The patient was gradually coming back to normalcy. Observing Rabinda's expression, the mother of the patient asked, "Are you fine? Will you have any tea?" Rabinda shook his head and after giving a little medicine to the patient, instead of going home, took the next available train to Hemayetpur. When he described the incident to Sri Sri Thakur, he laughed profusely. Rabinda said, "The patient's mother was telling me that I had gone there, and given medicine at a time when I was sitting here in front of you." Sri Sri Thakur with a smile replied with one of his favourite quotes from Shakespeare, "It has been said—There are more things in heaven and earth, Horatio, than are dreamt of in your philosophy." Whenever Rabinda described this wonderful event to Sri Sri Thakur, he would always laugh, and never answer.

When Rabinda returned home, he saw that a few robbers had burnt his entire house down, but his family was safe. The neighbours said, "Thank God, you didn't come home any earlier, or else these bandits would have murdered you." *(Being and Becoming)*

Sri Sri Acharyadev

In those days, Sri Sri Thakur had just begun work as a physician in Pabna. A woman from a well-to-do family had a carbuncle on her leg. He treated her and she was cured. After this, the patient developed such immense faith in Thakur that later she always used to say, "I will not go to anybody else except my Thakur-doctor." A long time passed. Sri Sri Thakur's Satsang Ashram had been established in Hemayetpur. He was no longer seeing patients. One day, he suddenly met that woman. She had come of age, and the family had lost all their wealth in the midst of unforeseen circumstances. The woman was unable to even manage two square meals a day. She was wearing tattered clothes, had an extremely frail body, looking like she could die any moment. She was the lone, surviving member of her family.

Sri Sri Thakur clearly remembered her great faith during the days of her treatment. With due respect for her faith and reliance on him, he brought her to the ashram. He fed her properly, giving her a feast of innumerable food items to choose from. In addition, he categorically told the other women at the ashram to incite her and quarrel with her. He knew that after a certain age, the angrier one is, the faster is food digested. At times, Thakur would also narrate some sensual and humorous tales to amuse her. Many devotees were confused about Sri Sri Thakur's way of dealing with the old lady. Little did they understand that all this was being done to help the lady digest her food, and revive her health. After many days, the lady passed away. Sri Sri Thakur said, "Whatever life the Supreme Father had granted the woman, she has lived not even a single day less." This lady went by the name of Raman Saha's mother. (Ritwik Conference, Gauhati, 1 January 2019)

This happened after the *Viswaguru Abirbhav Utsav*. Those days, Sri Sri Thakur was collecting five rupees from everyone for some important purpose. Whoever could offer something, considered themselves lucky. Truly, who would not be happy to fulfil His wishes! Then, Sri Sri Thakur's mother-in-law was staying with him for several days. She was an immensely devoted woman. She had heard many divine accounts of Sri Sri Thakur's *Lila*. Even she had saved five rupees to offer for Thakur's purpose. She thought, "He is receiving so much from his devotees, what if he refuses to take from me?" Her mind was preoccupied with such thoughts. One day, all the male members of the family were eating together. After the meal, Thakur washed his hands, and went away, but came back sensing that his mother-in-law wanted to tell him something. She asked if he would accept the five rupees she had kept safely for his work. At once, he knelt before her and stretched his folded hands. In a moment's time, the entire atmosphere was filled with a divine impulse of elation. His mother-in-law took out the money she had kept in a knot in her saree and gave it to him. Tears of love rolled down her eyes and fell on Thakur's hands. His eyes too welled up were filled with tears and everyone present there was overwhelmed with emotion. Seeing this, Sri Sri Borda said that he had never seen such a magnanimous manner of receiving an offering. He added that these were not tears of distress, but of sacred love. Whoever has seen is blessed. While describing this event, he wept like a child himself. (Satsang Vihar, Bhubaneswar, midday meeting, 12. 2. 2016).

PART TWO

1

BELONGINGNESS TO THE ENVIRONMENT, LOVE AND COMPASSION FOR PLANTS AND ANIMALS, ASSURANCE TO SERVE HUMANITY

His Concern for Plants

Sri Sri Thakur deeply loved all creation—plants, animals, and inanimate objects. It was in 1928 that the construction of several new buildings started at the Hemayetpur Satsang Ashram. Due to the summer vacation, the majority of teachers and students from Tapovan Vidyalaya, as well as many Guru brothers and workers of the ashram, joined the effort along with masons and labourers. Thus, it was possible to complete the construction of the two-storied Vishwa Vigyan Kendra within a short time. Sri Sri Thakur did not allow the building of a house for himself as the site would have entailed the felling of many trees. Subsequently, it was built at another location. After a few days, a cyclone blew off a few branches of a babul tree and dropped them on the road to his new residence. They were thorny and caused inconvenience to passers-by. Nafar Ghosh, a disciple, cut off several more branches and cleaned up the entire space. When it came to Sri Sri Thakur's notice, he was in utter shock and asked, "Nafraa, why did you do so, despite knowing everything? Go at once, and re-join the cut-off branches with the remaining tree using a bandage of straw, cow dung, and soil." After this incident, Sri Sri Thakur did not use that road for several days. When the branches grew afresh in the tree, Thakur was relaxed and resumed commuting on that road. (*Satwati,* June 2019)

In the Deoghar Ashram Sri Sri Thakur desired to build a house at a particular spot, close to Thakur-Bangla. Roof casting was done. One evening, he was walking towards the hillside mansion, where a mango tree had been cut beside it. He uttered, "Alas!...who committed such ruthlessness?" Khagen Tapadar, in charge of the construction, remained silent. It was his doing. For the convenience of the roof casting, a branch of that tree had been lopped off. Seeing it, Sri Sri Thakur could not move even a step. Pointing to another disciple, Pyari Mohan, who was accompanying him, he said with compassion, "Pyari, look what has been done to this innocent tree! Treat its wounds at the earliest, use medicines, or any other botanical treatment that is needed, so that new twigs can come up." Saying this, he turned back and walked towards where he usually sat. He avoided using that road for the next 15 days. One day, a devotee attendant informed him that many new twigs had come up on the tree. Elated beyond measure, Sri Sri Thakur went to see them at once. His joy knew no bounds. He resumed strolling to the hillside mansion. (Santosh Joyardar—Kaloda).

His Affection For Pets
(The Episode of *Kani,* the One-eyed Cat, and the Pet Dog, Tabu)

Kani was very dear to Sri Sri Borma. She had one eye only and hence was named *Kani* in Bengali. Sri Sri Thakur always left a portion of his meals for it. Kani would sit in the corridors of the big mansion (now known as Memoria) nestling between Sri Sri Borma's legs. On those days, Sri Sri Thakur showered at exactly 11:08 a.m. Thakur would be immersed in discourses with disciples and scholars from the break of dawn, and also deal with the problems of so many devotees who came from near and far. Therefore, his shower would be delayed. Kani would often get restless at such times, and feebly cry out to Borma with a shrill meow! Sri Sri Thakur, alert as always, would ask Borma what the cat wanted. Borma would reply, "Kani is hungry, and if he doesn't go and take a bath immediately, it will delay her lunchtime with you." Sri Sri Thakur, in his innocence, would feel guilty, and instantly go for a shower.

Sri Sri Thakur's youngest son, revered Kajalda, had kept a puppy called Tabu. Most of the time, when Sri Sri Thakur or Sri Sri Borda was at home, the pup would sit by their side. Tabu was extremely dear to Sri Sri Borda, He was then staying in Boral Bungalow (now Shorashi Bhawan), and whenever he fell ill, Sri Sri Borma would come to see him, and bring Tabu with him. The pup would sit at Borda's bedside, and would innocently stare at them during their long conversations, with an expression as if it understands everything. When Tabu breathed its last, Sri Sri Thakur, Borma, Borda, and Kajalda grieved for days together.

The Tale of the Majestic Goat

During 1945-46, Rairanjan Das, a resident of Kandi village in Murshidabad came to know that Sri Sri Thakur wanted a Majestic species goat from him. He received this message from a Hemayetpur Ashram worker, Rajendranath Majumdar. Rairanjan faced a lot of trouble to accomplish this task as it was a rare species of the goat family.

One day, he remembered that there was a dehydrated goat meat factory on the banks of the Ganges in Patna. He contacted an old acquaintance, a Muslim subedar working in the army, who lived in Patna. The subedar said he would keep his demand in mind and after a few days, informed Rairanjan that a consignment of hilly male goats would arrive in Patna the following month. Around 100 high-breed male goats arrived. Among them was one Majestic goat (*Raja Chhagol*). Rairanjan bought it and successfully convinced the Railway authorities to send it with Rajen Majumdar via Danapur to Pabna.

Sri Sri Thakur was very happy to see the goat. It proved to be a loyal pet in a very short span of time. It followed Sri Sri Thakur everywhere. At times, it sat quietly under his seat. Thakur named the goat Hriday. Its body was maroon, and it made a pitpat sound when it walked around the ashram with flair and grandeur. Gradually, it could understand Sri Sri Thakur's language, and followed his commands. When Sri Sri Thakur ate, it would stand at a distance and wait for a tiny portion of his food. One day, during Thakur's lunchtime, Hriday was absent. Sri Sri Thakur could not begin with his lunch, and the baffled devotees looked for the goat all over. At a distance, Sri Sri Borma and Sri Sri Borda stood speechless. Suddenly, a shout was heard that Hriday had been found. It had entered the room of revered Guruprasadi Devi (Sri Sri Thakur's sister). Unwittingly, she had bolted the door from outside, and the goat was locked in. When it was Sri Sri Thakur's lunchtime, a loud bleat from the goat was heard. Listening to Hriday's shrill cry, the people around immediately called out to Guruprasadi Devi, and when the door was opened, Hriday rushed to Sri Sri Thakur's dining area. Seeing Hriday, Sri Sri Thakur was happy and started eating. Once, while speaking contextually, Thakur uttered, "This goat is a very wise one." He paid a lot of attention to Hriday, and similarly, it too was sincerely devoted to him. Everyone in Thakur's family was shocked when he passed away; their grief was akin to the loss of a close friend or companion. (*Alochana, 2018*—Kripasindhu Rakshit)

Tending To A Goat's Distress

In Deoghar, Sri Sri Thakur was sitting in the Yati Ashram with Kestoda one day. Just then, a goat came running there bleating in distress. Sri Sri Thakur understood its pain, and tears rolled down his cheeks. He called for a devotee and directed him to find out why the animal was in pain. After a while, the devotee reported that the goat belonged to a woman called Sumati, and she had sold all of the goat's kids to a trader. Sri Sri Thakur immediately sent another devotee with some money to buy back the kids. He waited anxiously without rest, listening to the melancholic bleating of the mother goat.

The devotee returned with all the baby goats and returned them to their mother. The reunited 'family' lovingly caressed each other. Thakur was extremely pleased and said, "The agonized bleating of the goat was so full of distress that it broke my heart. I simply could not rest."(*Satwati*, February 2019)

Saving a Goat from Sacrifice

On 4 April 1919, close to the Hemayetpur Ashram, a tantrik in his rites of worshipping the Goddess of *Shakti* (power) organized the sacrifice of a goat in the local burial ground. He was aware that Sri Sri Thakur did not like such sacrifices. As soon as this came to Thakur's notice, he personally went to the tantrik and pleaded, "The Goddess is everyone's mother, including this goat's; can the worship of a mother be possible with the killing of her own child? Can the mother accept such worship? Kindly let the goat be." The adamant tantrik did not pay any heed. Thakur pleaded again, "Look, you are performing a sacrifice. A funda-mental ritual entailed in all sacrifices is that a donation must be made to Brahmins. I am a Brahmin, and as an offering, please give the goat to me." The tantrik replied angrily, "I cannot give this goat to anybody in any circumstances." Sri Sri Thakur fell at his feet and pleaded with folded hands, "Instead of the goat, offer me in sacrifice." Meanwhile, Manmohini Devi arrived at the scene and understood the situation's gravity. She caught her son's hand and took him back to the ashram. Sri Sri Thakur could not disobey his mother's command, but he was extremely restless, as he could not rescue the goat. Seeing his desperation, one of the devotees named Nafar sought permission to rescue the goat.

Manmohini Devi agreed but on one condition. "There should be no conflict with anybody over this." Twenty to twenty-five people had surrounded the goat. Nafar uttered "JaiGuru" loudly, rushed into the cordon, lifted the goat, and fled with blazing speed to the ashram. The people at the burial ground were dumbfounded. The tantric cursed saying, "Whoever disturbed the worship of the Mother Goddess has to pay for his sin." At the ashram, Sri Sri Thakur happily lifted the goat onto his lap and caressed it as if a mother had been reunited with her lost child. (*Manas Tirtha Parikrama*)

The Mark Of A Whip

Sri Sri Thakur was travelling in a horse carriage to Kushtia to meet physician Gobinda Chandra Saha of Baradi village. He was accompanied by Dr. Satish Chandra Joyardar, Birendranath Roy, and Gokul Mandal. The horse was weak and unable to pull the cart speedily with a load of four persons. The coachman whipped it to make it go faster; he did this thrice, giving the horse no respite from its agony. Sri Sri Thakur could not tolerate such behaviour. He got off and said, "The horse is in pain. We can all walk the rest of the distance." They paid the fare and walked on. On arrival, Sri Sri Thakur freshened up and rested for a while. An attendant devotee while massaging him saw three severe whip marks on his back. He asked, "Thakur, how did you get these whip marks?" Sri Sri Thakur remained silent. When the devotee asked the same question repeatedly he resolutely said, "While I was coming here by horse carriage, the carriage man whipped the horse thrice. I was greatly affected by it; I felt the whip lashing my back." The attendant was surprised and said, "The horse was whipped, and there are marks on your back! I am simply not able to understand." Sri Sri Thakur said, "It is as if I was feeling the horse's pain in my body. It is perhaps why you see these marks." (*Sri Sri Thakur Anukulchandra[1]*)

Language Not A Barrier

In Deoghar Ashram, everyday cows went on the narrow trail between the wide corridor and wooden thatched-roof house towards the kitchen for the surplus of food and boiled rice water. Sri Sri Thakur always looked at them with affection. Once, one of the cows halted for a while and looked at Sri Sri Thakur as if he wanted to say something. He also looked back at the dumb creature for a long time without blinking. A surprising moment followed. The cow waved its head in a unique gesture as if trying to say something. Sri Sri Thakur nodded in a similar manner. The cow managed to understand what he indicated, and perhaps it was the response it wanted. After a while, as usual, it left for the kitchen yard. The devotees present there enjoyed this silent conversation between man and animal. (*Priya Param*)

Pal Ma's Gift of Squirrels

Pal Ma was a sincere devotee of Sri Sri Thakur staying in Calcutta. She narrates this story in the first person as follows, "During Sri Sri Thakur's visit to Calcutta, he would sit for some time in Nani Bhangida's business house in Hatkhola locality. I went there often to see him. One day, he told me, "Ma, can you give me a squirrel?" I said, "Baba, to catch hold of a squirrel at this age is an extremely difficult task; they run very fast." Regardless, Thakur was insistent, "Yes Ma, I know, but can you still give it to me?" His asking was childlike. He repeatedly said, "Yes Ma, I know you will give me a squirrel, not one, but many." What could I do? Where was I supposed to find one? I was worried about it. For several days, all I thought of was how to catch squirrels. Sri Sri Thakur left for Pabna. One day, to my surprise, on my way to the market, I found a trader selling four baby squirrels for four rupees. I was taken aback. The sheer rarity of such an event was unprecedented. I immediately purchased all of them. It was only after I had sent them to the Hemayetpur Ashram through a devotee that was I able to make my mind normal. Afterwards, I went to the ashram and saw several squirrels running up and down a palm tree. Seeing this Thakur told me, "Look, Ma, these are the squirrels you gifted me; how have they multiplied to so many! This is how life is; in one moment there is nothing, and in the next there is plenty." What sort of Leela is this? I asked myself. What am I supposed to understand from this? I am simply unable to fathom it. The essence of such an act is only known to Him."
(*Dui Mayer Smriti Alekhya*)

A Home for Frogs

It was September 1956. In the Deoghar Ashram yard, the construction of a thatched-roof wooden house was in progress. It was monsoon, and the yard was full of water. The population of frogs had grown manifold. They were playing in the water freely, but a few of them were crushed to death under the feet of the workers. When Sri Sri Thakur visited the construction site, he was distressed, and the work halted. What could be done? It was suggested that some arrangement should be made for the work to continue without endangering the frogs. Nobody had a solution. At last, Sri Sri Thakur intervened., He instructed that a few small makeshift boxes be constructed in a corner of the yard. The frogs there jumped from one box to another. Food was placed in the boxes, and all the frogs started playing there happily. Sri Sri Thakur enjoyed this sight to his heart's content. (*Deeprakshi*, Vol. 2)

The Fate of the Cow dung Insect

Sri Sri Thakur started work for the Hemayetpur Satsang Ashram in the second decade of the twentieth century. Several cottages had been built on the banks of the Padma River. In those days, people did not have the means to have toilets in their homes. They went to the forest, or other open areas adjacent to the river to defecate. Very few people had service latrines in their houses. This entailed a lower-caste person coming to carry the faeces away. Sri Sri Thakur had this facility at his house, but, when he went there, he would look in the excreta for a particular insect (cow dung) that flew in and ate the excreta. In this process, most of these insects were buried in the excreta and unable to get out, eventually dying there. Aware of this phenomenon, Sri Sri Thakur set forth on rescuing these insects with a stick from the excreta. He would get so engrossed in this work that on some days his entire schedule would be postponed indefinitely. Even an insect was not deprived of his love!

One day, Sri Sri Thakur mentioned the strange fate of the cow dung insects. "Look, God has created this insect with such precision that when it flies, it seems as if an aeroplane is coming. God has made their bodies so well lubricated, that no rubbish in the world will stick to them. But when it falls into a dump of excreta or dung, it forgets the reservoir of its immense energy and forgets that by flapping its wings, it can get rid of any rubbish clinging to it. It is prepared to be suffocated to death in the pile of shit, but unwilling to be a little conscious about itself. Man is no different. Entangled in the passions and material attractions of the world, he forgets that he is the son of the Supreme Father, the offspring of Heavenly Might. If he wishes, he can save himself from the grip of great distress. However, the man never thinks in that way; instead, he considers himself weak and feeble and succumbs to the trials and tribulations of life. He ultimately perishes and meets the fate of the cow dung insect. (*Manas Tirtha Parikrama*)

A Love Story of Two Lizards

At Deoghar Ashram, at the sitting place of Sri Sri Thakur, a wonderful incident took place. Since midday, a lizard had been clicking loudly somewhere close to Sri Sri Thakur's bed. It would creep up one of the bed's legs, increase its clicking, and then come down. This cycle was repeated again and again. The devotees present around Thakur could not understand the story till then. Sri Sri Thakur laughed and said, "Wait, he is coming, don't worry." As afternoon approached, a devotee came from Malda, and bowed to him. He had brought with him a basket of ripe mangoes. As soon as he placed the basket in front of Sri Sri Thakur, a lizard rushed out of it, and ran up his bed, making intense clicking sounds. It finally met the lizard that was present there waiting for its mate. Sri Sri Thakur laughed again, and said, "Oh! Today is their wedding day. The bride lizard had been very worried since the groom was delaying the proceedings." (*Punya Prabahe*)

Narrator: A similar incident is described in the last part of chapter 15 of *Sai Satcharitra* (Hemadpant Dabholkar). One day, Sai Baba of Shirdi was sitting in a mosque, and a lizard was clicking continuously on the adjacent wall. Out of curiosity, a devotee asked him, "What is the meaning of such intense clicking by the lizard? Is it a good or bad omen?" Sai Baba replied, "The sister of this lizard will soon come here from Aurangabad. That's why it is swelling with joy." The devotee could not understand Baba's words and sat there silently. After a while, a man came on a horse to see Baba. He tied the horse nearby and opened a bag of fodder for it. Just then, a small lizard rushed out of the fodder bag and crept up the wall where Baba was sitting. Baba asked the devotee to observe. The small lizard slowly reached its sister. Both sisters embraced and kissed each other, running all around the walls in joy. Shirdi and Aurangabad are quite far from each other! How could Baba know that a lizard's sister was travelling in a fodder bag from such a long distance? It's a mystery.

Concern for a Street Dog

It was 1951; summer was at its peak. One day after a session of intense spiritual discourse, Sri Sri Thakur was returning from the Yati Ashram to his residence for a bath. At the gate, he saw a street dog in distress caused by a wound on its neck; flies in large numbers flitted around and on the wound and worrying the dog. Thakur was immensely concerned. He called the devotees following him and asked them to tend to the dog. One of them informed him about the nature of the wound. Sri Sri Thakur directed a devotee named Harenda to fetch a veterinary doctor, and stood there all the time waiting for him. It was long past his daily routine to bathe and eat. Regardless, he did not move an inch. One of the devotees requested him to go ahead, saying that the doctor would certainly come. But the devotee's counsel was of little use. Another devotee gave him a chair to at least sit down, but he did not do so, and said, "The dog is restless and in severe pain, and you are here asking me to sit in comfort? Take the chair away." After about an hour, Harenda returned with the doctor and soon treatment started. The doctor requested Sri Sri Thakur to go to his house.

He was now reassured, and slowly paced towards his residence. (*Satwati,* May 2019)

Rescuing the Insects

One day, Sri Sri Thakur, along with some devotees, was travelling from Hemayetpur to Kashipur. It was monsoon season, and they had to cross a stream. The water was three feet deep. Sri Sri Thakur noticed that a large number of insects were being carried away by the current of the stream. He was distressed and could proceed no further. He entered the water, stood there firmly with the water up to his knees, and rescued all the insects one by one, placing them safely on the ground. He earnestly requested his followers to help in this rescue operation and they did so.(*Sri Sri Thakur Anukulchandra*[1])

His Assurance to Serve Humanity

In this Life: During a discussion, Sri Sri Thakur said, "Those who come here and gain my company, their devotion shall never go in vain. By being here, they attain the blessings of the Supreme Father. When you come here, you stay within the boundaries of goodwill and good wishes. Those who come with good intentions, their virtues shall gain momentum. Even those who come with bad intentions, their vices will similarly get multiplied here, but, they shall never perish. No doubt, they will suffer for their past misdeeds, but their suffering, instead of persisting over a long period of time, shall now be short and swift, and in the end, they will be benefitted too. My disciples will never squander in darkness, they shall not be ruined."

Sri Sri Thakur continued, "There is no need to be fearful, I say this fervently. Some realisation is guaranteed to everybody who has come within the sight of the Super Soul. Even those who have not been able to dedicate their body, mind, and wealth entirely to the Lord's service, even their progress in life will not be hindered. Although they have not sacrificed anything out of their own volition, but by the virtue of their simple affinity with me, the

Supreme Father has *suo moto* accepted their offerings and granted them His blessings. For those who have not been able to practise the prescribed form of *Sadhana*, they shall not be entirely deprived of my grace, and attain some form of realisation through their dreams."

In the Afterlife: In a different context, Sri Sri Thakur talked to his disciples about the service he will offer them in the afterlife. Those who die here without being liberated from their earthly passions and attachments, the Sadguru with his presence will show them the path they are entitled to. They shall never languish in darkness, but will always be protected under His divine shelter. They are assured of a suitable birth in the next life, and all the progress they had attained in this life will be carried over to the next one in exponential proportions. All the consequences of their evil deeds shall be negated, and they will not be born as inferior beings, but as humans. Not only this, they are ensured to inherit an enriching character and personality in human society, by the virtue of their leanings to the Ideal. (*Amiyabani*)

3

THUS SPAKE SRI SRI THAKUR: GLIMPSES OF HIS PREVIOUS BIRTH, HIS ADVENT IN THIS WORLD, SRI JAGANNATH SWAMI, PURUSHOTTAM SRI RAM & BHAKTA HANUMAN, SRI KRISHNA, *THE BHAGAVAD GITA*, JESUS CHRIST, HAZRAT MOHAMMAD, EPISODES FROM HIS EARLY LIFE, THE FUTURE OF BHARAT.

Previous Birth

During a discussion, Sri Sri Thakur said, "My memory is the witness. Once upon a time, I was rowing in a river with my maternal grandmother. There were many turtles and fishes in the water. Another strange experience comes to my mind as well. Once, in the hills, there were many moonbeam flower plants and bamboo trees. The bamboo I saw was different to the ones we see in our area. I was there with my wife, and we saw a unique large stone. If you stood on it, your footprint would be etched on it. There were many trees with creepers entangled around them. A stream flowed nearby, across which lived several tigers and bears. I was immersed in meditation. The days I spent in another land also come to mind. It was called Manipur. I clearly remember a wooden house. It was a little distance from a crack-edged brick road that led to the market. My wife resided in this wooden house. I am certain if I go there now, I will find her there. From Manipur, I went to another country where people wore gowns with a veil covering their faces. Their garments were of different colours and there were many markets. I remember some sort of a mosque there, with several fruit stalls nearby. I met a tailor named Khalifa, and talked to him for a long time."

After this discussion, Guruprasanna Bhattacharyya (Panditda), a sincere devotee, asked a couple of questions to Sri Sri Thakur. That conversation is documented below:

Panditda: Do they seem real?

Sri Sri Thakur: I recollect another place. There was a hill, and beyond it were stones and water. Hearing your words, all those memories are refreshed.

Panditda: Do you feel bad remembering all this?

Sri Sri Thakur: No, not bad exactly, but a feeling of regret comes over me.

Panditda: Why?

Sri Sri Thakur: Although I remember those places vividly, I can no longer go there. So I think, is it my imagination or something else?

Panditda; Are the incidents not very clear to you, so that you separate reality from imagination?

Sri Sri Thakur (emphatically): It is all crystal clear. With a little help, whatever part of my memory is hazy will become vivid.

Panditda: Generally, what we have seen is difficult to imagine.

Sri Sri Thakur: Sitting here with you, I can visualise many events unfolding in the world. A person has his eyes fixated on me right now, I can clearly see him. (*Deeprakshi,* vol. 6, 8.5.1960)

On 5 October 1961, Sri Sri Thakur was sitting in the parlour of Deoghar Ashram. Kestoda's youngest son came with a basket full of moonbeam flowers and bowed to Sri Sri Thakur. He picked one or two and entered into a state of deep thought and reflection for some time. Then he said, "There were a lot of flowers like this on the banks of the Saryu River, in the midst of which, there was a cluster of bamboo trees. Crimson rays of the sun at dusk and dawn fell on these tiny flowers and gave them an appearance of varied colours. It looked very beautiful. There were many stones of different sizes on the edge of that river, and glossy in texture as much water flowed through that channel. I also remember women carrying pitchers of water on their heads instead of in their arms. If I can go there, I shall recognise all this." (*Smritir Mala*)

His Advent in this World

The description that Sri Sri Thakur gave about his advent on Earth as published in "*Amiyavani*" has appeared in an anthology published from the USA, *Cosmic Cradle* by Elizabeth M. Carman and Neil J. Carman, PhD, Sunstar Ltd., USA, 1999. In Chapter 32, Sri Sri Thakur's cosmic memory has been elaborated on:

"A spiritual master of India, Sri Sri Thakur Anukul Chandra, has been established as an unchallenged seer of the origin of Creation. On being asked how creation came into existence, Sri Sri Thakur Anukul Chandra said, 'As I have realised, a prime point being free from the centripetal force expanded, and as a result of this, millions of active atoms were created. Each active atom created millions of hyper atoms, and each of the hyper atoms created supra-hyper atoms in millions. As a consequence, an unbroken, invisible, and physically inconceivable point was created. That prime inconceivable point is the Great Soul. From its centre was created, like flames of fire, many innumerable worlds. The souls that were created will undergo the cycle of birth and death until they are able to liberate themselves from earthly bondage (*Maya*). The great earthly soul is indeed the Supreme Soul as well."

"Since the birth of Sri Sri Thakur in the corporeal form, until his rebirth as a human, his soul episodically shifted forms, bodies, and professions through a series of births. Of all these births, in the last three, he lived the lives of a cobbler, prince and an ascetic. The sorrow of his family at the end of each life left a mark on his memory and deeply affected him.

"Before his advent in this life, Sri Sri Thakur dwelt in an undefined higher realm. His landing on Earth began through undiscovered heavenly bodies. He came across a total of 44,000 stars and planets in space. Just as the planets orbit around the sun in our solar system, there are several other yet-to-be-discovered planets and stars that are ceaselessly revolving around bigger celestial bodies in other galaxies and solar systems. The expanse of our universe is unfathomable. Sri Sri Thakur, on His path of descent, saw a star that had been broken into pieces. One of these scenes is still fresh in his memory; it was an uncommon circle of stars; four stars moving around a bigger star. When they came near the centre, they looked red, and when they went far apart, they looked blue. He knew that the change of colour was due to the Doppler Effect.

While coming through circles of heavenly bodies, he halted at various stars. The celestial inhabitants in those stars welcomed him, and at the time of his departure sang songs full of pathos for him; this valediction caused him a lot of pain. The atmosphere on those planets was different from that of Earth; the inhabitants did not resemble humans on Earth. Towards the end of his journey, he entered the Sun through the path of light. The outer part of the Sun is hot, but its core is much cooler. While entering the Sun, on his left, there was utter darkness, and towards the right, there was a path of light in a giant corner through which 44,000 stars and planets were visible."

Narrator: What is the Doppler Effect? Normally speaking, let us assume a group of singers proceeding towards me from a distance. The nearer they come, the louder the sound. It reaches its pinnacle, and when they go back, the sound becomes lesser and lesser. The difference in this sound vibration due to distance was discovered by the Austrian physicist, Christian Doppler in the 19th century: "The difference of sound wave length was due to variations of distance." In the same manner, the wavelength of light is visible in different colours due to the change in distance.

Sri Jagannath Swami

Once, during a discussion, Sri Sri Thakur observed that Sri Jagannath (Puri, Odisha) is an evocative manifestation of God Almighty. He has no legs, or no hands, and only a pair of arms. He has no ears, he has a mouth, but even that is closed as if conveying to everyone who visits Him, "I could run towards you, but I have no legs. I have no hands like you; even if I wanted, could I embrace you? I am here static at one place, I have no words for you as well, for my lips are closed."

Sri Sri Thakur continued, "But Sri Jagannath has two big eyes without eyelids to close them. He is ever sleepless, observing the entire universe through his lidless eyes. You may deceive everybody in this world, but not His *Chaka dolas* (round eyes). He observes all your actions, no matter where you are in the east, west, north, or south. He is '*Sarvam Khalu Idam Brahma*', it is not possible to fathom His all-pervasive omnipotence within the scope of our thoughts. However, he has facilitated the realisation of His expansive wisdom by offering the symbolic rope of his divine chariot to the world at large. This offering connotes three principles to abide by in life, namely, Discipline, Obedience, and Introspection. Those who follow His rules of discipline, and are obedient to His ways through proper introspection, shall attain bliss. To follow the Ideal is the ultimate meditation. Whoever is truly sincere in this pursuit will find the extent of their knowledge equally rewarding. During Sri Jagannath's chariot festival, His benevolence is equally available to everyone. There is no difference between a king and his subject, a scholar and an illiterate, or the rich and the poor. He calls everybody to take shelter in His grace, in the same way, the Prophet of an era (the Ideal) calls everyone into His fold. We have to hold on to the Prophet with our own hands, we have to make the effort to realise the Ideal. No God can help us if a follower is not attached to the Prophet with all his commitment and devotion." (*Amruta Kahani*, and *Alochana Prasange*, vol. I, 26.12.1941)

Purushottam Sri Ram and His Bhakta Hanuman

Sri Sri Thakur said, "Ramachandra was God himself, but throughout the course of his life, he manifested what it means to be devoted to one's father. This is his greatness. Through such concentrated efforts, man can make possible what is impossible. Coming to Hanuman, one must admit he had a great presence of mind, the possessor of eight-fold realisation (*Ashta Siddhi*). He was a good singer, orator, and expert warrior, physically and mentally strong, conscious, non-egoistic, a knower of scriptures, and the greatest devotee of Sri Ram. His devotion to the Lord is inexplicable. His original name was Maruti, but since both the temple bones on his face had an unusual growth, he was called Hanuman. During the battle between Ram and Ravan, Hanuman reached Sri Ram's battle camp. He saw Sri Ramachandra holding his dear brother, Laxman, wounded with blood flowing out and crying profusely. He was deeply affected. In agony, Rama Chandra exclaimed, 'Hanuman, for whom shall I fight? After coming to this forest, I have lost my father, my beloved wife, Sita, and a dedicated brother like Laxman! What shall I achieve in this battle?' The renowned physician of Kishkindha, Shushena, examined Laxman lying in a desperate, dying condition, wounded by Indrajit's shot. He advised, 'If within a stipulated period of time, the medicinal plant *Bishalyakarani* that is found on the slopes of the Gandhamardan mountain could be brought here, then perhaps something can be done to save Laxman's life.' As soon as Hanuman heard this, with all his might he flew to the mountain at the speed of the wind and brought back the Gandhamardan range of mountains. Shushena then prepared a paste from the medicinal plant and smeared it all over Laxman's body. Laxman regained consciousness gradually. Sri Ram embraced him with great happiness, and tears rolled down his eyes. Looking at the smile on the face of Sri Ram, Hanuman said, 'All my exhaustion has been swept away by seeing this smile on your war-weary visage.' The only aim of Hanuman's life was to bring a smile to the Lord's face and make him happy. Sri Ram never really gave any command to Hanuman; he always understood what his Lord wanted, and did so accordingly. His only objective in life was to fulfil his Lord's interests. The characteristic feature of a devotee is to understand the indications and hints of the Lord. (*Alochana Prasange*, vol. 3, 3.6.1942, and *Amruta Kahani*)

Lord Sri Krishna

Sri Sri Thakur remembered his past days and said, "When I was meditating, repeating the Name, Lord Krishna used to visit me and play his flute enchantingly. As it seemed, he looked the same age as mine, but his complexion was not dark. He looked as if live grass had been covered for some days, and when removed, glowed like green grass."(*Alochana Prasange*, vol.1, 4.12.1941)

Sri Sri Thakur, while talking about the battle of the *Mahabharata* said, "Sri Krishna always avoided war, but his circumstances never allowed him to do so. The real war he waged was against death itself, the death of those who were living embodiments of murder and ravaging in order to save society at large, and in effect, the whole of humanity." Recollecting his past experiences, Sri Sri Thakur said, "One day while coming along the Kashipur Road, I saw there was bright light all around; the Gods were singing. The first two lines of their chanting are still in my memory, and now only one word 'welcome' (*Swagatam*) occurs to my mind." (*Alochana Prasange*, vol. 1, 3.12.1941, 4.12.1941, and 12.10.1939)

In the context of Sri Krishna's death, Sri Sri Thakur said, "As it occurs to my mind, Sri Krishna was sitting on the branch of a margosa tree with his legs dangling. He was immersed in his thoughts when an arrow pierced his feet. He fell to the ground, and after a while passed away. The entire incident happened suddenly, in a very short time. In the prevailing circumstances leading to his last moment, he had lost his will to live." (*Parama Uddhata Sri Sri Thakur Anukul Chandra*, vol. 2)

Srimad Bhagavad Gita

Sri Sri Thakur said, "Whatever is recorded in the *Srimad Bhagavad Gita* is the eternal truth. If you understand the Gita with its implications in life, gradually the gist of all the scriptures shall be visible to you. The adherence to the Gita in thought, speech and action, rectifies all misdeeds of one's life. The pursuit of the Gita's morals makes the path to Sadguru (the Ideal) simpler for an individual; or, at the very least, creates an urge in him to attain the Ideal, without getting entangled in the needless passions and complexes of this world. The essence of Gita provides solutions to not merely the problems of our present, but also that of our past and future."

Jesus Christ and Hazrat Mohammed

Sri Sri Thakur said, "When I think of Jesus Christ, I feel everything about him is graceful and good. See how beautiful his words, eyes, and hair are. Thus, I say, we should all be like him, our dress should be simple and clean, our face, hair, behaviour, the structure of our bodies, our laughter and cries, everything should be as sweet and graceful as him. I think Jesus is the monarch as well as the beggar of love. He was begging for this love from the man who was collecting taxes from the fishermen; he yearned for the same from Mary Magdalene." In this regard, an American once asked Sri Sri Thakur, "Do you believe in Jesus?" He replied instantly, "Mere belief? Had he been alive today, I would have become his first disciple." (*Answer to the Quest*)

Once, Sri Sri Thakur said that Rasul's life was unprecedented, "He was the most glorified among all prophets, there is no doubt about it. Not only Hazrat Rasul is very dear to me, but I also love the millions who follow him. It is also written in the holy Quran that a man who loves and follows Rasul and keeps him at the centre of his life, shall imbibe all the great qualities of Hazrat Rasul.

"I have heard of Rasul's saying, 'One who tries to differentiate among Prophets, places one higher or lower than the other, is an infidel.' There are a few people who believe in Allah, or God, but do not have faith in His living incarnation, the Rasul. They have been misled! People create differences between Hazrat Rasul, Christ, and Buddha. There cannot be a bigger blunder than this. A Prophet belongs to all communities, there are no differences among them." (*Alochana Prasange*, vols. 1, 2, 3, & 4)

Sri Huzur Maharaj

Remembering his boyhood days, Sri Sri Thakur said, "One day, I saw my mother coming out of Huzur Maharaj's temple. A divine glow radiated from her entire body. I kept staring at her for a while, and I realised that if I went to that temple myself, and meditated, perhaps Huzur Maharaj would be glad, and I may be able to attain a similar experience. I acted on my intuition and went to the temple. The portrait of Huzur Maharaj seemed illuminated. A strange delight was awakened in my being. When I finally came out of the temple, I could no longer hold onto my immense ecstasy. I ran all over the ground for a long time to release some of my energy, but it was not enough. Thereafter, I literally flung myself into the Padma River. I spent a long time swimming there. Afterwards, still in wet clothes, I immediately wanted to go and tell this to my mother, her happiness would be out of bounds." (*Pralay Majumdar*)

The Crazy Old Lady

Recollecting his childhood days, Sri Sri Thakur said, "When I was a boy, I came across a *Vaishnavi*, who had left a deep impression on me. It has stayed with me ever since, and now it suddenly came to my mind today in this old age. She never called God God or *Ishwar*; instead, she would address Him as *He* or *You*. Her insanity was unparalleled. However, she loved my mother very dearly. On my way to school, she would play games like hide-and-seek near the tall trees on the road. When she sat down to eat, she would point to the sky and talk as if she was speaking to God, "You haven't had your food yet? Look at me, this wretched old woman has already started eating. Being a woman she was followed by countless men. She had no particular address, but wherever she stayed, she always behaved like a kind mother. She was insane, yes, but in her insanity, there was consistency. Her love for God was so deep and sincere, it was as if His face would appear at all times in her mind." (*Deeprakshi*, 1.12.1954)

An Altruistic Sadhu

"I once met a sadhu in my childhood; he stayed at our village for a few days. I have never met a man like him since then. Often during his meal times, he would not start eating, or allow anyone else by his side to eat, until he had fed me to my heart's content. If anybody offered him any money, he would keep only a coin or two, just enough for him to survive on, dropping the remaining on the road. Children would follow him to pick them up. When he left our village, he looked at me with such fondness that my heart melted. He said, "Oh great boy, one day we shall meet again." (*Alochana Prasange,* vol. 1, 7.7.1941)

A Friend's Repentance

Sri Sri Thakur said, "If I wish to take revenge on anybody, I think I have to first win his mind. In my childhood, I had a playmate who became malicious towards me as we grew up. He never had any kind words for me and blamed me in front of others. Understanding everything, I kept quiet; when we met, I treated him with love and respect. I was never biased against him, but one day I silently resolved that I should dispel all his misunderstandings about me. Our strained relationship continued in this way for 12 years. One day, he came to me with tearful eyes, and said, "Brother! how great you are, and how insignificant I am in comparison. I could only understand this after such a long time. Please pardon me." I smiled and said let us forget all about it. (*Sri Sri Thakur Anukulchandra*[2])

About his Kith and Kin

Sri Sri Borma

Sri Sri Thakur was married to Shorashibala Devi, otherwise known as Sri Sri Borma on 13 August 1906. If during discussions with his disciples, her name came up, Sri Sri Thakur would lovingly say, "If your Thakur had been born a woman, his appearance and attributes would have been exactly like that of Borma's."

He continued, "She barely gets any time to sleep. In the household, her responsibility is greater than mine. Her sleep is so light, she wakes up at the slightest sound. She is extremely organised, disciplined, and tidy. Whenever I want something, she immediately finds it for me. Her eyes are ever vigilant and can detect everything. One of her other special attributes I admire is her frugal nature; be it a single paisa or half a coin, she would always keep it, and in my time of need, would give me much more than the required amount. Everyone should learn how to manage the household economically from her. What I should eat, what my body can digest, she knew all. Both my likes and dislikes, everything was known to her. She was the nurse of my stomach, and of my day-to-day requirements." (*Deeprakshi,* vol. 5 & *Alochana Prasange,* vol. 2)

Recalling another incident, Sri Sri Thakur said, "Once your Borma was cooking a meal for 300-400 people, carrying all the water required herself. This was nothing new for her; she has accomplished tasks more difficult than this several times in her life. The education to shape a household doesn't happen overnight; it is a responsibility that is garnered and learnt over the years, one step at a time. People like your Borma, who have had such a refined education, are fitting to be mothers of this country. The popular saying(Bengali) goes, "One cannot be a skilled mason by merely sitting on a bamboo platform. The real essence of life lies in action." (*Deeprakshi,* Vol. 1)

During the final stage of his life, Sri Sri Thakur told Borma affectionately, "You are my mother and the mother of this whole world."

Sri Sri Borda

Sri Sri Borda (Amarendranath Chakravarty) was born in Dhopadah village of Pabna (now in Bangladesh) on 21 November 1911. He was Sri Sri Thakur's eldest son. He took a deep interest in ashram work ever since his childhood. He shouldered the responsibility of Satsang's administration since 1948. During an intimate conversation, he said, "I don't have any power. However, the Supreme Father has kindly blessed me with the unique ability to understand what kind of an individual one is, as soon as I meet him. I am able to see through what he wants, and what he is capable of achieving." His analysis of *Satyanusaran* is masterly. He was entirely dedicated to the Lord throughout his life and remained the prominent architect of the silent revolution led by Satsang all across the country. With his supervision, several temples and Satsang centres were established all over India, and under his able guidance, the initiation of several thousand was done.

Sri Sri Thakur once endearingly talked about his son, and said, "He has great wit and compassion, his efficiency is unparalleled. However, he is a bit reserved like his mother. At first sight, people don't quite understand him, but as they get closer to him, the more they perceive the softness of his heart, the more they begin to like him. He has always had a benevolent attitude towards everyone. It does not matter whether he has had his food or not, at no cost will he allow people around him to suffer from hunger. He would first arrange food for them, and only then think about himself and his family. To bring up your children is a thing of joy, but at the same time, it is painstaking. I had no idea that my eldest son is so capable of achieving great tasks in his life. The way he is proceeding in life, with intelligence and skill, to bring difficult situations under control, I am certain Satsang will go to great heights under his leadership. He stands as a shield for the people, I am greatly pleased."

Sri Sri Thakur continued, "He also takes a keen interest in learning the language(s) of animals and birds, the behavioural patterns of cattle, dogs, cats, birds, snakes, frogs, tigers, and other creatures, their ways of action and skill are known to him, and I am not exaggerating when I say this, all of this is true. Moreover, he can perceive accurately what is the true nature of persons, and how they would react in certain situations. He sets forth to do every task with the same vigour and enthusiasm as I do." Sri Sri Thakur chuckled and said, "At times, I feel he is the father, and I am the son." *(Alochana Prasange,* and *Dinpanji)*

This great divine personality breathed his last on 5 August 1994 at the Puri Thakurbari in Odisha.

Sri Sri Dada

Sri Asoke Chakravarty was born in the village of Hemayetpur, Bangladesh, on 21 October 1933. Satsangis reverentially call him Sri Sri Dada. After passing his M.A. and LL.B. from Calcutta University, he immersed himself in the organisational work of Satsang. He utilises all his time and power in propagating initiation all over the country. By virtue of his direction, millions of people have been initiated in India, and abroad. This process has been further accelerated at present. He is a man of simple conduct, extraordinary compassion, and loving nature; therefore, thousands of people are attracted towards him.

His memory is extremely precise and sharp; once he meets anyone he remembers him for the rest of his life. His abiding interest and efficiency in freeing people from distress has given him a saintly image. Few things in this life can be as attractive as Sri Sri Dada's company. He is absolutely against self-preaching and has never claimed to be great. He has the unique quality of never becoming angry. He says, "I rarely get irritated, and even if I have said a harsh word or two to anyone, it was always for their own welfare, and never to cause them any harm, my advice brings good fortune in their lives."

On the occasion of his 84th birthday, Sri Sri Dada explained the main purpose of his life to the devotees. "As a servant of the Lord, the purpose of my life is to serve, and accomplish it through all of you. I wish to see everyone in this world in white (wearing white attire at all times is a way of life for Satsangis). By doing this, violence and envy gradually diminish from this world, and the ever-desired intimacy between communities grows." A few words from Sri Sri Thakur about his grandson are given below:

"Grandson! It is not good to roam outside with a bare upper body on early winter mornings, you may catch a severe cold. Go to your mother, and at least put on a vest, and please don't go and play in the middle of the road, but carefully on one side; it would be convenient for you as well as travellers. Moreover, when you play on the road, there is fear of accidents with all these cycles passing by." Looking at his devotees, Sri Sri Thakur continued with a smile, "I see myself in them, and hence care so dearly for their well-being. The child is very intelligent, sincere; also kind-hearted, and sweet as honey. He is but the third generation of our family. I have always felt, in the lineage of all families, that the third generation inherits the greatest attributes in the family's bloodline; he becomes a possessor of great qualities."

The Future Of India

On the morning of 4 July 1948, Sri Sri Thakur was sitting in the corridor of Boral Bungalow. Kestoda, Sushilda, and several other devotees were also present. He spoke very vividly, "Yesterday afternoon I dreamt of a large house with a mango grove in the backyard and a lot of people at a distance. Someone was singing a song. At that moment, a person came up, and I believe he alone can change the destiny of India. I told him everything at once and asked him to swear by touching my feet that he would do everything necessary to restore the glory of Aryan Dharma and Culture. He promised me accordingly and vowed to accomplish this task. He had indomitable courage, confidence, and devotion. In the brief conversation that followed, all my doubts and apprehensions were dispelled. On waking, I thought, "Oh! Is it really in my fate to see the India of my dreams?"

Sailenda, a devotee, asked, "What was the age of this man?" Sri Sri Thakur replied, "He was Bholanathda's age. He had a small beard and his complexion was like mine, not very fair, and he wore a silk coat. On seeing him, it occurred to me that he was an extraordinary personality!" *(Alochana Prasange,* vol. 12, 4.7.1948)

4

Sri Sri Thakur's group of prominent devotees: Anantanath, Nafar Chandra, Satish Chandra, Sushil Chandra, Krishna Prasanna, Prafulla Kumar, Pyari Mohan

Anantanath Roy

Sri Sri Thakur's childhood friend, Anantada, was two years older than he was. After completing medical studies, Sri Sri Thakur set up a dispensary at Hemayetpur. Anantanath left his job as a compounder in Calcutta to assist him. He also participated in Sri Sri Thakur's kirtan, but he felt kirtan alone cannot bring God realisation. Rigorous *sadhana* was necessary. Meanwhile, he lost his wife and son. He had taken initiation from a local Guru, Radharaman Goswami of Gayaspur in Pabna, and took up Sadhana with all earnestness. It never occurred to him that his childhood friend, Anukul Chandra was also a great spiritual master. He constructed two makeshift rooms covered with canvas near his house and spent most of his time there. He also minimised his food intake. When asked by Sri Sri Thakur why he was doing such rigorous austerity, he would simply avoid the question and laugh it off. Gradually, his abstention from food increased. At one point, it was only restricted to water. He had become emaciated, and his body looked like a skeleton. At nights, when he would meditate, ants would roam all over his body; his hut was full of white ant hills. He was on the doorstep of death. Eventually, the news about his deplorable state of affairs reached Sri Sri Thakur. He came to his hut, and asked him, "Why are you doing all this?" Anantanath replied, "I have seen the divine glow, I have heard the divine sound, but I am still anxious and restless. I must continue this rigorous austerity until the point when I truly attain God realisation."

Sri Sri Thakur laughed and said, "What is all this nonsense? Come and stay with me at home, you can even attain God realisation there." With proper care for some days, Anantada gradually regained his health. Yet, his mind was distressed. He thought that his present body was probably not fit for the attainment of God realisation. If he forcibly discarded it, the agony in his mind would come to rest. There was heavy torrential rain that night. At midnight, he twisted his clothes and towels into a rope to hang himself from a ceiling fan. Just when he was about to push the stool from under his feet, there was a knock on the door. Who could be calling at this hour of the night, he wondered. He ignored the caller. The door was then broken down, Anantanath saw a completely drenched Sri Sri Thakur, who entered and warned him, "Hey, are you in your senses? What are you up to? God himself is behind you!"

Anantanath was astounded. How could Sri Sri Thakur know about his attempted suicide? Discarding this heinous idea, he uttered, "Will you guide me?" Sri Sri Thakur accepted him as a disciple. His work now was to treat patients in Sri Sri Thakur's Hemayetpur dispensary and do kirtan in the evenings. He would visit patients on a horse instead of a bicycle. For this reason, Sri Sri Thakur lovingly called him Anant Maharaj. Next to mother Manmohini Devi, the responsibility of giving Initiation was bestowed on him.

In 1934, the auspicious period of taking a religious dip in the Ganges, known as 'Ardhoday Yoga' approached. It is a very important ritual in Eastern India. Anantanath sought permission from Sri Sri Thakur to go to Calcutta and take a dip in the Ganges. Sri Sri Thakur asked, "What will you gain?" and denied permission. After a few days, Anantanath set out with Kishori Mohan to propagate the Name and initiate in the areas around Pabna. After that was done, Kishori Mohan returned to the ashram, but Anantanath went on to Calcutta. He bathed in the Ganga and returned infected with smallpox. The vaccine for it had not yet been invented; hence, its mortality rate was quite high. Anantanathda could not be cured, and at the age of 48, he breathed his last. In his final moments, Sri Sri Thakur was beside him. Before passing away, Anantanath had only one appeal for everyone, "Fulfil the wishes of Thakur as far as you can." Sri Sri Thakur was so heartbroken at Anantada's passing that he could not muster the courage to step into the ashram for over one year. He stayed in a house a little away from the ashram gate. (*Parama Uddhata Sri Sri Thakur Anukul Chandra*)

Kishori Mohan Das

Kishorida was older than Thakur by eight years. He was his childhood companion, a prominent member of the kirtan group, a friend, and a confidant in Sri Sri Thakur's adulthood. Sri Sri Thakur gave him the following titles, 'Bhaktaveer' (brave devotee), 'Seva Bhikshu' (always eager to serve), and lovingly called him 'doctor.' After giving up his compounder's job in Pabna hospital, he was engaged in Homoeopathic treatment in his village, Pratappur. When Sri Sri Thakur Anukul Chandra came to Hemayetpur to begin his medical career, he came to know that his childhood companion, Kishori Mohan, had gone astray and was now an alcoholic. He had also taken to hooliganism and was friendly with the lecherous. Yet, despite all this, a great aspect of his character was his sweet voice, and his ability to perform kirtan. He had no idea about Anukul Chandra's spiritual activities. Even though he had heard about some of Anukul Chandra's miracles, he did not have the maturity to understand Thakur's proficiency as a spiritual guide and master.

The more he was involved in kirtan, the more became his desire for spiritual pursuits. He began searching for a spiritual guide. He consulted a respected and realised person, Thakur Haranath, and requested him to take him under his wing. Thakur Haranath tried to convince him that he was not his Guru and that Anukul Chandra of Hemayetpur was his guru, and he is the Purushottam (best fulfiler) and Sadguru of the age. However, Kishori Mohan did not believe him. He thought Thakur Haranath was avoiding him and considered him unfit for the spiritual endeavour. During one of Kishori's kirtan performances, Sri Sri Thakur miraculously went into a trance. Although Kishori Mohan was overwhelmed with his grace, he was still unwilling to accept him as his Guru. He was in a state of conflict, caught between Thakur Haranath's rejection and his hesitation to accept Thakur as his guide. In utter despair, late one night, he went to a graveyard and cried, "Oh God! Where are you? Please show yourself to me!" In that strange, utter darkness, a voice floated in the air behind him, "Doctor! Doctor!" Kishori Mohan was aghast. It was Anukul Chandra! He saw him standing behind him saying, "Come back, doctor! Come back." Walking home, Kishori Mohan kept a vigilant eye on Anukul Chandra's feet. He had heard that ghosts had reversed feet. However, in the dim moonlight, he had seen Anukul Chandra's feet pointed straight like any other human being. He was then certain that the figure he had seen and heard was not a ghost. He wondered if Anukul Chandra could hear his voice and come to him, he was indeed omniscient. Kishori Mohan's dubious nature drove him to test Thakur. He wished that if Thakur was omniscient, he should dip himself in the Padma River. He saw Thakur doing so saying, "I have stepped on some filth, let me go and take a bath." Kishori Mohan still doubted him. To test Thakur again, he wished that Thakur would dip himself again in the river. That too happened as Thakur did take a bath for the second time right in front of him. Days passed, but his doubts persisted.

Kishori was a stubborn person and was living hand to mouth. One night there was no food in his house. Two devotees from the ashram, Durganath Sanyal and Anant Maharaj, came to his house with flattened rice and rasgullas sent by Sri Sri Thakur. He was surprised and wondered how Thakur had known about his miserable condition from so far away. Now his faith was revitalised. After a long discussion with them, he took initiation and dedicated the rest of his life to Sri Sri Thakur.

One day, Kishori Mohan and Thakur were looking at a dyke along the Padma River. Someone had tied a cow to a pole on it.

Suddenly, because of the current, the cow slipped down the dyke and the rope around its neck was strangling it. It was struggling in pain desperately trying to free itself. Sri Sri Thakur directed Kishorida to untie the loop around its neck immediately. The cow was rescued, but the tightrope left a scar on its neck. Back home, Kishorida noticed that Sri Sri Thakur had torn a piece of cloth from his *dhoti*, and tied it around his neck. Kishori Mohan insistently asked why he had done so. When eventually Thakur untied the cloth, he saw a mark similar to what was on the cow. (*Taanr Katha*)

In 1943, a severe famine struck Bengal. People died of hunger in large numbers. Hundreds of them from adjacent areas of Pabna rushed to the ashram at Hemayetpur, merely for a handful of food. Sri Sri Thakur directed Kishori Mohan to arrange food for all those in and around Pabna. Kishori worked day and night tirelessly collecting rice from far and near. As long as the last person did not get some rice, he would not touch his food. He continued doing so for several months, without food or with only very little late in the night. His health deteriorated gradually, and eventually, he was bed-ridden and fell seriously ill. He breathed his last in April 1943.

Nafar Chandra Ghosh

He was a very faithful attendant and devotee of Sri Sri Thakur. He accompanied him to various places for *kirtan*. Thakur affectionately called him 'Nafraa.' When he passed away, Kiran Mukharjee and some other prominent workers came to Sri Sri Thakur after the cremation., He told them, "You know, while you were bidding adieu to his physical body, Nafraa was sitting beside me." After a few days, one morning Sri Sri Thakur said, "Today Nafraa has taken rebirth in the family of Chutu milkman in Berhampur." Hearing this, a devotee asked Sri Sri Thakur, how despite being at his side as a close assistant for so long, Nafarda had taken birth in a lower caste. It is important to mention here that Nafarda was a milkman by caste. Sri Sri Thakur replied, "In the ashram, it was difficult for him to manage without a little ghee, butter, or milk every day. Even during the final days of his life, he always desired a little dairy supplement in his diet. Thus, for the fulfilment of that wish, he had to take birth in a milkman's family again."

After several years, one day a Guru *brother* came to the ashram with a child and its mother. He bowed to Sri Sri Thakur. Looking at the child, Thakur said with a smile on his face, "Look, Nafraa has arrived." He asked them, "Where have you come from?" They replied, "We have come from Berhampur. The lady here is the wife of my elder brother, Chhotu the milkman, and the mother of this child." Sri Sri Thakur curiously asked the child's mother, "How does the child react when you repeat the Name?" She replied, "He dances in elation, and claps his hands." Sri Sri Thakur told her, "Keep this child with the utmost care, never give him any non-vegetarian food. Do not take him to anyone's house for a feast; do not feed him anybody's leftover food. A great soul has landed in your home; you must treat him with kindness and love." The woman said, "He is not even eating rice these days, he prefers only milk, cheese, and butter. We do not eat non-vegetarian food at our home, so you can rest assured about that." (*Pranara Thakur*)

Acharya Satish Chandra Goswami

Satish Chandra was a descendant of the 15th generation of Advaita Acharya, who had been a companion of Sri Chaitanya. His paternal home was in Shalgadia, Pabna district (now in Bangladesh). His father, Krishna Chandra Goswami, was a prominent scholar in that area. The attraction for studies, inquisitiveness about God, and warm, hearty feelings for the whole of creation were marked in Satish Chandra since his childhood. He qualified as a Vidya Ratna in Sanskrit. Sri Sri Thakur lovingly called him Gosainda. In course of time, Satishda became very active in the ashram's organisational work, and he had initiated several thousand people who accepted him as their ancestral family guide (guru). Now he made all of them followers of Sri Sri Thakur. He was engaged in many vigorous austerities, but that did not satisfy him adequately. He was deeply attracted to the kirtans of Sri Sri Thakur and wholeheartedly surrendered to him. Within a few years, he was completely immersed in kirtans and in the propagation of the *Name*. His conduct was marked with a such generous sweetness that everyone, old and young—men, women, and children—treated him adorably. According to Sri Sri Thakur's wishes, at Deoghar Ashram he accepted the *Pourahitya Brata* (priesthood) and became adept in Vaidic ritualism. He left this world in May 1962 at the age of 88. (*Mahamanaber Sagartire*)

Sushil Chandra Basu

Sushil Chandra Basu was from a noble Bengali family. He was a student of Philosophy and preparing for M.A. and Law at Calcutta University. His sister and her husband were living in Kushtia. During a visit to them in November 1917, he happened to meet Sri Sri Thakur. He talked to him overnight about his personal and social life and his preoccupation with the nation's affairs and got an appropriate response to his questions. The next day he was initiated. He was one of Sri Sri Thakur's most staunch followers, and subsequently became the secretary, and then the president of the registered body of Satsang.

He visited many places across the country searching for people who remembered their previous births. He invited some of them to meet Sri Sri Thakur. He always had engrossing and satisfying discussions with Sri Sri Thakur on various topics including meditation, culture, and dharma. The replies of Sri Sri Thakur are now compiled in three volumes of *Katha Prasange* (Bengali). In addition, he wrote three very good books—*Manas Tirtha Parikrama*, *Jatismara Katha*, and *Rajastaner Pathe*. He was married but at Sri Sri Thakur's suggestion, did not father any children. This great devotee breathed his last on 6 March 1969 at the age of 79. His wife had died several years before him. According to Thakur, after Sushilda's demise, both of them reunited.

Krishna Prasanna Bhattacharyya

Krishna Prasanna was born in 1894 in a conservative Brahmin family in Barisal district (now in Bangladesh). His father, Pt. Kaliprasanna Vidyaratan Bhattacharyya, was the principal of a Sanskrit college. Having lost his mother during childhood, he was brought up by his elder sister. Since early in life, he had been restless and fickle-minded, but showed signs of brilliance and a sharp wit. He was a gold medallist from Calcutta University for his M.Sc. in Physics, and joined as a research assistant with renowned scientist, Dr. C. V. Raman. He was so profoundly influenced by Sri Sri Thakur's discussions on Physics that he gave up his job and came to live in the Hemayetpur Ashram permanently in 1923. He concentrated fully on work for the development of Satsang. Sri Sri Thakur lovingly called him Kestoda. A deep hunger to acquire knowledge imparted by the great men of this world on dharma, philosophy, science, architecture, history, politics, literature, education, and linguistics was always in him. In the company of Sri Sri Thakur, this hunger only became stronger. In addition to his extensive studies, he put forth innumerable queries to Sri Sri Thakur, and incorporated the responses in *Anushruti, Nana Prasange* (several volumes) in Bengali, and *Magnadicta, The Message* (several volumes), in English. Looking at his never-ending passion for knowledge, Sri Sri Thakur once said, "How much can Kestoda possibly know? The more one knows, the more they suffer."

In 1917, Krishna Prasanna won the University gold medal for his Master's. One day, he asked Sri Sri Thakur, "Lord, I have been living with you all this while, and yet it took me 12 years to understand the meaning of your maxims. What is the reason behind this?" Sri Sri Thakur asked him in return, "How many gold medals did you get from the university?" He replied, "Only one that I had received when I became the state topper in Physics." Sri Sri Thakur said, "No, in reality, you got two medals." Kestoda asked, "How?" Thakur explained, "You got one as a topper, everyone has seen that, but you have carried another one with you all along, the medal of ego. It took you 12 years to get rid of it. When the ego dissolves, man becomes the possessor of many attributes."

In 1937, when Sri Sri Thakur constituted the Ritwik Association, Krishna Prasanna was given the responsibility of 'Ritwik Acharya.' He was a pioneer in the great task of publishing the vast literature of Sri Sri Thakur. He breathed his last at the age of 69 on 7 April 1963 in Deoghar. Sri Sri Thakur said at the time of his passing, "Without Kestoda, I am blind."

Prafulla Kumar Das

He was an initiated disciple of Sri Ramakrishna Paramahamsa's order. His indomitable urge for the holy *darshan* of his Guru in the corporeal form of flesh and blood induced him to meet Sri Sri Thakur. After that, he dreamt that Sri Ramakrishna had appeared before him in the form of Sri Sri Thakur. Hesitantly, one day he asked Sri Sri Thakur secretly, "I am a devotee of Sri Ramakrishna. Has he taken another birth somewhere?" Sri Sri Thakur responded, "Search for him, keep searching. One day you will find him." Prafullada asked, "A lot of problems and queries arise in my everyday life. Where shall I find solutions for them?" Sri Sri Thakur suggested, "Keep the book *Chalarsathi* with you always. Whenever a problem arises, simply pray, Thakur, kindly give me a solution, then open the book and you will find an appropriate solution there.' He found the correct solutions to his problems just as Sri Sri Thakur had said, and was flabbergasted. Once, when Sri Sri Thakur touched his chin affectionately, a divine impulse spread through him like electricity. His mind became introspective and rose upwards into a world of higher consciousness and stability. He found love and grace around him. His immense urge to see Sri Ramakrishna was eventually fulfiled. He has later written about this event, "One day, Sri Sri Thakur was sitting on a cane stool. I looked at him for a while and saw it was Sri Ramakrishna who was sitting right in front of me in precisely the same form and figure. I can never forget this precious, personal experience."

One of his most important responsibilities at the ashram was to write down Sri Sri Thakur's discourses. Thakur had named him as the 'Clerk of Narayana.' This documentation began in June 1939; he compiled Sri Sri Thakur's discourses named *Alochana Prasange* (Bengali) in 22 volumes of text. For a long time, he was also the editor of the Satsang journal in Bengali called *Alochana*. He breathed his last in October 2006. (*Bhakta Valaya*)

Doctor Pyari Mohan Nandi

Belonging to an affluent family in Bikrampur district of Bangladesh, Pyari Mohan (born 1901), passed LMP from Midford College in Dhaka. Hearing about Sri Sri Thakur from one of his friends, he came to visit the Hemayetpur Ashram, and overstayed. there for several days. His father, Prasanna Kumar Nandi, and his younger brother came to fetch him. They were extremely impressed with the behaviour of the ashramites, and their meeting with Sri Sri Thakur went off very well. His father wished to send his son to the Royal College of Physicians in London for higher studies. When he expressed his plans to Sri Sri Thakur, the latter responded, "If your purpose is for him to acquire expertise in the medical sciences in England, and work for the welfare of the common people, it can be fulfiled by staying here. Do you have any objections?" Sri Sri Thakur asked this in such a passionate and sweet manner that Pyari Mohan's father could not refuse. The father and both his sons were soon initiated. From that year, 1925, Doctor Pyari Mohan lived there as the physician of Sri Sri Thakur and all the ashramites throughout his life. Thakur affectionately called him *Pyaricharan*.

One day, while checking Sri Sri Thakur's blood pressure and pulse rate, he thought to himself, "As a physician, I have been treating Thakur intimately, and I do not see anything extraordinary in him by which to conclude that he is an incarnation of God." At that very moment, a beam of light emanated from Sri Sri Thakur's navel and illuminated the entire room. He then heard the sound of *Om* resonating from the light's origin. Moreover, he saw in the ever-rising ray of light, the figures of Sri Ram, Sri Krishna, Buddha, Sri Chaitanya, and Sri Ramakrishna, as if all of them were giving him their holy *darshan* together. Then they faded away. After seeing this, the doctor's heart rate and blood pressure seemed to have increased considerably. He bowed to Thakur with great satisfaction.

On the direction of Sri Sri Thakur, Doctor Pyari Mohan taught the nursing skills required for childbirth to many mothers in the ashram. Sri Sri Thakur sent many patients to him. He treated them with allopathic and homoeopathic medicines. He also used indigenous Ayurvedic medications in some cases. He realised that giving medicines for so many ailments and in such a variety of cases was not due to his proficiency in medical science but due to Sri Sri Thakur's blessings. After Sri Sri Thakur's demise, Pyarida was not even able to prescribe any medicines. It was just as Arjun did not have the power to raise his bow, Gandiv, after the death of Sri Krishna.

In the latter half of January 1969, Sri Sri Thakur asked Pyari Mohanda to take his sick wife to a renowned doctor in Calcutta for treatment. Although Sri Sri Thakur himself was not in the best of health then, his condition was, however, stable. Pyari Mohan did not wish to stay away from Thakur for even a moment. In deference to Sri Sri Thakur's wish, Pyari Mohanda went to Calcutta with his wife. After receiving news of Thakur's sudden demise on 26 January, he rushed back to Deoghar. However, by the time he reached, Sri Sri Thakur's earthly body had been cremated. He felt Sri Sri Thakur had knowingly sent him away during his final moments. Otherwise, His abrupt death without any serious underlying medical condition would have been blamed on the doctor's negligence. Sri Sri Thakur's very dear *Pyaricharan* breathed his last on 12 April 1978. (*Bhakta Valaya*)

5

Some prominent foreign devotees of Sri Sri Thakur: Spencer, Hauserman, Michael, Exman, Padlisak, Bob & Julie

Edmund Joseph Spencer

He hailed from a rich family in America, and was a professor of History at Harvard University. He came to Calcutta as a member of an ambulance core group during World War II. He happened to meet one Jatindranath Das, an engineer, there and came with him to see Sri Sri Thakur at the Hemayetpur Ashram in September 1945. Seeing him, Sri Sri Thakur said, "I shall bring you closer to Christ." He was elaborating the incidents of Jesus' life one after another, and Prafulla Kumar Das was translating it all for brother Spencer. Sri Sri Thakur was speaking about the day of judgement and the crucifixion of Christ. He described it all like an eyewitness, loading the cross on Jesus' shoulders, putting a crown of thorns on his head, and so on. By the end of this episode, Thakur's voice choked abruptly; he covered his face with a scarf and wept bitterly. It was then that Spencer came to realise that if Jesus were to be born today in our times, he would take birth in the image of Sri Sri Thakur. He was initiated subsequently and remained a faithful worker for the rest of his life. Sri Sri Thakur affectionately called him, Spence.

In August 1946, Hindu-Muslim riots had broken out. When Spencer wanted to return to his own country, Sri Sri Thakur said, "You must go and continue your research there." He went on, "There, you would reside in a hostel, in its basement. Another student will introduce you to his sister, who will be very rich, and will be staying in the same hostel. She will have a pet dog, but it will be against the hostel rules to keep it in the hostel room. So, she will request you to help her keep the dog in the basement. You will agree, and as a result, love shall bloom between both of you, and eventually, she will propose. However, you must agree on only one condition, that after marriage she will have to stay in

India in the ashram of your Master, and that she would never bear any children. Spencer returned, and the events transpired exactly as Thakur had predicted. That naturally deepened his devotion to Sri Sri Thakur. Margaret and Spencer were married. After Spencer told her the conditions laid down by Sri Sri Thakur, she hesitated but agreed. Spencer came back to Deoghar with her, and their pet dog, Ohm. Arrangements for their accommodation were made in a two-bedroom apartment at Golapbag. Margaret wished to be a mother like any other woman. But Spencer did not violate his Master's command. Thus, Margaret became increasingly depressed. After some days, she went back to America and sent a divorce notice to Spencer. Sri Sri Thakur directed him not to respond. Thereafter, the divorce was decreed.

In 1961, Sri Sri Thakur instructed Spencer, "Go on the road with one dress and no money," and he did so. That year, in August, while sleeping on the ground in Punjab, near dawn, he saw Jesus, and he could hear His *mantra* resounding within him. He came back to the ashram. Sri Sri Thakur was very happy to see him, and asked, "Did you get the *mantra*?" Spencer responded in the affirmative with tears of joy rolling down his cheeks. Sri Sri Thakur asked him to do research on Jesus' death, and find out everything. He said, "Like Buddha, I too believe that Jesus did not die on the cross." Spencer visited many places in India and America on foot. He found a lot of new information, still undiscovered by the world.

His mother and sister came from America to take him back home, but he did not agree. In the ashram, he was doing everything, small or big, with great interest, such as carrying bricks like a common worker, carrying rice in paper containers, and spinach on his shoulders to the homes of the poor, and so on. He had accepted Indian citizenship. He started the publication of the Satsang English monthly journal, *Ligate*, using stencils with a lot of difficulties. He also translated the *Bhagavad Gita* into English.

One day, Sri Sri Thakur asked Spencer, "Don't you have a torch?" He replied, "Yes, I have a small one." After a while, Sri Sri Thakur spoke softly, "No matter how small it is, always try to switch it on." Just as Buddha had said, "*Atmadeep Bhava.*"

He breathed his last in December 1996 at Deoghar.

Ray Archer Hauserman

He was born in Ohio, USA, in 1922. At the age of 23, he joined the Ambulance Division of American Field Services, and worked for two years in Burma (now Myanmar), after which he came to India. In 1945, while waiting for a ship at the Calcutta port to return to his country, he planned a short meeting with his friend, Edmund Joseph Spencer. By that time, Spencer had spent quite a lot of time with Sri Sri Thakur. Hauserman was so deeply moved by Spencer's experience that he decided to meet Thakur in person. . He travelled to Hemayetpur, met Sri Sri Thakur and following lengthy conversations with him on Philosophy, Medicine, and Literature, took initiation. He turned out to be one of Thakur's closest foreign devotees, and also a dedicated worker for Satsang. When Thakur moved to Deoghar, both Spencer and Hauserman accompanied him.

Once, at the Deoghar Ashram, during one of the discourses, he said, "By coming to Sri Sri Thakur I have become a better Christian, because of what he says: 'If I am not able to bestow your love and devotion as a Christian on Christ, then I am not your centre, or the Ideal.' Another day, he asked Sri Sri Thakur "Is God helpless?" Sri Sri Thakur replied, "God is helpless when his disciples are helpless."

Once, in Deoghar Ashram, pointing to somebody, Sri Sri Thakur said, "Ray, can you keep him with you?" Hauserman looked at the man; his clothes were dirty, his hair untidy, his face bearded, and his teeth yellowish. Hauserman accommodated him in the room he shared with Spencer, and told him to rest there, as he went out on some work. Returning at midday, Hauserman noticed that there were half-smoked *bidis* (leaf cigarettes), burnt matchsticks, and spit marks all over the room. Entering the bathroom, he saw that the man had used his towel and toiletries. He arranged some food for him and went out again with Spencer at work. Returning, he saw that both their wallets were missing.

After the evening prayer that day, he told Sri Sri Thakur about that man, and said he would not be able to keep him any longer. Sri Sri Thakur said, "You can bring a change in him if you wish to." The words resonated in Ray. If the devotee is helpless, God is helpless too. Without avoiding the responsibility, Hauserman kept the man with him. Gradually, he came to know that the man was an expert in making leaf cigarettes (*bidis*). He arranged for some capital and engaged him in that work and for making paper containers. He also arranged a room in the market, and the man set up a shop there. Gradually, his business grew so much that he employed three-four people to assist him. His poverty came to an end along with all his bad habits. When Sri Sri Thakur came to know these developments, He told Hauserman, "One day you asked how to conquer the world, and I say, this is the elementary course to that end."

In his book, *Ocean in a Teacup*, Hauserman has depicted the picture of food scarcity, lack of accommodation, and the distressing conditions that persisted when Sri Sri Thakur migrated from Hemayetpur to Deoghar. Yet in the midst of all these difficulties, Sri Sri Thakur was not perturbed or felt helpless. An excerpt from the book:

"Thakur himself gave no sign nor did he evince the slightest expression of his sense of loss. From five in the morning until well past midnight, he was engaged in planning, instructing, supervising, and counselling. Over and over again, we could hear his ringing injunction to a despairing disciple: "We have lost nothing, I tell you! All that we had—homes, land, machinery, and buildings—were created by your efficiency and ability. We still have them. With it, we shall build again. And this time it will be faster, for we have the benefit of our experience to guide and aid us!"

Between 1945 and 1970, Hauserman visited America twice.

His mother came to Deoghar, and availed the company of Sri Sri Thakur. It was only after Sri Sri Thakur's death that he returned to America in 1970. He got married at the age of 64 in 1986. He came to Deoghar again with his wife and son, Raymond, in 1990. He breathed his last in March 2000.

James Michale

He was a journalist from America who visited the Deoghar Ashram on 7 February 1954. After discussing with Sri Sri Thakur, he took initiation through Nanigopal Chakravarty. After that, when James and Nanigopal went to see Thakur, Nanigopalda told him to carry something to be offered to the Ideal. James replied, "Money is not the appropriate offering for my dearest Love Lord; I must offer that which is most precious to me. Nothing in this world is as dear as this watch that my father had given me before he died." On meeting Thakur, Michale gifted it and this proved his devotion to Sri Sri Thakur. Michale then said, "I hope I will be able to propagate my Ideal in America. Kindly bless me."

Sri Sri Thakur uttered exultingly, "You shall be a glowing example. Let thousands of people come to the Lord with you as their guide." After a brief silence, he said again, "Don't be afraid of suffering. Move on with the concentric goal of life, with patience and perseverance. Suffering will never deter you from your goals." (*Jiban Dyuti*)

Professor Robert Coming

Professor Coming taught at an American university for several decades and visited India in 1964 for official work. He had heard about Sri Sri Thakur earlier, and in August of that year visited Deoghar. He asked Sri Sri Thakur, "What happens when you surrender to the Ideal?" Sri Sri Thakur replied, "When the concern for the Ideal gets enhanced in an individual's life when feelings for the Lord become prominent in his eyes and words when all these aspects are manifested in his mannerisms and activities, then his *sadhana* becomes spontaneous. There will be both vision and sensation in it. In the word 'surrender', there is 'sur', which means 'above', and 'render', which means 'to give.' 'Surrender' means I have given myself to him, I have become His wholeheartedly, and I have therefore accepted him in all aspects of life. 'Surrender' is the highest form of love."

After residing for some days in the ashram, Coming was initiated by Sushil Chandra Basu. After it, he offered a moonstone to Sri Sri Thakur as an oblation. Sri Sri Thakur accepted it and asked him to give it to Sri Sri Borma. She held it in her hands and said, "What kind of a thing is this? So big!"

Bowing to Sri Sri Thakur and Borma, he said, "Thakur, you must guide me." Sri Sri Thakur smiled, "You love me, and that love shall dictate, how you must be guided." (*Smritir Mala*)

Eugene Exman

He was the chief of a renowned publishing agency, Harper and Brothers, in America. Ray Archer Hauserman had shown the manuscript of his book on Sri Sri Thakur, *Ocean in a Teacup*, to him for publication. Exman was so much influenced by reading it that he came to India to see Sri Sri Thakur. He was very cordial with the then president of India, Dr Sarvapalli Radhakrishnan. He came to Deoghar in September 1961, and stayed in the ashram for more than a week. He was greatly impressed by the prolonged discourses of Sri Sri Thakur on various subjects and was initiated in September 1961. He was all set to return the next day to the USA. Paying his respects to Sri Sri Thakur, he said, "If you come to America, a lot of work could be done." Sri Sri Thakur expressed his limitations, "I am unable to walk steadily. I am able to move with the help of my disciples. In any case, you are in the USA, and I am always there in spirit with you; you shall carry me in your mind wherever you go. I will wander from country to country through you all.' While leaving, Exman told those who came to see him off, (Hauserman, Janardan Mukhopadhyay, etc.) "Whichever corner of this world I may go to, I will speak about Thakur—that even now there is a man, centring around whom all surroundings have become full of love, camaraderie and cooperation and become normal and habitual, I am returning from here with the fulfilment of mind." (*Parama Uddhata Sri Sri Thakur Anukul Chandra*)

While returning, Exman was delivering a speech on Sri Sri Thakur at a meeting in Italy when a woman in the audience suddenly fainted. Exman placed his hand on her head and repeated the 'Name' (*Mantra*) he had got during his initiation. To everyone's surprise, she regained consciousness. She described the appearance of the great man who had revived her, and the description resembled Sri Sri Thakur. At that moment, Exman remembered Sri Sri Thakur's utterance, "You carry me in you to various places of this world, I will always be there in spirit with you." (*Manas Tirtha Parikrama*)

Dr Karrel Padlisak

He was an M.D. in Medical Sciences and a member of the UN medical team. He was born in Czechoslovakia and was engaged as a doctor in Geneva in 1966. He came to India on the invitation of the Central Government to research diseases of coal mine workers caused by prolonged work underground in a hostile environment. After staying for a few days in the Dhanbad coal mining area, he provided clinical treatment to mine workers. The Ritwik in that area, Shyamapada Mukherjee, brought him to the Deoghar Ashram to meet Sri Sri Thakur. He expressed his desire to be initiated. Judge Prafulla Banerjee and his wife were present there. Pointing to him, Sri Sri Thakur directed the couple to initiate Padlisak. After his siesta, Sri Sri Thakur was sitting in Nirala Nivesh when Prafulla Banerjee informed him that the Czech gentleman had been initiated at midday and was asking how anyone in Czechoslovakia could be initiated. Thakur responded, "If someone is genuinely interested, they shall be initiated through you. We can be in touch through correspondence, and I shall tell you precise details and directions to initiate others." (*Prophets and Prophecies*)

Bob and Julie

This American couple, Bob and Julie, decided to divorce mutually for various reasons. Bob had been initiated earlier. However, before their separation, Bob wanted to visit India once with the hope of changing Julie's mind. They came to Deoghar Ashram and met Sri Sri Thakur who was very happy to see both of them and asked how they had been, and whether everything was fine with them. Both bowed and sat close to Thakur. Looking at Julie, Sri Sri Thakur said, "Seeing you, I feel really happy. Did you face any trouble during the journey ?" She replied, "No, Thakur, there was no trouble. I am glad to be here."

Sri Sri Thakur continued, "The husband is the altar of God." He uttered this repeatedly and discussed the terrible effects of divorce. He spoke to Julie with immense affection and kindness. As a result, the complaints and doubts she had against her husband gradually melted. This change of heart could be seen in her expression. She drew close to Sri Sri Thakur, and said, "Thakur, I realise my folly, but you must tell Bob to behave with me like a husband." Sri Sri Thakur smiled, nodded his head with a gesture of consolation, and said, 'Of course! He should.' (*Jiban Dyuti*)

(As per available records, 27 foreign nationals came to see Sri Sri Thakur during his lifetime. Because of the limitations of this book, only seven persons have been cited here).

PART THREE

6

CREATION, EVOLUTION OF LIVING BEINGS, BRAHMA, ANIMATE AND INANIMATE, BEING AND BECOMING OF MAN, SPIRITUALISM, GOD, IDEAL, SADGURU, PROPHET, TAPASYA, SIDDHI, DHARMA, ETC.

Devotee: What is creation and why?[1]
Sri Sri Thakur: The Supreme Father willed, hence the Creation. The source of Creation is Word. He is the word that manifests Himself with all His properties into all that has manifested.

There are five basic elements in all that have been created: Earth/solid (*Kshiti*), Water (*App*), Sun or fire (*Tejas*), Air (*Vayu*) and Space (*Vyoma*). Among them, Space is the finest, Sound is the soul of space, and the soul of sound is vibration. Due to friction in the stream of vibration (waves), the sun, stars, constellations, the Milky Way, etc., came into being. From that, matter evolved. The sun is also a form of matter. The matter is the manifestation of energy. Energy cannot remain dormant. There exists a continuous play of radiation, contraction, stagnation, and expansion. In this process of attraction and repulsion of the finest atomic and subatomic particles, numerous things have evolved in the bosom of the beyond. The tune and potency of one are different from the other. The flow of evolution passed through many stages and phases, ultimately leading to Man, the best among beings.

Devotee: What are the characteristics of vibration?[2]
Sri Sri Thakur in *The Message*
Vibration
comes from the conflict of
stato-dynamic urge
evolving into sound
in a periodic flow
of positive and negative motion
which creates
with every orientation different devices and designs
of creation and dissolution
from the vibrating tremor of tuning adjustment
and it runs on resonating
within and without
in the form of a thrill of make and break;
discern,
know the clue and characteristics
of vibration,
apply it accordingly
to make and break
and have the desired effect of
creation or dissolution. (The Message VIII, 179-180)

Narrator: Yugacharya Sri Sri Borda observes, "Sound is Brahma and by the constant flow of primordial vibration, Creation sprouted in many forms. Man's inner self is pure, but as it is shrouded with many complexes and passions, he does not realise his original pure self, *sat-chit-ananda* (the divine). He throws himself into the mundane whirlpool of desires, distress and misery. To remind man of his forgotten self, the Supreme Father descends in human form. He shows the way; eternal memory-consciousness develops, and we know why we are here."

David Bohm (1917-1992), the American-Brazilian-British scientist observed the universe as made up of vibrations; they are not random, but highly ordered; they are coherent. Their order and coherence tell us that they are not the result of mere chance. Bohm used the term 'in-formed' to explain how deep the dimension of the cosmos is beyond space and time. He said that we, for that matter, are 'in-formed' clusters of vibration in space and time. (*The Undivided Universe*)

Devotee: Kindly explain what is Sat-chit-ananda?[3]

Sri Sri Thakur in *Magnadicta*:

He is the existence of all that exists
Thereby He, the Sat;
He is the responsiveness
of all that responds,
So Chit that He is;
He is becoming
of each that becomes
Thus He, the Ananda as known,
He made Him Himself,—
materialised within the matter
of Sat-Chit-ananda—
that of Him and His
which is and was. (verse 75)

Devotee: What was before creation?[4]

Sri Sri Thakur: (On the third day of his Samadhi, Ashadha-4, 1321 BS/June 1914 AD): When I was before, He was latent in me! When I was before, you were latent in me! When I was you, you were 'I'! I was the only one, I was latent in me. Think of yourselves. You were latent in me. The whole creation is you—no doubt, the Spirit. I was Sound. Sound was my creation. Therefore, you are created by me. Only Sound is your spirit, no doubt.

Devotee: What is the purpose of Creation?[5]

Sri Sri Thakur: Because of Creation, you and I are here, sitting together, chatting and enjoying each other's company. It is called 'Leela'—to accept and embrace. When we attach ourselves to the Ideal, we are active and energetic, and we expand. We stand as an example to others, and the environment changes for the better.

Devotee: What is Logos?[6]
Sri Sri Thakur in *The Message*
> *I do not understand*
> *theology*
> *but I understand*
> *the Logos of God the invoking urge of life,*
> *i. e., 'be'*
> *which turns into being*
> *the inherent stimulus*
> *in everything*
> *with different actions*
> *and attributes.* (*The Message*, VIII, 165)

Devotee: What is spirit?[7]

Sri Sri Thakur: Pure spirit is present everywhere all the time. Within Him, attraction-repulsion-stagnation goes on endlessly. Sometimes the contraction is extreme and at other times the expansion is the utmost; it is completely stagnant at other times. In this manner, Creation moves on. 'Raa' is Vibration, 'Dhaa' is Cessation, within these two, attraction, repulsion and stagnation take place non-stop. 'Swaa' is the outgoing force and 'Mee' is the ingoing force. I can explain this activity of Creation in terms of science like electrons, protoplasms, etc., but ultimately it is the activity of the Supreme Being. If I move towards Him with love and sincerity, all this will gradually dawn in my understanding. In this journey towards Him arises feeling and anti-feeling. Sometimes the mind moves closer to Him, and sometimes it recedes. All of this happens to all of us. (*Deeprakshi*, vol. 5)

Devotee: Is Spirit different from Matter?[8]

Sri Sri Thakur in *The Message*
> *What comes down*
> *from the motherly unison*
> *is matter*
> *and what aspires to exist*
> *is spirit;*

*I think, everything comes down
through motherly unison
and aspires to exist—
therefore, everything
includes matter and spirit.* (*The Message* vol. VIII, 161)

Devotee: How does Spirit move life?[9]

Sri Sri Thakur: Spirit is the vital force for which I exist, as I am, for that matter, everything. Again to exist as it is, the play (interaction) of two forces is required, the positive and the negative. The movement due to the attraction and repulsion of these two is Time. If we charge anything with a positive force, it emanates a positive current, and shall not allow the positive to move any further. But when a positive is with a negative, it will attract the negative. Electrons and protons have the tendency to unite; but there is space in between, like the stars, like father and son. A father is attached to his son but does not become one with him. Space is very important. It provides matter with life, shape, and motion. Space is the origin of matter.

Devotee: What is the primary element of Creation?[10]

Sri Sri Thakur: Protein is the primary materialization of beings. By its permutation and combination with other elements, so many beings that never existed earlier, are created. This process of Creation goes without a break. After many stages came Nebula. It moves in a circular flow. In its flow are two streams, positive and negative; one is thicker than the other. During the movement of these two streams, there is friction, but no separation. When the negative dominates the positive, there is a condensation of the negative and vice-versa. This is called Being, it includes even the tiniest dust particle.

Sri Sri Thakur describes how protein creates its variety.

*Protein is the offspring of
protolyte constituents
and this, with other, additions
creates its varieties;*

> *the constituent of many varieties*
> *in nature evolves into specific species*
> *with addition of*
> *different ingredients*
> *with the change of its various*
> *characteristics;*
> *so, protein*
> *is the body-building Substance.* (*The Message* vol. VIII, 196)

Devotee: In the Holy Bible (Genesis) it is mentioned, "The Spirit of God moved upon the face of the waters." What does it mean?[11]

Sri Sri Thakur: In the Hindu texts, a parable says: Narayana is reclining on a banyan leaf in the ocean of milk, and Lakshmi is massaging His feet. Brahma, the Creator, is born from His navel. The banyan leaf represents the idea of becoming. There is much similarity between the statement of the Bible and the concept of Creation in Hindu scriptures.

Narrator: Sri Sri Thakur has said that among beings with flesh and blood, man is the last in the scale of evolution and the best. According to the Bible, first came living beings in water, then animals, the birds, with man being the last. Charles Darwin stated that life started with aquatic animals and went on until man. The famous Odia poet, Jaydeva (12th century) in his epoch-making long poem, *Gita-Govinda*, mentioned, "Fish! that didst out swim the flood/Tortoise! Where on earth has stood/Boar! Who with thy tusk held'st high/The world that mortal might not die/Lion! Who hast giants torn/Dwarf! Who laught'dst a king to scorn/soul, subduer of the dreaded!/mighty plough man! Teacher tender!/of thine own the sure defender/under all thy ten disguises/endless praise to thee arises. (*The Indian Song of Songs, Gita Gobinda*, Sir Edwin Arnold)

Sri Sri Thakur describes the phases of creation in the following way:

(I)
The booming commotion
of Existence
That rolls
in the bosom of the Beyond
evolves into shooting
thrilling rhyme
and upheaves
into a shooting
Becoming of the Being
with echoes
that float
with an embodiment of energy
that is logos;
the Word—
The Beginning!

(II)
He the Word—
The Source of Creation—
Manifests Himself
with all His properties
into all that has manifested,—
But the Beyond
Comprehended Him not—
Though He shineth
in the bosom
of the Beyond!

(III)
It is Energy
which lies
in the embodiment
of World that remains
as He is—
though manifesting Himself

Into all that was created—
That is God
That is Word
That is Divine!

(IV)
The thrill of Existence
which occurs
due to Apathy and Sympathy
for what lies is Beyond
in a stream of Will
That tends to make the Word
to become conscious
in manifesting Himself into many
like Him albeit unlike—
by their mutual impulses—
moving
Spiro-elliptically,
one round the other!

(V)
The Beyond is what intervenes
to make the manifestations
unlike, different and discrete—
though the Affinity
that lies under
tends always to make
all to be One!

(VI)
The interaction of
manifestation of Word
in the Beyond
makes the unlike different
and discrete
instinct with life—

from fine to gross—
thus the Divine creates Himself
into life
surrounded with blood and flesh
which are enlivened too!
(VII)
In such a way
different, discrete, finer, and grosser
blood and flesh are manifested—
blood and flesh
are embodied with life
as beings, as creatures—
from which Man comes forth
by degrees—
discrete individuals with
other phenomena
become the environment
of every individual
and make it awaken
in life and consciousness
with the thrust of impulses
from mutual affinity
while on the other hand
He the Word
Became the Supreme Being
the father of manifestations
and the individual
Who comes forth
ever-enchanted
With sympathy and love
from the Supreme Being—
at the crying call
of panic-stricken sufferers
becomes the Beloved God in the flesh

the Divine,
the Ideal—
the way to rescue!
(VIII)
Only then recedes the Beyond
when sympathy invokes love—
To make one attached to Him
By Whom
Being and Becoming
is accelerated—
and then knowledge appears
with an illuminating zeal!
(IX)
And knowledge shines
And redeems the Being acceleration
fulfiling in concord
the Ideal, individual
and environment,—
towards Becoming—
towards a superior Becoming
with gradually unfolding
memory
Of the Father,
by service and surrender,
unto the Beloved!
(X)
And when wrappings
on the thrilling tension
of attachment to the Beloved
occur—
Due to the thrust
of environment
and complexes—

discretely and collectively,
the impressions rebound
and set in the individual
according to sympathy and apathy,
With a tremor of sensation
Into resultants
and are adjusted
with a solution
tending towards his interest,
thus knowledge grows—
With a gradual generalization
of experiences
into a subtler harmony
of the individual,
the Ideal and wisdom;
In this way—
as varieties of rapping
diminish gradually,
the individual
plunges into the Beloved
Through a grand generalization of Wisdom!
(XI)
The Sympathetic Affinity
that induces the opposite-equal
to dwell in herself
and breeds to beget him
measured in different shapes,
is Female;
whereas the entity that inclines
towards female
to fulfil her
is Male,
but apathy always resists the one
To become the other;

> *Female is the shelter*
> *that nourishes,*
> *absorbs,*
> *and reproduces one into many*
> *and the inclination of the male*
> *towards female*
> *without something to*
> *uplift existence,*
> *dwindles them*
> *to decease! (The Message, vol. I)*

Devotee: What is Time?[12]

Sri Sri Thakur: The advent of Creation creates time and space (*The Message*, VIII, 158).

Devotee: What is Space, and where does it end?[13]

Sri Sri Thakur: Space is not void. It is filled with so many...why only stars, there are atomic and subatomic particles. There is no end to space. I am the end.

Narrator: I. K. Taimni (1898-1978), the Indian scientist-scholar, observes: 'Space, though apparently appears empty, contains within itself an infinite amount of potential energy. It is filled with vibration and forces of various kinds—electromagnetic, gravitational, nuclear, and others yet to be defined including fields of dark energy and dark matter. Quantum Physics tells us that space is not empty and smooth, it is grainy, filled with waves and vibrations. Dynamically filled space could vibrate.' *(Man, God and The Universe)*

Scientific research now also confirms this. "There is no space without meaning or significance, for it is infused and 'in-formed' with a conscious cosmic intelligence. The new scientific paradigm reveals that consciousness is not confined to the human brain, rather, it is a gift, a quality of vibration that is decoded by the brain from a myriad of sensory data received externally." - (*The Intelligence of the Cosmos*)

Edwin Hubble discovered in 1929 that the universe is

expanding. He made his discovery by analyzing the spectra of light from distant galaxies and noticed a persistent red shift by which the radiation falling on the Earth from the galaxies is reduced. The expansion of the universe meant the expansion of space itself because the galaxies are embedded in this space.

Devotee: How do we understand the Supreme Being?[14]

Sri Sri Thakur: That Being, or the Entity who in its eternal motion, creates fine (subtle) or gross forms without a change in His self, I understand He is the Supreme Being with unfolded memory consciousness and manifests differently according to place and time. So He is the Supreme Father of Creation.

Devotee: What is the nature of the living being?[15]

Sri Sri Thakur: The living being is only a part and parcel of the Supreme Being. Whatever cells are there in the human body are in fine form in the astral body. The coherent integration in the astral body manifests in the physical body. To achieve a healthy astral body, unwavering adherence to the Ideal is necessary.

Devotee: What is life?[16]

Sri Sri Thakur: The fact of living is life. We live life. There is appropriateness in our existence which is harnessed in our spirit. The ability by which we experience things through our senses, and the capacity to discern, with continuous existence, are facets of life. Life is a particular wave—you can call it consciousness that exists in different degrees in all the creation that we see. The wavelength distinguishes one from the other. An entity of a particular wavelength produces another of the same wavelength— a drumstick tree produces another of the same variety but with different characteristics. It is the same with human beings; we are all the same, and yet are different from one another. So the distinctiveness with which we are born enables us to inherit our own subjectivity and thought. This in effect contributes to our growth. This process is nothing but life.

Devotee: How to achieve the aim of life?[17]

Sri Sri Thakur: He who performs, achieves; he who serves not but enjoys, becomes indolent and a pauper. (*The Message*, vol. IX, 71)

Devotee: What is the difference between animate and inanimate?[18]

Sri Sri Thakur: I don't think anything is inanimate. What we perceive as lifeless has a consciousness of a kind not yet fathomed by science. In the days to come, we may invent an apparatus that can tell us the presence of consciousness everywhere, even in a sand particle.

Devotee: How do you define matter, Sir?[19]

Sri Sri Thakur: Matter, by its very nature, constitutes two dialectic forces within itself. In reality, matter manifests in all that has a physical existence. We can perceive matter by the virtue of our senses. Matter by this design must retain its substance, the very life force that makes it what it is. I think the objects we use in our daily life develop a sort of affinity and warmth towards us—a relationship with the person who uses them. In the event of separation from their beloved, they are hurt, the same as we are. This is no exaggeration. Using a little insight, you or anyone else can see it for yourselves. The seas, rivers, mountains, bricks and stones, or for that matter, everything else, are indeed a replica of the Supreme Being. A person endowed with this knowledge is called *Brahmagyani* (the wise one).

Devotee: How to understand *Brahma* and *Brahma Gyan*?[20]

Sri Sri Thakur: *Brahma* created everything with different attributes but He is above all attributes. He is formless but assumes form. He goes on spending Himself, but doesn't diminish. He is always full. *Brahma Gyan* (Wisdom) is the realisation that everything in Creation with its own distinctiveness is part of *Brahma*. By the application of this wisdom, we can discern and deduce the nature and distinctiveness of all that exists. The epitome of *Brahma Gyan* is to bring this understanding into the realm of awareness.

Narrator: In the *Brihat-Aranyaka Upanishad*, Brahma is explained as:

> *He who dwells in all things*
> *Yet is other than all things*
> *Whom all things do not know*
> *Whose body all these things are*
> *Who controls all things from within*
> *He is your soul, the inner controller*
> *The Immortal.* (*Discourses on the Ideal*, vol. II)

Sri Sri Thakur provides a simple explanation of *Brahma Gyan*:

> *Can it be determined whether a man*
> *is a knower of Brahma*
> *by the standard of public opinion? This can't be.*
> *Rather it is by ardour in love and active following,*
> *the realisation of the Ideal's principles,*
> *and applying them through every faculty*
> *that the radiance of his wisdom may be felt.*
>
> *(Tapo Vidhayana)*

Devotee: In whatever manner you explain it, Sir, it goes above my head. What to do?[21]

Sri Sri Thakur: That's true. That is why Brahma is said to be beyond the comprehension of the human mind (*Abangmanaso Gocharam*). I remember two lines of a song by Swami Vivekananda: *Abangmanaso Gocharam bujhe pran bujhejara* (Beyond man's mind He exists, only the souls who know, they know). If I tell you about Brahma, I mean an ever-expanding universalization; by soul, I mean the entity in eternal motion, by Providence I think of Him who commands and controls all the resources that exist, by God I perceive the Supreme Being, having manifested Himself in all gross and fine forms in continuous motion. He remains absolute as He has always been; this explanation will always be incomprehensible to you. So, to simplify the understanding, Sri Krishna said, "Renounce everything and come only to me." Now the concept of Brahma comes within our perception. The abstract is personified. What was only hazy in idea is visible in its complete existence. Now we understand Brahma with the attributes and activities of Sri Krishna without much difficulty. However great He may be, He is approachable; it is not impossible to develop a relationship with Him that we can feel by our senses. Thus, the idea of Brahma is personified and clear before us. In this way, we understand the Supreme Being, God, Providence, etc.

Narrator: In the *Bhagavad Gita*(18/66), Sri Krishna says:

"Do all thou dost for Me! Renounce for Me!
Sacrifice heart and mind and will to Me!
Live in the faith of Me! In faith of Me
All dangers of thou shalt vanquish, by My grace;"
(Tr. by Sir Edwin Arnold)

Devotee: Does it mean to abandon one's religion?[22]

Sri Sri Thakur: No, no. Here *Dharma* does not mean religion as you understand it. It means to renounce all practices of self-realisation hitherto, our notions of sin and virtue, good and bad, truth and falsehood.

Devotee: What is the meaning of '*saranam vraja*' and '*mokshyayisyami*'?[23]

Sri Sri Thakur: '*Saranam vraja*' means to proceed in life by following Him, and Him only. We have desires, complexes, and passions, a tendency to worship many gods and goddesses and to run after several godmen. Sri Krishna wants us to stop all this, and put our hearts and soul in Him, so that He can save us. So the crux of the above directions of Sri Krishna is to find the Ideal and surrender to Him; no matter to which community, class, or place He may belong. He is the world-teacher. By following Him you will get rid of your sufferings, don't worry.

Devotee: In the Hindu scriptures, it is said that he who knows *Brahma* is a Brahmin. What does it signify?[24]

Sri Sri Thakur: Don't you know the story of Viswamitra, the sage? He was once a warrior king, became a sage through intense meditation, and appealed to Lord Brahma to be recognised as a Brahmin. He thought that he had already achieved *Brahmagyan*.

To his dismay, he was told that Vasistha was the authority for this purpose. Vasistha was also a sage and a man of wisdom and experience. He found that Viswamitra had an ego that did not allow him to realise Brahma, and hence was unfit to be bestowed with Brahmin Hood.

Viswamitra felt humiliated and was wild with anger. He tried to take revenge, but Vasistha would not retaliate. Out of desperation, Viswamitra decided to perform a sacrificial rite to end Vasistha's life (*Vasistha- Medha-Yajna*). At the end of the rite (*yajna*), Vasistha was to be offered as a sacrifice. Interestingly, he called Vasistha to perform the rite as a priest, and the latter agreed. On completion of the rite, when the time came to behead Vasistha, Viswamitra, to his utter astonishment, found that the priest was ready for it without any objection. Only now could Viswamitra realise the nature of a Brahmin, free from any animosity against any being. This is the true knowledge of Brahma in a Brahmin. Viswamitra's ego melted, and with tears in his eyes, he fell at the feet of Vasistha and profusely apologized for all the insults he had inflicted on the great saint. He begged, "I don't desire Brahmin hood any more, but, I pray, O great sage, may you live long." Now that the mind of Viswamitra was pure and bereft of ego, he was recognised as a Brahmin.

Sri Sri Thakur, after telling this story enjoined: Man cannot become God, but if with complete dedication and without any expectation, he loves God, his being becomes a temple, and God starts residing therein. When one surrenders at the feet of a person who is endowed with supreme knowledge (*Brahma Gyana*), he becomes a Brahmin.

Devotee: What is the process of attaining *Brahma Gyana*?[25]

Sri Sri Thakur: Self-knowledge is supreme knowledge. It exists in all of us in a dormant state. By self-analysis, we can remove the cover of ignorance from our minds. Every human being has existence-consciousness-bliss (*sat-chit-ananda*) present in him. Six disciplines are prescribed for a Vipra in this regard. They are: self-upliftment

(*Jajan*), nurturing the environment (*Jaajan*), study (*Adhyayana*), teaching (*Adhyapana*), donation (*Daana*), and acceptance of gifts (*Pratigraha*). I have introduced Jajan, Jaajan, Istavriti, Swastyayani, and Sadachar through a process of initiation (diksha). All these six ancient disciplines have been included in my tutelage for modern man. If this is practised sincerely, you shall derive the instinctive traits of your heredity, qualities that are ingrained in your being, and succeed in your field of interest. Along with this, a compatible marriage, and an Ideal-centric way of life is bound to bring a change for the better. In this way, there is a possibility that hundreds of souls with superior knowledge of the Supreme Being will be born in India and elsewhere in the days to come. If all of you can follow these basic guidelines I am giving, man can transcend himself to godliness in the coming hundreds of years. But remember, everything depends on how to control your passions and complexes. Be prepared to forsake your selfish endeavours.

Satyanusaran—The purpose of life is to drive away want completely, and that is possible only by knowing the cause. Exhausted in want, the mind seeks Dharma or the Supreme Being; otherwise not."What will remove want and how ?" From this thought, the question of the Supreme Being arises ultimately.

Narrator: Sri Sri Dada observes (Ritwik Conference 27.10. 2012): 'The Supreme Being (Purushottam) is beyond our perception. No one can understand Him. One can only love Him, and bind Him by love. He cannot be measured by the intellect. He is incomprehensible (*Abangmanasagocharam*). When evil is rampant, He comes to save us. Hand in hand, He takes us along the path of becoming so that we are saved from disasters and miseries. We are very fortunate. Now and then, we should ask ourselves, "Have I come up to His expectations?" He loves all and shows kindness to all. We should learn from Him to love and be kind to all. He does not have any enemies. If we really wish to follow Him, we should not have any enmity against anyone either throughout our lives.'

Devotee: What is spiritualism?[26]

Sri Sri Thakur: That which holds, enriches, and moves your soul is spiritualism. It is due to the presence of the Spirit that you are alive.

Satyanusaran—The idea and activities that lead man towards the Cause is Spiritualism.

Devotee: What is a body and where is the mind?[27]

Sri Sri Thakur: The conglomeration of vitalities results in the formation of the body, a father being the source. Life comes in contact with various external objects. We have actions and reactions to them. Such actions and reactions produce impressions in the brain cells. When the impressions start flowing, they give rise to feelings. Feelings are different ideas and emotions resulting due to interaction with outside objects. That is the mind.

Devotee: How is man different from the rest of Creation?[28]

Sri Sri Thakur: It is said that man is the wave of the mind. It has the potential for development. All material-spiritual developments originate from here. It is said that the mind is the ledger of Chitragupta, meaning the hidden picture. Whatever good or bad deeds a man does in life, the mind records it. It is difficult to control the mind. Thus, our existence is due to our body, mind and life force. The concrete manifestation of these three is the Being. The Being also includes everything in which you participate, like your family, your profession, your possessions, etc.

Narrator: Yugacharya Sri Sri Borda divided human beings into three broad categories—the lowest being men of gross intellect. They are concerned with only food, sleep, and sex. They refuse to budge an inch to a higher plane of living. The second is the class of persons who are guided by complexes. They are of a *Rajasic* temperament. The superior type is not content with just food, sleep, and sex; they are able to control their complexes. An artist is so engrossed in his art that he forgets food. A good singer who takes part in a music concert runs away from royal treatment in his in-law's house. These persons are of A-class and of a Satwik temperament, not polluted by worldly desires. They can progress well in spiritual pursuits. However, if all three categories accept the Ideal, and follow Him with sincerity, they can change for the better, sooner or later.

There are other divisions in the text, says Sri Sri Borda: the desperate (*artta*), the money-maker (*artharthi*), the knowledgeable (*jnani*), and the inquisitive (*jigyanshu*). Whenever Sri Sri Thakur saw an inquisitive person, he would be stimulated to discuss and start pouring out his enlightening talk. To an enthusiastic devotee, he would say in a soft, fatherly voice—keep reciting the Name, don't forsake it even for a moment! Sri Sri Thakur is known for talking in tune with the interest and receptiveness of the audience.

Satyanusaran—He who speaks less and does more is a first-class worker. He who does as he speaks is a second-class worker. He who speaks more but does less is a third-class worker and he out of laziness neither speaks nor does, is the worst type.

Devotee: Please explain intellect (*Budhi*), conscience (*Vivek*), and ego (*Ahamkara*).[29]

Sri Sri Thakur: All three reside in the human mind. Our conscious actions produce reactions; the impressions that these reactions leave are transmitted to our brains. The brain retains them in several layers, creating vibrations that nourish our consciousness. The consciousness subsequently attains awareness. The ability to give this awareness an expression is intellect. Using our intellect, we can differentiate the good from the bad, do's from don'ts; the choice varies with the nature of our intellect. The ability to prefer good over evil, creative over destructive is Conscience. Conclusively, Ego is banal, it always stresses the 'I', full of vanity.

Devotee: What is infatuation (*Moha*)?[30]

Sri Sri Thakur: When a man is guided by an egocentric, passion-dominated way of life and ignores the well-being of the self, it is infatuation.

Satyanusaran—Be wealthy, no harm. But be humble and

charitable. If a rich man is proud, he is drowned in distress. A rich man, arrogant and proud, generally lacks faith and the door to heaven does not open in his heart. A proud rich man is a slave to impurities, so he ignores wisdom. From an obsessed ego, comes addiction. From addiction comes ignorance and ignorance is misery.

Devotee: What is ignorance?[31]

Sri Sri Thakur: Man's ego without rein takes him on an unhealthy road of mere fulfilment of passion, which is detrimental to his well-being. Hence, ignorance is a lack of knowledge for the well-being of the self. In every step of your life, you should be careful in taking proper judgement conducive to your being and becoming. An ignorant man guided by the allurement of the mind misses the real, and deprives himself of reality.

Devotee: Kindly explain the meaning of deprivation from reality.[32]

Sri Sri Thakur: The urge for passionate desires and longings, destabilises the growth of the individual. It shadows conscience. That is why Sri Ramakrishna Paramahansa (1836-1886) said, 'Unless one observes *Brahmacharya* for twelve years, his sense of discrimination (*Medhanadi*) does not grow.'

Devotee: What is *Brahmacharya*?[33]

Sri Sri Thakur: *Brahmacharya* is the practice of ideal behaviour essential to one's being and becoming. In ancient India, education was imparted in centres of learning (*gurukulas*) run by seers and sages. The training was three-fold: education (*shiksha tapasya*), service to the environment (*seva*), and collection of alms (*vikshya*) for livelihood. Education meant proficiency in all subjects required for a superior state of living. Service meant taking care of the environment as a whole. The collection of alms was for self-preservation. In religious scriptures, we come across anecdotes about sages who had dedicated themselves to spiritual pursuits for twenty or thirty thousand years. It means that if a person aspires to spiritual knowledge on his own, it may take a very long time. However, when one follows a Master who is well-versed in knowledge, the time required may not take so long, proficiency comes soon.

Devotee: Who is a saint (*sadhu*)? What is meant by keeping the company of saints (*sadhu sang*)? Who is an ascetic (*sanyasi*)? What is asceticism (*Tapascharya*)?[34]

Sri Sri Thakur: *Sadhu* is a practical person who takes responsibility for the environment at large. He knows the prior and after of all matters and situations, and solves problems by guiding one and all. He does so of his own volition. Keeping the company of the practical man, loving him, and following him, makes one integrated into life. Integration makes the man understand the clue to face and tackle any situation. The Ideal is the *Sadhu*, an ascetic is he whose mind is totally Ideal-centric in thought, word and action. Asceticism is the practice of a way of life ordained by the Ideal or the Master and carrying out His commands without question, hesitation and doubt. In other words, the essence of asceticism is to make the outer and inner self adept in self-restraint and self-evaluation, so that life becomes existence-nurturing.

Satyanusaran—*No cunning is so good as simple honesty. Any person, whatever he may be, must be caught in this trap. "Honesty is the best policy." May thou be ascetic at heart. Dress not thyself as a hermit, and be not chameleon-like for nothing. Let thy mind roam about on the Source or Brahma, but not be busy to dress thyself in saffron robes or to paint the body; for then, the mind may incline towards these things.*

Narrator: *Taittiriya Upanishad* mentions: 'Self-discipline is the key to success.' Swami Vivekananda comments: 'No force can be created; it can only be directed. Therefore, we must learn to control the grand powers that are already in our hands, and by willpower make them spiritual instead of merely animal-like.' *(Upanishads In Daily Life)*

Devotee: It is said in the scriptures that the aim of life is emancipation (*mukti*) and realisation of God (*Bhagavat Prapti*). Will you kindly explain?[35]

Sri Sri Thakur: So long as man remains attached to his complexes, the bond remains. When he masters them, he is free. Emancipation would mean preserving, nourishing, and developing the being by overcoming negative thoughts and actions. Thus, emancipation is the proper use of complexes for being and becoming. When you follow a person who has achieved this freedom from the complexes in his life, your power to control, manipulate, and use the complexes in a positive way is achieved quickly. This is called spiritual realisation. It is not a commodity that the Master hands over to his disciple. It is a continuous journey with no end. The practitioner builds up energy (*taapa*) gradually, so it is known as *Tapasya*.

Devotee: It is said that one of the aims of man's life is prosperity (*Aishwarjya Prapti*). Is it the accumulation of wealth and power?[36]

Sri Sri Thakur: I don't think so. The Sanskrit word '*Aishwarjya*' means an Ideal-oriented life, active and agile, coherent and content. While making money, one has to see how much it serves him and the environment around him to exist and grow. While attracted towards women, one has to see how much he is attached to the Ideal, the source of his well-being. In short, money, power, and women, when acquired, should be put only to that use that is beneficial to the being; otherwise, they may create havoc.

Devotee: How to distinguish between truth and untruth, good and bad, virtue and vice?[37]

Sri Sri Thakur: Action which preserves, nurtures, and develops your being is truth, is good, and is virtuous. In the opposite manner, indulgence in which your preservation, nourishment, and growth are impaired, is untruth, is bad, and is a vice. An act by which we deteriorate is sinful. We are shaped by our actions. Actions ultimately make us. What we do becomes the guideline of our life and our soul. What we are doing in this life determines our existence here, and also indicates the directions our soul will pass through in the new world hereafter.

Satyanusaran—If you are good yourself, thousands of people will be good, seeing your example. If you are bad, you will find no one to sympathise with you in your distress because by being bad, you have made your environment bad. Attach your inclination to good; you will become good unconsciously. Be absorbed in good ideas in your own way. Your feelings will bloom according to your aptitude. As evil thoughts are revealed through eyes, words, dealings, behaviour, etc., so do good thoughts express themselves in the same way.

Narrator: The *Brihad Aranyaka Upanishad* states, "From untruth lead me to truth, from darkness (ignorance) lead me to light (knowledge), from death lead me to immortality. (*Asato ma sadgamaya, Tamso ma Jyotirgamaya, Mrityorma Amritamgamaya*)." Swami Vivekananda explained, "From the Unreal, lead us to the Real. From Darkness, lead us to Light. From Death, lead us to Immortality. Reach us through ourselves, and ever more protect us. O, Thou Terrible! From Ignorance, by thy sweet Compassionate Face." (*Upanishads in Daily Life*)

Devotee: It is said whatever is in the universe is also in the human body. Is this true?[38]

Sri Sri Thakur: Yes, it's a fact; think in terms of microcosms and macrocosms. Whatever is in the universe is also present in the cells of a body; not only there, it's also present in the smallest atom. The fine exists in the gross. The things you see in shape and form were not there before, though there was a possibility of their becoming so. This possibility of becoming something is the fine element within the gross matter. So, as there are many gross beings, there are also so many fine counterparts.

Devotee: What is the finest state of Existence?[39]

Sri Sri Thakur: The abode of the Supreme Being is the finest state, the source of flow for Creation. There exist only fine vibrations and nothing else. You may call it *Dayal Desh*, that is why there is no alternative to God, there is no other being like Him. He is the sole source of the universe. The elements present in Him are present in all that He has created. Every individual entity is a limited version of the Supreme Father. He is the Absolute, Indivisible, and Omnipresent.

Narrator: Sufi saint Jalal ad-din Rumi (AD 1207-AD 1273) said thus, "You are not a drop in the ocean, you are the entire ocean in a drop. Stop acting small, you are the universe in ecstatic motion." (*Rumi Quotes*).

With regard to the omnipresence of God, there is an anecdote about Guru Nanak, the saint and the first Guru of the Sikhs. He was walking all across the country. One afternoon, He went to a roadside temple to rest. The temple was closed. At dusk, the priest came to open the doors. He found a hermit reclining on the veranda, with his legs pointing towards the door and the deity. He shouted at him, 'Oh! Who are you looking like a mendicant and behaving so impertinently that you have no common sense? You are pointing your feet towards the Lord?" The saint calmly replied, "Panditji, please show me where the Lord is not present so that I can turn my feet in that direction." (*The Spirit of Indian Culture*)

Devotee: In the scriptures, it is said that God is everywhere (*Sarvam Khaluidam Brahma*). Then why does He not manifest?[40]

Sri Sri Thakur: A mirage gives the false impression of water. The thirsty goes on running endlessly and perishes. However, if he is with a camel, it carries him to where water is available and he survives. Similarly, we have to take the help of a person who is God-anointed to reach Him. Such a person is Brahma personified (*Brahmavid Brahmaiva Bhavati*). He alone can arouse dormant traits to blossom into a blissful existence (*sattva guna*) in man.

Devotee: There is a sect that worships space or vacuum (*Mahashunya Upasana*) and says it is the best. What is your view, Sir?[41]

Sri Sri Thakur: Why seek my view? Has not Bernard Shaw said, 'Be aware of the man whose God is in the skies.' To call God formless, attributeless, and omnipresent, are all abstract concepts. Where I and you are not there, how to understand and what to understand? God must exist as tangible in our consciousness, then only can we say: yes, He is. Let us not go about Nihilism (*Shunya Vada*), Monism (*Advaita Vada*), Dualism (*Dvaita Vada*), etc. Take the shelter of a true Master and everything will be revealed to you.

Narrator: George Bernard Shaw (1856-1950) was a noted Irish playwright and Nobel Laureate (1925); one of his other famous quotes, states: 'We are all dependent on one another, every soul of us.'

Devotee: Should we think of Sri Krishna, Hazrat Muhammad, and Jesus Christ as one?[42]

Sri Sri Thakur: Yes, of course. There are two aspects in all of them, divine and discrete. Divine is eternal, universal, and invariable, but discrete varies according to time, space, and circumstance.

Devotee: Are all prophets alike?[43]

Sri Sri Thakur: Remember, there are no two Gods. God is one and His messengers are one and the same. They come according to the need of the hour, all past prophets consummate in the present one.

Devotee: When Jesus said, 'No one comes to the Father, if not by Me', He meant, He alone is the Prophet. Isn't it, Sir?[44]

Sri Sri Thakur: 'Christ' means 'the Anointed.' Hence, all real Prophets are Christ since they are anointed with the Supreme Soul. This is the reason, I suppose, Christ declared, "Before Abraham was, I am", as well as "No one comes to the Father but through Me." When I use words like Prophet, Ideal, Love-Lord, Sadguru, Ishta, and Yugapurushottam, all mean the same, the divine personified. Christians call Jesus the 'Son of God.' How much the son will imbibe his father in him depends on the degree of his attachment to him. When the attachment is so deep that the father completely resides in the son, he declares 'I and the Father are one.'

Narrator: In the Bible, Jesus says, 'I am the way, and the truth and the life. No one comes to the Father, if not by me.' It is also mentioned in the holy Quran, 'None other than Mohammed is to be worshipped. He is the messenger of God.' (*La ilaha, illallah Muhammadur Rasoolullah*)

Devotee: Love of God or fear of God's wrath; which is more effective?[45]

Sri Sri Thakur: I feel that fear and hope lead the mind to knowledge. Then mercy and love lead to achievement. All Prophets made love prominent and a basis of their teaching, for it leads us to achieve and sublimate our soul normally. Thus, in the *Tidings of the Hebrews*, it is said, "Love is the beginning and the end of the Torah" and Mohammed has said, "If you love Allah then follow Me and Allah will love you...." (*Answer To The Quest*)

Satyanusaran—He within whom all the resources of the world knowledge, love, and activity are spontaneous and by the inclination towards whom the scattered lives of men and all the diversities of the world find a solution, is the God of men.

Devotee: Please tell us who is Ideal and what are His attributes.[46]

Sri Sri Thakur: In simple words, Ideal means a living man who, out of an irresistible love and maddening urge for his Superior Beloved, establishes Him in his own life, service, contact, and sympathy. In this process, he exalts the environment's life and growth with the aid of His varied experience, without caring for suffering. It is in Him that man finds his path by which he can, without tottering, embrace life and growth. (*An Integral Philosophy of Life*)

Devotee: How to identify the Ideal?[47]

Sri Sri Thakur: The Ideal fulfils all knowledge in the traditional trail of time, space, and circumstance, with a meaningful synthesis of the divine and discrete in His words and deeds. Only then can we know that He is not false or futile. He is rather the embodiment of the Fulfiler as the best, the Superior Beloved, nurturing and fulfiling the distinctive traits of everyone. He carries within Himself a flood of Love, and He is the Redeemer of Mankind! The Ideal is God manifested.

Satyanusaran—*The Master is the materialised form of Bliss and He is the Absolute. Follow only Him who tries by strength, skill, or tact for the welfare of all created beings. You shall surely achieve your good! Follow Him alone who does not cause grief to anyone in any way, yet does not indulge in evil. You shall achieve your good.*

Devotee: Has He come into our midst? What is His nature?[48]

Sri Sri Thakur: Yes, indeed. He sits here today, gorgeously simple, wisely foolish, and abnormally normal in some neglected corner of the world and with an atom bomb of love in His hand.

Devotee: Does He lead a worldly life?[49]

Sri Sri Thakur: Yes. He lives like an ordinary man; eats, sleeps, loves his parents, wife, and children, feels pain and pleasure, probably a little more than the common man due to His supersensory perception. Yet His active attachment to the source, the Supreme Consciousness, manifests verily in His character and guides Him at every moment. This is as natural and automatic as respiration is to life. Remaining in the world, He is unattached; yet attracts everyone to the noble road of salvation. All the past prophets converge in Him. Love towards Him is to love all in the worship of God. Yes, I say, He is the way, the truth, the light of Life.

Satyanusaran—*As the sparkle of a diamond, which remains in coal and dirt, can be seen after a thorough cleaning, so also He who lives in society as an ordinary man can illuminate the world with His sparkle only by the washing of love. The lover alone can know Him, so keep the company of lovers and worshippers of Existence. He must manifest Himself.*

Devotee: When and where was he born?[50]

Sri Sri Thakur: He comes when the suffering of mankind is on the rise, when there emerges a painful cry in man's heart. He descends to show Man the right way ahead. He is born to parents of a noble lineage, surrounded by a community of degraded lumpens. He may belong to any sect or community that is not detrimental to His cause. He begins His work of reconstruction of society from the most deprived and degraded sections. The wicked ignore Him, despise Him, and desist Him. He does good to them instead, but they act against Him. He does not retaliate, and never forsakes them. He tries to mend them and considers them as His wayward children. He sees in their hope, like he sees hope with everything else in the world.

Devotee: We find a plethora of godmen with everyone claiming himself to be the divine messenger. What do we do?[51]

Sri Sri Thakur: Being in touch with him, you can observe three attributes in his personality: His affinity towards all past prophets; He fulfils you according to your distinctive ability; He does not display His eminence, and is averse to self-publicity.

Devotee: - But what makes him sacrifice his life for others?[52]

Sri Sri Thakur: The Ideal is a living man, anointed with the Supreme Being; so he sees all creation as his own. Search him out, follow him to find out the clue to a meaningful existence.

Narrator: The Chinese sculptor-philosopher, Lao Tzu (2500 BC) on the nature of the Supreme Sage (Ideal) said: He is free from self-display, and therefore He shines; he is free from self-assertion, and therefore He is distinguished; He is free from self-boasting, and therefore His merit is recognised. (*Tao Te Ching*)

Devotee: Who are His followers?[53]

Sri Sri Thakur: The virtuous and the righteous follow Him; they may not be persons of wealth and power. It may so happen that the socially high profile are so enamoured of their own greatness and status that they are completely engrossed in it. Their time and energy are spent in self-aggrandisement. It prohibits them from pursuing the Ideal of a noble and enlightened living.

Satyanusaran—To be blind is unfortunate indeed; but to be without a staff is even worse, for the staff does much of the eye's work. The true guide has a light ego. He will never assert his own strength to you by Himself, and so will follow you according to your thoughts. These are the characteristics of a true Guide. If you really have a true Guide, whatever you do, no fear. You cannot be destroyed. Only be prepared for suffering.

Devotee: What are the broad categories of your followers?[54]

Sri Sri Thakur: There are persons who are prepared to undergo all hardships to rise to my expectation. They elevate themselves as they are completely dedicated to the Ideal even after his departure to the Acharyadev with untottering adherence. They are the God-intoxicated (*Iswarakoti Purusha*). There is another category that is mundane to the brim, totally in the clutches of passions and complexes which make them dull, tired, and frustrated. They don't show any interest either in accepting or following the Ideal. However, the Ideal follows them and goads them to higher strata of living. For this purpose, the Ideal undertakes any amount of hardship. This class is a passion-ridden class (*Jivakoti Purusha*).

Devotee: How does the Ideal elevate his followers?[55]

Sri Sri Thakur: The Ideal is aware of the past, present, and future of all things. He arouses your dormant ability, and makes you more active, agile, and disciplined so that you prosper in all aspects of life. You learn to manipulate any situation to your advantage, without hurting the interests of others. In short, you are best fulfiled.

Satyanusaran—One must take the Master as one's own. When one thinks of mother, father, son, etc., His face should appear in the mind. Going to school alone does not make a student and taking initiation alone does not make a disciple. The heart should always be kept open to carry out the orders of the Master or Teacher. Have firm faith within.

Devotee: Can't we carry our spiritual pursuit without the Ideal?[56]

Sri Sri Thakur: I don't think so. Even the possibility of one going mad and abnormal cannot be ruled out for such practitioners. You may achieve some power by the dint of your rigorous spiritual practice, and then rush to use them according to your whims and passions, making your downfall inevitable.

Hence, discipline and restraint ordained by the Ideal keep you intact in your spiritual journey. A novice with little results boasts loudly and thereby blocks his achievement. Without a true Master, it is difficult to reach the planes of fine and subtle vibrations. The help of the Master will be necessary for the realm of higher realisation. So, unless one is Ideal-centric, the spiritual practice may turn out to be futile or may not be congenial to personality development.

Satyanusaran—*Adopt the habit of the creeper and entwine yourself around the tree of the Ideal, fulfilment of desire shall be yours. Take to the feet of a true Master, go on taking the Holy Name, and remain in the company of devotees. Truly, I say you have no more to worry about your elevation.*

Devotee: As you learn from many teachers, what is wrong in taking the guidance of many masters?[57]

Sri Sri Thakur: A story goes like this: In a village, there was a cowherd tending to about twenty-five cattle. It was the rainy season, and as he was busy in the field, he told his young son to graze the cattle in a pasture near the jungle. He gave his staff to the boy to control the cattle. One day, while following the animals with the staff in his hand, a strange idea struck the boy. He thought that the cattle were of many colours and varieties. Instead of one staff for the whole lot, why not have separate sticks for each to better control them? To implement his idea, he ran to the jungle to procure the required number of staves. In his absence, the cattle strayed into the jungle. By dusk, when he came back with a bundle of sticks, he found all the animals missing. Nervous, he ran to his father and told him everything. With the assistance of other farmers, the cowherd could round up the missing animals. Laughing at the foolishness of his son, he cautioned him: 'One master staff is more than enough, many may create confusion.'

Devotee: There are so many temples, gods, goddesses, holy men, and godmen. You say, to stick to only one master (Ideal). How is it possible, Sir?[58]

Sri Sri Thakur: You are in the habit of visiting temples, worshipping many gods, and running after godmen, for fulfilment of your mundane desires; today here, tomorrow somewhere else. Your devotion lacks sincerity, your visits are for temporary gain. In such cases, be sure you are going on the opposite road to life and growth. Remember the caution of Lord Krishna: 'He is helpless for those with divided devotion. Don't blame God when you fail.'

Narrator: Sant Kabir (1440-1518) speaks of the futility of ritual worship without sincerity. He warns the Hindu priest by saying, "Oh Friend! You have been counting the beads of the rosary all your life, but doubts and hesitation cloud your mind. For God's sake, stop muttering to the count of beads, start counting the beads of your heart. "*Mala Ferat Janam Gaya/Gaya na manka fer/ Karka mala chhodke/manka mala fer.*" He warns the Muslim moulavi in the mosque thus, "Oh dear! I don't know how your Lord is; You utter your prayers at the top of your voice; is your Lord hard of hearing? Don't you know, the Lord can even hear the tinkling of the anklet of the tiniest creature? (*Na jane tera saheb kaisa hai? masjid bhita rmulla pukare kya saheb tera bahari hai? Chiunti ke pagne or baje so bhi saheb sunta hai*)." (*The Spirit of Indian Culture*)

Devotee: Then what do you want us to be, Sir?[59]

Sri Sri Thakur: I am told Greenland is a place frequented by cyclones and storms, often without warning. Rescuers are ever ready to meet the challenge. They put a strong rope around their waists and tie the other end to a pole so that wind does not blow them away. Likewise, tie yourself with the Ideal, with the chord of love, to save yourself from disasters in life. Lord Krishna says to Arjuna, "O son of Bharata, according to one's existence, under the various modes of nature, one evolves a particular kind of faith. The living being is said to be of a particular faith, according to the modes he has acquired."

(*SattanurupasarvasyashradhabhavatiBharata*
  shradhamayoyampurusho jo jatsradhasaebasa, Gita 17/3)

The Devotee: Can the Ideal bring amity in society?[60]

Sri Sri Thakur: The Ideal is the meeting place of all varieties of human beings. He alone can discover your inherent distinctive potency, and properly nourish it blossom fully. Thus, He is essential for your total growth. The fact remains that you cannot grow unless your surroundings are congenial. The restlessness, indiscipline, and violence prevalent in different communities are due to a lack of tolerance for each other. The Ideal brings in you a sympathetic tolerance and compassionate fellow feeling by teaching you how to love. He shows in His life how love can change the negativity of hatred to a positive attitude of acceptance and abidance. So, always keep the Ideal in the centre of your life and society. Loving, obeying, and following him are the *sine qua non* for peaceful co-existence and growth of various social and religious sects and creeds. It is also a fact that during the presence of the Ideal, many fake masters appear to create confusion.

Devotee: How are fake masters like?[61]

Sri Sri Thakur: They are foolish and disoriented. Their words and deeds never match each other. Without a centre, they are undisciplined, inconsistent, and incoherent. They pose as men of great virtue, and talk of righteousness and divinity left and right. Hearing divine words from their lips, the ordinary man mistakes them as genuine and completely succumbs to their deception. They ruin their followers; be careful of them. There is also another group of lesser devils—the quacks—who due to their inferiority complex cannot stand the Ideal, and hurl slurs at Him. Keep yourself away from them as well.

Narrator: Paramahansa Sri Ramakrishna compares a fake master with a cunning vendor of gold ornaments. The story goes:

The owner of an ornament shop is sitting in his shop with a *tulsi* rosary around his neck. A rural family, seeing such a devotional vendor, enters his shop. He was chanting 'Keshava Keshava' (Keshava is the name of Krishna). These words were actually meant for the salesman in his shop. He would understand the coded meaning behind this phrase and knew the owner only wanted to know if the customers were simpletons or intelligent. The salesman, after talking to them, uttered, 'Gopala, Gopala' (Gopala is the childhood name of Sri Krishna, and the clan of milkmen who are supposed to be simpletons). By repeating these words, the salesman conveyed to the owner that rural folks are gullible and can be cheated. After a while, the salesman cunningly shouts, 'Hari Hari!', this time meaning 'should I cheat them?' The hidden reply from the owner comes almost immediately, 'Hara Hara!', which implies, 'cheat the clients as much as you can.' This is an example of how in the guise of God's name, fraudsters fool innocent people. The fake master similarly hoodwinks his innocent followers.

Devotee: Like fake masters, are there fake followers as well?[62]

Sri Sri Thakur: Yes. Among the followers, there are many pretending obedience and devotion, but waiting for a chance to loot. It is like miscreants entering the marriage venue as members of the bridegroom party. After some time, somebody's purse is lost, someone's wristwatch is gone, and many cannot locate their footwear. The fake disciples exploit their association with the master to fulfil their wicked needs. However, they don't last long. There is another type. They are not hypocrites but lazy and lethargic. After some time, they also fall by the wayside as they are unable to undergo the rigour of discipline.

Devotee: In the *Bhagavad Gita,* Sri Krishna declares through Arjuna, "My devotee never perishes (*Kounteya Pratijanihi Na me bhaktah pranashyati—9/3).*" What does it mean?[63]

Sri Sri Thakur: Man perishes by excessive indulgence in desires, but when he loves the Ideal with all his passion, the adherence regulates his energy for creative purposes. Thus, the energy spent in fulfiling desires is no longer futile. This does not mean that the follower will not go through bad times, disease, or agony. They may come but cannot overpower him. He is shaken, but not swept away. On the contrary, he develops the courage to tackle them and uses them as experience to further his becoming.

Sri Sri Thakur in a verse:
From the adverse path of distress
Who hand in hand guides you to life and progress
Know for sure, your True Master
With Him by your side
You need not fear.

Devotee: Then what is your advice in this regard, Sir?[64]

Sri Sri Thakur: I repeat the message of Lord Krishna which is simple, straight, and easy to understand. I also like *'Vasudeva Sarvamiti'*; Vasudeva is the total, the Omni, the Absolute.' You love Him as the man who is the son of Vasudeva. You love Him for the sake of loving only. Let this love be your only love, it is the destination. It is the means as well as the end at the same time. The Ideal (Prophet) of a particular era is the Sri Krishna of that era. Remember one more thing: those who despite the sorrow, suffering, and distress do not lose faith in the Ideal, not due to compulsions of incapability or helplessness, but out of indomitable commitment towards Him; they are the genuine ones, no doubt. When a man, while passing through a period of untold adversities, remains steadfast in his love and affinity for the Ideal, he overcomes the stormy phase, and remains intact, or else he retrogrades.

Narrator: The complete verse in the *Bhagavad Gita* (7/19) '*Bahunam Janmanamante Jnanaban mam prapadyante/Vasudeva sarvamitisa mahatma sudur lava*'—After many births of spiritual practice, one who is endowed with knowledge surrenders unto Me, knowing Me to be all that is. Such a great soul is indeed extremely rare.

Devotee: Will you kindly simplify it further?[65]

Sri Sri Thakur: We feel happy when we are successful in achieving our life's goals. This is how we evolve. For this purpose, we have to take the guidance of a person who knows the clue to success. So an Ideal-centric person, though he may appear meek and mild, will ultimately succeed in his life, whereas a so-called smart and go-getter may not hold to the rhythm for long. It is also true that an Ideal-centric person would definitely secure rebirth in higher strata among men.

Narrator: Sri Sri Dada (Ritwik Conference 1.1.2012) spoke thus: "Whatever, I may be, wherever I may be, I am at the feet of my Master, the Love Lord. Our life's ambition should be to serve Him and establish Him. This we can do when we move, taking everyone along with us. The clue to this is *sadhana*, as Sri Sri Thakur has shown us through His life. He is Purushottam, fulfiler of the best, He is God personified, He is our preceptor, and teacher. He has taught us how to move, how to act, how to live, and how to achieve. If we move on the path shown by Him, we are fulfiled. We are content."

Devotee: What should be the aim of man's life?[66]

Sri Sri Thakur: The aim of our life is God-realisation, prosperity and bliss. Life moves on through the play of libido, sincerity, fellow feeling and sympathy. It is dynamic in nature. It is also known as an asexual creative journey.

Devotee: In the Book of Genesis (Bible) it is said, 'So God created man in his own image.' What does it mean?[67]

Sri Sri Thakur: To comprehend and feel Him in our limited being, the micro becomes aware of the macro.

Devotee: Why is man given so much prominence in Creation?[68]

Sri Sri Thakur: Living beings receive life-affirming currents from the cosmos through the brain. The brain is in the head, and the head is the root. The placement of the head in the physique of the being indicates its current receptivity. The higher a head is situated in the body, the more its ability to receive currents from space. The tree has the lowest potency as its root is below the surface. Above the tree, there are animals and birds, whose heads are horizontally aligned with the body. By gradual evolution, man's head is on the top of his physique, towards the cosmos. So, in nature's creation, man is destined to receive the maximum cosmic energy. It is our instinct to always keep our heads facing up. Suppose while reclining, you are discussing some topic and hear something important or interesting; you will immediately straighten your body with the spine erect and the head up.

Devotee: What is the way to achievement in man's life?[69]

Sri Sri Thakur in *Magnadicta*: Do meditate mantra on thy Lord dawn and night, Do repeat the Holy Name mentally and meaningfully. In all the moments of daily life. Do materialise the directions of the Guru in due time. That is Tapas— the way to achieve me! (verse 68)

Devotee: How to become great in life?[70]

Sri Sri Thakur in *Magnadicta*: 'To adore the great with devoted service is the way to be great because bliss is materialised in them through their devotion and worship.' (verse 242)

Devotee: If suffering in the present life is due to the bad deeds of the previous birth, can it be waived by following the Ideal?[71]

Sri Sri Thakur: One has to reap the fruit of the actions of his previous life. There is no way to waive or reduce it; that is the law of nature. But one thing is certain; when you adhere to the Ideal with all your passions and complexes, you are under his care and protection. Protection, because the negative forces are now resolved in a positive direction. It is as if the venomous teeth of a reptile have lost their poison. In essence, to diffuse the bad effects of unwanted deeds of the previous birth, and to succeed blissfully in the present life, you must welcome the Ideal, accept the Ideal, and follow Him ardently. That is *Yoga* and *Dharmacharya* (religious practice). If you are clever, you should not miss the boat.

Devotee: What is *Dharma*?[72]

Sri Sri Thakur: Doing that by which your being as well as the environment is best nourished is *Dharma*. Those habits, behaviour, and actions by which the individual, along with the environment, exists and grows best is *Dharma*. The perception framed by conscience, empathy, and fellow feeling for all in Creation, are broadly the facets of *Dharma*. Remember that when a person with Ideal-oriented motivation takes care of the self as well as all beings around him; he is highly religious.

Narrator: Sri Sri Thakur further says: 'That by which one's life and growth along with that of others is upheld, is called *Dharma*.' 'To live and let others live is *Dharma*.' 'All live and grow through *Dharma* and sectarianism is not *Dharma*.' (*An Integral Philosophy of Life*)

Devotee: What are the attributes of *Dharma*?[73]

Sri Sri Thakur: I feel that upholding, nurturing, and protecting existence with an apt resistance to evil are the core attributes of divinity.

Sri Sri Thakur in *Magnadicta* :
God cares little what one thinks,
but He sees how one behaves
and what one does.' (verse 228)
Do behave
as you think good,
and do sincerely
what is apt thereto. (verse 229)

Devotee: In daily life, I am very religious, Sir. A room in my house is earmarked for puja (worship). There I have kept photos of many gods: Sita-Ram, Radha-Krishna, Mother Kali, Mahadev, photos of saints like Sri Ramakrishna, Shirdi Sai Baba, and yours. Early in the morning, I decorate them with flowers, apply sandalwood, and worship with all my might with camphor, lamps, joss sticks, and offerings of fruits, sweets, etc. In the evenings too, I pray regularly. Am I not religious enough?[74]

Sri Sri Thakur in *Chalar Sathi: Religious you are! Every day you are worshipping God engrossed in rituals, prayer, and offerings but kindness, affluence, glory, life, lustre, contentment, and nourishment have never honoured your being. Your environment is not exalted by getting them from you, Know for sure, your religious paraphernalia does not invite existence and growth. So, you and your environment both are deprived of Dharma.* (verse 98)

Narrator: The famous Odia saint-poet, Bhima Bhoi (1850-

1903), had no formal education. He was one of the main propagators of Mahima Dharma(*Manabbadi Santha Bhimabhoi*)—worshipping Space through the Guru (*Shunya sadhana*). Two lines from a long poem:
> Immensurable are the woes of the afflicted
> How one can see and tolerate,
> Let my life rot in hell, to redeem the rest.

Sir Philip Sidney, a poet and soldier, is considered a bright example of self-sacrifice. During the Dutch war of Independence, he and another soldier were lying wounded on the battlefield. Both were extremely thirsty. His chances of survival were much less than the other soldier's. He passed on his bottle with little water to the co-soldier whispering, "Thy necessity is yet greater than mine." He died and the co-soldier survived.

Devotee: If this is Dharma, then how should we understand Religion?[75]

Sri Sri Thakur defines Religion thus: *The art of binding oneself with the Idea in love worship and admiration and living on accordingly in an acceleration of one's being and becoming is Religion to me. (The Message, vol. 1, 150)*

Religions may be many but the principle and realisation thereof are ever the same. (The Message, vol. 1, 238)

Narrator: Controversial spiritual mystic Osho says: "I call religion the art of living, Religion is not a renunciation of life; it is a stairway to descend deep into life. Religion is not turning one's back on life, it is opening one's eyes fully towards life...Religion is a total encounter with life." (*From Sex to Superconsciousness*)

Devotee: Hindu texts have this mantra '*Acharoparama Dharma.*' What does it mean ?[76]

Sri Sri Thakur: It means actions that are conducive to your being and becoming along with that of others; that is religion, the ultimate.

Devotee: In the *Bhagavad Gita*, Lord Krishna says: "Come and surrender to me alone." (*mâm ekam sharanam vraja*). In the Bible, the statement of Christ is: "None comes to the Father, but through Me." Should I follow Lord Krishna or Jesus Christ?[77]

Sri Sri Thakur: Follow the Ideal, the present Prophet in whom there is the consummation of all past prophets.

Devotee: Then why do people fight, hate and kill each other in the name of the prophets?[78]

Sri Sri Thakur: It is very unfortunate. Hazrat Rasul has spelled it very clearly. I also believe that one can follow Hazrat Muhammed and Jesus Christ more sincerely if he follows the Prophet of the present age.

Devotee: What is your opinion about conversion?[79]

Sri Sri Thakur: A truly religious man does not impose his faith forcefully on anyone. Religion is a matter of love and faith, not of compulsion and power.

Satyanusaran—The beauty and meaningfulness of life lie in being devoted to One with intensity and continuity. When liking for many cannot shake or sever the liking for One, that liking is the sister of love.

Narrator: Sufism and Baba Farid: Sufism is against conversion. They hold, 'No compulsion in religion.' To a Sufi, he who does not abide by the rules of conduct of the Holy Quran is an atheist, a coward, a *kafer*. Sufism started in the 7th and 8th centuries, first in Persia, and spread to other parts of the world. The term 'Sufi' is derived from the Greek word 'Sophos', meaning 'spiritual knowledge' or Gnosis. Sufis are very strict in following the rules and commands of the Quran. They shun luxury and royal patronage. They lead a very simple life and accept distress and suffering as a gift from God. They sing and dance in praise of Allah and remain in ecstasy. In 12th-century India, there was a great Sufi mystic lovingly called Baba Farid. His parental name was Farîd al-Dîn Mas'ûd Ganj-i-Shakar (1173-1266). 'Ganj Shakar' means store-house of sweetness. In his childhood, Farid liked sweets. There is an anecdote about him. His mother was a religious lady. She wanted her son to stay at home at sunset every day and join her in the evening prayers. To induce him, she used to keep a packet of sweets below his pillow every evening. After the prayer, he used to partake the sweet with relish. As the boy grew up, the prayer became a habit; his mother discontinued it. But, lo and behold! The sweet packet was below the pillow as before. This astonished his mother. She told her son: "Look, how merciful Allah is. When I stopped giving you sweets, He provided them to you. He loves you. You should love Him too by being merciful and compassionate to all beings." Baba Farid was immensely loved by Muslims as well as Hindus for his motherly affection.

7

Yoga, libido, fixing of libido, Nam and Nami, Raasaleela, Pranayam, Rise of Kundalini, Tantric pursuits, Mayavada

Devotee: What is *Yoga* and how is it practised?[80]

Sri Sri Thakur: Devotion and love for the Ideal is Yoga and complete adherence to Him is its practice.

Narrator: *Yoga* is now commonly used and understood by certain physical postures and breathing exercises for sound health. In Hindu scriptures, it means 'to unite with.' So Yoga should not be conceived as merely a physical and breathing discipline, rather it is a practice by which you unite with the Supreme Being.

Devotee: Patanjali states, "Yoga is the subjugation of passion (*yoga chitta vritti nirodha*)." Is it correct, Sir?[81]

Sri Sri Thakur: I would like to amend it a little: By union with the Ideal, the inclination to passion is subjugated. (*yogat chitta vritti nirodha*).

Devotee: Please clarify what are these Passions?[82]

Sri Sri Thakur: They are described as *Sada Ripu* (six enemies) in our scriptures: *Kama* (lust), *krodha* (anger), *lobha* (greed), *mada* (pride), *moha* (delusion), and *mascharya* (egoism-self-conceit). They express themselves through our sensory organs. A person under the influence of lust or anger or greed goes to any extent, even at the cost of his life. Delusion overpowers the conscience and ego hinders man's becoming. However, when we completely surrender to the Ideal, these enemies are tamed to serve and fulfil the Ideal, and gradually they become friendly.

Devotee: If anger, greed, and sex are so unwanted, why has God put them in us?[83]

Sri Sri Thakur: They are manifestations of our primordial energy; they are meant for providing pleasure but the trouble starts when we are overwhelmed by their gratification, and we become their slaves. Then they start dictating to us and, in the process, we deteriorate. As they become the cause of our deterioration, they are branded as our enemies. When they are controlled and used properly, they provide us with beneficial results and become our friends. With regard to sex, Sri Krishna says in the *Bhagavad Gita* (7/11): "Oh Lord of the Bharatas (Arjuna), in strong persons, I am their strength devoid of desire and passion. I am the sexual activity not conflicting with virtue or scriptural injunctions." We should regulate our sexual desires in such a way that they become clean, permissible, and enlivening. When we suppress them, they become more powerful and induce many physical and mental disorders. The suppressed emotions of sex, anger, greed, etc. affect the nervous system manifesting in various disorders of the mind and body. When we utilize these powerful warehouses of primordial energy in the service of the Ideal, that is, serving the environment to please the Ideal, they serve a greater purpose in life.

Narrator: Controversial spiritual exponent Osho says: The sex energy in human beings is greater energy, even than electricity, than atomic energy, but did you ever think how to transform it? It is sexual energy that transforms into love. However, everyone is against it and is inimical about it. Your so-called good people are against it. Coal never becomes a diamond because the acceptance that is needed for its evolution, for its process of transformation, is out of the question. The moment sex becomes, spiritual, it becomes love. (*From Sex to Superconsciousness*).

Devotee: Hindu scriptures talk of eight fetters (*ashta pasha*). What are they?[84]

Sri Sri Thakur: These fetters are chains that prohibit the movement of the individual towards his growth. They are hatred, shame, vanity, insult, infatuation, arrogance, malice, and cruelty.

They should be treated in the same manner as the other six enemies such as lust, greed, etc.

Devotee: In common understanding, virtue means abstaining from money and women. What do you say, Sir?[85]

Sri Sri Thakur: The infatuation for wealth and women does not go away by leaving their company. We have to acquire mastery over our sexual hunger, anger, greed, pride, delusion, and ego. Suppose we suppress our sexual desires, it resurfaces in the guise of abnormal anger for which Rishi Durbasha was known. So, keeping your mind away from wealth and women by compulsion would lead to various other abnormalities. It is better to keep them under control and lead a normal life of honesty and truthfulness. If an honest, straightforward and service-oriented man indulges a bit in women and money, he is still better than someone who gives a lesson on morality and yet engages in falsehood. To be honest, upright, and humble, a great amount of energy is required, and an abundance of moral courage is imperative. Only a coward indulges in falsehoods and lies.

Narrator: To illustrate that outward abstinence from desire and passion does not help, Yugacharya Sri Sri Borda tells a story: Two intimate friends come to know that a rare beauty has arrived at the brothel. One evening, at dusk, they went together to the brothel. On the way, they found a hermit addressing some people around him. What is going on? One of them ran to the crowd and was absorbed in what the hermit was explaining. He waved his hand to the other to go ahead. Of the two friends, one listened to religious discourses, and the other spent time with a beautiful harlot. They came home late at night and died early the next morning in their respective houses. Yama's messengers came to the friend who had listened to religious discourses to escort him to hell. Lord Vishnu sent his emissary to welcome the soul of the womanizer to His abode. What sort of justice is this? It was explained that the man with the hermit was physically listening to the discourses, but his mind was in the brothel thinking about the sexual enjoyment of his friend. On the other hand, the friend in the brothel's den was repenting and thinking of God. So, it is the attitude of mind which is most important in shaping human destiny. (*Discourses on the Ideal*, vol. II)

On this issue, let us hear the controversial Indian guru, Osho, "I have been amazed, I have come across prostitutes but they never ask anything about sex. They inquire about the soul and about God. I also come across many ascetics, monks, and holy men, and whenever we are alone they ask about nothing but sex. In public, they sermonize on the soul and about God, but within, they have the same problem as others." (*From Sex to Superconsciousness*)

Devotee: What is libido?[86]

Sri Sri Thakur: It is the fundamental magnetic force in every being. It is called *Yogabega/Surat* in Sanskrit. By this cohesive force, sperm and ovum join together to form a life cell. This impetus to unite is libido. I think in every creation there is a libido: male and female. The male is positive-prominent and the female is negative-prominent. They attract each other. When they meet, a sort of toxic excitement arises.

Devotee: How do the positive and the negative attract each other?[87]

Sri Sri Thakur: There is a saying (in Bengali): 'Wherever he goes, she follows.' This is an unimaginable and incomprehensible state of affairs. The negative can't exist without the positive. This is called centripetal attraction. Positive and negative unite to depart and depart to unite. This continuous process goes on without a break, creating stars, constellations, and universes beyond count. You direct this primordial urge according to your shifting state of mind, sometimes to women, sometimes to wealth, sometimes to power, etc. When you realise that the gratification you receive from them is transitory, you search for a union that is permanent and will take care of you in totality. This union with the Super Soul is Yoga, it subdues harmful instincts, and regulates them to productive use.

Devotee: Our method of *sadhana* is called *surat sadhana of 'Sant-mat.'* Will you kindly explain this, Sir?[88]

Sri Sri Thakur: In simple terms, it means when a man with all his heart and soul attaches his libido or the primordial attraction to the Ideal, ignoring the demands of passions, he takes the eternal path of becoming, by regulating and adjusting the passions to his utmost benefit. This journey of becoming has no end. I call it *Sant-mat*.

Devotee: In what way is it different from the spiritual practice of the Vedantins?[89]

Sri Sri Thakur: Reverend Huzur Maharaj has opined that at the most there can be a hairline difference between the two. In Vedantic pursuits, the ultimate realisation may happen to one in a crore, but in *Sant-mat* the possibility is more. By adopting *Sant-mat*, a practitioner, in his transcendental state will definitely realise the primordial sound.

Narrator: Sigmund Freud (1856-1939), the Austrian neurologist, was a major exponent of libido. He held it to be the reservoir of primary energy and the impetus for attraction between man and woman. However, subsequent psychoanalysts like Carl Jung and others have established that it is the totality of psychic energy, which is amenable to be turned towards more beneficial endeavours.

On how the craving for sex could be transformed into spiritual realisation, Sri Sri Thakur narrates the legend of Bilwamangal. He was born into one of the leading families in his village, but, by nature, was a debauchee. His infatuation with a prostitute named Chintamani was tremendous. Her residence was across the river. Most times Bilwamangal was with her, but his desire remained insatiate. It was a dark monsoon night. The village seemed awash with torrential rains, its thudding sound giving the impression it would never end. Ditches, pits, and channels overflowed. In the middle of the night, his desire for Chintamani goaded him to go to her. With great difficulty, he reached the river. It was flowing at full capacity; there was no boat anywhere.

Bilwamangal jumped into the swollen river and holding on to a floating dead body managed to cross. In the darkness, he trudged to Chintamani's house. The stairs were submerged in water; he caught a serpent to climb up to her abode. Chintamani was aghast to see Bilwamangal with his clothes covered with mud and showing a weird demeanour. She exclaimed, "My dear lover! Had you shown such madness for God, you would have surely met Him by now." The sarcasm of the sex worker struck a vital cord in him. In a flash, he realised how degraded and miserable he had become because of his lechery. He left but instead of going home, went to Vrindavan (a sacred place where Sri Krishna emancipated the gopis in the age of *Dwapara*). He pulled out his eyes, blaming them as the prime agents of his infatuation for beautiful women. He took to rigorous spiritual practices and, in a short time, was recognised as a saint. It also so happened that after that night, Chintamani abandoned hiring out her body, sold her properties, and eventually left for Vrindavan. She heard of saint Bilwamangal and went to meet him. Aware of her presence, Bilwamangal was overjoyed, and out of gratitude congratulated her, "Oh Great Lady! You are my first teacher to open the doors for my spiritual sojourn. I will remember you as long as I live."

Devotee: When does libido behave erratically and bring harm?[90]

Sri Sri Thakur: Libido leads to a downfall when it is damaged or distorted. In the case of Bilwamangal, the libido was damaged leading him to debauchery, but it is like a hole in a boat; when the hole is plugged, the boat sails without any threat. When a person with a damaged libido is attached to the Ideal, the job is done. Passions are tamed and such human beings stand up with all their goodness. However, the difficulty lies when the libido is distorted, there is a knot in the rope that cannot be unraveled. Persons having a distorted libido think negatively, they cannot tolerate good in anyone. They hallucinate that the world is against them. They try to edge over others to show their supremacy. As a matter of fact, they suffer from an intense inferiority complex. It is very difficult to handle them or improve them.

Narrator: Sri Sri Thakur wrote a long poem on libido, *Suratsaki*, describing the pious aspect of it. A stanza from there :

Libido is not salacious intoxication
but arouses rosy tenderness
unfolding of loving feelings
utterances of amative words
in pleasant activities it rests.

Devotee: How is the libido related to existence-consciousness?[91]

Sri Sri Thakur: By existence-consciousness, one becomes aware that he breathes, he lives, and he grows. Existence is fundamental to all beings. To exist, the being collects all that is necessary for its sustenance, he fights against all odds to survive. So when the libido is attached to the Supreme Being because of His guidance, it becomes easy to achieve a higher state of existence. In simple language, this is the charisma of spiritual realisation.

Devotee: What happens if the libido is not attached to the Ideal?[92]

Sri Sri Thakur: As I told you earlier, unruly and erratic passions are bloodsuckers; they deplete your vital energy. You go on losing energy, but seldom realise it, because you enjoy the harmful intoxication. You feel you are enjoying life. Sooner or later, you are bound to be depressed. Passion is compared with the venom of a snake; it can end life. However, by appropriate use as a medicine, it can also save lives. So the primary task is to mould the libido in the path of being and becoming. Sri Krishna did it for the gopis.

Devotee: What did Sri Krishna do for the gopis?[93]

Sri Sri Thakur: Sri Krishna wanted them to love Him with uncompromising loyalty. To love Him, not as a God, but as a human being, the son of Basudeva. This love was pure love, without any sexual connotations. The gopis accepted Sri Krishna as their Love Lord. The life ambition of the gopis was to take care of Sri

Krishna by sustaining Him, protecting Him, and abiding by Him. It was the simplest way to achieve wisdom. That is why, in the Vaishnava scriptures, the gopis' love for Sri Krishna was treated as the best form of devotion.

Narrator: In the 15th century, Thomas A. Kempis (1380-1471 AD) wrote his famous religious treatise "*The Imitation of Christ*" in Latin, explaining the real love for Jesus (a bestseller, and translated into many languages of the world). We quote a few lines relevant to the present subject: "Those who love Jesus for His own sake, and not for the sake of selfish comfort will praise Him in every trial and anguish of heart, no less than in great joy. They would continue to praise Him, and thank Him, even if He never offered them any comfort. How powerful is the pure love for Jesus, which is free from self-love and self-interest."

Lord Buddha makes a subtle observation by saying that pure love changes man so much that 'He is not the same nor is he another.' Torrence (1875-1956), the US playwright and poet, makes a similar statement: 'It is possible that a man can be so changed by love as to hardly be recognised as the same person.' (*Living Thoughts of Great People*)

Devotee: Who were these gopis? [94]

Sri Sri Thakur: Ladies of Vrindaban who dedicated their lives to the service of Sri Krishna are the gopis. Sri Krishna was in their blood, and the very beat that kept their hearts going. They adored Sri Krishna as Gopala. In Sanskrit, one of the meanings of the word 'Gopala' is the caretaker of living beings.

Devotee: What is the meaning of the name Sri Krishna? [95]

Sri Sri Thakur: 'Sri' stands for service, 'Krishna' signifies attraction. So he who dedicates his life to the service of all beings, and invites them to his fold to render service, is Sri Krishna. He holds a flute, which is a symbol of knowledge. Another name of Sri Krishna is 'Govardhandhari', as He holds the Govardhan mountain on his fingertip. This means he has taken upon himself the arduous responsibility to look after the whole of Creation. In his hands, he holds a conch, a discus, a mace, and a lotus. They symbolise love, discipline, spiritual practice, and bliss, respectively. The Prophet of a particular era is called the Sri Krishna of that era. In that way, the Ideal, the Prophet of the present age, is Sri Krishna for us. He alone is to be worshipped. By worshipping Him we worship all the past Prophets.

Devotee: What is *Raasa leela* (*rasakrida*)? [96]

Sri Sri Thakur: *Raasa leela* is *Sabda leela* (sound-vibration). By this method, Sri Krishna used to arouse the nerve centres of the gopis. When the nerve centres are activated, it creates heat, which is transmitted to the brain. The brain cells, in turn, are heated up and activated. As a result, one can experience the eternal sound (*anahata naada*) at the back of the head, and view the entire Creation through the inner eye.

Devotee: How did Sri Krishna enlighten the gopis by *Raasa leela*? [97]

Sri Sri Thakur: It was the onset of winter, on a full moon night in the month of *Kartik* (a holy month for Hindus), and the young Sri Krishna was with the gopis in a garden full of trees, bearing jasmine, iris, orange blossoms and tuberoses of enchanting fragrances. The gopis had been fasting throughout the holy month, consuming only a single meal in a day, preparing for their pious moment with Krishna. When the time arrived, all of them gathered around Him, and a rhythmical dance started. Gradually and surely, the dance gained momentum, and a spiritual trance enveloped all of them. Suddenly, to their surprise, the gopis found Sri Krishna missing. Where had He gone? The pangs of separation were intense and unbearable for all of them. Perspiring and crying, they searched for Sri Krishna everywhere. Their sole intention was to attain Sri Krishna, to be wholly owned by Him. To their utter surprise, each gopi found Krishna dancing and holding onto her alone. The same was happening with the other gopis. Sri Krishna's form had proliferated; he was with each of them. Their immense love for Sri Krishna made these multiple manifestations seem more real than reality itself. The pain of separation followed by an unexpected gift of togetherness elevated them to a state of ecstasy. They had a divine vision of glowing flashes and could hear the eternal sound deep in their ears. Due to the spiritual energy that started flowing through their brain cells, the gopis, in that ecstatic instant, could now see the whole universe, the massive expanse of Creation condensed in a halo of light. For them, the love for Sri Krishna was the means as well as the end.

Devotee: What is the eternal sound (*anahata nada*)? Physicists call it the 'buzzing of the cosmic hive.' Where and how is it heard? [98]

Sri Sri Thakur: During *mantra-sadhana* (meditation), the brain cells open up and the inner sound is heard, which is incessant and eternal. It is heard in the inner ear at the back of the skull, a little to the right. The sound heard on the left of the skull is passion-ridden, and hence needs to be ignored.

Devotee: Vaishnava texts speak of five modes of relationship (*Pancha bhava*) to worship the Supreme Beloved. What are they, Sir? [99]

Sri Sri Thakur: The first is the mode of tranquillity (*shanta bhava*); when one is immersed in contemplating the splendid attributes of the beloved, he goes into a state of peace and tranquillity. Thereafter comes the attitude of a servant (*dasya bhava*) towards his master; an alertness to serve the master. The third is to treat the Lord as the most loved friend; where a devotee cannot be separated even for a moment from God. This is called *Mitra bhava*. The fourth is to take care of your Love Lord as your own child, where the devotee assumes the role of a mother. This is known as *Vatsalya bhava*. The last is to assume the Love Lord to be a husband (*Madhura bhava*). Broadly, these are the five states of mind one has to go through according to the mental upbringing of the practitioner. Your love for the Ideal should be pure and selfless.

Devotee: It is also said in the Vaishnava texts that being (*jiva*) is the perpetual servant (*nitya-dasa*) of Lord Krishna. What does it signify, Sir? [100]

Sri Sri Thakur: It is an august and excellent statement. The Sanskrit word '*dasa*' means *dana*, a gift, and '*nitya*' means that which is eternal. So the meaning of the above statement is that being exists as an eternal gift from Lord Krishna. That is true. We are created by the Supreme Being, deriving our life force from Him, a sum of positive and negative energies interacting in a seamless, never-ending process. We have in us the urge for unity. Instead of wasting that urge needlessly, we should fix it on the Supreme Beloved (Sri Krishna for the *Vaishnavas*).

Devotee: It is said that to be immersed in noble thoughts is the best form of worship. Is it not so, Sir? [101]

Sri Sri Thakur: Thought without action is milk without cream. Saying this, Sri Sri Thakur told a story: There was a mendicant running a hermitage. The maintenance of the hermitage required a lot of money, so he decided to establish a banana plantation in the open area behind his place. In due course, stems with thick bunches of plantains emerged one after another on the trees. When they ripened, a colony of bats would flock and eat the ripe fruits and destroy the raw ones. The mendicant was sad at the loss of his fruits. He prayed to his deity, and in his mind, offered all the fruits of the plantation, hoping the deity would take care of the bats. However, nothing happened; the bats persisted. A young cobbler used to visit the mendicant in the evenings to smoke marijuana. He came to know about the predicament of the mendicant and said, 'Sir, you have offered all the fruits to the Lord, and naturally, it is now His property. How does it matter to you?' The hidden satire of the cobbler made the mendicant fume with anger. He shouted, 'You urchin, are you trying to be funny?' While leaving, the boy meekly remonstrated, 'Sir, you are very learned and I am a fool, but if you collect the bunches of bananas from the tree before they ripen, and put them in a closed room, they will ripen on their own. The bats will not be able to destroy them, and you will be able to market your produce. The mendicant now understood that thought alone is useless without proper action. Completing the story, Sri Sri Thakur said, It is the law of nature that we reap the results of our actions. We have to undergo good or bad times according to the deeds done by us. God does not come to your rescue to waive the penalty for your bad deeds. Only noble thoughts backed with proper action can serve as repentance, and lead you towards tranquillity.

Devotee: If we always think good for others, and pray to God for their well-being, is it not enough, Sir? [102]

Sri Sri Thakur: When the luxury of mere good thought devours a man, and he does not back it up with action, his life is useless. To show his goodness, he talks sweetly, but within him, his wicked faculties are active. Such behaviour is characteristic of a gambler. The common good is best achieved only when there is complete dedication to the Ideal. We overcome our ego and arrogance when we perform good work to satisfy the Ideal without expecting anything in return. Such an act makes us humble.

Sri Sri Thakur in *Magnadicta*:
> God cares little
> what one thinks
> but He sees
> how one behaves
> and what one does! (verse-228)

Edmund Burke (1729-1797), the Anglo-Irish statesman, economist, and philosopher, deplored lazy pious thoughts in his satire: "The only thing necessary for the triumph of evil is for good men to do nothing." (*Understanding Philosophy*)

Devotee: What is *Naam* (Name), and what is the proper way to chant it? [103]

Sri Sri Thakur: Name is a sound, it is called *bija mantra*. *Mantra* is the chanting of words, by the application of which a purpose is successfully accomplished. And *bija (seed)* is understood as that which sprouts within and outside. Repetition of the Name has the potency to rekindle the vital force so much that the things we experience and contemplate, come within our perception. In

Hindu spiritual texts, the *bija mantra* is divided into three broad categories. The first is that which is effusive (*bhavatmaka*)—'*Om kling vasudevaya.*' As we chant it, it brings to our mind the form and attributes of Lord Krishna. The second one is that of sound (*Dhwanyatmaka*)—'*Om hring kling.*' The third *bija-mantra* is vibration-potent (*spandanatmaka*). This is the Prime Name (*Adinaam*): the place of origin of all names. This is our vital force. It is also understood as a *radiant unit*. As radium continuously emits light, the Prime Name emits vital force incessantly. It is called *Dayal Desh*, starting from *Satya Lok*. Whatever is created in the universe is a manifestation of sound waves and the Prime Name contains its finest form. The Prime Name also contains in it the primordial vitality of all the names. When we repeat it in a particular manner, the latent talent in man awakens to its hilt. The experience of inner realisation of the Prime Name is different from the way in which the *anahata nada* (incessant eternal sound) is experienced. It is the sprouting state of Prime Sound (*Sabda Brahma*), where the attribute-less assumes many attributes.

Devotee: If the Prime Name is the place of origin of all the other Names (*bija mantras*), then that one Name is enough. Why do we have so many *bija mantras*? [104]

Sri Sri Thakur: Name (*Bija mantra*) is the arena of sound energy. A particular Name rekindles the level of consciousness of specified strata. Hence the need for various mantras. If one thinks of a mantra in the lower strata as the ultimate one, and sticks to it, progress is hampered. So, to get rid of all this confusion, I tell you time and again to accept the Name (*Bija mantra*) brought forth by the Prophet of an age as the potent Name (Mantra) for that particular era. Accepting such a Name, through proper initiation and prescribed way of repetition, can work wonders.

Devotee: Suppose, somehow we get to learn the *bija mantra* suggested by the Ideal. Won't chanting it to ourselves work? [105]

Sri Sri Thakur: Without accepting the Ideal of the age, when one practises on his own, he will continue to remain where he is.

Neither can he identify his deficiencies, nor can he overcome them. So it is said: '*Naama O Naami Aveda*' (Name and its exponent are inseparable). When you undertake the pursuit of *Adi Naam* (Prime Name), for its proper efficacy, attachment to the Ideal becomes a must. When the Ideal becomes the primary of your life, the Prime Name becomes the most potent. In Sanskrit, this is called: *kaivalya lava* (the acquisition of exceptional power).

Devotee: How does the inner change happen when *Naam* is practised with attachment to the *Naami* (the Ideal)? [106]

Sri Sri Thakur: The Name that is transmitted directly from the Naami is endowed with higher potency. It excites the brain cells. Due to excitement, they become more sensitive and more effective. The periphery of knowledge expands. Things that were opaque earlier, are now clearly visible. To give a concrete example, it is like a wireless photo transmission of television and sound transmission by radio. In a nutshell, existential consciousness goes on developing, and you achieve great accomplishments (*vibhuti*).

Devotee: What are those accomplishments, Sir? [107]

Sri Sri Thakur: In Sanskrit, these powers are called *vibhuti*. Vibhu is another name for the Ideal (Prophet); meaning whoever is competent to achieve what he desires. The first of these powers is *Anima*—the ability to become weightless as a bay leaf. Then comes *Laghima*—the ability to make oneself the thinnest of all. The third is *Vyapti*—the ability to expand. Then comes *Prakamya*—the ability to control desires, followed by *Mahima*—the proficiency of a higher order, *Ishitwa*—the ability to gain knowledge, *Vashitwa*—the ability to lead and command; and, finally, *Kamavashayita*—the ability to silence the demands of passion. When desires are controlled and demands are silenced, pure knowledge flows unhindered.

Narrator: In 1946, Sri Sri Thakur migrated from Hemayetpur with minimum belongings and little money to Deoghar. Properties worth crores of rupees in buildings, educational and research institutions, and small-scale industries were left behind. He was unperturbed. In later days, during discussions, he would say: When I left Hemayetpur for Deoghar, I did not have an iota of remorse. Whatever existed there, can be constructed here as well, and now it has happened, due to the kindness of the Supreme Father. I do not possess them, nor did I have them at any point in time. I am least concerned with property, wealth, money, etc. I am a beggar of men. Man is my desire, man is my demand, and man is my asset.

Devotee: Is it not a Herculean task to minimise one's wants?[108]

Sri Sri Thakur tells a story: Long ago there lived an eminent scholar of *Nyaya Shastra* in a village. His name was Ramnath. He was well-versed in logic and polemics (*Tarka shastras*), and devoted all his time to scholarly pursuits. He was so engrossed in his work that he did not bother with any worldly acquisition. He was content and happy. The king of the land was kind. Many pandits, scholars, and poets, would approach for favours, and were granted gifts of land, gold, and a permanent allowance from the royal treasury. However, Ramnath never visited the king. He knew that Ramnath was a great scholar, but was extremely poor. In his heart of hearts, he thought of giving something to Ramnath. The king sent for him, but Ramnath sent the messenger back saying: 'Let the great king rule the country and let me pursue my knowledge.' The king was flabbergasted. Out of respect for the scholar, he came to meet Ramnath. The king asked, 'Oh Learned One! I have come to take care of your necessities. Tell me what should I give you?' Ramnath replied, 'Oh great king! Who told your honour, I needed anything? I am very happy in this mud house I inherited from my father. I get enough rice from my paternal land. Please look at the tamarind tree in front of us. My wife prepares a soup of tamarind leaves daily and serves it to me with hot rice. I relish it. Why should I acquire anything more than my need and complicate my life?' He looked at the king with folded hands. The king, while departing, said, 'There is peace and prosperity in my kingdom because people like you live here.'

Narrator: Socrates (470 BC- 399 BC), the Greek philosopher known as the Father of Philosophy, lived in Athens. He believed simplicity and moral discipline should be the aim of human life. Once, he was returning empty-handed from the marketplace when an acquaintance asked, "What, Sir? What did you purchase?" Socrates replied, "I saw all the things in the godown, and I can certainly manage without them. So why carry an unnecessary burden?" (*Understanding Philosophy*)

Sculptor-philosopher Lao Tzu of China said the following:

'Always without desire, we must be found,
If desire always within us be,
Its outer fringe is all that we shall see.' (*Tao te Ching*)

Paramahansa Sri Ramakrishna Dev said: 'I don't accept money from someone greedy for riches. His money is wasted on four counts—litigation, robbery, doctors, and the extravagance of wayward children.' He went on to narrate an anecdote: A mendicant came to the palace of Emperor Akbar to beg for money, while he was praying. It was a royal instruction that if a mendicant comes when the Emperor is in prayer, he should be allowed inside and the emperor would receive him later. Emperor Akbar completed his prayer, and, on getting up, saw the mendicant leaving. He signalled him to wait, approached him, and asked why he had come. The mendicant replied, 'I came to ask you for monetary help, but instead found you begging for money and power from Allah. It dawned upon me why I should beg for money from a beggar. If I have to beg, I would beg from the Almighty Himself.' (*Gems from the Gospel of Sri Ramakrishna*)

In this context, we give below the translation of an oft-quoted verse from Sri Sri Thakur:

Money is not yours, but man,
Earn man as much as you can.

Devotee: In the Hindu scriptures, persons having spiritual attainment are divided into three categories, *Nitya-siddha*, *Sadhana-siddha*, and *Kripa-siddha*. Kindly explain them. [109]

Sri Sri Thakur: When a devotee takes the Ideal as his most loved one, his happiness lies in the happiness of his master, and in due course of time it forms a part of his nature. He engages all his passions and complexes in carrying out the orders of the Ideal. He has no self-interest. Such persons are called *nitya-siddha* (perfectly accomplished). There are devotees whose inclination of mind is divided. They serve the Master, no doubt, but are shrewd enough to look after their own interests at the same time. In their *sadhana*, surrender to the Master is not complete, so their progress is like the movement of a tortoise. A time comes when they rise up and become totally Ideal-centric. When they attain this state after a long process, they are called *sadhana-siddha*. The third category is rare. When a devotee is a beginner, his surrender to the Master is so enormous and genuine that the Ideal showers him with knowledge instantly. As this is due to the kindness and mercy of the Master, it is called *kripa-siddha*. These are the varied experiences of a *Sadhaka*.

Devotee: How to understand 'experience', Sir? [110]

Sri Sri Thakur: By thinking, analysing, visualising, and acting, impressions are created in our brains. We decipher them to know what is what. These impressions are stored in our brains in the form of memory. We call them experience.

Devotee: What kind of experience does one get by repetition of the Holy Name? [111]

Sri Sri Thakur: By continuous repetition of the Name, one enters the realm of knowledge where Creation is understood in its finest form as the interaction of positive and negative energy. In Yogic texts, it is called *Hiranyagarva*. When the mind is set there, the adept experiences his omnipresence, 'I am everywhere.' When somebody is hurt, you feel you are also hurt. When something good happens to anyone, you rejoice as if it is your own good. You are content with the happiness of others. So, to think good and do good to others becomes imperative for you. The feeling of 'ownness' expands beyond the limit. From here, the region of *Alakh, Agam Loka* starts.

Narrator: Rishi Aurobindo described this feeling thus,
A fourth dimension of aesthetic sense
Where all is in ourselves, ourselves in all.
(The Spirit of Indian Culture)

Devotee; All this is very difficult to understand. Kindly explain it in a simple way, Sir? [112]

Sri Sri Thakur: What we do in the world is action, its image goes to the brain, and is stored there in synergy with the existing ones. It is gross or fine, according to the level of our intellect. When the brain cells are activated, the ability to receive the finer aspects of an experience with all its sharpness increases manifold. In this manner, our knowledge expands and we know how to solve problems. When we enhance the elasticity of the brain cells by meditation in the prescribed manner, we climb step by step towards the state of ever-increasing consciousness. These levels are named differently according to the visualisation of different colours of light, and hearing of various sound rhythms in the inner ear. As heat (*Taap*) is generated in this spiritual exercise, it is called *Tapasya* (ascetic practice). However, it must be done under the guidance of an able master.

Devotee: In Yogic texts, there is a mention of three vital arteries—*Ida, Pingala,* and *Sushumna* (the central subtle nerve). Would you please explain how they function? [113]

Sri Sri Thakur: *Ida* and *Pingala* are a sympathetic autonomic cerebrospinal nervous system and *Susumna* is the hollow in the spinal cord starting from the bottom, parallel to the junction of the heart, ending at the base of the frontal lobe. It is full of spinal fluid. *Ida and Pingala* help to preserve the well-being and through *Susumna,* the *Kundalini* rises.

Devotee: What is *Kundalini* and its rising? Kindly tell us about your experience, Sir? [114]

Sri Sri Thakur: When the practitioner repeats the Name in deep meditation, he experiences the movement of the spinal fluid like the rise and fall of mercury in a thermometer. At that stage, he finds the environment to be blissful. This is known as the rising of the *Kundalini* (the creative spiral). There are different layers. When you press a sugar candy with your teeth, it emits a flash of light. For easier understanding, the flashes of light at the time of the *Kundalini*'s rise are more or less similar to this. They bear different colours at different plexus; the sound also varies.

Devotee: Will you please elaborate a little more about the plexus?[115]

Sri Sri Thakur: The base of the spine from where the nerve plexus with the ganglia starts and spreads, each junction is called a plexus *(chakra,* or the psychic centre). They are the pelvic plexus *(Muladhara chakra/*base of the spine, anal region*)*, sacral plexus *(Swadhisthana chakra),* solar plexus *(Manipura chakra,* navel region*)*, cardiac plexus *(Anahata chakra,* heart region*)*, cervical plexus or carotid plexus *(Vishuddhi chakra,* throat region*)*, and base of the cerebrum or medulla plexus *(Ajna chakra,* between the eyebrows and at the root of the nose*)*. Concentrating the mind on a particular region excites the corresponding nerves of that region, which in turn, stimulate the related brain cells. This stimulation enhances the sensitivity and receptivity of the brain cells. In Yogic texts, this journey through the six plexus is called *Shat-Chakra-Veda.*

Narrator: Arousal of the *Kundalini* in Yogic texts: The human body with its psychological and biological function is a vehicle through which the dormant psych-energy *(Kundalini shakti)* can be awakened to finally unite with the cosmic consciousness. A transformation and re-orientation of this dormant energy is only possible with the arousal of the *Kundalini* through the psych centres in the human body. The rising of the *Kundalini* in the language of modern science means the activation of the vast dormant areas of the brain. When it awakens to a higher spiritual plane, the individual is not limited to his own perception but participates in the source of light and sound. Neurologists call the dormant areas of the brain 'silent areas', which remain 'wasted assets', untapped and unutilized. Once these areas are completely active, one can communicate with his own higher consciousness. The unmanifested *Kundalini* is symbolised by a serpent coiled in three-and-a-half circles, with its tail in its mouth and spiralled around the central axis. *Chakras* are the psych centres in the etheric body and the points of contact by which the *Kundalini* rises. The first centre is *Muladhara Chakra,* ending with *Ajna Chakra* and finally, *Sahasrara,* the uppermost. The ascending planes of experience are called *Lokas,* starting from *Bhuloka.* (*The Tantric Way*)

A detailed account of Sri Sri Thakur's experience of *Shat-Chakra-Veda* has been given in the book, *Katha Prasange,* Part III (Bengali) by Sushil Chandra Bose. The author recorded an account of his conversation with Sri Sri Thakur in 1942-43. Sushilda, in the Preface, has written about the physical changes in Sri Sri Thakur when describing his experience.

Excerpts: It appears as if Sri Sri Thakur was in a trance and at the time of talking about a particular plexus, he was seeing the light and hearing the corresponding sound. His face was dazzling with inner light and each utterance was clear and firm. Sometimes, while describing, he lost consciousness for a while and regained it soon.

Another devotee, Ray Hauserman, in the preface to his book '*Ocean In A Teacup*', spoke of what he had seen for himself: "A north Indian Brahmin (Pandit) insistently challenged Thakur's level of realisation in 1953. Thakur in his disarmingly innocent way protested that he knew nothing and then proceeded to vividly describe the various lights, sounds, and scenes of each spiritual domain as he entered them one after the other, effortlessly demonstrating his presence simultaneously in and out of this world. When he described the three worlds of Triloka, his face grew radiant. When he talked of Trikuti, his voice seemed to come from a long distance. As he described Sat-Lok, it seemed that his entire body was surrounded by light, and when speaking of Alakh-Lok and Anami, his body was trembling. When he spoke of the brilliance of Radhaswami Dham, his voice changed. Unaware of the surroundings, he kept saying- 'I'm going...going.' He stopped. There was an awe-filled silence in the yard where we were sitting. Slowly Thakur's countenance regained its normal hue. The challenger was sobbing. He prostrated before Thakur with folded hands and said: 'Forgive me, Thakur, forgive me. I had heard in Agra that a saint can't be born in Bengal, so I was disrespectful. Truly, you have hidden yourself well.'

Devotee: What is *Pranayama*? [116]

Sri Sri Thakur: '*Prana*' is the vital energy by which the physique is enlivened with ceaseless growth, and '*ayama*' is the method by which the vital energy is regulated and utilised. So *pranayama* would mean regulated utilisation of life energy.

Pranayama: A short note by Yugacharya Sri Sri Borda

Pranayama is disciplining the flow of breath. If one repeats the name in the method ordained by Sri Sri Thakur, the breath is automatically regulated, and there is no need of doing pranayama. Sri Sri Thakur has said,"When you repeat The Holy Name with keenness, Pranayama becomes automatic." We are all worldly creatures. Thakur has asked us to live like an ascetic, even in our family life. While living in this mundane world, we have to do spiritual practice. Wherever we are, if we feel Thakur is with us, it is yoga. If we do *pranayama* regularly, it improves the circulation of air in our veins and arteries and ensures good health. A normal man breathes 18-20 times a minute. He exhales more than he inhales, and as a result, there is a loss of vitality. Due to this continuous process of less inhalation and more exhalation, energy deteriorates. By *pranayama*, this process is regulated, resulting in the availability of more energy and longer life. The practice is as follows: Count up to 4 while inhaling (*puraka*), and hold your breath counting to 6 (*kumbhaka*), then exhale and count to 8 (*rechaka*). When you perform the above 4-6-8 (*puraka-kumbhaka-rechaka*) it is one cycle of *pranayama*. When you complete three cycles, it is the full *pranayama*. Doing 12 times of full pranayama, it is *pratyahara*, 12 times of *pratyahara* is *Dharana*, 12 times of *Dharana* is *Dhyana*, 12 times of *Dhyana* leads to *Samadhi*. Generally, we inhale up to the length of 10 fingers and exhale up to 12 fingers length. Through the practice of *pranayama*, the excess exhalation stops. It can be reduced to a short length of 5 fingers. When your exhalation reduces by one finger and is at 11, you get control over your passions. Likewise, at 10, you experience bliss, at 9 poetic creativity develops, at 8 knowledge of the future comes, at 7 one gets a fine vision, when it comes down to 6 one can roam in space, and when it becomes 5, one sees distant objects. For example, when somebody's child is missing, an adept in *pranayama*, with his distant vision, can tell where the child is. *Pranayama* should be done under the guidance of a perfect master. In our system, when we move in life, keeping the Ideal in the centre and following his instructions to mould our living becomes a must; hence any other exercise becomes redundant. (*Ishta Prasange*, vol. 3).

Devotee: In the Tantric system, *Kundalini* is aroused in rituals involving wine (*madya*), meat (*mansa*), fish (*matsya*), posture (*mudra*), and sexual union (*maithuna*). What do you think about *Tantra* sadhana, Sir? [117]

Sri Sri Thakur: The prime impetus of life is food and sex. By appeasement of hunger, the physique is nourished, and by sexual union, one begets offspring to ensure progeny. A person with a high sexual tendency has an inclination for meat. Meat-eating whips the system adequately unlike vegetarian diets. A vegetarian, after tasting non-veg food, literally hankers for it. Of course, those who are culturally superior do not yield to it. To stimulate the excitement of meat-eating, wine was imbibed. Fish is used as a corollary of meat. Posture or *mudra* is the technique by which passion can be kept in check.

The exponents of the *Tantras*, to regulate passionate desires and direct them to being and becoming, introduced this system so that those interested in wine, meat, and sex are not deprived of spiritual practice. The *sine qua non* of this *Tantra sadhana* is to surrender to the Guru or the Master. The practitioner has to take the guidance of the Master at every step, otherwise, it creates havoc. In that system, the emphasis is on rules, regulations, discipline, and complete obedience to the Master (Guru). In this way, passions are regulated. So the aim of *Tantra Sadhana* is to get rid of passions by putting them under the guidance of the Master.

Devotee: Vedantin says 'neti, neti.' What does it convey?[118]

Sri Sri Thakur: 'Neti' means 'not this.' When a seeker reaches a level of spiritual realisation, he shares his experience with the Master and asks: 'Is this the end?' The Master tells him: 'No, it is not, go ahead, further ahead.'

Devotee: What is the meaning of *Laya*?[119]

Sri Sri Thakur: When the being merges with the Supreme, it loses its identity and becomes one with Him. This stage is called *Laya*.

Narrator: A devotee always desires to enjoy his ever-loving relationship with the Supreme Beloved. He wants to remain in that state of ecstasy. If he loses his identity, he is lost. The devotee does not wish to be lost.

The two lines of a popular bhajan of Sri Sri Dada indicate this:
Earth appeared desolate
Only you and I are left,
In you have merged the rest.

Devotee: What is *mayavada*?[120]

Sri Sri Thakur: *Maya* means the limited manifestation of the unlimited Supreme. It is also understood as a variable truth. If we accept the truth, we also have to accept its changing reality. The entity of truth is dynamic and because of its dynamism, the creation moves on. Whatever the proponents of various 'isms' may say, the fact remains that with intent, keenness, and inclination towards the Supreme Being, Creation is on the move, and so is the world.

Devotee: Sri Ramakrishna Dev has said, 'as many views, that many paths.' Which path should we follow?[121]

Sri Sri Thakur: Say Tantra, Vedanta, or Mayavada —whatever you may say, the easiest, most secure and invulnerable way of spiritual practice (*sadhana*) is that proclaimed by the Prophet of the age.

Devotee: How do you want us to proceed? [122]

Sri Sri Thakur: Repeat the Name and meditate as directed. You can start with concentration, and remember that concentration is not fixation. 'Con' means to be with, and 'centration' is used for 'centre.' So concentration implies being with the centre. The Scriptures talk of concentrating on the medulla plexus (*Ajna Chakra*: the middle point between the two eyebrows). That is the place of knowledge and perception. When a man is in deep thought, by reflex action he puts his fingertip there. If one practises according to the prescribed procedure, the base of the brain gets excited, the pineal gland becomes active, and we can perceive and understand many phenomena.

8

NIETZSCHE FORECASTS THE ADVENT OF SUPERMAN (THE PROPHET), BHAKTI YOGA, JNANA YOGA, AND KARMA YOGA

Devotee: How to uplift society? [123]

Sri Sri Thakur: You have to bring in a progressive mood among people. A progressive mood is the attitude of love and admiration for the Ideal. That is how King Ashoka could build a vast empire through his admiration for Lord Buddha. The King's admiration for his Guru percolated down to society and developed unity among people. You have to spread progressive ideas like Nietzsche, Marx, Lenin, etc., did.

Narrator: It is astonishing how, with so much ease, Sri Sri Thakur was able to talk about philosophers, saints, scholars, and scientists, as if he is well acquainted with them. However, there was no opportunity for him to learn about them from any known source.

Friedrich Nietzsche (1844-1900) became Professor at Bessel University, Germany, at a very young age. He also joined the army, but cut short his service due to poor health. He stayed home and Germany produced a great thinker of the nineteenth century. He said, 'Go back to the Greeks to revitalise the dying Western civilization.' Instead of scientific discoveries, he emphasised a cultural revolution. He felt that Western culture had reached rock bottom. Christian morality had made man weak through an overemphasis on sin and confession in the Church. He further said these are not the words of Jesus Christ but that of St. Paul. Confession brings down the tempo in man; he feels like a sinner, and thereby shatters his life. This is slave morality. He declares, 'The last Christian died on the cross.' The dream of Lord Christ ended in His crucifixion. The present Christianity is 'church-Christianity' and not 'Jesus-Christianity.' To clean up the mischief of the Church, Superman comes. His concept of morality would be very simple. He will make a man strong and energetic. Superman will bear an exemplary character, he will be very humble and fair. The vision of the advent of Superman by Nietzsche is akin to the statement of Sri Sri Thakur that the Prophet of the age has come, and the Ideal has come. The depreciation of the Church by Nietzsche inspired the Soviet writer, Fyodor Dostoyevsky (1821-1881), to write an anecdote in his famous novel *The Brothers Karamazov.* We try to briefly express the same in our own way:

Once, Christ had the desire to come to Earth to see how His message of love and compassion had spread to uplift mankind. He descended from His heavenly abode. His invisible chariot landed in front of the church of Bethlehem, right in the shade of a sprawling tree. He was enjoying the sight of people coming in numbers for the morning prayer. They saw Him, a man looking like Jesus, standing under a tree. Out of curiosity, they surrounded Him. Someone asked, 'Who are you? You don't look like a local. Are you an imposter of Christ?' In no time, the gathering swelled, and the hubbub attracted the attention of the pastor. He came and looked at the person resembling Christ. When their eyes met, he shivered. Without disclosing anything, he took him to the guest room at the back of the Church. He sat him on a chair, locked the room from outside, and disappeared. After the Mass, when the Church was empty, he stealthily opened the guest room and inquired of the Lord. He pleaded: 'Sir, what made you come here unannounced, uninvited? Things are fine the way they are here. Christianity is doing very well, and churches are growing in number, as is conversion. By your blessings, we, the preachers, are very powerful. We influence the ruling class. Your portrait is sufficient to achieve this cause. Your reappearance, however, will undermine everything. Now, like before, if you preach love, compassion, and forgiveness, then who will come to us? Who will care for us? O Lord! Kindly go back to your abode. We are propagating your word all right. A weak man listens to us and does what we say. Christianity spreads faster. Please do not interfere.'

Satyanusaran—'First of all, we must wage war on weakness. We must be bold and brave; for weakness is sin incarnate. Drive it away at once—this depressing, blood-sucking vampire! Say, you are bold, the offspring of might; believe, you are the son of the Father, the Supreme! Before all else, be daring, be sincere. Then it is clear you have the right to enter the kingdom of heaven.'

Devotee: Are you Nietzsche's Superman, the Ideal, the Prophet?[124]

Sri Sri Thakur: I am the last person to make such a claim. By calling me the Prophet of the age, or the Ideal, you really abrogate me from your midst. I am ready to go to heaven or hell along with you. I do not want to leave you. If you really love me, mend your ways and live life as I do. If you do not get out of your narrow selfishness and do not adopt the path of being and becoming, and merely call me the Ideal, is it not lip service? And then, how can you propagate me? How do you gain and what do I get? I am in search of a carrier who can shoulder me and reach the masses. I need a reliable shoulder to spread my man-making mission. However, I am not so lucky. I have yet to find such a man. Everybody is ready to take the burden of his wife and children, to carry the burden of his passion, but when it comes to me, he feels burdened and escapes. I expect you to adopt the way of living shown by me, and convey my message to the people without distortions.

Narrator: In the book of verse, *Adarsha Vinayaka,* Sri Sri Thakur very succinctly expressed: As light cannot say I am light, wind cannot say I am the wind, the earth does not say I am earth, so also in whose being the Supreme has materialised cannot say I am God. As you cannot see or speak about your own self, explaining what you are; it is only others who can speak of you as per their level of understanding. So you come to learn about the Ideal from the people who are attached to Him. Here again, the state of their understanding is commensurate with the depth of their attachment. (Verse 58)

Devotee: In the *Bhagavad Gita*, Lord Krishna has spoken about Bhakti-yoga, Jnana-yoga, Karma-yoga, etc. Will you please explain the essence of His enunciations? [125]

Sri Sri Thakur: Yoga means to unite. But with whom should you unite? The answer is simple. Unite with Him who is the master of devotion, knowledge, and action. When we follow Him with heart and soul, and offer ourselves in His custody, we start the journey of unity. Devotion enhances knowledge; by the expansion of knowledge, devotion grows, and the cycle goes on. Without activity, knowledge withers, without *Bhakti*, nothing flourishes; so *Bhakti* (devotion), *jnana* (knowledge), and *Karma* (activity) are all interrelated.

Satyanusaran—If there is no deep faith in the Ideal, there is no consistency, no devotion. And if there is no devotion, how can there be realisation? How can there be wisdom? What will he preach? Do light the lamp of truth with the wick of wisdom, soaked in the oil of devotion! You will see how you will be surrounded by so many grasshoppers and insects, so many beasts, and men.

Devotee: How to understand devotion (*Bhakti*) easily, Sir? [126]

Sri Sri Thakur: Devotion is your willingness to accept and serve the Ideal with body, mind and soul. His pleasure is your happiness. Sincerity and faith are two inseparable ingredients of devotion. Devotion has no comparison. Attraction to the Ideal takes birth in the mind and gathers momentum in due course. When it is without a break, it gives rise to a sense of belonging, that is devotion. Whatever you say, energy or knowledge, all flow from devotion. Love is devotion condensed. The devotion of a child towards his parents, the fidelity of a wife to her husband, the obedience of a disciple towards his master—all these are manifestations of devotion. Whenever you do something for God, it takes you to the arena of goodness and godliness. I have tried many ways but nothing is as simple and pious as devotion. Nothing is more filling than devotion. For those who have internalised simple devotion, it is easier for them to accept, and follow the present Ideal. Devotion can change a man in a moment. Knowledge follows devotion and action blossoms from it. Without devotion, actions turn out to be inconsistent and incoherent. The companions of devotion are faith and sincerity. Both these qualities eventually culminate in devotion.

Devotee: Does the fear of God lead to devotion? [127]

Sri Sri Thakur: God has no need to attract anyone with fear. Righteous men seek God of their own volition and opt for the spiritual way. They overcome all adversities and become happy and successful in life. They enjoy God, as God enjoys them. Love is entwined with life. Our basic urge is to live and exist. Love of life induces us towards becoming. The poet thinks, 'O sweetheart, be aware, love is the supreme knowledge.' In Dwapara Yuga, the gopis endowed themselves with knowledge through their sincere love for Sri Krishna.

Narrator: St. John observes, 'He that loveth not, knoweth not God; for God is love.' Sri Ramakrishna Dev said: As a true devotee cannot stay without his Supreme Beloved, the Lord cannot stay without his loving devotee. God is bound by the string of a devotee's love. It is of no consequence to ponder if God is formless or has a form, the basic need is to have faith, and be able to surrender to Him. Learning, knowledge, devotion, and companionship with the Master are ways to realise God. (*Gems from the Gospel of Sri Ramakrishna*)

Sri Sri Thakur in Satyanusaran—Though you have gained such power that you can move the sun and the moon from their courses, can break the earth into pieces, or make all people wealthy, but if you have no love in your heart you have achieved nothing.

An oft-quoted verse of Sri Sri Thakur:

Devotion gathers energy and perception ensures victory
To prevent decay, always carry the two by your side.

Devotee: Nowadays, devotion to parents is on the decline. Why is it so? [128]

Sri Sri Thakur: In the epic, The *Ramayana*, we find devotion to parents at its zenith. Sri Ramachandra was God incarnate. But, look, how he demonstrated his devotion towards his father. He accepted the royal order of fourteen years of banishment to the forest, and separation from His wife, and bore many untold hardships. Sri Ramachandra did not protest, or questioned the justness of his father's order; he simply obeyed. Chanakya is another example of devotion to his mother. He was the law-maker in the council of King Chandragupta Maurya. In his boyhood, an astrologer, noticing two big incisors of Chanakya had predicted that he would be a king or king-maker in the future, but would bring agony to his mother. Chanakya overheard it and ran to the kitchen. With a pincer he pulled out the front tooth before his mother could interfere blood flowed out; his mother was dumbstruck. Chanakya said, "If I am not for my mother, what will I do with the king's throne? Let the wicked teeth go."

Relating these two stories Thakur concluded, 'Devoted children are born only to devoted parents. The seed of devotion is generational, it is cultivated at home.'

Devotee: In the *Bhagavad Gita*, Sri Krishna says: 'Adoration brings wisdom. (*shraddhavan labhate jnanam*).' What does it mean, Sir? [129]

Sri Sri Thakur: Deference to the teacher bestows knowledge. The more one loves a teacher, the greater the acquisition of knowledge. Have you not heard the stories of Aaruni and Upamanyu?

Sri Sri Thakur tells the story of Aaruni: In ancient India, education was a mixture of learning the *shastras* and vocational training in agriculture and cottage industries, so that after the completion of studies, students could take up earning assignments. The centre of learning was called a *gurukula*, and was headed by a rishi (sage).

Acharya Dhaumya maintained paddy fields along with running the gurukul. It was monsoon and heavy torrential rains were a regular affair. The rush of rainwater from the hills broke a portion of the farm's dyke. The excess water would certainly damage the crop. Acharya Dhaumya sent his pupil, Aaruni, to the farm immediately to repair the damage. Aaruni took a spade and gathered soil and stones to fill the gap in the wall, but the pressure of the water washed out his efforts again and again. Ultimately, he stretched himself over the leaking dyke, and used his body to make an embankment. The flow of water stopped. and the crop was saved.

In the evening, Acharya Dhaumya noticed that Aaruni was missing. He took some students to the paddyfields to look for him. They found Aaruni lying near the damaged dyke like a corpse. He was rescued and brought back to the gurukul. He was given a hot water massage, and warm beverages to ward off pneumonia. The next morning, Acharya Dhaumya sent for Aaruni and very affectionately said: 'I am pleased beyond measure at your steadfastness to carry out the orders of your teacher, without caring for your own life. By the grace of the Almighty, knowledge of all matters shall come to you spontaneously. Your training is complete; you may go and take care of your household.'

Upamanyu: A roly-poly young boy, he was in charge of tending the cattle for the gurukul. One morning, Acharya Dhaumya asked, 'Upamanyu, what do you eat that you are so chubby?' With a shy smile, the boy replied, 'In my free hours, I beg at the doors of the villagers and manage my food.' Acharya reprimanded him, 'What you beg for, belongs to me. Henceforth you deposit the alms in the gurukul.' Upamanyu nodded in reverence. Days passed by. One morning, the teacher asked the same question and the young lad replied, 'I beg twice a day. First for the gurukul and then for myself.' Acharya Dhaumya looked at him in disbelief, 'Who permitted you to do that? You can't beg from a household for the second time in a day. It questions my goodwill. Besides, if you knock off all the alms by yourself, your fellow students will return empty-handed. Stop it.' The pupil bowed and left.

After some days, the Guru's eyes fell on Upamanyu again, and he enquired about his survival. He answered, 'I manage by drinking the milk of the mother cows.' Acharya lost his temper, 'The milk of the cow is meant for its calf. How dare you snatch it? Don't do that.' After a fortnight, when Upamanyu came face to face with his teacher, the latter asked, 'Hey, how do you manage your food now?' The young boy answered, 'I lick the milk foam that oozes out after the calf has sucked its share of milk from its mother's udders.' 'It is unhygienic', said Acharya. 'Besides, I don't permit it.'

Now all the means of food were denied Upamanyu. However, he was as jolly as ever. He did his usual duty of grazing the cattle and took to surviving on water only. The pangs of hunger became intolerable. He saw a bush with healthy green leaves and was compelled to consume those. As soon as he gulped the juicy leaf, he lost his eyesight. He could not gather the cows and bring them back to the gurukul. Confused, he moved around aimlessly and fell into a well. In the evening, when Upamanyu did not turn up, Acharya Dhaumya went with some disciples to look for him. They found him, and with a lot of difficulties, pulled him out of the well and brought him back. After preliminary treatment, Acharya urged him to worship God Ashwini Kumar for the return of his eyesight. Upamanyu followed the instructions of the Acharya word for word with tenacity. In due course, he recovered his vision.

Acharya Dhaumya blessed him and said, 'Boy, you passed all the difficult tests put upon you, and showed your uncompromising adherence to your teacher. Hence, with my blessings, all the knowledge of the Vedas will be revealed to you. You have attained wisdom; now go home and lead your worldly life.'

Devotee: The devotion of Aaruni and Upamanyu was sincere and steadfast. What happens when devotion is pretence and deceit?[130]

Sri Sri Thakur: A person with fake devotion has no coherence in what he thinks, what he speaks, and how he acts. Some of the characteristics of a true devotee are that he is not conceited, he is kind, well-behaved, and not envious. The prayer of Duryodhan before Lord Krishna was full of deceit when he said:

> 'What is right (dharma) I know, but cannot sustain
> What is wrong (adharma) I know, but cannot abstain
> O Hrushikesh (Sri Krishna)! You are in my heart
> So I do what you compel me to do.'

Satyanusaran—Exciting oneself in bouncing and pouncing or a little weeping on the impulse of dancing or singing, etc., is sometimes taken for devotion. However, this is not devotion at all. Momentary excess of emotion and outburst is not sign of a devotee. There must be some sign of thin ego, a sign of faith, a sign of honest thought, good behaviour, broadness, etc., in the character and conduct of a devotee, otherwise, the devotion is not true or pure.

Sri Sri Thakur added, One of the characteristics of devotion is to love variety in the interest of the unit. You can also love one for the interest of the variety.

An oft-quoted verse of Sri Sri Thakur:

> 'You are for the Lord
> Not for others,
> You are for the Lord,
> And so for others.'

Narrator: Yugacharya Sri Sri Borda gave two concrete instances from the life of Sri Shankardev, differentiating genuine devotion from a deceitful one.

Sri Shankardev, before starting his all-India pilgrimage with a group of followers, approached some of his wealthy devotees for contributions. The first devotee he approached was a known miser. All of a sudden he found the Master at his door, was taken aback, and enquired about the purpose of the visit. Sri Shankardev answered his question. The miserly devotee, after requesting the Master to rest for a while, disappeared from the scene. The people thought he had gone away to avoid contributing. But, lo and behold! After an hour, he returned with a bagful of gold coins. Sri Shankardev was surprised and asked how he had mustered such a big amount in such a short time. The devotee replied, 'Sir, I have mortgaged all my properties and secured this amount. Please accept my little share for your pious sojourn.'

Another wealthy devotee of Sri Shankardev was very vocal about his self-sacrifice. He would say, 'Though I possess many properties, nothing belongs to me. Everything belongs to my Guru, the God Incarnate.' While walking in the huge teak garden at the back of his mansion, Sri Shankardev explained the purpose of his visit. He pointed to a full-grown tree and asked the devotee to cut it down, and arrange for it to be donated. It was a bolt from the blue for the devotee. With tearful eyes, he pleaded, 'Please don't ask for that, Sir. It is an expensive tree. I will arrange for some funds and come to you to give it myself. For now, let me be.' (*Ishta Prasange*, Part I)

(Sri Shankardev, the saint-poet of Assam, was a contemporary of Paramhansa Sri Ramakrishna Dev and lived for 120 years. His religious tour of India over a period of twelve years was a legendary one.)

Devotee: How to identify a deceitful devotee? [131]

Sri Sri Thakur: When you find that a devotee is not enjoying the company of the Master, and rather, avoids him; when his mentor does not attract him, but still boasts of devotion, be certain that his devotion is bereft of love and dominated by lust.

Devotee: What is 'love' and how is it different from 'lust'? [132]

Sri Sri Thakur: I think the *sine qua non* of love is the desire to give, Your only real satisfaction is in bestowing, and pouring out to the Beloved. It is unrelated to the idea of give and take: 'If you love me, then I love you.' This mentality does not exist in real love, there are no expectations, and no hope of getting anything in return. Love is the ultimate outcome of devotion. The lover is greedy for the love of the beloved. Love says: adore the master, while lust says: neglect all and stick to women. Lust is just the opposite of love. It is the desire to get. Lust demands, deprives, and neglects the Beloved. Where there is lust there is lethargy, complaints, unwillingness to sacrifice, reluctance to give, and the inability to exalt or nurture. No matter how much a person might say, 'I love you', that love is based on his passion and need.

Without love for the Ideal, man is shattered by the demands of lust. In devotion, service of the Ideal is always preferred over service of self-interest. All actions of the devotee are for the gratification and glorification of the Ideal. All activities then become auspicious and lead to great achievements. Sri Sri Thakur continued, with determination, even a man from lower social strata can reach the pinnacle of devotion. He narrated an anecdote from the life of Sri Ramanuja:

One among the several disciples of Sri Ramanuja was a scavenger. He was older than the other Brahmin disciples and was staying with his wife in the ashram. Both were attending to the domestic needs of the Master like providing water, washing clothes, etc. They were always alert to his needs. They had an unwavering adherence to Gurudev. Their close proximity to Sri Ramanuja made the other disciples envious. There was subdued indignation and slandering against the couple. Sri Ramanuja became aware of it. One day, he called the group leader and asked him, 'My boy, can you do a job for me?' The youth readily agreed. Thereupon, Sri Ramanuja murmured in his ear, 'Let us teach a lesson to that scavenger. Tonight you steal all his belongings, along with the ornaments of his wife, and bring them to me.' The leader was very happy. After midnight, he stealthily stepped into the couple's room. As they were sleeping, he gathered all the items and packed them into a bundle. He then slowly started taking off the ornaments worn by the lady, one after another. One silver bangle was tight, and would not slip out. At this instant, there was a sound outside, and the youth panicked. He left the bangle and hurried out with the bundle. He was aghast to find the lady running after him, 'O brother! Don't leave the bangle. Wait for a while, I will remove it myself, and give it to you.' The thief ran as if he was on oiled wheels; the lady could not match him.

The next morning, Sri Ramanuja called for another student and told him, 'Go and wear your group leader's dhoti that is drying in the veranda, but do not tell him anything about it.' The leader after his morning bath, could not find his dhoti, and searching for it, saw it on another disciple. Angrily, he rebuked the boy in filthy language and was about to hit him when the other disciples intervened. Later in the day, Sri Ramanuja called the disciples and narrated the two incidents: In the first case there is pure love for the Master, and so for everyone, including the thief. And In the second case, there is intolerance, arrogance, and anger—the products of lust. It was now clear to the disciples why the Master preferred the couple over them.

Narrator: Sri Ramanujacharya (1017-1137) was born in Sriperumbudur in Chennai. He was a major exponent of Vaishnava philosophy. He wanted to eradicate unhealthy caste superstitions. We find a similar incident with Sri Ramakrishnadev: There was an old sweeper, Rasiklal, cleaning the surroundings of Dakshineswar Temple where the Master stayed. Every morning, while sweeping, he would notice the Master walking in the garden, talking to devotees and, at times, hugging someone or the other. As he was a scavenger, he could not muster the courage to go and prostrate before him. In his heart of hearts, he longed to touch the feet of the Master. But he knew it couldn't happen. One day, when he was looking down and sweeping the premises, Sri Ramakrishnadev came in front of him unexpectedly. He was puzzled. He prepared to flee from his presence, but in no time found himself being embraced by the Master. Pure devotion brings the impossible into the realm of possibility.

Devotee: How was the devotion of Hanumanji? [133]

Sri Sri Thakur: Sri Ramachandra had a strong group with him, like Hanuman, Sugriva, Jambavan, Nala, Nila, and others. Each of them was a strong unit with uncompromising adherence to the

Master. When Hanuman was offered the chief ministership in the cabinet of King Sugriva, he rejected it outright. He was a Dravidian, a great pundit, and worked like a bull. His tolerance was boundless. Laxman rebuked him, left and right, but Hanumanji never reacted.

Devotee: We are ordinary people, not like the powerful Hanuman. What do we do? [134]

Sri Sri Thakur: It is not right to think like that. Manliness lies in tolerance. People talked ill of Saint Kabir Saheb, but he did not retaliate. He tolerated the slanderous gossip silently. Mirabai, the legendary devotee of Sri Krishna, faced criticism and wrath throughout her life, but never lost the balance of her mind and her ecstasy. St. John used to sit beside Jesus Christ all the time, without uttering a word. If someone asked what he was up to, he would reply: "Please don't disturb me. I am immersed in love as I am looking at Him. If you cannot love, at least pretend to love for some time, and it will sprout in you."

Devotee: How does that happen? [135]

Sri Sri Thakur explains this with a story: At dusk near a pond, a bird hunter was aiming to shoot a few homecoming birds close to a nearby tree. He saw a monk, who bathed in the pond and sat in a clean place to meditate. To the utter surprise of the hunter, the birds flocked around him. He pondered: If I pretend to be a monk and sit at the bank, I can get many birds in one stroke. After the monk left, the hunter pretended to be a monk. He too bathed in the pond and sat at its edge as if meditating. Birds gathered in large numbers around him. Suddenly, a noble idea flashed in his mind. He thought, if just pretending to be a monk can bring so much, what would I not achieve if I actually became one? He gave up hunting and went in for spiritual endeavour.

Sri Sri Thakur remembered the days of his youth, 'In those days, I often visited Kolkata to see a drama in Star Theatre. Actors of a mythological play would observe many disciplines like a vegetarian diet and live in a pious way. One night, the actor playing the role of Lord Buddha in '*Buddha Charitra*' (written by Girish Ghosh) identified himself with the qualities of Buddha to such an extent, that after the play, instead of heading for home, he proceeded to become a monk. The pretension of devotion can sometimes be good, but, mind you, it's different from bluffing.

Thereafter, He recollected the example of Haridas, a follower of Sri Chaitanya. Haridas found his friends going into ecstasy with tears rolling down their eyes during kirtan. But his eyes remained dry. So he used to put black pepper powder in them to induce tears. Continuing this for some time, it so happened that he was eventually able to reach a state of ecstasy, and really shed tears.

Sri Sri Thakur quoted William Cowper: 'England, with all thy faults I love thee still, My country!' and said we should pray similarly: 'Lord, I shall love you and serve you with all my life.'

Devotee: Is it wise to love someone, even after knowing their faults? [136]

Sri Sri Thakur: Before loving someone, one should enquire about them. The growth of your character depends on the kind of person you choose to love. So, be wise when you love, it determines the exaltation of your being.

Narrator: There is a saying 'Love is blind.' The complete phrase is 'Though love is blind, it is not for the want of eyes.' The author is unknown. It suggests, if one loves being aware of the faults and shortcomings of the other person, and does so for sensual pleasure only, that love is blind. Shakespeare made it popular. A dialogue in the drama *The Merchant of Venice*: "But love is blind and lovers cannot see the follies that they themselves commit."

Sri Sri Dada in his address to workers (321st *(virtual)* International Ritwik Conference), on 29 October 2020, said, "Accept my good wishes on this auspicious and unique occasion of our International Virtual Workers' conference. Man is perceived by the Ideal he adheres to. There are two ways to achieve self-realisation. You may do whatever is necessary for your self-fulfilment, so that people will know how successful a person you are, or you may accept and follow the Ideal which brings peace and salvation to all people on earth. Your adherence to such an Ideal shows that you are a lover of life and becoming. We come upon the earth and after some years will return to nothingness. When we love and serve the all-fulfiling Ideal, people remember that here was a person who loved his Lord. Love Him, and achieve whatever he has asked you to achieve, not by using a sword but by true love. Remember, the mightier your Ideal is, if you follow him with true love, you shall gain accordingly. Your very compassion for mankind will make you a messenger of light and life. Never hate anyone, love all. Remember that you are for the Lord and only for him, and as you are for him so you are for others too. The message of Thakur to survive against all odds must be spread to all mankind. You should convince others, and show them the way of total becoming of the being. Don't waste a single moment of your life. Use yourself in such a manner that your Lord will feel that your love for Him is true and sincere. Peace, peace, peace. *Bande Purushottamam.*"

Devotee: Please tell us what is love in simple terms. [137]

Sri Sri Thakur: That mental state which fulfils being and becoming, I call that love. When inclination, coupled with eagerness, tickles our emotions, our emotions act as a stimulus to do something meaningful for the beloved. The desire to nurture and nourish the beloved, I feel, is the foremost in love.

Devotee: What is the relationship between love and devotion?[138]

Sri Sri Thakur in *Satyanusaran*—Love is the gradual development of devotion. The concentration of devotion is love. The thinner the pride, the bigger the place for devotion. How can one succeed in avowed activity, without devotion? Devotion alone can bring success. As faith is never blind, so is devotion never stupid. In addiction, there is the gratification from self-interest. In devotion, there is satisfaction from interest in others. Devotion is concentric to the Source. Addiction seeks satiety in self-interest or ego. Addiction is the wife of passion and devotion is the younger sister of love. Devotion brings wisdom. In wisdom, there is a sense of self creation. When there is this realisation of self in creation, non-violence emerges and from non-violence comes love. To the extent you possess any, you possess all.

Devotee: How to love the Ideal, Sir? [139]

Sri Sri Thakur: If you desire to love Him, declare so and act accordingly.

Narrator: Sri Sri Dada observed (Ritwik Conference, 15-07-2012): "In Bengali love is called '*Bhalobasa*', meaning 'live well.' Wherever Thakur is present, there lies bliss and no sorrow. Do not create sorrow for yourself. Create an atmosphere of bliss. Exalt everyone by making them blissful. *Paramananda Madhav* has come to conquer sorrow. Thakur does not stay where there is animosity among people. Once he turns his face, he does not respond to your calls any more. That is why you should not have enmity with anybody. You should live happily and let others also live happily: that should be the aim of your life. Move forward with this determination. This is *sadhana*. Without acting on anything concrete, if you beg Thakur only with the words: 'Be kind, be kind', will he ever shower his kindness on you? Do you think, He is so foolish, can't he see through your deceit? He does not tolerate it. Call him with all intensity, and sincerity, "O Thakur, make me blissful."

St. Francis de Sales (1567-1622), a noted seventeenth-century philosopher said: 'You learn to speak by speaking, to study by studying, to run by running, to work by working. In the same way, you learn to love by loving.' (*Living Thoughts of Great People*)

The Persian poet, Omar Khayyam (1200 approx.) wrote in his famous poem, '*The Rubaiyat*':

> *Ah, Love! could thou and I with Fate conspire*
> *To grasp this sorry Scheme of Things entire,*
> *Would not we shatter it to bits—and then*
> *Remould it nearer to the Heart's desire.*

Sri Sri Paramahansa Yogananda has given a spiritual interpretation of the above stanza: "If man could but harness his innate divine will to God's pure Infinite Intelligence immanent in creation as Divine Love and to the Cosmic Law that governs all happenings through cause and effect, he could wield that wisdom and power to shatter the sad circumstances of karmically-set patterns, and remould the effects of earth's untoward dualities into circumstances nearer to the ideal plan that God intended." (*Wine of The Mystic*)

Devotee: What are the facets of love? [140]

Sri Sri Thakur: Non-oscillatory sincerity and doubtless faith are essential. By faith, I understand the firmness of belief. When our love lacks any question whatsoever, our libido is properly set on any man or matter giving a full scope of enjoyment.

Satyanusaran—To remove doubt and establish faith is to attain knowledge. If you have firm truth, no contrary idea, no incantation, and no power other than that of your own faith can overwhelm or bewitch you. Know this for sure.

Narrator: Yugacharya Sri Sri Borda said: When faith is matured, unbelievable things happen. He recalled the story of a milkmaid: She crossed a river every day to sell milk in a village. The village temple festival was going on. A pundit was invited to give a spiritual discourse in the afternoons. He was lodged in the guest house on the temple premises and bought milk from the milkmaid. On a fine morning, she reached the lodging of the pundit with milk. He queried: 'How could you get the boatman so early to ferry you?' The maid replied, 'Coming to the river, I found no boatman there. Then I remembered your words. Did you not say the other day, 'If one repeats the name of Hari with full faith, he can achieve any impossible task.' I reposed my whole faith in Hari, and walked across the river.' The pundit did not believe her. He told her to show how she did it. The milkmaid, reciting the name of Hari, easily walked across the river. The pundit tried to do the same, but after a few steps, he drowned. (*Ishta Prasange*, vol. II, 30.11.1975)

Sri Sri Dada recollected his own experience: One evening, Sri Sri Thakur was sitting in Nirala Nivesh (Deoghar). When I sought permission from him to go to Calcutta, He sent me to Baba (Sri Sri Borda), who was in a thatched cottage a little further away. Baba said: Today is the full moon, you can go tomorrow. I brought it to the kind knowledge of Thakur, and on my way back, while passing through the *Jamtala Sriangan*, I stared at the full moon rising on the eastern horizon. Most of the night, I enjoyed the sight from my terrace. Those days, it was my hobby to gaze at the moon and stars. I left for Calcutta the next day, stayed there for a couple of days, and returned. During a conversation with my mother, she said that we are in the brighter half of the lunar month, which started a few days ago. I immediately retorted: what are you saying, Mother? There was a full moon the other day. She would not agree. We placed a bet. The almanac was brought out, and the information was verified. I lost the bet. How could it happen? I thought to myself and ran to Baba and told him everything. He said: "As you believe me completely, you could see the full moon even though there was no moon in the sky." (*Atma Janer Katha*)

Sufi saint Hazrat Nizamuddin Auliya (1238-1325) talked of three layers of faith. He compares the initial stage of faith with a client approaching his advocate. Explaining the facts of his case, while handing over the relevant documents, he says: 'Now it's your baby, Sir.' In the initial stage, a devotee narrates all his woes and sorrows to his Master. He feels that He alone will handle the rest. As faith deepens, it moves to the realm of a mother-child relationship. The child completely relies on his mother for his security and upbringing. He thinks that even if a tiger comes, nothing will happen to him as long as the mother is there. Similarly, the devotee in the company of the Master is not afraid of any eventuality. Then comes the final stage of the surrender of the devotee to his Master. The wish of the Master is the wish of the devotee. He is at the complete disposal of his Master like a corpse; before cremation, it is bathed, clothed in a new fabric, and accepts all that is done.

Sri Sri Thakur in a verse says:
No more questions,
all arguments lay,
Only to obey your command
to withhold death and decay.

Devotee: Sir, what is fundamental to devotion? [141]

Sri Sri Thakur: Devotion towards parents, husband, Master (Guru), etc., are all based on the same fundamental principle; unwavering adherence. Knowledge flows automatically to a true devotee. For example, here is a story: One afternoon, a Brahmin was studying the Vedic scriptures under a banyan tree on the outskirts of a village. A crane on a branch above excreted on his head. He stared at it with blazing eyes, and the bird burst into flames. Such was his power.

Another day, while begging for alms in the village, he called out at a closed door of a house. A voice was heard from within: 'I am feeding my ailing husband. Please wait.' The Brahmin was impatient and felt insulted. When the mistress of the house came with a handful of rice, the Brahmin shouted and accused her of impertinence. The lady humbly said: 'I am not that crane, that your anger will burn me.' The Brahmin was flabbergasted. How did this illiterate lady know about the crane? With remorse, he asked, 'How did you know that, Mother? Please tell me.' The lady replied, 'I have not read much, but my parents told me to serve my husband with sincerity, without being bothered about any inconvenience or pain; I do only that, I do not know anything more. However, when I come across a person, I am able to instantly know everything about him.'

Completing the story, Sri Sri Thakur enjoined: Steadfast and assiduous inclination is devotion, and that is the soul of penance (*tapas*) and spiritual power (*siddhi*). Though the lady was illiterate, her dedication to her husband was the key to her knowledge. The surrender of self should not be confused with self-sacrifice. It is the throne of love. In surrender, love for the beloved dominates; his pleasure and satisfaction become the aim of one's life.

Narrator: Yugacharya Sri Sri Borda referred to the aphorism of Sri Ramakrishna Dev. According to Him, the combined force of a wife's loyalty, a miser's craze for wealth, and a mother's attachment to her child constitute the adherence of a true devotee. Sri Sri Borda further said, 'His protection is complete when our surrender is total. When the surrender is total, he guides us to overcome the problems we face in our everyday lives. He should be our only goal and our single demand. Only then will we succeed.'

Satyanusaran—If you long for good, give up the conceit of knowledge. Listen to everyone and do whatever helps to expand your heart. No other passion creates such a hindrance to knowledge as does the conceit of knowledge.

Narrator: On the conceit of knowledge, Yugacharya Sri Sri Borda tells the following story: Once a great pandit was being ferried across a river. He asked the boatman: 'Do you have any idea about the creation of this universe? How big is Earth? How does it revolve around the sun? How do solar eclipses occur? How far are the stars?' The boatman humbly replied, 'To whom are you asking all these, Sir? I am a fool. Am I as fortunate as you are?' The pandit adopted an air of superiority, 'What is the use of your living? You know nothing. Fie upon you!'

When the boat was in the middle of the river, the sky darkened suddenly, and a fierce wind began blowing. The boat could sink at any moment. The boatman was puzzled and asked Panditji, 'Do you know how to swim, Sir?' The pandit was scared, 'No, no, I do not know.' The boatman now cautioned him, 'O Learned one! What is the use of your vast learning? If the boat capsizes you are finished.' After some time, torrential rain fell along with the aggressive wind. The boat overturned; the boatman swam to the bank, and poor Panditji was unfortunate.

Devotee: We come across the dictum 'Work is worship.' What do you think of it, Sir?[142]

Sri Sri Thakur: Remaining busy all the time with work that brings only material benefit, is not worship. We are not born in this world for mere selfish pursuits; rather, our purpose is to do something beneficial for the self as well as for others. Our task is to build a world, where people learn to give before they take. This is what the Ideal teaches us; it is what makes him happy.

Narrator: Thomas A. Kempis (1380-1471), a great exponent of Christian spiritualism, observed: He does much who loves God much and he does much who does his deeds well and he does his deeds well who does it rather for the common good than for his own will. (*The Imitation of Christ*)

Devotee: While working for the common good, Jesus said, 'Resist not evil.' (*New Testament*). How is it, Sir? [143]

Sri Sri Thakur: Jesus was against impropriety, unfairness, and injustice throughout his life. He was strongly against shopkeepers who trespassed into the temple premises. One great thing we find in the lives of great souls is that they are prepared to sacrifice their lives even for the smallest creature; they do not fear for their own safety. They always think, 'Thy necessity is greater than mine', and don't hesitate to make even the supreme sacrifice. That is the reason why devotees and disciples around him must shoulder the responsibility for his safety. When he was to be arrested to be later crucified, Jesus instructed His close disciples not to interfere. They, in obedience, remained passive onlookers, but it was Mary Magdalene who stood up, protesting against the injustice towards her Master. For her, the Master's life was more important than the consequences of disobeying the Master's orders. She was prepared to go to hell for her efforts to save the Master. That is true adherence. The question of morality, or any semblance of sin, does not arise here. I have heard of a similar incident in the life of Sri Krishna. He once fell unconscious, and the Gopis came to know that he could be revived if dust from a devotee's feet was applied to his forehead. No one came forward, but the Gopis immediately did it and saved Sri Krishna.

Narrator: The fact that the followers of Jesus Christ, on the pretext of obeying His commands, did not raise a finger against the injustice towards Him, is echoed in a poem of Khalil Gibran (1883-1933) '*We and You*'; a few lines from the poem:
"*You crucified Jesus and stood below Him,
Blaspheming and mocking at Him; but at last
He came down and overcame the generations,
And walked among you as a hero, filling the
Universe with His glory and His beauty.*"

(Khalil Gibran Reader)

The complete statement where 'Resist not evil' occurs is: "But I say unto you. That ye resist not evil, but whosoever shall smite thee on thy right cheek turn to him the other also." —Gospel of Matthew in the *New Testament* (5:39). Commentators of the *New Testament* opine this as a counter to the 'eye for an eye' phrase in the *Old Testament*.

Swami Vivekananda, in a detailed discussion on this issue, observed: 'If we do not resist evil, the world will be swept away. Satan will overpower the genuine.' According to him, 'Resist not evil done to yourself, but you must resist evil done to others.'

Yugacharya Sri Sri Borda quoted these relevant lines from *Satyanusaran*: "You stay in Truth, try to bear injustice; do not resist it, soon you will achieve eternal well-being." Explaining the above he said: 'I will bear the injustice done to me. I will not resist. It is said he who exists, must tolerate. But if I do not resist torture meted out to you before me, I am effeminate.' So the view of Sri Sri Thakur in this regard is clear: To establish the Ideal, I am prepared to undergo injustice and torture inflicted on me, but if somebody else is the victim, there is no alternative but to resist and protect him. (*Ishta Prasange*)

Devotee: From many reported incidents from your life, we find that the people you help, have more often than not landed you in trouble. So why do you help them? [144]

Sri Sri Thakur: A father always looks after his children, and guides them to success. It is a paternal urge. It does not leave me. When I was in medical practice, I treated a Muslim patient from a nearby village. After partial recovery, nobody from the family turned up to fetch more medicines. I was sleepless and deeply worried. When the patient came to me, I lost my temper and reprimanded him for not sending his family to get further medicines from me. He listened silently to my scolding and said: 'Sir, I would not have tolerated all this from anybody else. But your scolding is so sweet! Go on, Sir, it's very pleasant.'

Devotee: How can a scolding be sweet? [145]

Sri Sri Thakur: I cannot utter harsh words to anybody. I always think that if by my admonition, a man dies, there will be no end to my suffering. This fear possesses me like a ghost; I cannot wriggle out of it. Of course, it does not mean that I tolerate evil. I think there is no difficulty in being uncompromising, but sweet. A good scolding should encourage an individual to improve. I am happy if I can encourage you to grow. We should teach people how to efficiently manoeuvre the obstacles on the road to success. That will inspire them to activity and achievement. When you do good to others, you are indispensable to them; your esteem grows in their mind, and that is your honour.

Devotee: How does one enhance one's diligence? [146]

Sri Sri Thakur: When we encourage a worker, his efficiency grows, and he crosses the fatigue point. The work he performs is no longer a burden or boring for him; he enjoys it. We call him an honest and hard worker.

Devotee: How to enhance competency in a man? [147]

Sri Sri Thakur: Sincerely follow a Man of competence, take refuge in Him. It will bring introspection that makes you aware of your follies and shortcomings. You can rectify them, and mend your ways.

Devotee: What if I am competent, but the others around me are not, and the work fails? What am I supposed to do? [148]

Sri Sri Thakur: One who sincerely follows the Ideal and never blames others but himself when he fails. Stop blaming others, and try to imbibe this in your character. To achieve your goal you may face insurmountable difficulties, but do not lose heart. Once you start working diligently with patience, you will eventually overcome the odds. As you go on, overcoming each difficulty shall bring you satisfaction and self-confidence. This brings about the realisation of contentment with work (*shramasukhapriyata*). The pleasure in work should be so powerful that you feel like you are conquering the world every day. The pleasure of name, fame, and wealth is no match for it. Once you are engaged in work that the Ideal wishes for you, you no longer perform it to reap any selfish benefit, but instead, for the satisfaction of the Ideal.

Narrator: Yugacharya Sri Sri Borda wanted us to be Ideal-worshippers. Ideal worship does not mean placing his photograph on an altar, decorating it with flowers, burning incense sticks, and making big paraphernalia of your devotion. On the contrary, worship means your unflinching determination to fulfil him. (*Taanr sannidhye, 16.12.1974*)

Devotee: How to develop unflinching determination?[149]

Sri Sri Thakur: You should have the stubbornness of a pig to carry the work till completion. I remember an incident from my youth. It was a burning summer day, I decided to go to Kushtia, which was 15 kilometres away, and started the journey from Hemayetpur Ashram without an umbrella or shoes. The road was dusty, burning like coal. I covered some distance, but it was unbearable. I was thinking of cancelling the trip. However, a determination came over me and prevented me from retreating. I reached Kushtia, and looked at my feet, completely red with rashes and blisters. The next day at noon, I again resumed my walk back to Hemayetpur. The blisters started bleeding and turned into wounds. The pain was unbearable, but I was extremely satisfied that I could accomplish the task. Whenever you are afraid of the obstacles that you may face ahead, develop the stubbornness of a pig to conquer them. On completion, you realise joy as never before. Listen, my children, develop the attitude to overthrow failure. Once you cross the fatigue layer, your capacity to work increases so much that you astonish not only yourself but others as well. A person who crosses the fatigue layer is not aware of it. It becomes usual and normal for him.

Narrator: The Fatigue Layer is a unique situation conceived by Sri Sri Thakur. When one does not abandon work in spite of extreme exhaustion and ends up completing it, he crosses the fatigue layer. Success builds great self-confidence; we become capable of taking up more difficult tasks. Self-confidence reaches new heights, and so also efficiency. Nothing succeeds like success.

Devotee: What is the Ideal's work? [150]

Sri Sri Thakur: When work is done for the public at large, it becomes the Ideal's work. The enthusiasm for the work overpowers passions. This is called dispassionate work (*Nishkama Karma*), and whosoever succeeds in performing achieves '*Naishkarmya Siddhi.*' This is the first step in your spiritual sojourn. Good work often creates a desire for recognition, reward, and popularity. So, when any work for the public good is undertaken to please only the Ideal, things like pride, ego, and appetite for recognition, are subdued. Your endeavour becomes Ideal-centric and Ideal-dedicated.

Devotee: What is the mission of your life? [151]

Sri Sri Thakur: My life's mission is to rectify the erring man. Each one of you belongs to me. To set one man on the righteous path, I do not hesitate even to sacrifice a kingdom. In my lifetime, if I can see you build up to an Ideal-centric, culturally refined, and socially amicable human being, then my life's ambition is attained. Needless to mention, for this, your passions and complexes must be under control. Firstly, you must change your-self, only then can you think of revamping society. This is not for my mirth or merriment, but the fundamental urge of my life.

Modern man is depressed, disintegrated from within and without. A lot of debris has gathered in society, in the country, and in the world. To bring integration into society, all of us must unite under the flag of the Ideal. This is the only way. All our efforts to bring social justice, sectarian friendship, and international amity are bound to fail unless we agree to unite for the Ideal's sake. Time is running out. Each one of you can do the work of a thousand men, if you are properly groomed and disciplined. Otherwise, there is no purpose in your hobnobbing around me, no stakes gained for me either.

Devotee: Sir, who will listen to all this? In Dwapara Yuga, even Sri Krishna was ignored, and the Mahabharata war brought mass destruction of life and property. Why do you think this happened? [152]

Sri Sri Thakur: When an arrogant and haughty king does not agree to peaceful co-existence with his neighbours, war is inevitable. Religion is used to justify war at times that can lead to the worst possible outcomes.

Narrator: The Crusades, a series of religious wars waged by Christians against Mohammedans, resulted in great loss of life and property. An important place of worship for both Muslims and Christians, the city of Jerusalem was then occupied by the Mohammedans. Under the leadership of Peter the Hermit, Christians raised war to free the land from the clutches of their adversaries. It was claimed to be a holy war with the support of many European Christian kings. The war was fought eight times over a span of three centuries (1095 to 1271). The Christians did not succeed. Historians call it the height of idiocy, because it is said: When the king is on an idiotic rampage, even Jesus cannot stop the war.

Sree Maa of Pondicherry tells us a story: 'As it was said that Jesus raised the dead, healed the sick, made the dumb speak, gave sight to the blind, so one day an idiot was brought to him to be made intelligent, and Jesus ran away! Why did you run away? He was asked. 'I can do everything', He answered, 'except give intelligence to an idiot.' (*Stories Told By The Mother*)

Devotee: How to make a man wise? What is wisdom? [153]

Sri Sri Thakur: I do not understand wisdom, without the conception of a man who embodies it. Where can you find knowledge, if not in a living entity who carries it? Any knowledge is futile unless it is applied in the world and put into action. Scholarly discussions, debates, and theoretical assumptions cannot bring a clear conception, unless we go to a person endowed with knowledge and clarity of conception.

Devotee: What do you mean by the clarity of conception, Sir? [154]

Sri Sri Thakur: You may call it scientific analysis. A superior person with the extraordinary power of solving all problems of individual and collective life should be followed. By doing this, both the individual and society are integrated in their minds. It is the easiest way of attainment.

Devotee: If the Ideal is so indispensable, why don't people simply follow him? [155]

Sri Sri Thakur: People seek God for fame and power. They run from one temple to another, to several Godmen, spiritual quacks, and fortune tellers for only one purpose—their fulfilment of material desires. Very few realise the real aim of life. They only accept, believe, and follow the Ideal. They acquire contentment and bliss.

Devotee: How to place the Ideal in one's life? [156]

Sri Sri Thakur: Love Him intensely. That love gets priority over anything else in your life. Unless the dedication is total and attachment is single-minded, your passions will intrude and play mischief. You must tame your passions, and be pure in your inclination to the Ideal.

Devotee: What about ritualistic worship? [157]

Sri Sri Thakur: Ritualistic worship, although not paramount, nonetheless preserves our traditions and customs. They don't harm, rather they build a healthy social fabric. It brings the lower strata of society into the spiritual fold. These people do not aspire for a higher spiritual realisation, but if you discard ritual worship, they will even stop the little religious activities that they practise now. So what happens ultimately? They could not go for any higher spiritual realisation; rather, they were also discouraged from the minimal religious practice they were engaged in. You must keep in mind that nobody should lose their way because of your actions or words. In the *Bhagavad Gita*, Sri Krishna ordains: *Na buddhi bhedam janayet* (Do not hamper intelligence).

9

EDUCATION, ELEVATED INTELLECTUALISM, DEVELOPMENT OF PERSONALITY, NURTURING THE ENVIRONMENT, NATIONALISM, TRADITION AND VARNASHRAMA (HUMANS, ANIMALS, AND BIRDS), INTERNATIONAL SCENARIO- MILITARIZATION-WAR AND AUTO-EXCRETION, UNIVERSAL VARNASHRAMA AND LANGUAGE, AND THE CONCEPT OF ONE-WORLD VILLAGE (*VASUDHAIBA KUTUMBAKAM*)

Devotee: What is real education? [158]

Sri Sri Thakur: Teaching the clue to meaningful living is the essence of real education. Real education imbibes Dharma: the key to being and becoming. A man inherits instincts from his parents and forefathers; we call it heredity. His environment nurtures it. To bring up a child, the common participation of both parents is essential. In the same way, instincts, and environment determine the life of the individual.

Sri Sri Thakur in Magnadicta:
'Literation makes the
complexes facilitated
whereas education enlightens the being
hence its index, habits and behaviour
glows on in a sonorous rhyme.' (Verse 103)

Devotee: How does a child start learning? [159]

Sri Sri Thakur: A newborn baby receives sensations from the outer world through its eyes. It looks around and observes everything. Such observation creates impressions in the brain. Subsequently, its ears open, and the other sensory organs are activated. The way its parents live influences it. It keenly observes the relationship between its father and mother; if it is loving and soothing, the child inculcates love in its character; on the contrary, when there is no love or attachment between the couple, the child is deprived of love in its nature. When it grows up, it is prone to lead a passionate, distorted, and undisciplined life. So, education and culture start from the parents and develop through them. By culture, I mean what one imbibes in the path of elevation and upliftment.

Devotee: When and where does a child's education begin?[160]

Sri Sri Thakur: Before the child turns five, it should be guided towards good habits, behaviour, and urges. The sense of adoring life should be effulgent in the child. That should be the basic aim of education. When the parents are attached to the Ideal, we can see its good effects on the child. When the child sees that his parents are respectful to their superiors and elders, it follows automatically. Literacy is secondary in education, the most important are habit, behaviour, urge, sincerity, self-confidence, and good character. When the child acquires these qualities, he becomes efficient in all fields.

Devotee: What are the aspects of learning at home?[161]

Sri Sri Thakur: What we preach to others, we don't follow at home. We presume that our child will learn everything on its own, without taking the effort to inculcate in it these values. The thrust should be on making the child sensitive, receptive, and inward-looking. There should not be any compulsion, rebuking, or beating. Everything should be taught through love.

Devotee: - Is it not the duty of the parents to see that the child does well in studies?[162]

Sri Sri Thakur: Parents should not pressurise the child for academic excellence; rather they should ignite interest in him towards the realities of life and be at home with the environment. If a child rears birds, develops a kitchen garden, learns to swim, climbs trees, rides a bicycle, makes a toy, paints well, sings well, acts in plays, or if he loves feeding beggars, removes a stone from the middle of the road, if he knows the mental state of a person just by seeing him, if he observes the change of seasons keenly, if he becomes immersed while listening to a story, or alert when he distinguishes good and bad in his surroundings, if he develops the ability to mould himself from bad to good, you can be sure that the foundation of a good man is definitely being laid in it. Hence, the responsibility of the parents and elders is enormous in shaping the future of a child. When the child grows up, the parents should inspire it by their own example to lead an Ideal-centric life, through initiation and Swastyayani. I feel it will arouse in it the eagerness to stand out in academics and more than that for all-round excellence.

Narrator: Noted philosopher Jean-Jacques Rousseau (1712-1778) echoed the same ideas: "The child should be led into learning rather than be forced into it, and be allowed to develop along its own lines and in its own way." He wanted education to be not artificial, but as natural as possible. He saw it as a development of capacities rather than an imposition of ideas, nurtured by love and understanding, not by compulsion. He thought it would be best to employ the naturally good impulses of the child, and not have to present knowledge as hedged by duties, obligations, and commands. "Children ought to learn by imitating their parents, but it must be the parents' virtues and not their vices they are learning from." (*Understanding Philosophy*)

Sri Sri Thakur on Real Education:
> *Education in its real form*
> *is to unfold the characteristic faculties*
> *that are latent within*
> *by attachment to an Ideal embodied,*
> *and through the glimpse of expressions*
> *those which come forth as impulses*
> *from his experiences*
> *during periods of exposition*
> *to follow with services*
> *to learn with attention*
> *to do in accordance therewith—*
> *in a word,*
> *to take those impulses in, with sense—*
> *to unfold and adjust.* (The Message, vol. I)

Devotee: What is the responsibility of a teacher? [163]

Sri Sri Thakur: The role of the teacher is extremely important. A strong interest in building responsibility within the child's character must be inculcated at school. Interest in studies can be awakened through practical activity. A lack of self-confidence in a child does not allow it to develop its latent talent. A child needs appreciation. Even the slightest progress in studies, behaviour, and activity should be appreciated by teachers and parents. This motivates the child to put more effort into his work so that he can receive more kudos. Also, a teacher should not malign other teachers in front of the students. In such cases, students lose respect and admiration for teachers.

Devotee: What happens if the teacher does not have a living Ideal? [164]

Sri Sri Thakur: Ideal-centrism is the key to man-making and nation-building. If the teacher does not have an Ideal and does not lead a disciplined life, how can he influence a student's character? A teacher with an Ideal in his life can easily inculcate high moral standards in his students; he is therefore able to nurture their inherent goodness.

Devotee: Sir, education is a lucrative business today. Where does one get the Ideal teachers you have in mind? [165]

Sri Sri Thakur: Teachers bereft of character, and actiOn bereft of a cause, are doomed to fail. A teacher who has no Ideal to follow, carries a demeanour that is lacking and uninspiring, and also has no leanings for culture; in that case, he is not developing a pupil's character. Such a teacher's undisciplined way of life spoils the individual, as well as the collective life of society, and pushes the nation towards debility and darkness. In such cases, it is better to remain uneducated, than be ill-educated.

Devotee: Yet, there is great demand for learned teachers. How is that possible? [166]

Sri Sri Thakur: He who knows how to nurture the existence of the being is really learned. To understand how the being exists, one has to accept a living Ideal, surrender to him with adherence, and serve him. By ignoring this vital fact, no learning can happen, no matter how high a person's academic qualifications are. Decorations of so-called degrees and titles without sublimation prepare an arrogant and confused personality unsuitable to guide the youth.

Devotee: Such people are successful teachers today, helping students to secure well-paying jobs. How can you deny it, Sir?[167]

Sri Sri Thakur: A lot of distortion has crept in everywhere. There is nothing such as real education today. The aim of education has never been to produce a crowd of money-makers. Education has failed to bring alive the innate qualities in students, and inspire a love for their culture and tradition. That is why students are not evolving into integrated personalities. We have failed to be proud of the glorious past of India, but tom-tom our poverty and misery across the world with the sole motive of gain. The inferiority complex never forsakes us.

Devotee: Is there no getaway from such self-disgrace?[168]

Sri Sri Thakur: The great teachers of our country, the seers of Bharata, have discovered the clues to achieve all-round success in a man. They have discerned how to synchronise our inner being with the external world. We have to learn such clues and techniques from the wisdom of our progenitors. We have to bring elevated intellectualism in education to ensure the admiration of our culture. Learn to admire the heroes of this land.

Devotee: What is elevated intellectualism?[169]

Sri Sri Thakur: Students must be made to learn what is beneficial or harmful for their growth. Education should never teach us to envy or criticise others. We should not only be convinced, but develop strong convictions on such matters.

Devotee: According to you, what is the aim of education, Sir?[170]

Sri Sri Thakur: It is eight-fold: meaningful adjustment of complexes, concentricity, alertness, agility, inquisitiveness, judicious attitude, presence of mind, and a cordial way of life.

Devotee: What is your opinion about an objective type of education?[171]

Sri Sri Thakur: Along with science, physics, chemistry, literature, psychology, geography, history, etc., students also need to be taught how to be practical, resourceful, and gain self-confidence. The aim of elevated intellectualism is to dissuade the student from salaried jobs. I call it a slave mentality. Students should be encouraged to undertake jobs that suit their innate instincts and ability.

Devotee: Why are you against salaried employment?[172]

Sri Sri Thakur: While in a salaried job, a man develops only one aspect in his life, all other options die out, whereas, when one is engaged independently to earn money in a creative job or profession, he has myriad options in front of him to substantially grow with his ability and expertise. Another thing, the salary mentality percolates down to the progeny. This is the most harmful. If a person goes for salaried service, the tendency continues one generation after another.

Sri Sri Thakur in Magnadicta:

A servant for money
is often disqualified
to master the same,
hence wealth mourns away
with insignificant glow. (Verse 91)

Devotee: What about women's education, Sir?[173]

Sri Sri Thakur: Along with formal education, women should be taught to be devoted and serviceable, learning and implementing activities to nurture their family and surroundings. Devotion is important for female children. When they marry, it will make them devoted wives. Whether married or not, we must not forget that devotion to the Ideal is primary.

Devotee: So do you think their system of education should be different from boys'?[174]

Sri Sri Thakur: Both girls and boys should be highly educated.

The difference is only with regard to their temperament. During the time of education, they should be taught separately with an eye on their distinctiveness.

Devotee: What do you think of co-education? [175]

Sri Sri Thakur: I think before adolescence there is no harm if boys and girls study together. At that age, a lady teacher is more suitable for them. When they grow up, the manner of their learning should be different. Male education should be of a fulfiling nature, and education for girls should be of a servicing nature: one towards fatherhood, the other towards motherhood.

Devotee: How to impart sex education to youngsters? [176]

Sri Sri Thakur: It must be done in a very careful and coordinated manner. Undue secrecy in these matters is detrimental to a healthy understanding of sex; it should be conveyed in a simple and sacred manner, making them aware of the pitfalls, distortions, and abnormalities in sexual relationships. They should treat sexual urge as a natural phenomenon; they need not feel guilty about it, but channellize it in a healthy manner in order to bring about progressive change in life. Knowledge of the do's and don't s of sexual acts should be explained to them; this is a must for health and hygiene.

Devotee: Student indiscipline is on the rise. How do we tackle it, Sir? [177]

Sri Sri Thakur: Unless teachers, parents, elders, and people of high social stature become disciplined and interdependent, it is futile to expect discipline among students. Discipline comes from discipleship. When different varieties meet with the meaning of unity, it is a University. "The motto of a University is to love variety in the interest of the Unit, or to love one for the interest of the variety."

Sri Sri Thakur in Magnadicta:
> *'Where the disciples are of the same principle*
> *with every sincerity discipline is automatic.'* (verse 112)

Devotee: How to induce love for the Ideal in youth? [178]

Sri Sri Thakur: Firstly, parents, elders, and teachers need to become 'unit-centric.' Teachers have to become ideals in the eyes of their students. It cannot happen to them just by reading books. If teachers take discipleship, their influence will induce students to know the source of their discipline. Only then can they inculcate Ideal-centrism in their students. The same holds true for parents and elders. To put it briefly, as a husband and wife unite to bring a child into this world, parents and teachers similarly need to collaborate in an integrated manner to bring an ideal education. Where this cooperation is dull, education is insufficient. Only investing money in education will not help. When a dog has a master, it is trained. Everything in it gets adjusted according to the command of the master. We see a similarity in the case of human beings for developing real conceptions.

Devotee: What is real conception? [179]

Sri Sri Thakur: As I have said earlier, you have to explore minutely to know more and more about a subject. You have to consider all aspects in a coordinated and meaningful way in the arena of your knowledge in a particular subject. It is the essence of science. Where science is present, philosophy too is present with all its possibilities. Science helps us to study the positive and negative sides of everything, to observe everything minutely, and to know its fundamentals and specialties. It makes us look for an object's existential relevance and meaning. If you get a grip on everything in this manner, your conception will also evolve accordingly. The more you improve your conception, the finer aspects of science will be revealed to you.

Devotee: A number of Indian students are going abroad. What is your opinion on this? [180]

Sri Sri Thakur: This is good, but the exchange of culture must be mutual between nations. I want thousands of students from our country to go abroad, and a thousand more to come from abroad to study in India. Sometimes, I find that an Indian educated abroad has an aversion towards our glorious culture and tradition. That is not good.

Narrator: Once (14-02-2014, Deoghar) a student came to Sri Sri Dada for his blessings to go to the USA for higher studies. Sri Sri Dada blessed him saying: 'Go to America, Germany, Russia, or even to the moon, but do not stay back. Come here to serve your country. If not, your higher education is self-centred and useless for us.'

Development of Personality and Nurturing the Environment

Devotee: I have heard that for the development of one's personality, there should be a coordination between *Daiva* (destiny) and *Purushakaar* (vigour). Kindly explain it. [181]

Sri Sri Thakur: '*Daiva*', the Sanskrit word, means destiny in a nutshell. Our innate qualities and instincts are manifested as we grow. This is known as our character, the basis of our intellect. Our character and intellect mould our life in a particular way. Accordingly, we think, speak and interact with our surroundings. A qualitative addition to our surroundings elevates our life. Take an example: By instinct, you go for a particular profession; a doctor, an entrepreneur, a scientist, or a leader. We say we are destined for it. But how to be an excellent doctor or extraordinary entrepreneur depends on your inner strength backed by hard work. That is your vigour. So destiny does not restrict you to rise to the pinnacle in your chosen field of interest. The determination to rise is called Purushakaar (vigour) in Sanskrit. So your success is equal to your destiny and your vigour.

Sri Sri Thakur in Magnadicta:
'To think
all is determined
is the outrage
to terminate God
the Infinite.' (verse 168)

Devotee: From where do we derive vigour? [182]

Sri Sri Thakur: Vigour is acquired through action. To sit without action and blame destiny is foolishness. The action paves the way to achievement, we call it fortune. We become disciplined when we follow a divine man of perfect discipline. Our vigour is commensurate to our love and devotion to the Ideal.

Sri Sri Thakur in Magnadicta:

> *'Baffled are the traits*
> *that are not regulated*
> *through surrender*
> *to the divine man.' (verse 170)*

Devotee: Without attachment to the Ideal, can't we acquire vigour? [183]

Sri Sri Thakur: I do not think there is any other way. Unless anchored to the Ideal, your efforts will be scattered, and knowledge half-baked, leading to an inharmonious experience. Ultimately you achieve your goal in bits. When you are attached to the Ideal, you shoulder a big responsibility. When you betray somebody, people will blame your Master, before they blame you. So you become careful with every action you perform to save your Master from the spectre of suspicion. Unaware, you build up a character of honesty and dignity. That is why I say: you should always be conscious that you are carrying Thakur in your personality. The more this consciousness becomes active, the fewer faults you commit. Unless you develop this responsibility for your Thakur, how can you take responsibility for others? Your dedication to the Supreme Beloved is the only path to make you responsible and respectable.

Devotee: Jesus has said: 'Seek ye first the kingdom of heaven and all else shall be added onto you.' (The Gospel according to St. Matthew). What does it mean? [184]

Sri Sri Thakur: Jesus was able to discover the 'Kingdom of Heaven' in Him, so He said: The 'Kingdom of Heaven' is inside every one of us, but to discover it, you should surrender to the person who has already discovered it. By discovering it in yourself, you love everything in Creation.

Sri Sri Thakur in Magnadicta:
Whoever serves the environment
for his own sake
shall lose it
and he who does it
for the Lord's sake shall be crowned. (verse 50)

Narrator: Sufi saint Hazrat Bayazid Bistami (804-874) in answer to the question, 'Who is the Emperor (Sultan)?' replied, "The man whose only choice is God, and who feels Him everywhere, is the Emperor." (*Islamic Mysticism in India*)

Devotee: During a trance (Bhava Samadhi) you said, 'He who gets my touch will be elevated in body and mind to the kingdom of Heaven.' Please explain it.[185]

Sri Sri Thakur: First, establish me within you, without any deviation or inconsistency. Your absolute love for me will pave your way to the kingdom of Heaven. I am only the motivator, the effort must be yours. In spite of your physical closeness to me over a long period of time, can you be sure that your attachment to me is total? When you achieve that, and are truly the nearest to me, even if you are physically far away, you shall find completeness in your being, the taste of heaven.

Devotee: How to know one's total commitment to you?[186]

Sri Sri Thakur: The test is his dedication to serving the surroundings. One who claims he loves me, but is callous to the environment, his love for me is superficial.

Narrator: The German philosopher, Meister Eckhart (1260-1328) made a similar remark: 'A person must do one of two things; either he must learn to imbibe God in his work and hold fast unto Him, or he must give up his work altogether. Since man cannot live without activities that are both human and various, we must learn to keep God in everything we do and whatever the job or place to keep on with Him.' (*Living Thoughts of Great People*)

Devotee: We are all mundane people. It is very difficult to completely surrender to the One. What to do?[187]

Sri Sri Thakur: Take from me an easy clue to success. Try to love your parents with obedience, and go by their advice in all your ventures. Don't consider their view obsolete and old-fashioned. Your personality will be more integrated than before, there will be harmony in your thought, word, and deed. Do not lose heart if you fail, try again and ultimately you will succeed. Life is an endless journey of learning. You only need a thread to transform sugar into candy, and a bunch of flowers into a garland. A thread is necessary for the cohesion of your personality. Parents come first and with them the Ideal. Immediately you would argue, 'How is that possible? Such and such a genius does not obey his parents, nor is he bothered about the Ideal, so how is he adored?' I tell you all your so-called geniuses live a fragmented haphazard life, bordering on madness. That is why I insist: Hold fast to a divine man. He shall grow an unthinkable genius in you.

Devotee: How to make the Ideal our own? [188]

Sri Sri Thakur: As you obey, so you grow. The more Ideal-oriented you are, the more your personality will bloom. Hold on to a perfect man.

Devotee: Why does one try to exploit others? [189]

Sri Sri Thakur: To fulfil his self-interest. I call such characters 'fly-like men.' Beware of them. Whatever good you do to them, they are so nasty that they will forget it and malign your character undoubtedly. There is another category of men, of course, the number is not very high; I call them 'bee-like men.' They see only good in your character and they locate the honey in you and bring it forth before others. If you come across such people, never leave them.

Devotee: Kindly explain this quote from the Bible. Jesus says:
'Ask and it shall be given to you;
Seek and you shall find;
Knock and it shall be opened to you.' (The Gospel: Matthew)[190]

Sri Sri Thakur: Jesus here spoke of enhancing your proficiency and energy by following the most accomplished, the Son of God, and the Ideal of the time. When the energy is concentric to your being, the success achieved is proportionate to it. Your little success inspires you to put more effort into your ventures. This eventually results in an endless spiral of success, with the Ideal at the centre. Be honest to yourself, do not behave like that conceited woodcutter.

Sri Sri Thakur now narrates the story: A wood-cutter was cutting a tree near the river. His axe suddenly slipped into the river. He was upset, and prayed to God Varuna: 'Without the axe, how can I cut wood to feed my family?' The god of the waters appeared, and offered him a golden axe. The woodcutter refused humbly: 'It's not mine. I cannot cut wood with this.' The god vanished to reappear with a silver axe, but, as before, the woodcutter again refused to take it. The god now came with three pieces—gold, silver, and the lost axe. The woodcutter identified his axe and begged for it. The Lord told, 'I am pleased with your honesty. Take all three.' Another woodcutter saw this episode from a little distance and knew how wealthy one could become by losing an iron axe in the water. He pretended to slip and threw his axe in the water. On his prayer, the sea god manifested with a golden axe, and asked the cunning woodcutter, 'Is this yours?' He replied, 'Yes, yes, give it to me.' The Lord disappeared into the water, never to come back again. The greedy woodcutter thus lost his axe. On completing the story, Sri Sri Thakur said, 'Work honestly, you will get what you deserve.'

Devotee: How does one achieve comprehensive development of personality? [191]

Sri Sri Thakur: I think it can be done through integrating the material and spiritual development in a human being.

Devotee: Generally it is felt that materialism and spiritualism are poles apart. Money is the biggest cause of trouble. (*Arthamanartham Bhavaya Nityam*—Always think of money as the root of all mischief). What do you think of this, Sir? [192]

Sri Sri Thakur: I think money leads to mischievousness due to our greed and avarice. Your wealth and your prosperity are meant to serve the surroundings so that people think of you as their own. The aim of spiritualism is a glorious augmentation of your personality. If your material performance is dismal, your spiritual progress is bound to be gloomy.

Devotee: What are the qualities of a glorious man? [193]

Sri Sri Thakur: To me, the foremost quality is Ideal adherence. When you are with the Lord at a moment, you are there for others. You derive happiness by making others happy. You never hurt anyone with your words, deeds, and behaviour. That does not mean a spineless and weak personality, a shallow yes-man for everything. A man of character is sympathetic and resists evil and injustice done to others. Remember, unless you are honest in your character, your pretension of honesty will not last for long

Devotee: Why does a dishonest man masquerade to be good? [194]

Sri Sri Thakur: He does so to hide his follies. For example, I entrusted you with a job with great hope, but you took it lightly and transferred the responsibility to someone else. Ultimately, the job could not be done. However, shamelessly you came before me, and blamed the other person for his negligence, forgetting that your response to my request was insincere and treacherous. So it is said in the Bible (William James): 'With mere good intentions, hell is proverbially paved.'

Devotee: What is the character of such persons? [195]

Sri Sri Thakur: Lumps of disintegrated, unadjusted experiences, and nothing else. In life, they are unsuccessful and blame Providence. They never admit their insincerity and dishonesty which bring grief and misery. To put it briefly, as long as you engage yourself in multifarious activities, thinking them to be conducive to your material growth, you are a confused person. You will not find any headway to solve your day-to-day problems and requirements. You will blame God for all your failures, rather than analysing the causes thereof in order to succeed in life.

Sri Sri Thakur in Magnadicta:
> 'When they find none to blame
> they blame one—
> that's God;
> only then Satan looks at him.' (verse 124)

Satyanusaran: *After a little progress you make, you will find some have come to find a Master in you, some are calling you a 'great man', some, a prophet, etc.; on the other hand, some call you 'Satan' or 'scoundrel'; some 'a professional', etc. Beware! Pay no heed to them. They are all ghosts to you. If they are heeded, they will sit heavily on your own shoulders, and it will be very difficult to get them off. Work on it in your own way, come what may.*

Devotee: Why does a man always try to be one up? [196]

Sri Sri Thakur: It is pauperism. Such a man takes credit for a job without doing it. He aspires to greatness overnight. Such characters are always disrespectful and envious of others. They cannot tolerate anyone's progress, and react in evil ways immediately. They betray others. They are on the lookout to annex the wealth and property of others. To achieve that, they take recourse to false submissiveness. Often, in their words of consolation, there exists an inherent sense of fear. In this manner, they exploit you for their own selfish advantage. Through this cunning habit, they become good for nothing in society. Their poverty never leaves them.

Sri Sri Thakur in Magnadicta:
> 'Ingratitude, selfishness
> and mean-minded service
> make a good beverage for Satan
> and the unfortunate.' (verse 121)

Devotee: Why do some people not mind giving to others, but have a problem while contributing to their patron? [197]

Sri Sri Thakur: That is simply because they are ungrateful. A person who abandons the source, in him envy rules, for his self-aggrandisement he belittles others. A criminal behaves innocently. If you find someone reprimanding another person beyond measure for a small fault, be certain that the fault lies in him to a great extent. You also see the contrary in a person supporting the criminal. Both situations arise out of an inferiority complex.

Devotee: What about treachery? [198]

Sri Sri Thakur: It is the root of all sins. As the sex urge is primordial, treachery is the gateway to hell. All evil starts from there; evil is that which knocks down the growth of our being. The root of treachery is to disown the benefactor in front of others for selfish gain. I know a person who was gleefully delighted in poisoning my ears against others. I had to bear it in silence.

Devotee: In the dictionary, "go-between" means middlemanship, but you have used it to mean treachery. Is it not, Sir? [199]

Sri Sri Thakur: Yes, by "go-between" I mean a person who does not live up to his word, and squanders money for purposes other than for which it has been earmarked. He mistakes appreciation for reproach. All forms of treachery reside in such a go-between state of mind.

Devotee: The Hindu scriptures talk of eight fetters *(Astapasha)*. What is it? [200]

Sri Sri Thakur: They are: contempt *(ghrina)*, disgrace *(lajja)*, hunger for name and fame *(maan)*, insult *(apamaan)*, infatuation *(moha)*, arrogance *(dambha)*, malice *(dwesha)* and brutality *(paishunya)*. They reduce man to the size of a cockroach; they diminish his character.

Devotee: Why is speaking evil so despicable? [201]

Sri Sri Thakur: Malice within the mind is far more horrific than its affliction outside. Speakers of evil indulge in scandalous malpractices; they condemn others to prove their innocence. Gradually, it pulls them from progress. Never speak ill of others. Whoever despises you, or whoever praises you, take both of them with aloofness, and mind your own business.

Sri Sri Thakur's view in this regard:

Never become
a pot of venom,
with milk on the surface
It will poison you first,
then disseminate it to the rest.

Narrator: In the Bengali treatise 'Adarsha Vinayak', Sri Sri Thakur speaks of six dos' and don'ts:
- Never kill anyone
- Do not be immoral (exploiting others for selfish gain)
- Do not steal
- Do not bear false witness
- Love your parents with due service
- In your own way, love everyone in your surroundings. (verse 10)

He also prohibits 11 criminal acts:
- Speaking ill and malign of Prophets and Spiritual Masters.
- Returning loyalty by being ungrateful and treacherous.
- Immorality/misconduct—to exploit others by illegitimate means.
- Dereliction of responsibility.
- Secretive destruction and abduction of others' property and dignity.
- Devastating or destroying others for self-aggrandisement.
- Suspecting the fidelity of chaste women merely on hearsay.
- Failure to provide security for your proteges; unduly tormenting them.
- Compromising the interests of others for gain.
- Failure to fulfil your obligations, and to be biased towards undeserving individuals.
- To punish and humiliate others on false allegations. (Arya Pratimoksha, vol. 9)

Devotee: What is morality? 202

Sri Sri Thakur: Abiding by rules and regulations, where a man is endowed with perpetual goodness without depression and deprivation is morality. For example, alcohol may save lives in rare situations, but its addiction is dangerous for the self as well as society. The after-effects of drinking are depressive; that is why the intelligent have considered drinking immoral. So, morality facilitates existence towards becoming, and that hinders this process, is immoral.

Devotee: Today man often goes into depression. What to do about it? [203]

Sri Sri Thakur: It is worthwhile to analyse the cause of depression. Wishful thinking without appropriate endeavour may be one of the reasons. Ideas only, but no effort. When we act against our conscience, the mind weakens; the result is depression. When we fail to do unto others as we wished to be done, we feel depressed. The unexpected blows and beatings from the surroundings like harsh words, slander, cheating, betrayal, treachery, etc., cause depression.

Continuing the conversation, Sri Sri Thakur laughed a little and said: Be prepared to receive deplorable blows from life-long beneficiaries, so that when you get such reciprocation from someone in the future, you will be less affected and depressed. Your expectation of good returns for good deeds done to others may be belied. Don't worry. There is Nature's law of reciprocation—return comes from unexpected quarters at the time of your need, even if your ungrateful beneficiaries do not come forward. It is said, 'Nature abhors a vacuum.' When you are with the Ideal, believe in Him and do not harbour doubts.

Satyanusaran: As soon as faith is overwhelmed by doubt, which is again supported by the mind, depression sets in. If one gives up contrary ideas, and hears and accepts arguments favouring faith, doubts vanish and depression cannot remain. No contrary thoughts can shake faith after it has ripened. What can doubt or lethargy do to a true believer?

Devotee: How to get over a discontented mood? [204]

Sri Sri Thakur: Don't sit idle and brood over anything; rather mingle with your friends, and share your problems, and you will get relief. When ill health eats into your volatile self, take proper treatment to eradicate ailments. Try to be cheerful in all adverse situations. When you are cheerful, you can bring happiness to others.

Devotee: How to always remain cheerful? [205]

Sri Sri Thakur: The biggest enemy of cheer is jealousy. A jealous man pretends to be happy at someone's success but burns from within. Never go for such a disposition. The lesser the malevolence, the greater your peace of mind. Do not be a cynic to always find fault with others. It is as evil as malevolence. Cynicism is associated with blindness to one's own faults, causing an inferiority complex, and meanness. All of them together put you in distress.

Devotee: What does Vanaprastha (self-exile on spiritual pursuit) signify? [206]

Sri Sri Thakur: It does not mean retreating from the world, and to live a solitary life like in a jungle away from society. Rather, it means expanding the scope of your family to a multitude of people beyond your kith and kin. It makes you a real ascetic. At this stage, adherence to the Ideal gets intensified. As the intensity grows, you go to sainthood, and then to *Nirvana* (Emancipation).

Devotee: What is *Moksha* (Liberation)? [207]

Sri Sri Thakur: *Moksha* does not mean a state of nonchalance or aversion to the world; rather, it connotes a mental state in which we include society and the environment into the fold of our family, to regulate it, discipline it, and make it an amusement ground for the Supreme Father. In other words, you promote this world to become an ideal place of being and becoming. I think of the chronology of life in this way: Disciplined education *(Brahmacharya)*, family life *(Garhastya)*, self-exile *(Vanaprastha)*, sainthood *(Sannyasa)*, and liberation *(Moksha)*.

Devotee: What do you think of your followers? [208]

Sri Sri Thakur: By the grace of the Supreme Father, none of my children are blind or one-eyed; they possess good vision. But what's the use? They always keep their eyes closed. They always behave like minors, extending their hands for my help. Instead of using my help to get a thing done; they sit idle. When they fail, they come to me with a concocted explanation for their failure and seek further help. I look at their morose faces and help them again and again. Do you know how my nature is? Suppose you are teaching somebody to swim, if you always hold onto him, he won't learn it in a lifetime. You have to push him into the water so that he overcomes fear and starts swimming on his own. My problem is I can't loosen my hold over you, lest you drown. I do not allow you to struggle that much. You may ask why so? Here lies my tenderness. I always think: Let all the troubles come to me, but all of you should be happy.

Devotee: In spite of your concern for us, we are unable to give up many bad habits. What to do? [209]

Sri Sri Thakur: Decide to leave, and then leave it at once. Do not dilly-dally., Chop off the tree with one stroke. I remember a good anecdote in the Sri Ramakrishna Charitamrita: "One evening, a village couple was discussing a pious man of the village. The wife was praising him sky-high, 'Look at the man's devotion; he wants to adopt Vanaprastha (self-exile for spiritual sadhana), but is unable to find an auspicious day to leave worldly life behind.' The husband retorted: 'It is not done that way.' 'Then how is it done?' she asked. The husband stood up, put a cloth on his head, picked up a staff, and marched out of the house never to return.

Sri Sri Thakur in a verse:
> *Whatever good you think to do,*
> *do it with no delay,*
> *Walk your living on that path*
> *That is the right way. (Bibidha Sukta)*

Devotee: Can you change someone's nature? [210]

Sri Sri Thakur related his experience: One evening at Hemayetpur, I was talking about the possibility of changing somebody's nature. Suppose a man commits a theft, do we ever inquire about the circumstances that made him a thief? Do we ever place ourselves in his position? Instead of hate and punishment, have we ever taken the responsibility of moulding him into a normal human being? Can anybody say that they have tried? While I was speaking, a thief was eavesdropping. He did not disclose himself at that time. However, at around midnight, he came and knocked at my door and said, 'Sir, I have no other way to get by except stealing. Today you discussed the problems of a thief in a manner I have never heard before. Several times, I have stolen so many things from your house; some I have disposed of, but here are a few left that remained unsold. I am returning them to you.' I responded, 'No need of returning them, keep them.' After that incident, I helped him when he was in dire need of money. Gradually, we became close friends. One evening he came to me in an agitated state and confided that Kshitish Mazumdar (a wealthy villager) had withdrawn one thousand rupees from the bank, and kept it in his house. He said, 'Tonight I will steal it. Sir, kindly don't say no to me.' I said to him: 'Why should I stop you? It is your livelihood. I don't mind joining you.' He was initially taken aback, hesitated a little, and then agreed to my proposal. In the dead of night, he came with a black cloth for me. It was pitch dark when we left the house. On our way, I casually asked him, 'Is the door of your house properly bolted from the inside?' He laughed and said, 'Sir, What are you talking about? A thief always leaves the door of his house open when he goes to steal, so that in case of an alarm, he can run back immediately.' I asked, 'During this time, if someone enters your house to steal, or violates your young wife, what will you do?' For him, it was a bolt from the blue. He sat down on the road and said: 'Let us go back. Today I will not go to Mazumdar's house.' From then onwards, he swore off stealing. In due course, he became a very faithful worker at the ashram.

Devotee: Is repentance always helpful, Sir? [211]

Sri Sri Thakur: If someone genuinely repents, he will not repeat the same mistake. The attitude which leads a man to commit misdeeds can help him walk out of it. Repenting, and then repeating the same misdeed, is no repentance at all.

Satyanusaran: Repent, but see that you have not to repent again. When you are repentant for your misdeeds, you will be pardoned by the Supreme Father and you will understand it by the heavenly consolation you find in your heart. That will make you courteous, peaceful, and cheerful. It should be understood that he who repents but commits the same blunder again must soon fall into extreme misery. To repent in words alone is not repentance at all. It is rather an obstruction to feel repentance at heart. When real repentance comes, all its signs express themselves in varying degrees.

Devotee: Why do religious scriptures prescribe penance? Is it not a punishment? [212]

Sri Sri Thakur: It is a physio-psychical treatment. By observing the rules of penance, the impaired nerves of the culprit are rejuvenated. The fundamental idea is the cleansing of the heart.

Devotee: In *Satyanusaran* you have said, 'Faith, reliance, and self-sacrifice are the three signs of bravery.' Kindly explain self-sacrifice. [213]

Sri Sri Thakur: You have your own wishes, desires, and vocation. The more you engage yourself to fulfil them, the lesser will be your zeal to work for the Supreme Father. When you are preoccupied with your own matters, you have no time for others; you are stuck. I will give you an example: Suppose I become friendly with you, with an eye on your purse and somehow you get an inkling of it. Will you ever trust me? However, if I consider your interests as my own, and work sincerely for you, if I am willing to traverse troubled waters for your sake, if my fondness for you is beyond measure, only then will your inner soul realise that 'yes, here is a man whom I can call my own.' But while you are good to others, don't do it at the cost of your own well-being. When your being is poorly nourished, how can you look after others? Your main source of nourishment is from the Ideal. So, for doing good to others, you have to keep yourself active and agile, deriving energy and vibration from your love for the Ideal. When you reach a stage where you are restless to save a being from distress, your mutuality with him is at its apex. You derive enormous self-satisfaction, in front of which the desire for *moksha* (liberation) appears trivial. Such persons are always God-intoxicated *(Iswarakoti Purusha)*. They bring glory to Earth.

Narrator: American Psychoanalyst Dale Carnegie (1888-1955) observed, To get what we want from another person, we must forget our own perspective, and begin to see things from the point of view of others. When we combine our desires with their wants, they become eager to work with us and we can mutually achieve our objectives. (*How to Win Friends and Influence People*)

Satyanusaran: As long as you feel pain in your body and mind, keep trying to remove it even in an ant. If you don't do this, who is more deficient than you? Try to give others as you desire to have. To proceed with this understanding is enough. Everyone will like you and love you spontaneously.

Narrator: Swami Vivekananda, in relation to the conquest of selfishness, quotes from the Brihadaranyaka Upanishad, "Subdue the senses, do acts of charity, be compassionate. Practise the three virtues: control of the senses, charity, and compassion" and he adds: "Selfishness is a sin when we always think of ourselves first. He who thinks, 'I will eat first, I will have more money than others, and I will possess everything. is a selfish man. The unselfish man says, 'I will be the last, I do not care to go to heaven, I will even go to hell if by doing so I can help my brother.' *(Upanishads in Daily Life)*

Devotee: I go on helping a friend in his difficulty, but invariably he harms me. What should I do? [214]

Sri Sri Thakur: Forgive him.

Devotee: I have done so, but he is incorrigible. Should I forsake his company? [215]

Sri Sri Thakur: Forgiveness has many merits but only one demerit; whoever forgives may be misunderstood as timid and weak. But you should not bother much about it. For the virile and sturdy, forgiveness is adornment. So it is said: Don't be foolish while excusing one of his faults.

Devotee: What if a friend goes astray? [216]

Sri Sri Thakur in *Satyanusaran:* Do not abolish friendship; otherwise in your distress, you will neither get sympathy nor consolation. Even if your friend is dishonest, do not give up on him; rather give up his company if necessary. But with affection in your heart, help him in his distress and danger, in thought, word, and deed. Embrace him when you find he has become repentant. If your friend has gone astray and you do not try to bring him back, or if you give him up, its punishment will not forsake you either.

Devotee: The Ishopanishad mentions, "Enjoy the object by its sacrifice" *(Tena Tyaktena Bhunjitha)*. It appears to be a paradox. Is it not? [217]

Sri Sri Thakur: It means, removing the hurdles of true enjoyment. Conscientious enjoyment enhances our will to sacrifice. Here, sacrifice means renunciation of passionate desires. When a man is obsessed with sensual desires he is addicted, but let us not enter into theoretical discussions. The simple fact is that we want to enjoy ourselves through an object. For true enjoyment, there should be a distance between us and the object. That is called detachment. So it means enjoying it with the approval of conscience, and a sense of detachment.

Narrator: The meaning of the total verse in the Ishopanishad is: All this, whatsoever moves on the Earth, should be covered by the Lord. Protect (yourself) through that detachment. Do not covet anybody's wealth. Swami Vivekananda has explained, 'God is in everything. Where else shall we go to find Him? He is already in every work, in every thought, in every feeling. Thus knowing, we must work; thus, the effects of work will not bind us.' *(Upanishads in Daily Life)*

Devotee: Life is full of suffering. Where is enjoyment? [218]

Sri Sri Thakur: It depends on in what direction you want to move in life. Centripetal, or Centrifugal? When your movement is centripetal, the centre being the Ideal, the passage is smooth, but when you adopt a centrifugal movement in life, you are bound to be attacked by complexes and passions. This movement will alienate you from yourself. It will disintegrate you and deluge you in catastrophes. In the mirage of so-called progress, we annihilate ourselves. Be careful.

Devotee: Why do you insist on the transformation of the Individual? [219]

Sri Sri Thakur: Yes, that is the road to nobility. From the individual to the family, from the family to society, and from society to the country; this is how civilization grows. So the root is the Individual. Unless we have good men, how can we expect an ideal society and country? Without good individuals and a good society, the country will perish sooner or later. The knowledge one derives from being useful to others is real knowledge. Whether you come to me or not, be devoted to your parents. Such devotion will save you from many calamities. If you can extend your devotion to the Ideal, you further mould yourself in goodness.

Devotee: Anger, greed, sex, etc., are they the real enemies then? [220]

Sri Sri Thakur: The five elements like food, sleep, fear, sex, and pride are inherent in human nature. They are classified as spiritual, mental, and physical. Another classification is *satwik* (balanced), *rajasik* (energising), and *tamasik* (passionate). The Ideal teaches us how to aptly use the primordial forces to glorify one's life. When passions are employed to fulfil the interests of the Ideal, they become tamed and suitable for public welfare.

Devotee: How can I propagate your message? [221]

Sri Sri Thakur: Apart from lectures and circulating my literature, propagation is best done when you imbibe my message in your character, qualities that are prescribed by the Ideal for a better human being. People will see you and learn. There is no question of projecting me as God before the public. Call me God or not, I am what I am. Of course, good ideas can be propagated through the arts and literature as well as life-encouraging prose, poetry, plays, theatre, operas, and cinema.

Devotee: What is the role of literature? [222]

Sri Sri Thakur: Literature establishes ethics and guides us towards the goal. Literature that does not enunciate ethical living is not at all useful to mankind. I talk of elevating literature that arouses beneficial inspiration in us. There are writers who prefer a tragic end to their stories, novels, and poems, but it is very destructive as it may lead a reader down a ruinous path.

Sri Sri Thakur on Art and Literature:

What makes one Luminous
with an enthusiastic unfoldment of ideas
that elate the mind—
with a pleasure push to service and success
in the way of becoming by means and skill
that operates
with an
uphill sensation
is Art and Literature. (The Message, vol. I)

Narrator: I. B. Singer (1903-1991), the Polish-American writer, in his address during his felicitation on receiving the Nobel Prize, said: 'Moreover, belief in God and His Providence is the very essence of literature. It tells us that causality is nothing but a mask on the face of destiny. Man is constantly watched by powers that seem to know all his desires and complications. He has a free choice, but he is also being led by a mysterious hand. Literature is the story of love and fate, a description of the mad hurricane of human passions and the struggle with them.'

Devotee: J J Rousseau (1712-1778) in his famous book 'The Social Contract' wrote: 'Man is born free, but he is in chains everywhere.' Is it a fact? [223]

Sri Sri Thakur: Man has three bindings: family, social, and legal. When I talk of serving the surroundings, it is not due to any binding. There is no philosophy or 'ism' in it. I believe social change depends on the change of the individual. This consciousness can be aroused by Dharma only. Social service then becomes a part of individual upliftment. Serving the milieu is serving the self. Whatever good is inherent in any human being is aroused by loving all, and serving all. Otherwise, the incidence of crime would be on the rise, and no law or provision for punishment can check it.

Devotee: Why does one commit a crime? [224]

Sri Sri Thakur: Proneness to crime can be segregated into three categories; hereditary, due to evil company, and inadequate education. Criminals of the second category can be rectified easily, but inborn criminals are stubborn towards any rectification. For them, punishment and appeasement can be tried depending on the situation. In case they do not relent, they should be made sterile, unable to produce more criminals. Reckless marriages are a major cause of social violence and crimes. I feel it is the foremost duty of social leaders, albeit the state, to regulate improper and incompatible marriages. It will restrict the birth of ill-bred children.

Devotee: Exploitation of the lower class by the upper class is the main cause of social violence and hatred. Untouchability is also a cause of concern. What do you think, Sir? [225]

Sri Sri Thakur: I think it is our first duty to serve the people of the lower strata, and elevate them. Untouchability is to be despised always, at any cost.

Devotee: What is the parameter to know whether a civilization is in progression or recession? [226]

Sri Sri Thakur: When civilisation deteriorates, there appears to be an inadequacy of inquisitiveness and an absence of cohesion among people. With material prosperity, man becomes selfish. He runs after easy and quick money, rejects simple living, and prefers to live in comfort and luxury. Sectarian fanaticism grows in the name of religion, and so do crimes. A fanatic is worshipped as a hero in the sect he belongs to. The meanness and intolerance among sects bring indiscipline which also percolates into families; there is bound to be chaos. A wave of despondency pervades the country.

Nationalism, International Militarism and Auto-excretion

Devotee: In ancient times, India was known as 'Devabhumi', but first the Mughals, and then the British came to do business in India and subjugated the country for more than five hundred years. Why did it happen, Sir ?[227]

Sri Sri Thakur: The meaning of the word 'Devata' is 'enlightened.' Bharata was a place where the people were enlightened. They obeyed the rishis. The degradation came from the time of Emperor Ashoka. Buddhism was diluted. The principles of Varnashrama (instinctive classification of society) were flouted. Sri Shankaracharya's Mayavada proclaimed that only the Supreme Truth was real, and the rest was an illusion. The idea of a totality was lost. Due to infighting among rulers, the unity to resist foreign invasion disintegrated. Now, if all of you follow the Ideal, and leave your selfishness and sectarian meanness, then Bharata will rise again to indomitable glory.

Sri Sri Thakur hummed a stanza from a Bengali patriotic poem by Dwijendra Lal Roy:

On that day from the deep ocean blue
  rose our mother
  Bharata dear!
  What a day!
  What a clamour!
  What splendour!
  What a joy!

Devotee: What do you think of India's development?[228]

Sri Sri Thakur: Let Bharata be Bharata. There is no gain in trying to make our country like England, America, or Russia. With a lack of knowledge about the exigency of an Ideal, a rishi, the

West with all its power and capacity is digging its own grave. If we imitate them, the same consequence awaits us. If we maintain our originality, India is bound to guide the world with its banner of love, compassion, and wisdom embedded in our culture. The day is not far off when the whole world will begin to beg, "O Bharata, our passion-dominated living has torn us to pieces, it has parched our lives. Teach us the mantra, the clue of meaningful living."

We have to usher in a materio-spiritual development of our country; the village should come first. The development of the village is the development of India. Manufacturing agrarian products using modern techniques should be our top priority. As a result, agro-based small-scale industries will reduce the unemployment problem. Capital-intensive industries and factories should be at the minimum; that will avoid the present labour unrest. The excesses of industrialisation should not disturb the ecological balance.

Narrator: Sri Sri Thakur's message of India's development was echoed in the statement of former Indian Prime Minister Atal Bihari Vajpayee (1999-2004). He raised a pertinent question: When will India become Bharata? In this small question, many issues are embedded: the cause of India's subjugation, the war of Independence, the lack of care for rural India, and the growing disparity between the rich and the poor. He realised what Sri Sri Thakur had said. India grows when her village rises. The first and foremost is communication. He started the unique programme of the Prime Minister's Gramin Sadak Yojana. This project made the most remote villages accessible for carrying out developmental activities. The upliftment of rural India gained momentum. Because of his foresight, the country will remember him with reverence for ages to come.

Devotee: However, following the messenger of God or the Ideal is a sort of regimentation. It goes against liberal thinking. Does it not, Sir? [229]

Sri Sri Thakur: Free and liberal thinking, by ignoring the prominence of the Supreme Being, is bound to create chaos and anomaly in society. When the reservoir of empathy gets depleted in man, his heart becomes parched. With a dry heart, no matter how much we nourish our sense of reasoning, we shall not find bliss.

Devotee: No Ideal, no rishi, but still the advanced countries are reaching new heights. How is it possible? [230]

Sri Sri Thakur: Those countries are no doubt advancing with the inspiration of their egoistic ambitions. Inventions are taking place very fast, and materialism gallops. Due to egoistic ambitions, war is inevitable. The devastation of war creates a terrible state of frustration and lamentation in the human heart; then comes the realisation. Human society searches for a guide, by following whom the world will limp back to peace, love, and life. Man does not want to deteriorate, nor does he want to decay. He wants to live in peace and harmony. That is only possible by following the messenger of God, the Ideal.

Devotee: Now, rapid industrialisation and militarisation are accelerating the war psychosis among advanced countries. What is the remedy? [231]

Sri Sri Thakur: Today, capitalism exerts pressure on the ruling class. The ruling class, to remain in power, depends on mass support. When the rich and affluent do not come forward to sacrifice their wealth for the benefit of the masses, no social gain can be achieved. This is the story of developing countries. The developed countries due to their egoistic ambition are aggressive against each other. They will not be friendly with neighbouring countries. So humanity as a whole, instead of elevation, will be dragged towards annihilation. When the world as a whole goes towards annihilation, the process of auto-excretion starts to bring back peace.

Narrator: At the time of writing this book, the Russia-Ukraine war has persisted for months. This is a bright instance of egoistic militarism of two superpowers causing loss of life to thousands and mass devastation. Hundred years ago, Sri Sri Thakur had predicted, regardless of the progress in advanced countries, that they would always end up waging wars. This is probably the beginning. Jane Goodall, Ph.D. DBE, an English primatologist and anthropologist, has summed up the present world scenario: "What have we done to the planet—deforestation, pollution, loss of biodiversity, shrinking fresh water supply, the effects of chemicals used in agri-business and industry, the damaging effects of climate change; everywhere we find racial discrimination, hatred, exploitation, greed, and corruption. There is ethnic violence, terrorism, and war; the world is a mess." (*The Intelligence of The Cosmos*)

Devotee: What is auto-excretion? [232]

Sri Sri Thakur: When milk accumulates in excess in the udder of an animal, it hurts the creature. On taking out the excess milk, the pain subsides. Similarly, when society is oppressed by internal turmoil, it comes forward to accept the Supreme Personality of the age, because there is no other way for being and becoming. Human society accepts the Ideal, and follows His discipline for coexistence.

Varnashrama versus Classless Society

Devotee: It is claimed that in ancient India social coexistence was achieved by Varnashrama. What is Varnashrama, and how did it achieve this coexistence we talk about? [233]

Sri Sri Thakur: In ancient Indian society, there were four classes: Bipra (the scholarly class), Kshatriya (the warrior class), Vaishya (the business class), and Shudra (the service class). Bipras were busy learning and researching, formulating laws and regulations and drawing up various policies for administration, inventing methods to come up with equipment that increased agricultural and industrial production. Kshatriyas were suitable for warfare. They looked after law and order and national security. Vaishyas were experts in trade and commerce. The last category provided support and service to the other three categories.

Devotee: What was the basis for the above classification?[234]

Sri Sri Thakur: The hereditary germplasm creates man's tendency and urge, which lie embedded in his very being. This constitutes the inborn instinct and distinctiveness in every individual, each different from the other. However, men with broadly the same instinct and distinctiveness form groups. These groups are called *Varnas*. These *Varnas* are generationally passed down according to their work suitability.

Devotee: Could the person of one class adopt the work of another class?[235]

Sri Sri Thakur: Yes. This classification was not watertight, but flexible. Scholarly persons in other classes were taken into the first category of the *Vipras*. The road to improvement was always open. Social status was determined not on the basis of possession of wealth, but on culture, behaviour, and social competence. Theoretical knowledge without practice was not given any importance. The council of ministers under the king was formed of representatives from the four classes. There was a healthy gradation in society, no ambiguity existed with regard to the suitability of a person for a particular work.

Devotee: The proponents of Communism are not in favour of class discrimination, they think of a classless society without injustice and exploitation. What is your view, Sir?[236]

Sri Sri Thakur: I do not understand what a classless society is. Man is classified according to heredity, genetic distinction, etc., and adopts the culture of the family. The concept that all men are equal is a misnomer. In God's creation, no two beings are identical. It is unscientific not to realise this basic truth. Without considering hereditary instincts, if a man is pushed to take up a particular profession, he may not fit in it. For a compatible marriage, heredity, culture, etc., are to be considered. If not, it may lead to failure. You and I may not live to see it, but I can give you an undertaking: "If the world desires to survive, the fundamental principles of *Varnashrama* should be followed."

Devotee: Is not the caste system an offshoot of *Varnashrama*?[237]

Sri Sri Thakur: Class division *(Varnashrama)* and the caste system are not one and the same. Distortions in class divisions should not be confused with *Varnashrama*. It can be compared with different organs of the human body working coherently for its total well-being. This classification according to hereditary capacities is prevalent even in groups of animals and birds.

Narrator: Social classification in families and bond groups in elephants. An elephant family consists of one or more usually related adult families and their offspring. Above the level of the family unit, the second tier of relationship may exist within what is termed a bond group. Like the family, bond group membership is also usually determined by genetic relatedness. A bond group may include as many as five or more families, and up to fifty or more individuals. Elephant families and bond groups are ruled by matriarchs. The matriarch makes most of the decisions which are followed by others. A matriarch is usually the oldest and most respected female in the family, or in the bond group. Members of a family or bond group show extraordinary teamwork and are highly cooperative in group defense, resource acquisition, and offspring care. The cohesion of different families and bond groups varies significantly and depends on a number of factors including personalities, the degree of relatedness and friendship, and the strength of the matriarch's leadership.

Male elephants after their growth anywhere between nine to eighteen years leave their natal family and form another group. Independent males are often seen in small all-male groups, and they form lasting friendships with each other. During the sexually active period, males rove from one family group to the next in search of a receptive female. Their interaction with family members is gentle and courteous. Once a male has located a receptive female, he will competitively try to consort with her for a period of two to three days and then will move on in search of another female. Thus, the elephant population grows.

Researchers have found that elephants are intelligent, and highly social mammals, accumulating social and ecological knowledge over decades throughout their long life spans. (elephant voices via Instagram)

The wolfpack: It is a perfect mechanism of social organisation. A pack of wolves usually comprises a dominant Alpha, a lone wolf, or a couple. The next is the Beta, following in importance, and most likely to replace the current alphas; they are individuals in the middle ranks, followed by wolves of the lowest rank, Omega. The alpha commands the whole group, while the beta directs the mid-level wolves to take charge of the remaining pack of the lowest-ranked wolves. Wolf pups remain outside this complex ranking system until the age of sexual maturity, while females always play second fiddle to males of equal rank. As befits a leader, the dominant wolf exhibits an attitude and stands to match its status, standing tall with head and tail held high and ears erect. The alpha also demands important privileges such as the right to feast on prey before the other members of the pack. Less dominant wolves will act submissively to the alpha, licking their leader's muzzle, often lowering their bodies and positioning their heads, tails, and ears lower than the higher-ranking pack member. The omega is considered the lowest and only allowed to feed on the prey left over. When hunting, they form a collective team, working together as one intelligent unit to take down their prey. Sometimes there are conflicts within the ranks, and a wolf is driven out of the pack, or leaves of its own accord—becoming a so-called lone wolf. The collaboration of the pack for self-preservation, as well as their complex community structure, ease of body language, and howls, convey the magnitude of their intelligence and the depth of their emotions. (Almo Nature Fondazione Cappellino)

Devotee: How to understand birds and animals? [238]

Sri Sri Thakur: We always hear the chirping of birds and the howls of animals, but we choose to ignore them. If we make a habit of listening to their sounds and trying to decipher them, we can very well understand their meaning. We have a lively relationship with all that exists in creation: animals, birds, insects, earth and water, light and wind, trees and plants, the sun, the moon and the stars in the sky. In the past, in universities like Nalanda, lessons were given to decipher the language of animals and birds. I feel a common language for human beings, birds, animals, etc., can be worked out scientifically.

One world village *(Vasudhaiva Kutumbakam)*

Devotee: Can the principles of Varnashrama (instinctive work specialisation) be applied to all human societies in the world?[239]

Sri Sri Thakur: Yes. All the societies of our world can be broadly arranged into these four (scholar, warrior, business and service classes). Interpersonal relationships can be developed within the same class throughout the world; for example, an Indian warrior family can build a relationship with their German counterparts. Thus, the world will become a great village. Needless to say, for a disciplined society to emerge, the acceptance of the Ideal by one and all is crucial as well as essential. This concept transcends the barrier of race, nationality, and ethnic resentment.

Devotee: Will our traditional concept of *Vasudhaiva Kutumbakam* (the world as one family) be realised through this practice? [240]

Sri Sri Thakur: To my little knowledge, this appears to be the most appropriate way for unifying the world.

Narrator: The German philosopher, Immanuel Kant (1724-1804) was the first thinker to dream of a global state in which every individual would be a citizen. It was to be reached through a federation of nations. Kant was of the view that without a powerful international authority, there could be no international state. With the creation of the League of Nations, and now with the United Nations, his dream appears to be taking shape. However, when disputes between various states, and especially the superpowers arise, the UN is supposed to provide solutions. But, since it does not have the power to implement its decisions, its role is extremely marginalised. According to Kant, every human being is in possession of love and compassion. John Stuart Mill (1806 -1837) also argues along a similar line of thought: "Selfishness is very much a part of human nature, but if he learns to sacrifice it for the common good, his contentment would be hundredfold." *(Understanding Philosophy)*

Satyanusaran—Know this for certain, you are responsible for the present and future of your own self, your family, your environment, and your country.

10

WOMEN, WOMEN'S RIGHTS AND LIBERATION, MAN-WOMAN RELATIONSHIPS, MARRIAGE, CONJUGAL RELATIONSHIPS, CHASTITY, FAMILY, CHILD CARE, DIVORCE, WIDOW REMARRIAGE.

Devotee: Sri Ramakrishna Dev (1836-1886) said, "Keep away from money and women." Sri Sankaracharya (788-820) was supposed to have remarked on women as a gateway to hell. What do you think, Sir?[241]

Sri Sri Thakur: We have to look into the context in which the above statements were made. Probably the proponents wanted to convey that when a woman is singularly seen as fuel for passionate enjoyment, she paves the way to degradation. That is right, but why should we give so much importance to this abnormal situation? Why should we think of a woman only as a tool for our sexual desires? The woman's dignity lies in nurturing her family and inspiring them to a healthy life. Her role in society is tremendously important; she is the mother, the wife, the nurse, and the conscience-keeper.

Sri Sri Thakur observed:
> *Females are effeminate*
> *in structure*
> *in construction*
> *they are adjutant to the male,*
> *in conception*
> *they are agreeable to offspring,*
> *in conduct*
> *they are soothing to the male,*
> *in cooperation*
> *They are interrelated."* (The Message, vol. 7)

Narrator: The American poet and critic of the last century, Lousie Bogan (1897-1970), in her famous poem, *Women* (1923), held women in high stature. A few lines from her poem:

Women have no wilderness in them,
they are provident instead,
content in the tight hot cell of their hearts
to eat dusty bread.

The great Sanskrit poet of ancient India, Bhartruhari (approx. 7th century), was famous for his three *Satakas* on women (*Sataka* is a collection of one hundred verses). There is an anecdote behind this great creation. Bhartruhari was the king of Ujjain. Among several queens, he was very fond of queen Anangasena, and after her, queen Pingala. In the city of Ujjain, there lived a floozy harlot named Rupalekha, the king's paramour. Once, a hermit came to the king's court, and presenting him with a fruit, secretly, said, "O King! On my rigorous *tapas* for several years, I have been blessed with this magical fruit, it gives one eternal youth. I am a mendicant, but you are a compassionate ruler, brave and judicious; so if you eat this fruit, you can retain your youth forever and it will immensely benefit your countrymen. The king, taking the strange fruit, thought, 'if I present this rare gift to queen Anangasena she will understand my deep love for her.' Queen Anangasena was in love with Chandrachuda, the chief charioteer. She presented the fruit to him to avail his youthful fervour for a long time. Chandrachuda was philandering with Rupalekha. The fruit reached her. She was very learned. Like the saint, she thought that the king deserved the fruit for the benefit of the country, and eventually the fruit came back to the king. He was thunderstruck. Queen Anangasena committed suicide, Chandrachuda was ousted from the country. Devastated by this incident, the king went into a state of depression; he did not attend court and ignored his royal obligations. Hoping to elevate his spirits, the council of ministers arranged a hunt. The king hesitantly complied, and accompanied by a group, went into the forest and shot a deer. As soon as the animal fell to the ground, another deer leaped out from behind a tree, and in utter shock, died then and there beside its partner. It was a female deer. The king brought the two dead deer, male and female. He narrated the story to queen Pingala. She replied, 'Isn't it natural?' The king quipped, 'Will the same happen to you?' She gave a short reply, 'Of course.' Time passed, the king could not quite forget the remark of queen Pingala and wanted to test her. One day, on the pretext of hunting, he went out of the palace, and in the evening sent his blood-soaked dress with his soldiers to her. They showed her the clothes and narrated the horrible incident: 'During his attempt to shoot, the king was attacked by a tiger and was killed instantly. The tiger dragged his body deep into the forest. Here are the remnants of his final battle for life.' Queen Pingala clasped the pieces of clothing to her chest, and breathed her last. The repentant king cursed himself for playing this dirty trick on his faithful queen. His repentance had no end. Based on the lives of these three women: Queen Anangasena, the amorous one, queen Pingala, the righteous, and Rupalekha, the loyal harlot, he wrote three *Satakas: Srungara Satakam* (sentiment of lovemaking)—Anangasena, *Niti Satakam* (sentiment of righteousness)—Pingala, *Vairagya Satakam* (sentiment of renunciation)—Rupalekha.

Devotee: Does passion for women obstruct Ideal orientation?[242]

Sri Sri Thakur: Followers can be divided into three classes. The best is the passion-pervading class. They employ their passions and complexes only to serve the Ideal. The second class is passion-compromising: Attachment to the Ideal and attraction to worldly enjoyment go hand in hand for them. The third class uses the Ideal to fulfil passion: 'O Thakur, I follow you with heart and soul; if the girl I have in mind reciprocates well to my advances.'

Devotee: Man and woman, what is the basic difference between them?[243]

Sri Sri Thakur: Adam and Eve, the male fulfils and the female inspires. Woman augments the man, so that man can expand. The man's desire is for the woman, but the woman's desire is to boost him. The sphere of man's activity is large and wide, whereas a woman's sensibility is deep-rooted. The width of activity of the female is restricted as she enjoys the world through the male. Therefore, her activities are inward and vigorously concentrated. She is satisfied serving her father, brother, husband, and children. A woman's inner tendency is embedded in motherhood. Her upbringing should be conducive to her inner qualities. Man's character is to fulfil the woman with his acquisitions, and woman's fulfilment is in nourishing the man.

Devotee: Nowadays women are doing well in all jobs that men did. Is it good? [244]

Sri Sri Thakur: Yes, it is. When the necessity arises, women can go for all kinds of jobs. In the past, girls were trained to fight in the war; but it does not mean that their distinction lies in warfare, maintaining law and order, etc. I hope I am able to make you understand my viewpoint, i.e. women should be made capable to take up any job as needed, but their basic nature is to boost man to a larger sphere of activity, to nurture him and guide him so that the home is congenial and harmonious.

Devotee: How does love grow between them? [245]

Sri Sri Thakur: In the girl's mind, the inclination to love sprouts first. She becomes eloquent in her admiration for the man she likes. She never says to him, 'If you love me, I will also love you.' Love is inherent in her nature. The mother loves her offspring before the child learns to love his mother; when he grows up, he understands the love of his mother and tries to reciprocate by doing things that please her.

Devotee: What should be the way of living for women?[246]

Sri Sri Thakur: I think her living should be modest. She should be veiled. But her movement among men should be dignified. The behaviour of girls mingling much with boys of the same age, or a little older than them, or even with a young teacher, should be transparent, and preferably in the presence of her parents and guardians. Meeting in lonely places, even with elders around, should be avoided unless those meetings are with close relatives.

Devotee: In our society, we create relationships such as godfather, godbrother, etc. Are they real? [247]

Sri Sri Thakur: Girls should never be allowed into such relationships. Be careful of people who bring such propositions, unless they are related by blood. The desire for sex proliferates under the guise of such pretentious relationships. Be careful of outsiders who propose such a relationship. Women by nature are flexible, easily sympathetic, and vulnerable to influence. Sex maniacs may exploit the simple mind of a woman through such fake propositions.

Devotee: Today, women's security is at stake. Cases of rape and child abuse are fast increasing. What to do about it? [248]

Sri Sri Thakur: In cases of rape, the culprit should be compelled to accept the victim as his wife; otherwise, he should take responsibility for her maintenance. The laws of the land should be stringent on such matters, with quick adjudication of offences.

Devotee: The husband-wife relationship, they say, should be passionate. What do you think about it, Sir? [249]

Sri Sri Thakur: No doubt, passion is a gift of Providence, but its excessive expression brings dullness and deterioration in the body and mind. Hence, one should be modest and restrained.

Devotee: Is such restraint possible? [250]

Sri Sri Thakur: I believe that when passion sucks the source of life, disintegration absorbs existence. However, when passion serves life, existence becomes meaningful with love. Existence with proper use of passion becomes active with serviceable ecstasy for others. Only then with thrilling care and affection for life, you will be an emblem of care, hope, and charity to your progeny and society. Unless the female solicits, the man should not make any advances for physical union. When the initiative comes from the male, and there is no reciprocation from the female, it amounts to sex coercion. When the woman is enthusiastic about physical union, she begets healthy children; if she enlivens the godly attributes in her husband, there is a good chance of giving birth to noble souls. If salacity dominates the mind, performance becomes poor, and enjoyment becomes retarded and haphazard. A wife seldom likes a lecherous husband. That is why I say, without attachment to the Ideal, a man should not marry. You may call me old-fashioned, but you can see for yourself the way civilization is in the doldrums. The country in which noble souls were born in every family is now desperately searching for a good man.

Devotee: In the case of animals, which sex initiates the physical union? [251]

Sri Sri Thakur: In their case, the male is generally indifferent. The female woos the male first, and upon seeing the aroused female, he runs after her. In our case, without an invitation from the female, when the male wants to engage with her sexually, there is a possibility of vitally weak progeny, and the birth of a female child. The male must be revered by the female.

Devotee: A relationship must be mutual. A wife can't go on revering and serving her husband without any gratitude or love from him. Is it not correct, Sir? [252]

Sri Sri Thakur: Selfish expectations are pebbles in the jar of existence that resist the wine of life. Though love is seldom mutual, it has a magnetic pull to nurture the beloved's existence. So I always say, stick to your mate with an immortal, unbreakable tie, and both of you surrender to your Lord with progressive and concentric service.

Devotee: A woman is generally considered inferior to a man. So the women's liberation movement started in the West and has subsequently come to our country. What do you think of it, Sir?[253]

Sri Sri Thakur: Nowadays, we are talking of women's liberation and liberty. By liberty, I understand cooperative, interdependent, and serviceable run of life. I have heard that due to a lack of mutual understanding and tolerance, divorce has become common in Western countries, so children suffer. I must tell you, where is peace in this type of doubt-prone, contentious, conjugal relationship? I think we are better off even in our poverty. When a caring wife prepares food, even if it is meagre, and feeds her husband, elders, and children, her affection touches their hearts and opens up the cells of their minds. If the lady of the family is amative, she inspires her husband to undeterred development. I am lucky in this aspect, *Bada Bou (Borma)* is even alert to my sneezing. A woman in Indian society is revered as the Goddess of Prosperity (*Laxmi*) and Goddess of Learning (*Saraswati*). In a land where women are held in such high esteem, what kind of woman liberation is absent that we need to learn from others?

Narrator: Maya Angelou (1928-2014), a well-known American poet, wrote: 'The sadness of the women's movement is that they do not allow for the necessity of love. See, I do not personally trust in any revolution where love is not allowed. (*In California Living*, May 1975)

A similar view has been expressed by British journalist Polly Toynbee (1946): Feminism is the most revolutionary idea there has ever been. Equality for women demands a change in the human psyche more profound than in anything else that has been dreamt of. It means valuing parenthood as much as we value banking. (*Guardian*, 19 January 1987).

Devotee: What happens if the wife is ill-natured and malicious?[254]

Sri Sri Thakur: There is a risk of giving birth to sickly and weak children.

Narrator: The great Greek philosopher, Socrates (BC 470-399), married twice; the second time to Xanthippe, a shrewd woman who screamed at him repeatedly and often hit him, sometimes even in public. When asked why he put up with such behaviour, he replied, 'It was good training because if you could stand her, you could stand anything else that might happen to you.' When someone asked him once whether to marry or not, Socrates replied, 'Either way you will repent it.' (*Understanding Philosophy*)

Devotee: Why do you lay so much emphasis on compatible marriages? [255]

Sri Sri Thakur: Disconcerted marriage brings chaos. When they are antithetic and incoherent, the children are wayward and fickle-minded. It is very difficult to change them through education, sympathy, or punishment. They are lost causes by birth, what to do? That is the reason why I emphasise compatible marriages, according to the rules of genetics. Unless there is the purity of genes, it is difficult to carry forward any noble work. The genes of the mother work as a nurturing agent, and unless it is compatible with the genes of the husband, the child seldom inherits an unabridged personality. For a compatible marriage, the details of lineage, nature, culture, behaviour, customs, and traditions of both families need to be considered. Everything revolves around marriage because a congruent marriage is the source of good progeny.

Devotee: What is the role of a mother? [256]

Sri Sri Thakur: I understand that to be a mother means 'to measure', for she is the measure of the child's personality. She builds up the child step by step with great patience and perseverance.

Devotee: What is your opinion on chastity? [257]

Sri Sri Thakur: Without spiritual and mental chastity, physical chastity alone does not have much value. When the husband is Ideal-centric, and the wife thinks of him as indispensable, she surrenders completely, and along with him loves the Ideal; chastity is then spiritual. When the wife takes care of her husband in his work, adjusts her food or clothing preferences, and other requirements to suit the social and mental tendencies of the husband, chastity is mental. Although physical chastity comes last in the order of priority, it is the foundation, and without physical chastity, conceiving good souls is near nigh impossible.

Devotee: Society expects chastity in women, but overlooks the lack of it in men. Why does this hypocrisy exist? [258]

Sri Sri Thakur: Virtue in man is vital to existence, no doubt. Chastity is specially indicated in women as she is the mother who conceives; the cradle of life, happiness and peace. It is she who initiates every flowing good from paternal existential wealth. It is her discerning intelligence and affectionate goading that develops good character in children, according to the essential resources of the father that dwells within.

Devotee: Does chastity influence motherhood?[259]

Sri Sri Thakur: Unless there is a deep attraction between the husband and the wife, the bond with the child becomes superficial.

Devotee: But how is Ideal-attachment related to the chastity of women?[260]

Sri Sri Thakur: Single-minded devotion with all passions reserved for the Supreme Being is the *sine qua non* of chastity. Chastity, pious service, and pleasing manners are the radiant lustre of a woman that takes mankind to the development and growth of wisdom. If there is no pious worship and dignity in behaviour, chastity alone is incorporeal. Where the wife lacks passionate impetus and respect for her husband, day-to-day family life has to face ruinous devastation; be aware of this hard fact.

Narrator: The famous poet-philosopher, Khalil Gibran, exhorts newly married couples to be always conscious of the presence of God in their relationship:

> You shall be together when the white
> wings of death scatter your days
> ay, you shall be together even in the silent
> memory of God
> but let there be spaces in your
> Togetherness,
> And let the winds of the heavens dance
> between you. ('On marriage' in 'The Prophet')

Devotee: What should be the criteria for a compatible marriage?[261]

Sri Sri Thakur: The match should be equal but opposite, two families coming from the same clan. Along with the nature and qualities of the bridegroom and the bride, the tradition of both families is of paramount importance. It is better if the bride is from a lesser social stratum than the groom. In short, this is called a compatible (*Anuloma*) marriage. When the situation is contrary, it is incompatible (*Pratiloma*).

Narrator: In Western society, a marriage between a groom of a higher social rank than the bride is called a morganatic marriage. This is a marriage between a man of high birth (such as from a reigning, deposed, or mediatised dynasty) and a woman of lesser status (such as a daughter of a low-ranked noble family or a commoner).

Devotee: What are the shortcomings of an incompatible marriage? [262]

Sri Sri Thakur: The wife, coming from a higher status, will have no regard for her husband and his family. Even when we take cows and dogs to breed, we look for a higher pedigree in the male, but ignore this in our own case. It is funny and unfortunate that the progeny of horses and dogs seems to be more important for us than that of human beings. If this trend continues, man will be devilish, mean, jealous, and treacherous. I think if someone decides to destroy a civilization or a country, the quick and easy way is to sneak in an incompatible system of marriage. In the name of free will and liberty, the state should not encourage incongruous marriages. When a marriage takes place ignoring biological compatibility, the state must intervene to set the fault right.

Narrator: Social science talks of two types of marriages, homogamy and heterogamy. Homogamy is marriage between individuals who are, in some culturally important way, similar to each other. It is a form of assortative mating. The union may be based on socio-economic status, class, gender, caste, ethnicity, or religion. Heterogamy refers to a marriage between two individuals that differ in the above criterion.

Devotee: If the issue of marriage is so exigent, why do leaders overlook it? [263]

Sri Sri Thakur: The national leaders of every state have to ponder over it. These are matters of science, genetics, eugenics, heredity, and the experience of sociology. It is high time they think about it, or else we must be prepared for the downfall of the human race.

Devotee: Is it not possible to simply educate our children to be good human beings? [264]

Sri Sri Thakur: There is a heaven-and-earth difference between knowledge through acquisition and knowledge by instinct. Newton was a mathematician by instinct. There might be better-qualified mathematicians than him, but they cannot possess his mathematical instinct. Instinct is how the heart beats, ears hear, eyes see, nostrils inhale, and feet walk. Good children should be produced; rearing goodness has its own limitations.

Devotee: How can we produce good souls? [265]

Sri Sri Thakur: Firstly, the marriage must be compatible. After the male sows the seed, the responsibility of the female starts. The state of her mind during pregnancy influences the formation of psychological traits in the child. In a Hindu family, a number of religious ceremonies are performed to keep the mind of the woman serene and pure. When the husband and the wife maintain a cordial relationship with Ideal-orientation, the possibility of getting a good child is high. Attachment to the Supreme Being undoubtedly enhances the inner wealth of both husband and wife; when they are exalted, a noble soul arrives.

Sri Sri Thakur on marital relations:
> *Marital relation*
> *with proper distinctiveness*
> *which fulfils each other*
> *with every happy coupling*
> *is a source of*
> *distinguished progeny.* (The Message, vol. VII)

Devotee: In the sperm, it seems many souls are present, but only one goes into the ovum; what happens to the others? [266]

Sri Sri Thakur: I think every sperm is a being in microcosmic form; When it is wasted it is like killing a being in the same microcosmic form. By nature's design, only one sperm that enters the ovum survives, and the others don't. This cannot be helped. But one should realise that semen contains living sperm, which should not be wasted by sexual indulgence for pleasure.

Devotee: What should be the age difference between the husband and the wife? [267]

Sri Sri Thakur: The husband should be older than the wife by 15 to 20 years. When I speak of this, people often say this age difference is similar to that of a father and daughter. No doubt it seems awkward in today's day and age, but it carries a lot of benefits. In Sanskrit, the husband is called '*Pati*', and the father is called '*Pita*'; both these words originate from the same etymology. '*Pita*', or the father, cannot provide sexual nourishment to his daughter, whereas the husband can. So the husband or '*Pati*' is supposed to be a fatherly figure who can sexually nourish the female. When they are of the same age, or with marginal differences, the deterioration is equal and simultaneous; none of them is nourished. Due to the equality of age, knowledge, and earning ability of the wife, she seldom treats her husband with respect. They are more like friends, the relationship becomes one of 'give and take.' In such a relationship, love weakens easily. Perhaps that is why the rishis of India had recommended such a difference in age.

Devotee: Why did Jesus advocate monogamy, and was against divorce, and yet there is provision for divorce laws everywhere? [268]

Sri Sri Thakur: It is for the simple reason that monogamy begets good children. To sustain the growth and healthy upbringing of children, divorce or separation of parents is a peril. Divorce is always a civil adjustment. Divorce laws in various countries are legal sanctions to commit debauchery. Children that are born after divorce are condemned to ill-fated progeny.

Sri Sri Thakur on divorce:
> *Lust longs for divorce,*
> *divorce makes people unchaste*
> *the unchaste assemble and look for liberty—*
> *the liberty that liberates debauchery—*
> *Satan smiles there, and molested love*
> *looks to heaven with fear.*
>
> *(The Message, vol. VII)*

Narrator: The Bible says: "And I say unto you, whoever divorces his wife, except for sexual immorality, and marries another, commits adultery; and whoever marries her who is divorced commits adultery."

The English poet and novelist, Alfred Alvarez (1929-2019), wrote, 'Divorce and suicide have many characteristics in common with one crucial difference: although both are devastatingly public admissions of failure, divorce, unlike suicide, has to be lived through.' (*Life After Marriage*, 1962)

A similar view has been expressed by American novelist Erica Jong (b. 1942) when she wrote: 'There is a rhythm in the ending of a marriage, just like the rhythm of a courtship—only backward. You try to start again but get into blaming over and over. Finally, you are both worn out, exhausted, and hopeless. Then lawyers are called in to clean the corpses. The death occurred much earlier.' (*How To Save Your Own Life*, 1977)

Devotee: When one of the partners is neglected and tortured, there is no alternative but to stay apart. What else to do? [269]

Sri Sri Thakur: Love demands patience. Does any scripture suggest deserting a beloved when marital relations get complicated due to misunderstandings? No, never. True love never commits any harsh deed against a beloved; for love flows with total compassion and binds the beloved with an immortal adherence.

Devotee: Don't you approve of divorce even when conjugal life is hell and a curse for the children? [270]

Sri Sri Thakur: Physical separation in cases of extreme incompatibility can be accepted as a last resort to relieve conflict and sorrow. Yet I believe, divorce is an awful insult to humanity, especially to the progeny. It decreases the sentimental greed for life and makes them uncharitable. It is a filthy morale that scatters in the environment, a sin, the satanic solution that deprives the existence of Godliness.

Devotee: Should people remarry after divorce? [271]

Sri Sri Thakur: It should be a conditional exception, where all the parties involved must vow to amend their earlier wrongs. In any society where divorce persists and makes the marital relationship unrighteous, upon remarriage the partners must cleave together with love for each other and for the Ideal. They must strive to mould themselves with forbearance, sympathy, and understanding in happiness, sorrow, and suffering. Furthermore, they should keep their children from repeating the same mistake as their parents; they should be brought up idealising the institution of marriage.

Devotee: Why do differences and misunderstandings arise in marriages, resulting in divorce? [272]

Sri Sri Thakur: There are three root causes: sex complex, money mentality, and egoistic tendency. The prime suspect is lust. Undesirable rapacity for money destroys the clarity of the mind and conscientious decision-making. When the ego of the wife is hurt, she becomes furious; mutual hate and an inferiority complex drives the couple to the gates of hell.

Devotee: In some cases, the wife prefers to stay at her parents' home. How do you look at this phenomenon? [273]

Sri Sri Thakur: When absolutely necessary, she may do so; however, her appropriate place always lies in the husband's or his family's abode.

Devotee: Sir, you say divorce is awful, but what about the remarriage of a widow? [274]

Sri Sri Thakur: In the past, marriages in Indian society were arranged between boys and girls at a very early age, and if the boy died and the girl did not know her husband in person, she could marry again. However, if a widow with children remarries, the marriage may not be compatible, and there is a risk of losing the affection of her children.

Devotee: After a child is born, when and how does it start learning? What is the role of a mother in this process? [275]

Sri Sri Thakur: A child's learning begins before the age of ten. These are matters of psychoanalysis, and the science of eugenics. The mother is the first teacher of the child, and hence we find it is greatly attached to the mother; this is called the 'subject of tension.' Learning from a mother arouses a receptive attitude in the child; however, motherhood imposes a difficult task on the lady who has given birth to a child. Poet Ramaprasad (Bengali) aptly said, 'Is motherhood a small matter? Only begetting does not make a mother.' The child learns almost everything from his mother, habits of cleanliness like brushing the teeth, use of the lavatory, regular bathing, hygienic way of consuming food, and not using the items of others like towels, plates, and bed sheets. It also learns about cutting hair and nails regularly, etc. The child asks many questions of his mother and believes the answers she gives. Unless she knows the proper answers, she should not bluff, but find the proper answer to satisfy the child. In short, mothers should be careful, vigilant, and enduring.

Devotee: When a child grows up, what are the prominent complexes in his character? [276]

Sri Sri Thakur: A man's character is shaped according to the prominence of one of the four complexes, or a combination of them. To put it in a simple manner let's first discuss the Oedipus Complex; it manifests in the form of attachment of the child to its mother. The next is the Narcissus Complex, manifesting in self-love, self-confidence, and self-respect without a trace of any inferiority complex. The third is the Homosexual Complex; its positive aspect is man's sense of social service. It has other negative aspects as well. The fourth is the Hetero-sexual complex: this is expressed in the attraction between men and women, and love and understanding in conjugal life; it has many perversions also. Even if all the complexes are present in every human being, one of them is very prominent. If you watch a man's actions and behaviour, you can easily know which is salient. Before dealing with anybody, if you can comprehend his complex, it will be easier for you to win him over.

Devotee: How to know the lineage and heredity of a person?[277]

Sri Sri Thakur: A man with a good ancestry invariably takes interest in the upliftment of the self vis-a-vis others, but a man of a poor genealogy is self-centred and susceptible to passionate cravings, which ultimately ruins him. Heredity should not be confused with social status. A man with a high social status may have a low clan lineage, and reversely a socially insignificant man may be very good by birth. If you look deep into a man's character, you will know where he comes from.

Sri Sri Thakur on the science of good heredity:
Character
with adherence,
allegiance and active service
efficient compassionate urge,
with a farsighted view,
conscientious consideration
and valorous go—
are the simplest signs of a man
of good heredity. (The Message, vol. VII)

Devotee: Can a man of low heredity be upgraded? [278]

Sri Sri Thakur: This is possible only when he makes the Ideal the centre of his life, and surrenders to Him. Whatever was ugly within him, transforms itself into grace and dignity. On the other hand, no matter how scholarly or erudite a person may be, if his knowledge is not used for fulfiling others, it ends up like the cosmetic makeup of a widow. When a so-called foolish fellow devoted to his parents and the Ideal becomes an emblem of glory for society and mankind, he is adored by all.

Narrator: A popular anecdote from the life of Saint Ravidas (1450-1540): Ravidas was born into a cobblers' family. He had no interest in studies and spent most of his time with Acharya Ramananda, his Guru later. To improve his son's acumen, his father, who had a shoe shop in the town, taught him how to make and repair shoes. In due course, Ravidas took over the management of the shop during the absence of his father. In the shop, he was so absorbed in chanting the name of Hari that customers used to cheat him left, right, and centre. The father, out of disgust, threw him out of the shop. Ravidas then left his home and stayed in the ashram of Acharya Ramananda. He was initiated and with his earnest devotion acquired many spiritual powers about which he did not have the slightest knowledge. To earn his livelihood, his friends arranged a separate shop for him in the market. Within a short time, he did very well for himself, for the simple reason that he would accept whatever the customer paid for a new pair of shoes, or for repairing old ones. So poverty never left his side, but he used to cure people suffering from many afflictions miraculously. Once a pandit on his way to the Ganges river came to collect the shoes he had given for repair the previous day. Ravidas gave him a copper coin and said, 'Panditji, put this coin on my behalf in the holy waters of Mother Ganga.' As soon as the Pandit did so, a splendid hand emerged with a golden bangle, and a voice was heard: 'Give it to my son, Ravi, on your way back.' Panditji was stunned and puzzled. Greed overpowered him. He thought he would get much money and property by selling the precious bangle, and that Ravidas or anybody else would not know about it anyway. He sold the bangle to a goldsmith, and eventually, it reached the queen. She was very fond of it and constantly pestered the king, 'Get me one more to make a lovely pair.' The king tried to get a similar bangle from the best goldsmith in his kingdom, but nobody could make one with the same elegance. He searched for the source of the bangle. The pandit was traced. The king came to know that it was a divine offering from Mother Ganga to Ravidas in exchange for a coin. Ravidas was summoned. He humbly refused any royal patronage. The king was kind, and since the queen wanted another similar bangle at any cost, he decided to visit Ravidas' shop. His presence attracted a huge crowd. The king begged Ravidas with folded hands, 'O Great man, the queen is hell-bent on having a similar bangle as offered by Mother Ganga.' Ravidas now knew the whole story. He took another copper coin from his small cash box, threw it into a wooden water tub used to dip shoes to soften the leather, and said, 'O Mother, you are omnipresent in all water. Give me one more bangle so that I can please the king and the crowd will disperse.' An elegant hand with a similar golden bangle appeared. The king was pleased and asked the saint, 'How could you do it so easily?' Saint Ravidas replied, 'When the mind is pure, we realise Mother Ganga even in dirty water.' (*Man changa to kotouti me Ganga*). Saint Kabir had praised Ravidas for his steadfast and assiduous devotion to his guru.

Devotee: A couple has five children but everyone is dissimilar. Why is it so? [279]

Sri Sri Thakur: The mental plane of the father and mother at the time of union determines the character of the child to a large extent. I have heard about a couple that witnessed a theatrical play on Sri Chaitanya and were deeply moved. At home, they talked about it and went into union. The lady gave birth to a child highly receptive to devotional songs (*bhajan*). On the contrary, if a couple unites with bestial thoughts, the child will inherit that tendency.

Devotee: I have seen fathers thrashing their children to discipline them. Is it good? [280]

Sri Sri Thakur: No, not at all. It badly affects the child's ego. If it is continuous, the child becomes obstinate. The love of parents inspires the child to learn more and more. No matter if the child is a little disobedient; talk to it about the greatness of your ancestors, and of the Ideal, provide him with books that have simple narrations of the Ideal's behaviour, and his personality will be sublimated.

Devotee: Nowadays, husband and wife both work outside the home. What do you think of this? [281]

Sri Sri Thakur: We have become spendthrifts and conscious of our social status. The traits of simple and frugal living are fast disappearing. When the mother goes out to work, she leaves the house in a shambles, and eventually, it is the children who suffer.

Narrator: Mother Teresa (1910-1997) said: "Everybody seems to be in such a terrible rush, anxious for greater development and greater riches and so on, that children get very little time from their parents. Parents have very little time for each other either, and in the home begins the disruption of the peace of the world." (*Living Thoughts of Great People*)

Devotee: Instances of the negligence of parents by their children are increasing. It is also seen that the woman cares for her grown-up son more than her husband. What are your views? [282]

Sri Sri Thakur: If you neglect your parents in their old age, your children will definitely do the same to you. Moreover, you deprive yourself of an integrated character, and a lady who ignores her husband in favour of the son, loses both in the long run.

A few lines from Sri Sri Thakur in this regard:
At his beck and call she serves,
Pleases the son on all counts
Careless for her life's mate
She pushes the progeny down the gutter,
Restless tumult is her fate.

11

REBIRTH, LIFE AFTER DEATH, COMMUNICATION BETWEEN THE LIVING AND THE DEAD, ASTRAL BODY, GHOST CLAN, OBSEQUIES RITES (*SRADDHA*) AND LIBATION (*TARPAN*), MEMORY CONSCIOUSNESS, PAST LIFE RECOLLECTION AND REGRESSION-VIPASSANA, INTUITION AND CLAIRVOYANCE

Devotee: How does rebirth take place? [283]

Sri Sri Thakur: I think rebirth takes place in the same circumstances and astrological position in which one departs. If we reverse the astrological positions in one's horoscope, we can discern the reality of a previous life. However, for this, one should know the exact point of reversion.

Devotee: I heard of an incident: one night, before falling asleep, a couple was having a sentimental discussion about a close friend's demise, and they mated thereafter; the soul of the dead friend landed in the woman's womb. With his past life's memories intact, he could be identified. Is this really possible? [284]

Sri Sri Thakur: Yes, it is possible. Our scriptures prescribe a peaceful lonely place for the union of the couple, so the soul is not disturbed by other impulses while entering the womb.

Devotee: What happens to the soul after death? [285]

Sri Sri Thakur: The soul remains in the astral or causal body. It is so fine, even fire cannot burn it. For example, when any liquid turns to a gaseous state and becomes vapour, we only see its form. The astral body is composed of a similar fine matter; it is also called the Ectoplasmic body.

Devotee: Is it only for humans or all beings? [286]

Sri Sri Thakur: I think whatever happens in the case of humans, also happens to trees and plants, dresses, clothes, utensils, and bricks. It makes me believe that after death the ectoplasmic human body can wear astral clothes, and even eat something that is possible to consume in such a state. All these questions are normal: what exists after death, what one does and thinks, how does he live? Man is a conglomeration of ideas; after death, he lives in the astral body with the impression of ideas at the time of death. It may be pleasant or painful.

Narrator: Here is an interesting episode about the love affair between George Bernard Shaw in his ectoplasmic body and Ms Patricia: She was a Canada-born English writer and novelist who met the famous playwright, Shaw, in a hotel near a lake in Ireland. They fell in love with each other. After some years, in 1950, Bernard Shaw passed away. She claimed that after his death, Bernard Shaw used to come to her apartment in his ectoplasmic body. Over course of time, both of them developed a special set of syllables to communicate with each other. Ms. Patricia called him by his nickname, 'Berni.' According to her, they got married after Shaw's death. He presented her with a special ring that shone on one of her fingers. She claimed that she became the mother of a son from Bernard Shaw even ten years after his death. According to her, whatever she has written was inspired by Bernard Shaw. She described that there was a large photograph of Bernard Shaw in her bedroom in a dark corner. He used to appear there and communicate with her in the dim light of a lamp. She disclosed all these facts when she was 46. *(Pitru Purush*—Hindi/Odia*)*

When we read this episode, we remember Sri Sri Thakur often quoting the Shakespearean dialogue in *Hamlet*: 'There are more things in heaven and earth, Horatio, than are dreamt of in your philosophy.'

Devotee: If a man is an aggregate of ideas why does he hanker to have material possessions? [287]

Sri Sri Thakur: Man is born with a physical body. With his physical body, he encounters his surroundings; the mother being the first subject he sees. Over time, impulses from the mother, and his surroundings are recorded in his brain. Hence, the aggregate of ideas comes to life to fulfil the self through the surroundings.

So life is a continuous process of transforming abstract ideas into material manifestations.

Sri Sri Thakur continued with a smile, "I have given and shall go on giving messages and dictums, both in prose and poetry, on various subjects concerning life. At the moment, they are ideas. One day or the other they will be analysed and applied for their relevance in society, only then ideas will transform into material manifestations. He chuckled and exclaimed, it may so happen that in my next birth, as a student I would be asked to go through these ideas and explain them. If I fumble, the teacher may beat me. Am I taking all this trouble to be beaten up in my next life?"

Devotee: How does the ectoplasmic body carry ideas? [288]

Sri Sri Thakur: At the time of death, the deepest impression becomes prominent and the link to all other impressions gets disconnected. The deepest impression with which a person dies continues to be with him after death, in the ethereal mind. This ethereal impression determines the next birth. The soul searches for a homogeneous thought-platform for its rebirth. To some extent, you can compare it with wireless photo-transmission.

Devotee: What does the astral body do with the deepest ethereal impression? [289]

Sri Sri Thakur: It does what it desires to do. Suppose the deceased loved someone very dearly, but did not approve of some of their activities. Now, in the ethereal plane, the same thing happens. Before death, you asked your wife to fetch a glass of water, but before she could bring it, you departed and the thirst remained. You will feel the pain of thirst in your ethereal existence in the same way. When you are very happy at the time of passing, the same feeling persists on the ethereal plane and vice versa. For this reason, to keep the mind calm and cheerful, religious scriptures are read, and devotional songs are played near a departing soul.

Narrator: This is an account of the After-death-experience (ADE) of Bertrand Russell, conveyed through the testimony of an expert soul communication medium, Rosemary Brown, "You may not believe that it is I, Bertrand Arthur William Russell, who is saying these things, and perhaps there is no conclusive proof that I can offer through this somewhat restricted medium. Those with an ear to hear may catch the echo of my voice in my phrases, the tenor of my tongue in my tautology; those who do not wish to hear will no doubt conjure up a whole table of tricks to disprove my retrospective rhetoric.

"After breathing my last breath in my mortal body, I found myself in some sort of an extension of existence that held no parallel as far as I could estimate in the material dimension. I observed that I was occupying a body predominantly bearing similarities to the physical one I had vacated forever; but this new body in which I now reside seemed virtually weightless and very volatile, and is able to move in any direction with minimum effort. I began to think I was dreaming and would awaken all too soon in that old world, of which I had become somewhat weary to find myself imprisoned once more in that ageing form that encased a brain that had become exhausted, and did not always want to think when I wanted to think.

"Several times in my life [Lord Russell continued] I had thought I was about to die; several times I had resigned myself with the best will I could muster, so I could cease to be. The idea of B. R. no longer inhabiting the world did not trouble me unduly. Befitting, I thought, to give the chap (myself) a decent burial and let him be. Now here I was, still the same I, with the capacities to think and observe sharpened to an incredible degree. My earthly life suddenly seemed very unreal, almost as if it had never happened. It took me quite a long time to understand that feeling, until I realised at last that matter is certainly illusory although it does exist in actuality; the material world now seemed nothing more than a seething, changing, restless sea of indeterminable density and volume." (*The Intelligence of The Cosmos*)

The after-death experience of Victor Solow, filmmaker, USA: Victor Solow, in his 56th year, was reported to have died from cardiac arrest in 23 minutes. A team of doctors declared him dead, but a last desperate attempt, however, achieved the improbable, and he regained consciousness for one last time. Here is what he said about what had happened to him when he died:

"For me, the moment of transition from life to death was easy, no time for fear, pain or thought...I was moving at a high speed towards a net of great luminosity...vibrating with tremendous cold energy, as I found myself in a grid. The sensation was neither pleasant nor unpleasant, but completely consuming, an experience of transforming from the form into formlessness, beyond time and space. Now I was not in a place, nor even in a dimension, but rather in a condition of being. This new 'I' was not the I that I knew, but rather a distilled essence of it, yet something vaguely familiar. This 'I' had no connection with ego; it was final, unchangeable, indivisible, indestructible, pure spirit. 'I' was part of some infinite harmonious and ordered whole. I felt I had been there before...

"When resuscitated, a tough period followed, I could not connect to the world around me... it seemed that by chance I had been given this human body and it was difficult to wear...Was I really here now, or was it an illusion? Was the other condition of being I had just experienced the reality, or was that the illusion

"A recurrent nostalgia remains for that other reality, that condition of indescribable stillness and quiet, where the 'I' is part of a harmonious totality. Memory softens the old drives for possession, approval and success...I am glad I am here and now. But I know that this marvellous place of sun and wind, flowers, children and lovers, this murderous place of evil, ugliness and pain, is only one of the many realities through which I must travel to distant and unknown destinations." (Victor Solow, *"I died at 10.52 am"*, *Reader's Digest*, October 1974)

The Devotee: Suppose an adept had reached a high level of proficiency in some sphere; can he enhance it through the astral body? [290]

Sri Sri Thakur: No. To go to a superior state of consciousness, beyond what he has achieved, he has to come back again, and take refuge in a physical body.

Devotee: Do you believe in ghosts, Sir?[291]

Sri Sri Thakur (4-1-1942): I don't know what a ghost is. But I remember an incident from my boyhood in Hemayetpur. A little bit away from my home, near the residence of Prasanna Singh, there was an enormous *Sahada* tree, adjacent to a narrow path, leading to an open field, and a jungle thereafter. We have heard ghosts lived there. One afternoon, to get rid of the fear of ghosts, a few of us boys started to beat the trunk of the tree with strong staves. Suddenly, a big boulder came from the air and fell near us. A while later, it was followed by another, but nobody was hurt. We made a thorough search for the miscreant in the area around, but there was no one to be found. On another occasion, I was surrounded by a group of devotees, opposite the Chemical Works Building of the ashram, and someone among the group told us about a ghost menace in the house of one Badal Bairagi. When the discussion was gathering momentum, some stones fell close to us as if from nowhere. Obviously, no ashramite could have dared to do so. Hence, I say, not only ghosts, but so many things happen in our lives, the causes of which we do not pursue, nor observe astutely to fathom.

Narrator: Paramhansa Nigamananda Saraswati (1880-1935), a revered saint of eastern India, held that ghosts are altogether a different species of fine beings, not visible to the human eye. When they are hurt or dissatisfied, they may harm human beings. They prefer to stay in dilapidated houses, trees overspreading with thick foliage, and jungles. They marry, beget children, and of course, die. They stay as a family, with their wife and children, in their own society. We exist in a holistic form, but there are so many others who exist simultaneously with us in extremely fine or semi-fine forms. It is only natural. We cannot see them with our eyes. In the old days, people used to worship ghosts as the goddess of the graveyard *(Masanichandi, Yaksha* and *Yakshini).* By pleasing them, the worshipper could utilise their powers for beneficial or harmful acts. *(Sri Sri Thakur Nigamananda)*

Devotee: While performing obsequies, cooked food and water is offered to the departed soul. But if the soul cannot consume it, why do we offer them? [292]

Sri Sri Thakur: Suppose you offer some food to your loved one, and if he relishes it, you feel content. This is a similar case. The soul of the departed is always in tune with his close kith and kin, like son, grandson, etc. When they offer him food, and think about the departed, the soul derives a fine satisfaction in consonance with his astral existence.

Devotee: What is the purpose of obsequies? [293]

Sri Sri Thakur: The departed soul during his lifetime was loved by his progeny, by other near and dear ones, friends and admirers, etc. In his physical absence, when his good qualities are remembered and talked of, he derives a sense of fulfilment, solace and peace. When the near and dear talk of the love, kindness, compassion, and fellow feelings of the departed soul, their minds and heart gets cleansed as well. That is why the provision of feeding only these people is provided for in the Hindu scriptures. No big feast is organised because one is not sure whether someone in a mass gathering may talk ill of the dead, which would hurt the departed soul. A particular number of scholarly Brahmins are also fed as part of the obsequies.

Devotee: On completion of the mourning period, male members with direct blood lineage get themselves tonsured. Why? [294]

Sri Sri Thakur: On the death of a member, the whole family is disturbed and depressed. During this period almost all the relatives gather in the house of the deceased. They console and comfort the bereaved to bring them out of their depression. Tonsuring, I think, has physiological effects; perhaps the head in its clean-shaven form is able to absorb sufficient ultraviolet rays to help reduce the agony of the bereaved. Similarly, the prescription of tonsure as a religious rite is to remind the practitioner to strictly follow the discipline without any compromise.

Devotee: What is the motive behind water-libation (*Tarpana*) to the departed and the ancestors? [295]

Sri Sri Thakur: For Hindus, it is a daily practice. By doing it, we remember our forefathers, and their benevolent character. In doing so, we remember their noble qualities and in effect get an impetus to mould our own characters.

Devotee: It is believed in India that if the obsequies are performed in Gaya city, the liberation (*moksha*) of the departed soul is ensured. Is this true? [296]

Sri Sri Thakur: In Sanskrit, the meaning of the word 'Gaya' is knowledge, recapitulation of noble acts. The geographical location of the city is believed to be filled with vibrations from the cosmos. Indicatively, it is described as a place sanctified by the lotus feet of Lord Vishnu; a place congenial to freedom from the bondage of all passions. Whoever goes there is charged with divine feelings and vibrations, and when he remembers the departed, it resonates with their soul. Don't you know how hypnotism works? If you are hypnotised by looking at a button, you get the same effect even after fifteen years by simply glancing at a button without the hypnotiser. These are vibrations that cannot be proved by arguments, but can be felt. Along with the remembrance of the departed, you remember Lord Vishnu; it facilitates the integration of the ectoplasmic body with the protoplasmic body at the time of a soul's rebirth in that body. I think the lotus feet of Lord Vishnu symbolise the transcendence of our inner selves to a higher level.

Devotee: How to avoid rebirth on this planet? [297]

Sri Sri Thakur: One has to come back to Earth again and again to complete his *karmic* obligations; Every action, good or bad, has its own effect. Accordingly, you enjoy the result of good actions, and suffer for your bad deeds. While doing so, you create new actions and you have to go through its results. Thus the cycle is never-ending. When your action is selfless and you keep yourself unconcerned, you are no longer connected with the results of such an action. This is possible only in the case of realised souls. They come to Earth to perform noble deeds, to guide human beings for emancipation from passions and complexes; they do not expect any return for their good deeds, and so the *karmic* obligations do not apply to them. Life can be compared to a dream. In the dream, you may ride a horse, and visit several places. When the dream is over, there is neither the horse nor any place. Likewise, a soul experiences different states of existence as he desires. For a realised soul, there is no desire. When there is no desire in you, you reach the state of *Nirvikalpa Samadhi*, popularly known as *nirvana* by Buddhists. The birth of such souls on this planet becomes a rarity, unless ordained by Providence to guide humanity to being and becoming.

Devotee: Can the soul travel out of the physical body and come back to it again? [298]

Sri Sri Thakur: I will share with you an experience of my life. One day, while resting in my room I went out of my body. On the road I met the milkman and requested him to do a job for me, then I loitered around, and re-entered my body. The next day, I found that the milkman had done the job according to my instructions. It all happened while I was snoozing. So, I do think, out-of-body travel is possible. However, more scientific research is required in this regard.

Narrator: An anecdote of Sri Sankaracharya's out-of-body travel: Sri Sankaracharya was a great exponent of monism (*Advaita vada*): Absolute is the truth, and the world is an illusion (*Brahma Satya Jagat Mithya*). In ninth-century India, Vedic ritualism (*Karmakanda*) was practised extensively. Pandit Mandan Mishra was an authority on ritualistic knowledge and practice. His wife, Uvayabharti, was also highly learned on the subject.

Sri Sankaracharya, during his all-India tour to propagate

monism, once came to the city of Vidarbha, beside the river Narmada where Panditji lived. At that time, Sankaracharya challenged Pandit Mandan Mishra to prove how the philosophy of Vedic ritualism was superior to Advaita Vada. Both agreed on a duel of arguments over which Uvayabharti would preside to decide the winner. The verbal duel went on for sixteen days in the presence of eminent scholars. Sri Sankaracharya's argument was so logical that Pandit Mandan Mishra was declared defeated.

Before the declaration of the winner, Uvayabharti dared to pose a question to Sri Sankaracharya: "The wife is the better half of her husband. So, in the fitness of things, you shall have to defeat me in debating as well." All the scholars agreed with her. The debate started. The learned Uvayabharti slowly dragged the discussion towards sexology (*Kamashastra*). Sri Sankaracharya was well-known for his aversion to women. Without any experience, he fumbled and asked for an adjournment for two weeks.

On his way back, he saw the funeral procession of King Amruk, who had died of snakebite. In a flash of thought, he decided to enter the body of the dead king to gain all the knowledge about sex. He instructed his close disciples to take care of his lifeless body till he returned. The dead king, to the astonishment of all, rose to life on the bier. The information about the king's resuscitation spread like wildfire in the city; celebrations and joy were all around. The next day, King Amruk resumed his royal duties. The council of ministers observed how the king was more active and prompt in announcing decisions. His knowledge of religion and logic appeared superb, something never seen before. However, they also noticed that the king was not taking any interest in his queens. They thought it might be due to loss of memory regarding conjugal pleasure. Word was sent to the palace of the queens to indulge in eroticism to restore the sexual appetite of the king. It worked. The king was so immersed in love play that he forgot that the soul of Sri Sankaracharya resided within him. As the final days of the second week were inching close, the disciples of the saint thought it would be wise to remind their Guru in the king's body of the debate that was due to be in a few days' time. A disciple went in the guise of a dancer, and with a song, reminded the king about his soul. Thereafter, Sri Sankaracharya left the king's body and entered his own. Now, with practical knowledge of sexology, Sri Sankara took part in the debate with Uvayabharti. After a long duel of words, Uvayabharti admitted defeat before the august audience. Subsequently, Pandit Mandan Mishra and his wife became staunch followers of Sri Sankaracharya.

Devotee: How does the brain function in the ectoplasmic body?[299]

Sri Sri Thakur: Let us think of it this way. Our physique is similar to a radio receiving and transmission unit; impulses from the outside create sensations that the brain records and transmits at every moment. At the time of death, this mechanism collapses totally and takes place on a subtler plane as thought waves. After death, we continue to live in that subtle plane. For easier understanding, let us say that our physical existence is particles of ether and our after-death existence is ethereal waves depending upon the psychical arrangement. We are born as progeny to such a couple, who are akin and congenial to our ethereal vibration.

Devotee: Sometimes we see that the progeny of a noble couple turn out to be wicked and mischievous. How does that happen?[300]

Sri Sri Thakur: It happens when the wife's state of mind fails to come at par with her husband's. The rule of nature is that the tree grows according to the potency of the soil. If the wife does not love and have noble feelings for her husband during consummation, she fails to imbibe in the child the good traits of her husband.

Devotee: Why do good souls generally have a short span of life? [301]

Sri Sri Thakur: Life span or longevity is determined in the mother's womb. It depends on the comprehensive coherence and harmony between the husband and wife at the time of union. It may so happen that they reach an ecstatic level during their consummation, but if the link to that level is weak and fragile, the ecstasy cannot be sustained for long. It has its effect on the soul that arrives afterwards. His life span is cut short, but nonetheless, in most cases, these souls leave behind a distinguished legacy.

Devotee: Death is so painful. If God created man in His own image, why did He make him mortal? [302]

Sri Sri Thakur: Death is no doubt painful; we lose a person from our midst forever. According to the Hindu scriptures, there is existence even after death, but we cannot communicate with the dead. This is agonising, and hence the clamour for immortality in order to conquer death. If we can develop memory consciousness, we can claim to have conquered death to a considerable extent.

Sri Sri Thakur's dictum on this subject:

'Do never die, nor cause death, resist death to death.'

Devotee: How do you think memory consciousness can outrun death? [303]

Sri Sri Thakur: To win over death means to overcome the fear of death. It is possible only when I know the details of my past life, and what corrections I should make in the present one. I call this 'being and becoming.' In the *Bhagavad Gita*, Srikrishna said to Arjuna, "Many many births both you and I have passed. I can remember all of them, but you cannot, O subduer of the enemy." (*Gita*, 4/5)

We are destined to die, but the meek acceptance of this fact is an insult to man's prowess. Victory lies in getting rid of the fear of death. The primary cause of all our miseries is passion-induced activity. When one develops a love for the Divine and the Ideal, he knows the root cause of his misery and does not blame God for it. When we understand that the sufferings of the present life are the effects of evil deeds committed in the past, realisation dawns upon us to refrain from repeating such actions.

Narrator: Swami Vivekananda in his booklet *'Life After Death'* mentions, When you develop memory consciousness you will know that this world is only a dream and a big theatre. Then a sense of detachment will grow tremendously in you, because you shall know how many times you have come to this Earth; how many millions of births you have taken as mother-father-son-daughter-husband-wife-friend and spent your time with power and affluence. How many times you have gone very high and how many times you have been thrown to the abysmal depths of despondency? When your memory will bring all this before you, you will stand as a hero and say: O Death! I do not care about you. How can you frighten me?

Devotee: How can a soul ascend to a higher state of existence on rebirth? [304]

Sri Sri Thakur: We are often obsessed but seldom awakened. When we are awakened, we try to adjust and fit in. For instance, you take a female dog to a pedigree male to be bred, much after its several engagements with stray dogs, what happens then? The female dog in due course gives birth to black, black-and-white, and white pups as usual; because the past impression of its mating with stray dogs continues to remain in her. Similarly, the impressions of our past lives come in the way of our awakening. When we awaken, real observation in the form of realisation begins. In awakening, there is self-surrender. When we accept the Ideal as the guide of our lives and follow him sincerely, knowledge follows its course. We have to obey his commands, we have to nurture him, nourish him and maintain him. When this change takes place in one's life, whether he is a thief, a dacoit, or no matter how pitiful his character may be, the impressions of past lives do not affect him, he becomes exalted and worthy in all aspects of life.

Devotee: Some children have a photographic memory, whereas others are past masters in music; some others are born singers or recite *The Ramayana* from an early age. How is this possible? [305]

Sri Sri Thakur: There is a prerogative for merit and competence. The impressions of our efficiency in a particular field are stored in the form of knowledge. When one dies, he is immersed in the deepest level of that knowledge. That is the sum total essence of all his past life abilities. That is why someone sings very well from childhood, whereas someone else speaks many languages at an early age. So, when we develop our proficiency in a particular aspect in one birth, we carry it to the next. Of course, it is easier for an Ideal-centric person.

Devotee: Some people are memory-conscious. They can recollect the activities of their previous life. How does this happen?[306]

Sri Sri Thakur: We come across a number of such cases. On enquiry, it was ascertained that they are born into ordinary families. It is also found that in their clan, marriages were compatible. I do not think they have undertaken any extraordinary pursuits in their previous life to carry the flow of memory to the next. It appears to have happened in the normal course, but there is something, some link between their past and present which is extraordinary. If we can discover that, all of us can develop such a consciousness.

Narrator: On the basis of newspaper reports, Sri Sri Thakur, in 1939, sent his devotee, Sushil Chandra Basu, to various places in North India to locate the whereabouts of people carrying past-life memories and get their details. Sri Basu collected all the detailed information possible, and reported them to Sri Sri Thakur, and later published a book on the subject in Bengali. We cite a case from that book. The case history of Shanti Devi: Shanti was born in 1925 in Delhi. When she was eight, she told her parents that she had been the wife of Pandit Kedarnath Chowbey of Mathura in her previous life. The location of Chowbey's residence, his business, the name of their son, etc. were described vividly by the young girl, which, on verification, were found to be true. She could even recognise the younger brother of Pandit Chowbey staying in Delhi.

She said that in her previous life her name was Lugdi Devi, the second wife of Kedarnath. She was very fond of her son, Navneet. Both father and son came to Delhi to meet her. On seeing Navneet she embraced him and started sobbing. She gave him all her toys. She was not prepared to leave them, and conceding to her request, the father and the son had to extend their stay at Delhi. By this time, a committee was formed in Delhi to carry on the inquiry. Some members of the committee went with young Shanti and her parents to Mathura when Pandit Chowbey and Navneet returned home. She could recognise the different rooms and small details of the household.

She had recollected her after-death experience (ADE) as follows: Right after my death, I felt pitch darkness, followed by a bright light, just like smoke I was transported out of my body into the air. I started moving upwards; I found four saffron-clad boys coming to escort me in a bowl-shaped vehicle of 15 centimetre radius. They took me to a place that was peaceful with the pleasant light of the full moon. I found different strata. There were no buildings or houses there, but it was a very pleasant place to stay. When I was taken to the first strata, I found it was like a big field with a boundary wall and a gate. Those present said to the escorting boys, 'Her place is in a higher strata. Take her there.' We reached the second strata. I found an empty throne surrounded by males and females, their bodies floating in the form of light. They gave directions to take me higher. In the third layer, I found male and female monks with bodies of brighter light than those in the previous strata. Even they directed me to proceed to the next higher strata. There, I found the king of Dwarka (Lord Krishna) sitting on a throne surrounded by sage-like beings emanating still brighter light. In that strata, everybody is given a report card type document where the actions of their past life and henceforth were written in detail. As of now, I am a devotee of Lord Krishna, and so was I in my past life. When I presented my report card, I was intimated about my next birth as the daughter of my present parents in Delhi. They said this will be my final birth.

In that realm, I found all the existing things were in the form of light; it was all very soothing and enlivening. There was no sectarian division like Hindus, Muslims and Christians; tranquillity prevailed everywhere. I also felt, after this strata, there may be higher places, but I could not gather any information about them. In all the strata, there was absolute silence and no talking. Hunger and thirst were absent. There was no experience of happiness or pain. In my previous life, I had constantly read the *Upanishads*, *Puranas* and the *Bhagavad Gita*. I had almost learned them by heart. After receiving the report, I was taken to a place like a dark narrow lane. My carriers left me there. I found myself lying in a place, surrounded by an obnoxious smell and air. I then took birth. I could remember all this in my mother's womb. I was missing my husband, and my son, Navneet, and was anxious to join them.

In eastern religious orders like Hinduism, Buddhism, and Jainism, reincarnation is accepted as a sojourn of the soul from life to life, but the predominant religions of the West like Christianity and Judaism hold the view that this is the only life for which we will be judged. Reincarnation is incompatible with their way of thinking. Henry Ford (1863-1947), in an interview published in the *San Francisco Examiner*, August 1928, viewed reincarnation as a matter of complete satisfaction. He said: Work is futile if we cannot utilise the experience we collect in one life in the next. When I discovered reincarnation, it was as if I had found a universal plan. I realised that there was a chance to work out my ideas. Time was no longer limited, I was no longer a slave to a clock. Benjamin Franklin (1706-1790) said: "When I see nothing annihilated, not a drop of water wasted, I cannot suspect the annihilation of the soul, or believe that God will suffer the daily waste of millions of minds readymade that now exist, and put Himself to the continual trouble of making new ones." (*The Works of Benjamin Franklin 1856*, Vol. XX.)

Sri Sri Thakur, during his conversations with disciples, hinted that in Buddhist meditation the method to achieve past-life memory can be found. The rebirth doctrine in Buddhism (Tibetan) asserts that after death, rebirth may take place in six realms: *Deva* (heavenly), *asura* (demigod), *manusya* (human), *tiryak* (animals), *preta* (ghosts), and *naraka* (resident of hell), according to the *Karma* or activity of a particular birth. In the Buddhist texts, it is reported that on the night of his enlightenment, Buddha gained the ability to recall his previous lives. It is said that he remembered not just one or two but a vast number of them, with details of what his name, caste, profession, and so forth had been in each. Buddha stated that he could remember at least 91 aeons of his previous lives, one aeon being roughly equal to the lifespan of a solar system.

In Buddhism, the meditation method is called *Vipassana* (Sanskrit). It literally means special seeing or super-seeing. The practice begins with the preparatory stage, *Sila*, the practice of morality, giving up worldly thoughts and desires. The practitioner then engages in *anapanasati*, mindfulness of breathing, to simply watch the breath. Then the practitioner pays attention to any rising mental or physical phenomenon to become aware of how sense impressions rise. The practitioner also becomes aware of the perpetual changes involved in breathing. This understanding leads to insight; thus, the meditation continues. The meditator first explores the body and mind and then develops *Vichara*. From *Vichara*, he develops *jnana*; *jnana* leads to joy which disappears in due course, there is only happiness and concentration left. In concentration, the practitioner develops equanimity, and the desire for freedom takes place.

Sri Sri Thakur has given a system of meditation in which the Holy Name is repeated rhythmically concentrating on a living being (Ideal). We believe that by concentrating on a living entity, the journey of elevation is accelerated. While taking *Sankalpa* (Resolve) of *Swastyayani*, we pray to the Supreme Father to provide memory consciousness.

Apart from persons carrying immediate past-life memory *suo moto*, past-life regression has been made possible by hypnotism. Cases are reported where memories of more than one previous life could be unearthed.

Hollywood actor Glenn Ford (1916 -2006) was hypnotised, and could go back to four previous lives. In his first previous life, he was Charley Bill, a trail boss born in 1855 in Cheyenne, Wyoming. In his second previous life, he was Charles Stewart, teaching piano in Elgin, Scotland. He died in 1840 at the age of 38. In the third previous life, his name was Emile Langevin, a French soldier who lived from 1680 to 1704. In his fourth previous life, he was a sailor on a British merchant ship. He died in 1666, a victim of the great plague of London. It has been verified in history that during that year plague was rampant in London. (*Americans who have been reincarnated*)

This hypnotism technique was also practised in the past ages millions of years ago. An episode from *Yoga Vasistha*, in which Rishi Vasistha tells a story to his disciple, Sri Rama, when he was a young boy.

A long time ago there was a prosperous kingdom, Uttara Pandava, ruled by a virtuous king, Lavana. One day a yogi came to the court of the king and said he would show something extraordinary that he had never seen. Saying so, he raised his eyes at the king, and when their eyes met, the whole world appeared topsy-turvy to the king. He was no more a king, no royal paraphernalia, his court, and the council of ministers had all ceased to be. All of a sudden, everything vanished. He found himself on an erratic horse running at high speed, not amenable to rein. The horse went berserk, crossed the borders of the city, and entered a deep forest. Two days passed, but the cavalier could not bring the horse under control. At night, when the horse was passing through a dense grove with high trees, the cavalier caught hold of a strong branch of a tree and left the running horse. He remained suspended in the air for some time, and with a lot of difficulties managed to touch the ground. After a while, the day broke; the cavalier was extremely hungry and thirsty. He had no energy to proceed; he lay down on the grass looking at the nearby forest path with the hope that some passerby might rescue him. Around noon, from a distance on the narrow jungle path, he saw a woman coming towards him. When she came closer, he found that she was carrying two earthen pots on her head. After a while, the woman came close to him. She was startled and asked with fear and astonishment, 'O! Who are you? You do not seem to be a local.' The cavalier looked at her. She was young, but untidy and ugly. Ignoring her question, the cavalier beseeched her, 'I will tell you all that later but what are you carrying in the earthen pots on your head?' The woman replied, 'My father is a woodcutter, and has gone deep into the forest for firewood. I am carrying food and water for him.' The cavalier pleaded, 'Give me a little water and save my life.' The woman said, 'I cannot do that, sir. You appear to be a person of a high caste. I belong to the lowest class, and by custom, it would be a blemish on my part to touch your food and water. If I give this water to you, I will commit a sin. But if you die out of thirst, the sin will not be mine as I am in no way responsible for it.' Saying this, the young woman resumed her walking. The cavalier desperately shouted, 'O lady! Don't be so cruel. Have pity on a dying man.' The woman stopped, thought for a moment, and said, 'There is only one way out.' The cavalier eagerly asked, 'What is it? Tell me quickly.' The woman looked at the ground coyly, and said in a low voice, 'As such, I am in no hurry to marry, and clearly am not fascinated by you. But if you marry me, you will be converted to our caste, and then I will be able to give you water.' The cavalier instantly looked at the sun and said, 'Let the sun be our witness. I am marrying you here and now.'

The lady gave him water, along with a part of the food that consisted of some stale coarse rice and a piece of roasted dry pork seasoned with salt. The cavalier relished the meal. Now both of them went to her father, and the lady broke the news. The old man said to the cavalier, 'Why did you opt to marry such a wretched and lousy girl?' After dusk, all of them returned to the mud hut of the woodcutter in the forest hamlet. The couple started their worldly life. The cavalier helped the old man to raise crops of grains and pulses on the family land. As time passed, the old man died, and four sons were born to the couple. Three sons were married and left the hamlet to rear their own families and in search of livelihood in distant places. Now the couple was at an advanced age; only the adolescent youngest son was living with them. They were very fond of him. Due to an ongoing drought for three years, there was a severe famine. All the villagers had already migrated to the foothills in search of a better livelihood. The emaciated old cavalier was also compelled to leave the village with his ailing wife and skeletal son. For two days they walked, carrying their baggage on their heads. The little food they brought from home was eaten on the first day itself; for the second day, there was barely any water left in the almost dried-out streams. The young boy had no energy to walk any further due to exertion and hunger. He sat down on a stone near the forest path and pleaded, 'O Father I can't move any more. I long to eat the soft meat of a deer kid. Can you get it for me, Father?' The cavalier with tearful eyes consoled the boy, 'Don't worry, my son. I will go into the forest and fetch the roasted soft venison, but I will keep it near a tree in a leaf bowl. When I call, come and collect it. Don't forget to share it with your mother. I will be going to search for water, and if I am late, ask your mother to keep walking; I will join you later. Saying so, he went deep into the forest with a chopper. He severed his two legs from below the knees, took the soft portions, roasted them in a forest fire, and put them in a leaf bowl, and called his son to collect them. Then he rolled himself to the nearby ravine and slipped down.

The king opened his eyes, and looking confused, asked, 'Where am I? Where am I?' The chief minister standing nearby replied, 'His majesty is very much on the throne. He dozed off only for a while.' The king looked towards the yogi. He was not there; he searched for him but failed. The whole of his past life could be experienced by the king in a fraction of a moment. (*Stories from Yoga Vasistha, Retold*)

Devotee: What is intuition? How to acquire intuitive power?[307]

Sri Sri Thakur: Intuition is the knowledge obtained from experience. Suppose I ask you to cut a branch from a tree, place it before you and ask you to guess the number of leaves on it. Your guess may not be accurate. However, if you go on trying, again and again, you may tell the number to near accuracy. This is your sixth sense. You will achieve better results when you are less dominated by passions and complexes.

Devotee: How to develop clairvoyance?[308]

Sri Sri Thakur: One day, I had a vision of a sailing ship on fire; newspaper reports confirmed it a little later. Our brain is a wonderful mechanism, for it is highly receptive. The more receptive the brain is, the more it can catch finer impulses of incidents from far-off places. The brain's receptivity can be increased by spiritual practice. When the brain receives the finer impulses, the visual centres are excited, and the vision of the incident appears in the inner eye.

Narrator: A psychologist from California, Helen Stewart Wambach, PhD, in her research paper has mentioned a peculiar case of clairvoyance.

She had a student named Sheryl in her abnormal psychology class who, as part of her homework assignment, described a dream. In it, she had seen herself in a car with several fellow students. The car was moving very fast; it missed a curve and crashed. She then saw herself standing above the crash scene, looking with a sense of horror and wonder at her body lying on the road with its head separate. A few months later one of Sheryl's classmates informed Wambach that Sheryl had been in an automobile accident in which she had been killed. Her head had been partially severed from her body. (*Americans who have been reincarnated*)

Devotee: What is telepathy?[309]

Sri Sri Thakur: One morning, I found that the tobacco for my hookah had finished. In my mind, I thought of somebody to go and fetch some more. After a while, a devotee came to me with a packet of tobacco, although nobody had asked him to do so. This happens due to mental tuning. The wave which is released from a wireless transmitting centre is received by another centre in tune with the parent centre.

12

MIRACLES, SCIENTIFIC ANALYSIS, AND THE COSMOS

Devotee: What is a miracle? [310]

Sri Sri Thakur: When something out of the ordinary happens, we are amazed by its occurrence, and call it a miracle. It does not mean that there is no cause behind the occurrence. Anything that happens around us is the effect of a cause, we have to discover it. I do not know shorthand. When one writes, I look at the signs with awe. It is a miracle to me. As our knowledge expands, and we come to know the causes behind an event, miracles vanish. So I think the concept of a miracle is anti-spiritual; it conveys the idea of ignorance.

Sri Sri Thakur in *Magnadicta*:
*Miracle, mercy or might-monging
is the indolent,
weakling tenor
of ignorance
that may dupe one
to the dogs
without imparting sincere, tenacious adherence
to righteousness
That zeals character. (Verse 79)*

Devotee: Seeing a patient from a distance, you know the disease he is suffering from. What is the clue behind it, Sir? [311]

Sri Sri Thakur: If the mind is concentrated with sincerity about a particular thing, the sense perception expands, and it works as an instinct. Probably that is what happens to me.

Devotee: There are many instances where you get a flash of the past, present and future of a person merely from his appearance. How do you achieve it, Sir? [312]

Sri Sri Thakur: It is due to *Namdhyan* (meditation by repetition of the Holy Name). Continuous inward repetition of a word activates our nerves. In turn, they excite the brain cells, enhancing their sensitivity and receptivity. Along with this process, single-minded attachment to the Ideal, who is the embodiment of the Name, brings about various aspects of his character, like his love, and his teachings to our mind. We imbibe them in our personality, and the sphere of our understanding expands.

Sri Sri Thakur in *Magnadicta*:
> *More alive the adherence*
> *to the Ideal*
> *more is man*
> *unshocked*
> *and unshaken. (Verse 13)*

Devotee: It appears when you see an animal, you are reminded of a person you know. Conversely, when you look at a person's face, you find a resemblance to an animal. Is this true?[313]

Sri Sri Thakur: Yes, even I wonder what it is, have I gone mad?

Devotee: How to understand vibration in the human body?[314]

Sri Sri Thakur: This is the vital *(pranic)* vibration. In the human body, there are atoms, electrons, protons, etc. Electrons go on throbbing continuously; in effect, emanating from the vital vibration, because of which we are alive. We also have complexes; all these conglomerations of intercellular adjustment can be interpreted in terms of arithmetic.

Devotee: Aditya Mukherjee (son of Late Shyamacharan Mukherjee, ex-secretary, Satsang) a devotee, and a nuclear scientist living in the USA, reported that a current of one-fortieth volt runs in the nervous system of a human being. Is it so?[315]

Sri Sri Thakur: Not only is there current due to the presence of atoms in our veins, its voltage also fluctuates. It happens to all of us. When we see a person, and suddenly try to recall his name, we draw a blank. In most cases, after some time, we remember it. This is due to the fluctuation of voltage in the flow of vital current. Where there is no balance in the flow of our vital current, a man becomes abnormal.

Devotee: How do you define science? [316]

Sri Sri Thakur: I understand science as "See-ence", action through seeing. I have hinted about many scientific truths yet to be discovered. Those are compiled in a book called *Bigyan Bibhuti* (available in many languages). If research is undertaken on the basis of those clues, it might lead to many discoveries. The suggestions given by me are based on my practical observations.

Devotee: You have added a new dimension to Newton's First Law of Motion. What is that Sir? [317]

(Newton's First Law of motion states that if a body is at rest, or is moving at a constant speed in a straight line, it will remain at rest, or keep moving in a straight line at constant speed unless it is acted upon by a force. This postulate is known as the Law of Inertia.)

Sri Sri Thakur: Imagine there is nothing on this Earth except me and a ball. If I roll the ball in a straight line, it will go with the same force, and complete its movement. It will come back to my hand again. It can't go anywhere else. Everything must return to its origin. It is not only in the case of a ball, but everything else as well.

Narrator: Newton is silent about the ultimate fate of the ball in motion, which Sri Sri Thakur has clarified. Further, Sri Sri Thakur has also said that this principle of movement is for all gross and fine entities.

Devotee: In the last world war, the atom bomb created havoc. Can it be diffused? [318]

Sri Sri Thakur: A bomb is a combustible material; it annihilates the target area completely. When such a thing can exist, its antidote also certainly exists. It has to be experimented as to how sodium interacts with uranium. I think Russian scientists have got the clue, but they have kept it a secret. Experiments can be conducted using sound, because Creation started with the vibration of sound.

Narrator: In November 1957, a devotee, Debi Prasad Mukherjee, read out to Sri Sri Thakur a news item from a daily paper that Russia was on the verge of inventing a rocket moving at the speed of light. Sri Sri Thakur enjoined: I have said so long ago. I also added that we can make trains that can move at the speed of light, but I could not find a suitable person to do research in this field. During 1922-23, Sri Sri Thakur told a devotee-scientist, Krishna Prasanna Bhattacharyya, that there is a layer of electricity in the atmosphere, which if tapped, will be able to harvest electricity perennially at a lower cost. Experiments were done by flying kites with silver wire. The kite consisted of points to be charged with electricity. When the kite was flying high in the electric layer, the transmitted current was felt by the hands of the winder. So it was established that there is electricity in the atmosphere, which can be harvested for our use. At that time due to the paucity of funds, the Satsang Ashram could not go for machinery and instruments to carry the experiment forward.

On the directions of Sri Sri Thakur, experiments were also conducted on a wind-driven dynamo, and it was successful. During that time, Krishna Prasanna informed Sri Sri Thakur that some eminent scientists were of the view that as inanimate objects were getting transformed into finer elements, as the distance between the constellations go on increasing, as they appear more and more feeble, in due course of time, Creation would come to an end. Sri Sri Thakur replied, "There is no end to Creation. If one universe is wiped out, another will sprout, that is the law of nature. I don't know what the scientists say, but I see in my own eyes that in the depleting universe with constellations distancing from one another, a new creation sprouts in the form of condensed cosmic energy." On hearing this, Krishna Prasanna was amazed and said, 'Yes, yes, I have read somewhere that scientists have located new constellations between the existing ones.' Sri Sri Thakur nodded, 'Yes, that is it.'

Devotee: You have said that before coming to your mother's womb, you started your journey from an 'unidentified' region, passing through many constellations and arriving at the sun. You stayed there for some time. How is it inside the sun? [319]

Sri Sri Thakur: I felt the same soothing and gentle atmosphere that we have here. The beings residing there are completely different from ours. I cannot describe them to you as there exists no analogy between them and us. I saw many luminous hills. They appeared to be real and positive. In them, there were deep pits beyond imagination. The solar atmosphere is dynamic like ours; there are plants and trees. Had there been very high temperatures, everything inside would have melted. The sun is no doubt torrid, but habitable; inside there are places as pleasant as the springs here on Earth. There are also places with excessive heat. I found many spots bringing delight and bliss to the mind when I stepped in there.

Devotee: Will the sun die out someday? [320]

Sri Sri Thakur: I don't think so. There is a mechanism in the sun that replenishes the amount of heat energy it radiates immediately. The sun has two motions; it rotates as well as revolves. The sun and the entire solar system revolve around the centre of our galaxy, the Milky Way. Because it rotates, electromagnetic waves are created by induced friction. The incidental rays of the sun on our planet are reflected back to the sun. The sun itself is a reflector. The Earth receives energy from the sun and restores it back to the sun. We have a summer solstice (northward movement), as well as a winter solstice (southward movement). The effects of the sun's rays are different in these two periods. In a regulated and balanced way, the stars and planets exchange their rays. So many stars are simultaneously revolving along with the sun, but they never collide, in which case they would have gone still farther from each other. That is due to cosmic symmetry.

Devotee: Where did the moon come from? [321]

Sri Sri Thakur (on 24-12-1964): I think a star was once passing very close to the Earth. Its tremendous pull of attraction pulled out a portion of the Earth that became the moon, and the huge torn-off area on the Earth's surface is now the Pacific Ocean. One night, I continuously looked at the moon, and it brought forth so much inertia and stagnation in me, I felt as if I would lose consciousness any moment. Suddenly, I found myself on the moon. The side of the moon facing the sun is illuminated, and the other side is dark and glaciated. On the borderline, there is life. I saw wide roads, arches, and gateways; walking is very easy there. With one jump, you can reach the top of a mountain. The trees are very high, slim and smooth, and so also are the mountains. (Scientists have calculated that the gravitational force of the moon is one-sixth that of the Earth).

Devotee: What about Mars? [322]

Sri Sri Thakur: Mars is nearest to our planet. Its inhabitants have been trying to establish contact with us by sending continuous messages, but as our science is not so advanced, we are unable to receive or reciprocate.

Devotee: Have you been there? How do you know all this, Sir? [323]

Sri Sri Thakur: Yes, yes. I have been there. I stayed there. I mingled with them and talked with them as I am doing with you now.

Devotee: How are they? How is the atmosphere? [324]

Sri Sri Thakur: The facts of that planet are so dissimilar and discordant with ours. The nature of existence is so different, their description is humanly impossible. When I was there, I became like them, when I am here I am like you. They are well advanced in science. When our science develops to match theirs, we can communicate with each other.

Devotee: How do we send messages to them? [325]

Sri Sri Thakur: We can send messages through the ether layer, by a developed wireless mechanism that can be deciphered by them. That is why I have been talking about a universal language. Can't we invent a mechanism to record the voices of various animals and birds, and from that derive common alphabets to create a language through which we can communicate with them? If we are successful in this experiment, we can think of having a common language between the habitants of two or more planets.

Devotee: Is there life on other stars and planets? [326]

Sri Sri Thakur (on 28-3-1942): I have a dwelling place everywhere, not only on this Earth but in all planets, stars, and even in the Milky Way. A seer gets an inkling of all these in deep meditation; not in an abstract manner, such as whatever is there in the universe is also present in the tiny cells of an atom, but in reality. Those places do exist; we can move there, live there, and roam there. When our science develops to that extent, I am certain we will establish contact with them.

Narrator: In 2012, scientists confirmed the detection of the long-sought Higgs boson, also known by its nickname the "God Particle", at the Large Hadron Collider (LHC), the most powerful particle accelerator on the planet. This 'God particle' signals an invisible energy field present throughout the universe that fills other particles with mass. The research was carried out by the European Council for Nuclear Research (CERN), Geneva, assisted by many nuclear research centres of the world, including BARC and TIFR of India.

Sri Sri Thakur had spoken about this 'God Particle' almost a hundred years ago, in the first quarter of the last century. He called it "Chid-Anu." He explained how this God Particle (Chid Anu) was created, and how it provides mass to other particles. In verse. 17 of *Bigyan Bibhuti,* He says, "This Brahma manifested. By the attraction and repulsion of the primary element, by its coruscation, different varieties of fine and gross matters are created in this process from Chid-Anu to sub-atom, and then to atoms, and finally to particles which find expression in the formation of matter."

Devotee: Do you think a synthesis of science and spiritualism is possible? [327]

Sri Sri Thakur: First, you must keep your hereditary distinctiveness intact. You must be ready to follow the Supreme

Being of the age, and practise *Jajan, Jaajan, Istavriti* and *Swastyayani* with all earnestness.

Narrator: Swami Vivekananda said, 'Live for an Ideal, and that one Ideal alone. Let it be so great, so strong that there may be nothing else left in the mind, no place for anything else, and no time for anything else.' (*Upanishads in Daily Life*)

PART FOUR

13

SOME OF HIS DIVINE TIDINGS—HEMAYETPUR ASHRAM

(1). I hear you

Sri Sri Thakur was sitting on the veranda of Yati Ashram. In Sanskrit, 'Yati' means Rishi. A householder in their spiritual practice leaves their home for a particular period to undertake rigorous meditation in a secluded place. At that time, there were six such practitioners. There was an ongoing discussion about *Sadhana*. Suddenly, Thakur looked at one devotee by the name Harinandan Prasad and said, "I am the best fulfiler of Sri Ram, best fulfiler of Sri Krishna, best fulfiler of Buddha, of Jesus Christ, of Hazrat Muhammad; and what not!" He said lyrically:

"Whenever you shout
I hear you.
Whenever you call
I will appear with you."

Harinandanda asked, "Why not before you?"

Sri Sri Thakur replied, "Yes, it may happen when the situation demands so." (*Alochana,* Feb-Mar 1997)

(2). *When you call, I listen and come*

The infant Anukul started walking in his seventh or eighth month after birth; he could, to everyone's surprise, even talk a little at that age. In the nearby village of Haripur, lived Umesh Chandra Lahiri, a close friend of the family. Mother Manmohini Devi visited their house when little Anukul was about 10 months old. Umesh Chandra was an ardent devotee of Sri Gopaljew (Lord Krishna in his childhood) and performed the rituals with utmost sincerity. One fine morning after finishing his rituals, he sat in deep meditation in front of Gopaljew. The faint sound of some bickering disturbed his meditation; opening his eyes he saw infant Anukul sitting in the Lord's place quietly smiling. Umesh Chandra immediately called Manmohini Devi to come and get hold of her child. However, this was very disconcerting for Umesh Chandra. The purity of the process had been interfered with; the entire worship space had to be sanctified, and all the rituals had to be repeated, including the *Naibedya Nibedana* (where you request the Lord to come and accept offerings of food and gratitude.)

At last, Umesh Chandra could resume his meditation. After a little while, again there was a disturbance. Umesh Chandra, as if falling from the sky, saw infant Anukul again in the same spot, having dethroned Gopaljew, and sitting there himself. Umesh Chandra was sad, desperate, and angry. He thought, 'What an undisciplined child! It's about to be afternoon, and all my worship has gone in vain.' He loudly called out again to Manmohini Devi, and showed her the nuisance of her son urging her to keep Anukul in check until he had finished his rituals.

Umesh Chandra, with a faint heart, began his rituals for the third time, fearing that constant interruptions might be a bad omen and forerunner of some bad happening. Nonetheless, he reorganised all his worship materials and completed the rituals, and sat down to meditate. The same tinkering sound bothered him again. He opened his eyes and was dumbfounded to see young Anukul had sidelined Gopaljew and was sitting on his throne, smiling. Impatient and furious, he pulled infant Anukul down from the throne and slapped his cheek, saying, 'Why do you repeatedly intrude in my worship today?' Little Anukul, with tears rolling down his cheeks, exclaimed, "Why do you call out to me so many times? When you call, I listen and come."

The resonance of the words of little Anukul's statement reverberated within Umesh Chandra's soul. In meditation, he was calling Gopaljew to manifest Himself. He was in rapture, overcome by a sense of wonder; there were goosebumps all over his body. He called Manmohini for the final time and told her everything. Tears of sheer euphoria and elation rolled down his face. He looked at infant Anukul with folded hands, "Have you finally heard my prayers and come to visit me? Who are you? What are you!" (*Sri Sri Thakur Anukulchandra*[1]).

(3). Memories of Bose Ma (Sushilabala Bose)

Sushilabala Bose, known as Bose Ma later, was Manmohini Devi's neighbour. When she was fourteen years old, she was invited to Manmohini Devi's mother Krishna Sundari's house along with her mother-in-law for infant Anukul's *Annaprassana* (an auspicious Hindu ritual, which marks the first intake of semi-solid food by the child). Infant Anukul was only six months old then. That was the first time Bose Ma had seen him and was filled with so much love that she wanted to take him into her arms and cuddle him. But she had been newly wedded and visiting someone's home for the first time, that too with her mother-in-law, so she had to control herself. Given the circumstances, she thought to herself, 'If only I could take such a beautiful child into my arms!' All of a sudden, baby Anukul started crying. No matter what, his crying wouldn't stop. He was fed his mother's milk. Many neighbourhood women took turns to cuddle him, rubbed his back, and patted his shoulders, but the crying continued. Even in the harsh winter, the continuous crying made little Anukul sweat. Bose Ma, unable to contain herself, said, "May I hold the child for a while, Ma?"

Her mother-in-law agreed. Bose Ma gently asked Manmohini Devi's permission. To everyone's astonishment, little Anukul not merely stopped crying, but even fell asleep in Bose Ma's arms. Everybody asked, 'The mother couldn't stop his sobbing, nor did her milk work; how come this child fell asleep in an instant in your hands? Perhaps in the previous birth, you must have been his mother!' After this event, Manmohini Devi would often leave little Anukul with Bose Ma, saying, "Take care of your son; let me finish my household chores."

Baby Anukul at that time had started crawling. A child who at the time of birth had no hair, now had a head with a lush growth of hair. A beautiful, shining face, with mushy cheeks, akin to that of Bal Gopal (the childhood incarnation of Lord Krishna). Bose Ma would often comb Anukul's hair and make a crown of it at the top of his head, similar to little Krishna's hair bun in paintings. Bose Ma's family garden was full of flowers; before twilight, most of them would bloom. She would make a garland of flowers, and tie it around little Anukul's neck, hands and feet. She would look at him and wonder how the child had so much resemblance with Lord Krishna, except that the colour of his skin was fair. As she thought this while looking at little Anukul, the colour of his face and body would change a little dark, like that of Krishna. This scared Bose Ma; she would be worried and immediately carry the child to the open veranda space with more sunlight. Even there, she could see the child's complexion alternating between fair and dark. The child was still looking at Bose Ma and smiling innocently. She was out of her wits, scared and bewildered. She called out to Manmohini Devi, "Come and see what has happened to your son?" Manmohini Devi came running, and saw little Anukul completely normal, playing on the veranda as usual. She asked Bose Ma, "Why did you have to shout and call out to me like this?" She replied, "What can I say? Such a fair child turned dark in front of my eyes. See for yourself, right there." Manmohini

Devi looked at the child for a while, chuckled faintly, and quipped, "You are quite a character!"

Once, a devotee, Manilal Chakravarty at Satsang Deoghar earnestly requested Bose Ma to tell him a few incidents of Thakur's childhood. Bose Ma complied. 'When Thakur was a toddler, I once placed him on my lap. He would get up and try to slip away. I would pretend to be angry, and pull him back. After a while, I observed that every time I pulled him back into my arms, his body weight would gradually and significantly increase. In no time he became as heavy as a huge rock, and when he sat on my lap, my legs hurt. I was as shocked as I was in pain; my mind stopped working, what should I do? Whom should I call? I couldn't think of anything. When the pain became unbearable, I thought I had made a mistake by being annoyed at our little Lord; now I must make amends and show him some love. I talked to him lovingly and embraced him with affection. After a while, there was a warm smile on the child's face, and the weight of his body slowly decreased.'

This is a story from another day. I was holding little Anukul's hands, and teaching him to walk. I don't know how or when, I must have uttered something in anger to him. I suddenly saw that his height had monumentally increased in seconds, as tall as a coconut tree. His face was not visible to me any longer. I was scared to death. I exclaimed in utter fear, "I can't see you, I am very afraid."

'Listening to my pleas, he came back to his normal size. Then only I took him in my arms and started running. After that day, I made it a point never to be angry with him, even in pretence.'

Bose Ma reared Sri Sri Thakur Anukul Chandra in his childhood as her own son like Yashoda did for Sri Krishna. When Sri Sri Thakur moved from Hemayetpur to Deoghar, she accompanied him. She stayed there along with his family. Once, Sri Sri Thakur told Bose Ma: 'A time will come when many people would like to know about my childhood days from you. You must tell them everything accurately.' (*Kato Katha Monepare*)

(4). Across the Padma River with mother

It was during the monsoon torrential rains, a hail storm was brewing with gusting winds. The Padma was swollen with excess water. One morning, Manmohini Devi with little Anukul in her arms, set out for Kushtia along with her mother, Krishna Sundari Devi. On one side of the Padma lay Hemayetpur, on the other was Kushtia. By the time they returned, it was already evening. They had barely crossed part of the river when suddenly, the intensity of the storm increased with lightning, thunder, and heavy rain. It was uncertain whether the boat carrying them would stay afloat for long. Both the boatmen were scared and unable to control the boat; they jumped into the river. Now, only the three of them were in the rocking and swaying boat—Manmohini Devi, her aged mother, and in her arms the child, Anukul. Both women were devotedly praying "Gurudev.Gurudev.Gurudev." The boat was still afloat. Just then, little Anukul spoke, "Get off the boat right now, Ma, we are all getting down here."

At such a moment of crisis, on Anukul's word, all of them got off. The part of the river they were in was shallow, the great depth of Padma did disappear for a moment. The water was only knee-deep. Cutting through the utter darkness, amidst the furious winds they trudged towards Hemayetpur. The storm was slowly receding. On their way, at some spots, the water was knee-deep, and at other places, it came up to the waist, but their lives were saved. The boat seemed to have floated away to a distance; they could not see it. After a little while, another boat brought them to the shore in Hemayetpur. Manmohini Devi remembered Gurudev and expressed her immense gratitude with folded hands. She and her mother clenched Anukul in her chest, drenched in the rain, and they finally reached home. (*Sri Sri Thakur Anukulchandra*[1])

(5). Meditating on His image

One day, Manmohini Devi inquired of a devotee, Satish Chandra Joyardar, "Why do all of you sit in front of the photo of

Anukul and meditate?" Satish Chandra replied, "We do so because whenever we think of Lord Krishna, or any other gods, we see your son." Upon listening to this, Manmohini Devi asked with satire, "Is it really so?"

On the same day, at lunchtime, Manmohini Devi put leaf plates and bowls on the veranda adjacent to the kitchen, and asked Anukul Chandra and his devotees to sit down. Traditionally, one has to offer the first morsel of food to God. Anukul Chandra had to offer to God his first morsel of food and then the others would start. Instead of doing so, he called his mother and said, 'Why don't you take the first morsel from my plate and offer it to God yourself? Only then I will start eating.' Manmohini Devi was busy in the kitchen, so she shouted out, "I don't have time, do it yourself." But Anukul Chandra insisted, "Ma, if you don't come, I won't feel good. Only after you offer it, will I start eating."

This bizarre insistence of her son astonished Manmohini Devi. She came and sat beside him, and started the ritual (*Nibedan*). When she picked up a handful of food and remembered God, the mental image that surfaced in her inner vision was that of Anukul Chandra. Highly elated, she asked Anukul Chandra on a lighter note, "Do I now also have to eat your leftovers?" Sri Sri Thakur replied, "Why do you say so, Ma? Why would you ever have to eat my leftovers?" Everyone present understood why Sri Sri Thakur had done so. With a sense of communion and happiness, they started eating. Manmohini Devi could now understand why people wanted to meditate in front of her son's photo. *(Sri Sri Thakur Anukulchandra[1])*

(6). A Real Devotee

Sri Sri Thakur was marching with his circle of devotees along the village roads. He strode with big steps, and the company behind had to run in order to keep up with him. Sri Sri Thakur suddenly stopped and stood still; in front of him, there was a large poisonous snake with its hood erect.

Sri Sri Thakur with a smile looked at His devotees, "What do we do now?" The snake was only a couple of feet away from Him. Some devotees who had come a little closer to keep up had now receded into the background. Someone remarked, "The snake is trying to scare and stop our Lord; can a snake really harm God?" However, no one would go near him. Out of nowhere, Sri Sri Borda came running and immediately pulled Sri Sri Thakur a few steps backward.

Later during the after-prayer discussion with Sri Sri Thakur this topic came up; devotees had differing opinions. Sri Sri Thakur listened to them quietly, and remarked, "This is precisely the test to know the character of a devotee." If he sees his Guru in peril, he cannot stay calm, and acts. Hanuman did not leave Lord Ram alone in his hour of need, assuming he is omnipotent. During all his trials and tribulations, Hanuman stood steadfast with him, always ready to assist. (*Satwati, March 2014*)

(7). With Lord Vishnu, face to face

Once at the Hemayetpur house, Sri Sri Thakur was meditating in a room. It was late at night, and all of a sudden, there was a flash of light; an image of Lord Vishnu materialised with His *Shankh* (Conch), *Chakra* (discus), *Gadaa* (Mace), and *Padma* (Lotus) [the four objects seen in each of Lord Vishnu's four hands, symbolic of his responsibility as the guardian of all Creation]. Charged with emotion and elated, Anukul Chandra looked at this divine entity smiling. His eyes were fixed on this magnificent presence of Bhagwan Vishnu, as if someone was actually standing in front of him. There was a strange chill that ran through him; after a long time and after Darshan, Vishnu's presence dissolved away.

Sri Sri Thakur thought to himself, was all this really true? If it was so, then let Him reappear again. And there He was. Sri Sri Thakur was stunned and kept looking at the marvellous figure. This time it also disappeared after a while.

Sri Sri Thakur opened the doors of the house and went outside; it was pitch dark. On seeing the enchanting vision of Vishnu, he was stunned. He wasn't ready to believe what he had seen. He came back in, closed the doors, and prayed as earnestly as he could: "If you truly were Lord Vishnu, please appear before me again." His wish was fulfiled; the figure was there once again.

Anukul Chandra would now plead, "If you have come this time, then please do not leave."

This was not meant to be. The sight of Lord Vishnu faded away after some time. Flabbergasted, Sri Sri Thakur was charged with divine ecstasy, and could not sleep through the night. (*'Mahamanaber Sagar Tire'*)

(8). Far ahead of his time

In October 1945, Sri Sri Thakur suffered from a lung ailment. The efforts of doctors from Pabna and Kushtia had not worked well. Therefore, a renowned cardiologist from Calcutta, Dr. Jagdish Chandra Gupta, was sent for. Apart from his own domain in modern medicine, he was also proficient in Astrology. He studied Sri Sri Thakur's horoscope carefully and said, 'His environment, the epoch that he lives in, is not yet prepared to understand him and give importance to his towering personality. You are way ahead of your time.' With an example, he explained that despite being born as a *Rajarajeshwari* (princess) to a great empire, due to the inappropriate time and circumstances, he would have to live the life of a maid. It will only be long after his departure that the world will come to realise his contributions. In a sense, his arrival on this planet is a rare phenomenon, but due to his advent before His time, he would be a sad man. He would always be miserable in some sense or the other, for his objectives and mission for our society can never be realised in this age. In many ways, his destiny and character are like that of Lord Sri Ram. Among a thousand friends, he is lonesome. This, we may call it, is the tyranny of destiny. *(Sri Sri Thakur Anukul Chandra and Satsang)*

(9). A lively dialogue

At sunset, Sri Sri Thakur was sitting on the bank of the Padma River. Slowly, he was soon surrounded by a circle of devotees. The making of the ashram was in its initial phases; the most important was the construction of the ashram building. Sri Sri Thakur would frequently ask for updates about the progress. Looking at one of the masons approaching him, he excitedly asked,"What's the news? What is the progress?" The mason sarcastically replied, "You don't have the money to pay, but you want all the work done!"

Sri Sri Thakur: "You are right."

The mason: "I went to the office, but they didn't pay me and said, there would be no payment today. On my way out, I have only come here to tell you that I won't come to work from tomorrow."

Sri Sri Thakur: "Have you gone mad or what? Why are you talking like this?"

The mason: "How else should I talk? I come to work so that I can feed my family. If I don't get my wage at the end of the day, why should I work here?"

Sri Sri Thakur: "What kind of madness is this? If someone gives you a lot of cash, can you eat it or feed your people with it?"

The mason: "Why would I chew the money? With it, I would buy rice, dal and other things that I can take home, right?"

Sri Sri Thakur: "So why don't you say so? What do you need? You specify the quantity, we will make arrangements for it. You can manage today with it. If we do not have sufficient money today for your wages, tomorrow you will get some payment. Let us see what awaits us tomorrow. But if your anger dominates your good sense, everything will go in vain."

After listening to Sri Sri Thakur, the mason's anger subsided. He was returning to normal. Sri Sri Thakur could sense the metamorphosis in his temperament and asked, "Could you just look once towards the Padma River?"

Then Sri Sri Thakur asked, "What do you see?" The mason replied, "A dry river bank."

Sri Sri Thakur continued the conversation. "Today the river is dry. But the work cannot stop at any cost, do you understand? Don't worry, tomorrow the tides will come again, and the river will be brimming with water soon, what do you say?"

The mason smiled and said, "That is right, sooner or later water shall indeed come back."

Sri Sri Thakur then asked, "Tell me where pointless anger leads us to? What good ever comes of it? The head gets hot, the body perspires, and work suffers."

The mason replied, "Sir, Your words are so sweet that when one listens to you, he will be happy to carry out your instructions; those people in your office, the way they talk, it hardly takes seconds for anger to shoot up."

Sri Sri Thakur: "Don't allow anger to remain in your head for long. However, never let your mind be completely empty; be careful not to burden it with confusing and stray thoughts."

The mason nodded and said in a pleasant voice, "Tell me, Sir, what am I to do?"

Sri Sri Thakur: "All that is required for your family today—lentils, rice, salt, oil, etc.; make a list with quantity and hand it over to Bankim. He will supply the items. You will go home now, hand over these items, and come back. But the work must be completed before the stipulated time. I would suggest continuing the work at night, too." Now, upon seeing the mason happily walking off, Sri Sri Thakur said to him loudly, "Now do you see your stamina? What incredible inner strength you have! You have worked the whole day, you would go home and deliver all this ration there, and come back soon to start your night shift. I will instruct some ashramites to provide you with light and help. Go ahead."

The mason replied, "Yes, Sir."

Sri Sri Thakur moved up to the walking mason, put his hand

on his shoulder, and affectionately whispered, "This anger was going to create havoc for us a moment ago, wasn't it?"

Listening to Him, the mason chuckled. Sri Sri Thakur chuckled with him, and said, "My mad boy, now go home. Return as soon as you can, I shall be with you tonight."

The mason was apologetic and said, "What can I do, Sir? What is the way out when fury overpowers you?"

In the meantime, Bankim came with a jute bag full of the supplies the mason had asked for and handed it over to him.

The mason was highly pleased and obedient.

To further encourage him, Sri Sri Thakur said, "You are an extraordinary man with immense resilience. You must return soon. As you know, once the tide comes, you will see for yourself, there will be wave after wave."

After the mason had left, Sri Sri Thakur told all the devotees present there in a jovial tone, "Conversation after all is quite a skill. If you can do it right, you can raise the efficiency of a person beyond imagination. Good behaviour overcomes many hurdles."
(Premal Thakur)

(10). Amending human nature

During the monsoon of 1925, the Padma River was in a spate. On one side of the river was Pabna, and on the other, was Kushtia. That evening, there was no rain, the sky was clear, and the stars were visible. Each corner of the ashram was lit up. Many devotees had gathered for a darshan of Sri Sri Thakur and listened to his enlivening words. For the last few days, due to incessant rain, it had been impossible for them to come to the ashram.

This quiet, sublime atmosphere was terribly disturbed by a commotion. Soon, Sri Sri Thakur was told that two workers from the ashram had had a serious fight over something. They were Charuda (Charuchandra Sarkar), and Jashodada (Jashoda Goswami). In the heat of the moment, things had gone so far that Charuda had slapped Jashodada across his face. Jashoda Goswami came from a family that traced its lineage to Mahaprabhu Chaitanya Deva.

The news of this incident hurt Sri Sri Thakur immensely. He shouted loudly and broke into tears. He looked at Kishori Mohan, a sincere devotee, and with a roaring voice called out to him, "Doctor, a place where Bhagaban Chaitanya Dev was humiliated, could I even stay for a moment? I will abandon this place and leave, doctor!" Saying this, he instantly ran towards Padma, and jumped into its swirling water. This was so immediate and unexpected that everyone was aghast; wailing and screaming could be heard all around. Without much delay, Kishori Mohan jumped in as well. Many others followed him.

They managed to bring Sri Sri Thakur from the deep waters. It was a very long unfortunate night; no one wanted to leave the ashram courtyard apprehending another mishap. Both Charuda and Jashodada felt guilty and ashamed. With tears in their eyes, they presented themselves before Sri Sri Thakur seeking and begging for forgiveness. Sri Sri Thakur with a heart as large as the ocean was quick to forgive them. In a tone that only expressed understanding and love, he said to them, "Be good human beings, and always try to inculcate goodness in the rest of humanity." *(Purushottam Prasanga)*

(11). Flouting the Master's word

In 1940, the erstwhile Secretary of *Satsang*, Shyama Charan Mukherjee (Gopalda) along with another ashramite, Durgacharan Sarkar, sought permission from Sri Sri Thakur to go to Faridpur to complete important work. The local devotee, Pramatha Ganguly, was supposed to help them. Sri Sri Thakur initially refused, but after a lot of pleading and persuasion, he yielded; however, he wanted them to return anyhow by August 3 to the ashram without fail. Gopalda and Durga Charanda promised to and left.

Gopalda learnt upon meeting Pramathada in Faridpur that he had to go to Calcutta to get a job for the latter's relative. In those days, Gopalda was well acquainted with the British officers who were supposed to be in the selection panel for a government job. Gopalda by nature was a simple and loving man. He had completed his M.Sc. with a first-class first from Calcutta University. He had become very influential among the English ruling elite of the city, so much so that he could even bring the most dreaded Governor of Bengal to the ashram to attend a function in 1935.

His devotion to Sri Sri Thakur was matchless. Once, an astrologer, after examining Sri Sri Thakur's horoscope, found that he would face great danger. He advised wearing a special diamond ring to nullify the bad effects of the malefic stars. In those days, the ashram's finances were in such a bad state that affording a diamond ring was out of the question. Upon coming to know of this, Gopalda, on the pretext of going to Calcutta, left the ashram and instead went to his village, mortgaged his ancestral property, and arranged the money to buy the ring.

Gopalda agreed to Pramatha Babu's request to go to Calcutta to arrange for the job. However, if he went, it would be impossible to make it back to the ashram before August 3. Pramatha Babu was a cunning man; he enlisted Durgacharan to achieve his objective. After the death of his first wife, Durgacharan married Phula, called Phula Ma by the ashramites. He had a soft spot for his second wife; he would always try his best to keep her happy. Women's weakness for costly sarees and jewellery is known to all. Before Gopalda could make up his mind, Pramatha Babu gave a lot of money to Durgacharan to take care of their tickets back and forth and a good sari for Phula Ma. To avail the gift of a good sari, it was imperative that they go to Calcutta. So Durgacharan began convincing Gopalda to make the trip. He said, "Sri Sri Thakur always instructed us to help our Guru brothers in need. If, by the virtue of your influence, a Guru brother gets a job, wouldn't that make Sri Sri Thakur happy? Please don't hesitate. We will go to Calcutta and return as soon as our work is done. We will board the earliest train to Pabna." Gopalda retorted, "If we do so, then we will be late and reach Pabna after the third. Do you think it'd be right to disobey the orders of Sri Sri Thakur?"

Durgacharan was not someone to back down. He persisted, "Sri Sri Thakur has always advised us to go out of our way to help our Guru Brothers; now if we don't stand by that responsibility, wouldn't we be disobeying his instructions? If we have to go by his present instructions, it would mean ignoring His fundamental intentions." Gopalda had no other way.

Gopalda and Durgacharan boarded the night train and left for Calcutta. The situation in Calcutta was not feasible for the work to be accomplished in time. On their way back, the Dhaka Mail and North Bengal Express derailed in a freak accident and both Gopalda and Durgacharanda died. The news reached Sri Sri Thakur. He lost both his heart and spirit. No appetite, and no sleep; he wept day and night. All efforts to persuade him back to a state of normalcy failed. Even Gopalda's mother came forward, and expressed her grief saying, "If you fall apart in this way, to whom shall we look up to for strength?" It took a very long time for Sri Sri Thakur to overcome his grief.

After Gopalda's demise, the ashramites were perplexed with one question: How could a committed devotee like Gopalda lose his life in this way? Couldn't Sri Sri Thakur save Gopalda and Durgacharanda? Sri Sri Thakur learned about this and said, "If you don't give the handle in my hand, I am undone. If I have the handle and the control, I may even overturn your destiny. Without any hesitation, he who listens to my word, and follows it will be saved; though he may look like a fool, he is a man with real knowledge. And he who lives according to his own whims and preferences, his knowledge is of no use; he remains a fool. If you have any strong attraction or liking for anyone or anything other than me (Thakur), it is always a great threat to you."

Everything was right with Gopalda, but he had a great liking for Durgacharan. And Durgacharan was obsessed with keeping his wife happy at any cost. So the inevitable happened. *(Sri Sri Thakur Anukul Chandra[2]).*

(12). *Curing Durganath of his ailment*

Durganath Sanyal hailed from Nazirpur, a village close to Hemayetpur. He had been suffering from a severe stomach ailment for a long time. Gastroenterologists of Calcutta could not diagnose his severe pain. He also tried homoeopathy in his village and many other places to no avail. In 1913, fed up with life, he went as a last resort to Deoghar, a famous pilgrimage of Lord Shiva, where He is worshipped as Baidyanath (the Divine Healer), who could cure terminal diseases. Traditionally, an afflicted person would lie down at a secluded place within the temple premises without food and water, praying to the Lord. He would not get up unless the Lord informed him of the remedy in a dream. As Durganath was desperate, he decided either to be cured or die in the premises of the Great Divine Doctor. After some days of such penury, Baba Baidyanath passed down his instructions in Durganath's dream: "Why have you come here? Go and approach Anukul Chandra, who lives near your village."

Following the instructions, Durganath went to Sri Sri Thakur and told him his problems. Sri Sri Thakur assured him and told him to stay at the ashram. For Durganath's sake, Sri Sri Thakur requested his mother to cook for him in their kitchen. The menu suggested by Sri Sri Thakur was: thick brown rice along with Bengal gram (chickpea) gravy. Manmohini Devi bit her tongue in astonishment and exclaimed, "Have you gone mad? Are you seriously asking someone with chronic digestion problems to eat thick brown rice and Bengal gram? This may well be the end of him." Sri Sri Thakur confidently replied, "Nothing of that sort will happen. Please prepare the food as I said and feed the patient." Durganath sat down to eat with grave fear on his face. Noticing it Sri Sri Thakur assured him, "Please trust me; nothing awful is going to happen to you. Start with your meal! Come on!" Despite his fears, he really enjoyed the food. It was after a long time that he had eaten such relishing items. Sri Sri Thakur patted his back and advised him to go confidently and rest. Three hours passed. At around 4 in the afternoon, Sri Sri Thakur asked Durganath whether he had pain in his stomach. He said, 'No.' After a few days, he recovered completely. A person who was having at least 15-20 loose motions a day was now going to the toilet only once a day and experiencing a normal bowel movement. In due course, Durganath was cured, and after initiation, he left for his village. Nobody in the ashram had any clue of how an anti-diet would cure a chronic ailment.

Another day, Sushilchandra Basu (the then Secretary of Satsang), nonchalantly asked Sri Sri Thakur, "How did you manage to cure Durganath's prolonged stomach ailment by prescribing food that was rather dangerous for his condition?"

Sri Sri Thakur replied, "To diagnose a case, the doctor should have the patience to enquire how the disease started. I came to know that for a long time Durganath desired to have thick brown rice along with Bengal gram (chickpea) gravy, but due to various reasons, he wasn't able to have it. It was the repression of this long-standing desire of his that caused the abdominal pain. The digestive tract created this anomaly, indicating that he must satiate the craving to get rid of the problem." Sushilda asked again, "What kind of insight is required of a doctor to make such a diagnosis; where will we ever find such doctors?" Sri Sri Thakur replied, "Why not? If people really try, this will be possible in the years to come." (*Manas Tirtha Parikrama*)

(13). Master appears to the blind

Trailokya Nath Chakravarty was an ardent devotee of Sri Sri Thakur. His mother was very old and had lost her eyesight. She asked Trailokya Nath, "My son, is it not possible for me to take Thakur's initiation (*Diksha*)?" The matter in due course came to the knowledge of Sri Sri Thakur, and on his instructions, Trailokya

Nath completed the initiation of his mother. At the time of initiation, a person had to see a photograph of the Master, but the old lady was deprived of this vital aspect of Diksha because of her blindness.

One fine day, Sri Sri Thakur asked Trailokya Nath to cook delicious food of many varieties for his mother. After doing so, he woke up his mother from a deep slumber, and said, "I have cooked many recipes for your lunch." The mother, still drowsy, replied, "I am more than full. In my dream, a fair, handsome man with glittering eyes, and a sacred thread around his shoulders had come. He held my hands and lovingly insisted that I should eat a number of delicious items that he was carrying on a plate. I couldn't refuse him. I ate to my heart's content." Trailokya Nath did not give much importance to his mother's dream and said, "All that is in the dream. Can a human being satisfy his appetite in a dream? If what you are saying is real, then tell me what all did you have?" All the curries and desserts she mentioned were precisely the same as that Trailokya Nath had prepared. He was taken aback and exclaimed, "Mother, you are extremely fortunate. I have been very sad since you lost your eyesight. You could not know how *Sri Sri Thakur* looks. Nonetheless, he has compensated you for this, and has himself given you a divine view." (*Smaranika*, 2020; Chitroptala Satsang Vihar, Lemalo, Odisha)

(14). The Foresight of Sri Sri Thakur

It was the time of the Second World War. The war was becoming more aggressive and destructive. The movement of food supplies and other basic necessities was hampered in our country. They became scarce and expensive. In wartime, the British Government made the farmers migrate to other places. They lost their homes and land. It affected the production of food grains. By 1943, life had become extremely miserable in Bengal. The supply of food grains had become scanty. Fearing famine, large quantities of food grains were hoarded by businessmen to sell at exorbitant rates at the opportune time.

For a long time, Sri Sri Thakur had been asking people to save and stock extra grain for future use, but no one gave much importance to his advice. He also reminded a number of His followers, through letters from the ashram, but the matter was still not taken very seriously. In 1943, six months before the famine had set in, he wrote personal letters to a large number of Guru brothers of Bengal to collect and save as much food grains as they could. As the famine worsened, Sri Sri Thakur instructed a few of his close devotees (Sushil Basu, Prafulla Kumar Das, Jiten Mitra, etc.) to go to Calcutta immediately, and collect 50 tons of rice with the help of Guru Brothers there and transport it to Hemayetpur Ashram. He wanted nobody in the 15-km radius of Pabna Town to die of hunger.

For this purpose, a permit had to be obtained from the government authorities, Praful Das was entrusted to get it. He went to Calcutta and met the Chief Controller of Civil Supplies, (Mr. Iyer, ICS) at his official residence. He elaborately explained to him about Sri Sri Thakur, Satsang Ashram, and the reason for his visit. Iyer Saheb listened to him, and couldn't resist his laughter. He said, "Do you think it is humanly possible to collect so much rice in these circumstances? And who will issue a permit for such an impractical proposition?" Prafullada humbly replied, "Saheb, I do not know all this. How are we supposed to obtain and collect such vast amounts of rice, I don't know; but since this is Thakur's (my Master's) wish, it will happen somehow, even though it seems a near impossible task. Sir, I call upon you to simply arrange for this permit, and kindly tell me about the logistics of this operation." These assertions made by Prafullada toned down Mr. Iyer's dismissive temperament. He said, "Please come and meet the head of the Civil Supplies department tomorrow in our office; we will see what can be done." The next day, Prafullada went and met two top officials in the Civil Supplies office, (Mr. K. Sen and

Mr. A. K. Ghosh, ICS), and explained the situation to them. In the history of the Civil Supplies department of Bengal Presidency, for the first time was such a permit issued for the free distribution of relief food grains in the district of Pabna. All the Guru brothers in and around Calcutta were able to collect and transport 50 tons of rice to Pabna. (*Smriti-Tirthe*)

(15). *From a terrorist to a freedom fighter*

Nanigopal Dey was from the village Bagabaeed of Mymensingh district in undivided Bengal (now in Bangladesh). He has been a fierce nationalist since boyhood. When he grew up, he became a part of the Indian freedom struggle (Swadeshi Andolan), and joined an anarchist party. Soon he was declared a hardened criminal by the British Government, and wanted by the police. He remained underground most of the time, concealing his identity. When a police bullet hit him in the arm, he narrowly escaped and somehow reached his younger sister's house at Kushtia. On the advice of his brother-in-law, Shashank Mohan Dey, he went to Hemayetpur hoping for shelter. There, Sri Sri Thakur sent him to Anant Maharaj to be initiated (*Diksha*). Soon after, Sri Sri Thakur, through another devotee, intimated to the District Magistrate that a terrorist had come to the ashram to take refuge. The next morning, policemen in white uniforms came and arrested Nanigopal. Completely disgusted with Sri Sri Thakur's betrayal, on his way out, he shouted, "So, at last, you entrapped me? Had I had a revolver with me, it would have only taken a single bullet to get all this nonsensical godman business out of your head." Sri Sri Thakur calmly replied, "For your sins, go and spend a few days in jail. Don't lose heart." Nanigopal now cried, "They are not going to let me out. If they don't hang me, they will send me to Kalapani (life imprisonment in Andaman). Nobody returns from there." Sri Sri Thakur remained quiet. The police dragged Nanigopal away. He was put in Central Jail, Dumdum, Calcutta.

Three months passed. One day, Sri Sri Thakur called Bholanath

Sarkar, an attendant devotee, and directed him to go and fetch Nanigopal from the jail in Calcutta. Bholanath reached Calcutta in very bad weather. It was a night of severe torrential rain and thunderstorms. The metropolis had come to a standstill; all human activities stopped. All night, Bholanath chanted his *Guru's* name, feeling diffident about the difficult responsibility he had been entrusted with. The next morning's newspaper mentioned that the Dumdum central jail had been severely damaged in the storm and that large parts had crumbled. The British laws of the time had a strange rule. If due to any natural calamity, the premises of a jail were destroyed, all prisoners would be let free; even the ones sentenced to death. So Bholanath rushed to the central jail and found a crowd of prisoners with their relatives who had come to receive them. After a prolonged search, he was finally able to trace Nanigopal, and said, "Sri Sri Thakur had sent me to take you back to the ashram." Nanigopal was amazed that Sri Sri Thakur knew of this event beforehand. After three months in jail, a grateful Nanigopal returned to become a permanent ashramite.

Those were the formative days of the ashram; there was not much money to even arrange two meals a day for the ashramites. They were contributing physical labour for different structures to come up. Mother Manmohini Devi would aggregate the rice and lentils obtained through alms (*bhiksha*) and boil them to make ball-shaped morsels, one for each ashramite for the whole day. Despite this scanty diet, everyone would soon be back at work. Nanigopal was working all right, but could not stand starvation. He decided to sneak out of the ashram at night. Late in the evening, he packed his belongings, and around midnight, was about to leave. Just then, there was a knock at the door and Nanigopal found a messenger calling him to meet Sri Sri Thakur on the bank of the Padma River. Nanigopal had no other way but to accompany the messenger. He found Sri Sri Thakur talking with two other devotees. Looking at him Sri Sri Thakur said, "For only a few more bites of food, you would abandon me, Nani?" Nanigopal thought to himself. When he had not disclosed his intentions with anyone, how had Sri Sri Thakur known? Sri Sri Thakur's words were full of paternal love, it worked wonders in his mind. He immediately fell at Sri Sri Thakur's feet, his eyes swelled up with tears, and he cried, "Please forgive me, Thakur. I will never again think of leaving you." Sri Sri Thakur was happy. In course of time, Nanigopal excelled in conducting *kirtan* (singing of bhajans with dancing).

As Nanigopal had spent three months in jail, he was declared a freedom fighter eligible for a pension in the post-independence government. He was given a lifetime free pass to travel in the reserved coaches of Indian Railways all over the country. He accompanied Sri Sri Thakur to Deoghar and stayed in the ashram till he breathed his last at the age of 92. (*Swasti Sevak*, January 2020)

(16). The Strange Reformation of Hemakavi, the great Bengali poet

In 1934, Sri Sri Thakur was in Calcutta for treatment of an infection in his ankle. At that time, Sri Sri Thakur lived in a rented house at Haritaki Bagan Lane. A devotee named Baidyanath begged him to see and save a dear friend, Hem Mukherjee, a famous singer-poet. He was famous for his lyricism and choice of words, which were sublime and sweet. But this rare genius poet had one great weakness—alcoholism. He disappointed his friends in their efforts to save him with medicine or counselling. Hemkavi declared that he personally intended to spend the rest of his time dead drunk and advised his friends to do so likewise as a gesture of true friendship. One afternoon, Baidyanath brought Hemkavi to Sri Sri Thakur. He was dead drunk, his eyes were bloodshot. There was an untidy stubble on his face and his dhoti was soiled. Approaching Sri Sri Thakur he declared, "I know there is some trick afoot to reform me but I was bored and curious, so I came along." Whereupon he sat down with a thump, crossed his legs, and winked mockingly at the unsmiling audience. Sri Sri Thakur replied, "I too was curious, I have heard a great deal of praise for your singing and had been hoping that you would favour us with your talent." Hemkavi scowled, "I am not in the mood today. You cannot compel an artist." 'True, true,' Sri Sri Thakur replied and turned to his disciple requesting for refreshments to be served. The man returned shortly with a tray of glasses of fruit juice, an open bottle of whisky, and an empty glass. Hemchandra's eyes widened with surprise and a grin spread across his face.

"Scotch is fine", Hemchandra said, pouring himself a glass and quaffing it in two gulps, neat. He drank several glasses quickly; with a thickening tongue he rambled on disjointedly about the jaded harlot called Life. When his language became abusive, his friends tried to take him out. While leaving, clutching the bottle to his chest, Hemchandra said, "Thakur, I like you! I really like you! You are the first person I have ever met who did not give me a sermon on the evils of drinking...."

"Oh! Why should you stop? Since I am confined to this room, it would be very pleasant for me to have your company tomorrow", said Sri Sri Thakur.

Thakur's outraged disciples lost no time in seeking out the unhappy Baidyanath, and upbraiding him for bringing such a disgusting person to Thakur.

The next afternoon, Hemchandra arrived by himself although he had been drinking; he had shaved and wore a clean dhoti. He was in a gay mood and told Sri Sri Thakur, "I have a song for you." He clapped his hands and started humming:

Oh, the man who can feel his brother's thirst
I say is a saint through and through
If a roll is called, this man will be the first ...
Down the hatch, Thakur, here's to you!'

The group of devotees stared at him in horrified disgust, but Thakur clapped his hands with pleasure and called for refreshments which again included a bottle of whisky for Hemchandra. As long as Thakur was in Calcutta, Hemchandra showed up every afternoon and received his bottle of whisky with exaggerated pomp and thanks. When Thakur bid him farewell, Hemchandra was visibly downcast. He was then invited to Hemayetpur. Shortly after he arrived, Thakur arranged for the poet's accommodation and resumed the afternoon sessions with the daily gift of a bottle of whisky. Those nearest to Thakur were alarmed at the poet's arrogance and complete lack of respect for their Guru. He composed songs around incidents that occurred in the ashram lampooning them.

Early one morning, the devotees arrived to find their Guru seated quietly on the veranda, his usually immaculate white clothes covered with vomit. The worried disciples sat around him and wondered about this strange situation. Just before lunchtime, the poet, bathed and looking fresh, arrived. He stared at the vomit in horror and turned angrily to the disciples, "What are you fools sitting there for? Can't you see he is desperately ill? Send for the doctor. Get some water immediately! Get clean clothes!"

No one moved. Hemchandra moved hesitant towards Thakur sitting in stern silence and asked, "Are you all right?" Sri Sri Thakur said, "I am fine, but you, my friend, are you all right now?" Hemchandra's lips moved stiffly, "Why wouldn't I be all right?"

"You were very very ill. Don't you remember?" Sri Sri Thakur said. "You came to me after I had retired and asked for one more dose of intoxication, which I gave. All this will wash away, it is not important. Your well-being is the main thing."

With an anguished sob, Hemchandra stumbled blindly away from there. That afternoon as he did not appear for his usual visit, Thakur sent for him. He came reluctantly, his eyes on the ground. Reaching Sri Sri Thakur, he dropped to the floor and prostrated himself for the first time. Thakur called for refreshments. Hemchandra averted his eyes from the bottle and said, "I don't feel like drinking today."

Sri Sri Thakur agreed pleasantly, "As you like. But take the bottle with you. Perhaps you will enjoy it later." Glumly, the poet accepted the gift and left for the Padma River, and threw the bottle into it. The next afternoon, he arrived promptly, knelt, and touched Thakur's feet with no sign of embarrassment. "I wanted to come and tell you not to waste any of your money on liquor for me. I am finished with drinking."

Thakur said, "You've been ill. Take the bottle from the tray when you've recovered; you will probably feel differently. Save it."

'I will never feel differently', Hemchandra cried. "If I have to take the bottle, I will smash it." Hemchandra took the bottle, walked a short distance away, and smashed it against a rock. Returning to Thakur's presence, he approached Anant Maharaj and asked, "Give me initiation. I shall try to be worthy of it."

That evening, he joined the villagers as they settled around Thakur to seek guidance for their problems. During one of the silences that were common to these evenings as the people stopped to ponder the words of their Guru, the poet's tender voice rose in a song:

> Oh, Friend beloved, knower of my true desire,
> Dweller in the secret regions of my heart
> See how my emptiness is filled with blossoms
> Palpitating every joyous hue
> Breathing a fragrance that sweetens my tears,
> Soothing with a lullaby of knowing you,
> Pulsing with desire and life...to serve you.
> *(Ocean in a Teacup)*

(17). A very precious gift

It was function time in Hemayetpur Ashram. Devotees and followers gathered in numbers. A very old lady from a village in the nearby Kushtia district came to the ashram. It was customary to come to Thakur with an offering, but she was too poor to afford anything worthy for Thakur. There was a little paddy in the house. She processed it, and deftly pounded it. She could get approximately 600-700 grams of rice flakes that she packed neatly in a white cloth and started walking the distance. At the gates of the ashram, when she set her eyes upon Thakur, she saw a huge crowd around him. People had brought lots of vegetables, and so many fresh fruits from Calcutta; some had even brought jewellery, and even more expensive things. Thakur welcomed everyone and thanked them with a smile. Seeing this, the old lady's heart sank. In the face of so many expensive gifts, how much could her little rice flakes be worth? Just then, Thakur saw her standing in one corner. He called out to her affectionately as if he had known her for many years. He insisted that she come near, "Ma, what took you so long to reach here? Is everything well with you? Please come closer to me, let me see what you have got for me?"

Overwhelmed with Thakur's love and kindness, with tear-filled eyes she revealed her offering, saying, "Thakur, I am an unfortunate, poor old lady; I couldn't get anything of real value for you, all I could manage was these flattened rice flakes. If I offer just this to you, would you accept it?"

Sri Sri Thakur with a gleeful face expressed his jubilance as if he was receiving the most precious gift of his life. He extended his hands and took the packet of rice flakes with the utmost care, and handed it over to an attendant with the instructions "Look, take this carefully and give it to your Borma to serve me for breakfast tomorrow." The next day, just as she was about to leave, she met Borma, who told her how much Thakur had enjoyed her rice flakes for breakfast. He had eaten it with relish and even asked for a second helping. Borma now asked the old lady, "Are you happy?" (*Jiban Dyuti*)

(18). Eternally Grateful, Sri Sri Thakur

Sri Sri Thakur had a difficult childhood. He was a young student in the local school. His father, Shiva Chandra Chakravarty, had been bedridden for quite some time, and there was no money in the house. Mother Manmohini Devi and grandmother

Krishnasundari Devi took loans at very high rates of interest to run the household. Money was urgently required for Shiva Chandra's medicines. Without disturbing anybody, Thakur went to Pabna town hoping to get some hand loans from friends and acquaintances. After trying three-four houses, he reached the house of the landlord. As he was crossing it, he saw the landlord's son, Jogesh, who studied with him, coming out of the gate to board a horse-driven coach. Seeing him, Thakur's eyes blazed with hope and happiness. He thought he would now get some money to buy the necessary medicines. He took Jogesh aside and asked softly for a little money. Jogesh was arrogant over the wealth of the family and thought of Thakur as no more than a beggar. He grinned, grimaced, and in wry amusement, kicked a four-anna coin towards Thakur. The thin edge of the coin hit Thakur on his forehead and it fell down. Droplets of blood oozed out and Thakur wiped them off before anybody could see. He brought the medicines pleasantly, surprising the family.

Days passed, and so did years. In 1946 Sri Sri Thakur wound up the huge ashram of Hemayetpur, and came to Deoghar (now in Jharkhand). He and the devotees who accompanied him tried to build all that had been left at Hemayetpur. Soon, with his planning and hard work, the new ashram took shape and things were getting organised. One day, he was sitting outside the building of Baral Bungalow surrounded by a group of devotees. From afar, he saw the figure of the erstwhile landlord; old age had not been kind to him. In tattered clothes, and a bent back he was trying to enter the ashram. Sri Sri Thakur immediately asked a devotee to go and escort him. All arrangements for his food and stay were done. He was provided with new clothes.

A devotee who had come from Hemayetpur to Deoghar inquired of Thakur, "As far as I remember from your stories, isn't he the man who had humiliated you in childhood? Why are you showing so much concern and kindness towards him?" Sri Sri Thakur calmly said, "Listen, had I not got the four annas that day, can you imagine what would have happened to my father? Do you also realise that had my father not been there to support and raise me, you wouldn't have had your Thakur sitting with you here today?"

Sri Sri Thakur never forgot the people who had helped Him earlier. All such people were always supported. Several money orders would be sent to a list of names from the ashram every month. Even after Sri Sri Thakur's demise, this tradition was carried forward. (*Richinandan Chakravarty*)

(19). Padma River changes its course

It was July 1923. For the last few days, the rain had been heavy, and incessant, making the sun invisible. The whole area near the Padma river was flooded. The river was threatening to enter Hemayetpur village. If this happened, Satsang Ashram would be the first to be affected.

The sky was downcast with black clouds. Sri Sri Thakur was sitting below a neem tree on the bank. He was surrounded by a group of staunch devotees. Among them was a senior barrister of Calcutta High Court, J. N. Dutta, with his wife (known as Dutta Ma). There was a discussion on how to avert damage by the flood. Sri Sri Thakur looked at the overflowing water and said:"We have to build an embankment as soon as we can, or else I don't know what can save us from the Padma's wrath." Engineer Srish Chandra Nandi was present. He estimated the cost of the embankment at 11,000 rupees. Justice Dutta was quick to emphasise, "Thakur, how is it possible to collect so much money quickly? Moreover, today is Saturday. By the time we arrange the money and start work, it will be at least Tuesday."

Sri Sri Thakur replied, "Tuesday will be too late for all of us. I hope you understand how important it is to start work immediately." Hearing this, Dutta Ma removed the expensive gold chain from her neck and put it in the hands of a devotee (Nanibhangi) and suggested it be pledged and the money be used for the embankment. That is precisely what happened. Essential materials like cement, bricks, etc., were arranged for, and work started to gather steam. All the workers and devotees at the ashram—men and women—put all their might and labour into the job. Sri Sri Thakur was with them throughout the process. Not only did he provide minute instructions, but kept cheering and motivating them to complete such an uphill task. After immense effort, a considerably massive embankment was built to protect the ashram. Its premises were now secure from the forthcoming floods.

After this disaster was averted, the flood waters that had reached the embankment now slowly receded. Many months later, an extraordinary event occurred. Slowly, the Padma went back from its course farther from the ashram. (*Satwati,* April 2014)

(20). Panchananda's offering of jackfruit

Once, an ashramite, Panchanan Sarkar, went to his village to meet his elder brother and mother. In their family orchard was an all-season enduring jackfruit tree. Panchananda's mother had plucked a jackfruit from the tree that would be ripe in 2-3 days' time, and had kept it aside for both her sons. His brother, upon seeing such a beautiful fruit, asked their mother, "Such a majestic fruit, and at this time of the year? Please keep it aside for Sri Sri Thakur." But what their mother did instead was to pluck another jackfruit and place both fruits together. Panchananda exclaimed, "I don't think this jackfruit would survive for such a long time. On my way, I have to visit Calcutta. I will reach the ashram about 10 days from now." His brother was quick to respond,"What do you mean that it won't survive? Since it is meant for Thakur, until the fruit gets to the ashram, it will not ripen."

On the third day, one jackfruit ripened, but the one that was kept for Sri Sri Thakur had not. It took Panchananda 16 days to reach Hemayetpur from Kushtia via Calcutta. By the time he reached, the jackfruit had ripened. He was supposed to reach the ashram by 3 p.m., which would be long after Thakur's lunchtime. He thought, "I am not fortunate enough to offer this jackfruit to Thakur today." From afar, he could see Sri Sri Thakur standing at the ashram gate, as if waiting for someone to arrive. The moment Panchananda came to him and greeted him, he called out to his mother, "Ma, see, the ripe jackfruit has finally arrived." Hearing this, Ma Manmohini Devi called out to *Badabou* (Borma), and said, "Come, serve the fruit, Anukul is ready to eat." Returning home, all Panchananda could think of was how on earth a plucked jackfruit could survive that long, and what made Thakur wait for it. (*Amar Jibane Sri Sri Thakur*)

(21). *The ill-fated Zamindar*

It was the summer of 1939. In the evening, the landlord of Muktagacha, Jatindranath Acharya Choudhury, came for *Darshan*, and offered *Pranam* and obeisance to Thakur. He frequently visited the ashram. A Brahmin by caste, whenever he came, he would stay for a couple of days and enjoyed preparing various recipes at the ashram for Thakur. However, this time, he wanted to go back the same night for some important work. Sri Sri Thakur was adamant, "Nothing doing. I cannot let you go so late at night. Let your car go back along with the person who had accompanied you, and report for your urgent work tomorrow morning. You can leave for Calcutta early in the morning in the ashram's vehicle." The landlord was insistent and pleaded for permission to go. Sri Sri Thakur remained silent. The Zamindar left the ashram after dinner, and on his way back (near Ishwardi) the car crashed against a roadside tree. Jatindranath died on the spot.

A few days after this event, many devotees inquired of Sri Sri Thakur, "Why did you not stop Jatinda that night; why did you not tell him the consequences if he left then, since you knew his fate?" Thakur responded, "That night when Jatinda had come to me, I could see that it wasn't him, but indeed his ghost. He had already made his mind up. I repeatedly asked him to stay back, but he wouldn't listen. Whatever grief falls upon people as a consequence of ignoring my advice, I suffer twice the hurt. What can I possibly do? It is not my right to force anybody to do anything. To assume that I precisely know all your futures would be a futile theoretical exercise. Rather a simple way to avert the misfortunes of your life would be to simply adhere to what I say, "If my Thakur doesn't like, or objects to a certain kind of action, I shall not do it at any cost; this itself will save you from many disasters.

"Regardless, had I forced Jatinda to stay, his life may have been saved, but he would have still incurred financial loss. He wouldn't have got to know that I had saved his life, and rather would have blamed me for his loss. As a consequence, his faith, and sincerity towards me would have come into doubt. This by itself is a greater peril than death. Why I say so is because the soul which has no faith and sincerity in its being loses all meaning and essence in this life and the afterlife; whereas if someone departs this Earth with sincere faith in their hearts, the doors of a good afterlife open for them. It is my burden to meticulously think before every decision I take. I have to look for a far greater purpose that should not be disturbed due to immediate, present-day concerns of life."
(Sri Sri Thakur Anukulchandra[2])

(22). The Escapade of advocate P. R. Banerjee

The second World War had already started by 1940. Sri Sri Thakur directed his secretary, Prafulla Kumar Das, to send messages to all initiates in Burma that they come back to India as soon as possible. He did not allow Prafulla to ask questions on this issue. The puzzled Prafulla began the work of addressing hundreds of postcards with Thakur's strange and unexplained message. The postcards caused consternation among the Burmese initiates. The vast majority had explicit faith in Thakur; they accepted the warning and obeyed it without question. Within two months, devotees in Burma had dwindled to a few hundred. They sought further details in this regard from the ashram but received a cryptic reply, 'Thakur said what he understood, now you do what you think is best.'

P.R. Banerjee was also among the initiates who had received the second message. Mr. Banerjee's profession was well on track, fighting important cases in the Burma High Court. Along with his wife and children, he could afford a spacious and large bungalow with 12 rooms in Pegu. Needless to say, he was also a devout believer in Sri Sri Thakur and his ways. His daughter was suffering from the fatal disease of Nephritis, and most doctors from Rangoon had given up. She recovered through the medicine that Sri Sri Thakur had prescribed. As soon as he received Thakur's orders, he sold off some of his property and deposited the money in the bank, so it can be of help when needed.

January 6, 1942. That night Banerjee went to bed worried about the forthcoming dangers. After a moment's sleep, he heard, "Banerjee, leave here immediately." Someone murmured it in his ear. Lying beside him, his wife was in deep slumber. The atmosphere in and around his house and neighbourhood was silent. He thought it must have been a dream, and returned to bed. He had just pulled over his sheet to go back to sleep when he heard the voice again; this time almost a scream, "Leave here immediately, abandon this place."

Banerjee was shivering now. Even if he had never personally met Sri Sri Thakur, in that instant he understood that this was indeed his Guru's voice. He immediately woke up his wife and told her that they had to leave immediately. He instructed her to fetch the servants, and as they moved towards the garden his wife, confused and frustrated, asked, "Is the house on fire, or what?" Banerjee firmly ordered her to do as he said, "Get the kids, pack whatever you can, and come to the garden as soon as possible." Banerjee along with his four-year-old daughter, Kamala, left the house. All the domestic help and his wife followed him. They ran up to the farthest part of the vast garden and stood there.

His wife now asked, "What happened? Why did we all run away from the house in such a hurry?" Mr. Banerjee wiped the sweat off his face and said, "I don't know. Thakur has asked me to abandon this place at the earliest. And that's what we will do." His wife said, "Couldn't it have been a dream?" Banerjee was firm, and said, "It wasn't a dream. I was fully awake, he said in my ear, "Leave this place immediately."

In a few moments, they saw the night sky explode and rain fire. Japanese forces were bombing the city of Rangoon. It took only a while for an explosive to hit their house, turning it to ashes in seconds. Mr. Banerjee along with his family went up through the turbulent pathways of Kamayut, finally reaching Ferry Ghat. They saw a huge number of refugees gathered there. Banerjee asked his son and wife to stand in the queue, while he rushed to the bank to get as much money as possible before all banks shut down. This effort went in vain; the banks had already shut their doors. By the time he returned, all the boats had filled up. No one had any idea when the next one would leave.

From there, the Banerjee family managed to travel to Markatila by train. There they met many Satsangis. Everyone then went to Mandalay. They put together some money to buy a bullock cart, in which they went up to the Chindwin River. This long arduous journey resulted in many refugees dying of amoebic dysentery and beriberi. (Thiamine deficiency). In May 1942, the refugees finally crossed the Chindwin River, and reached Imphal, Manipur, safely. After three weeks of travel, along with 141 refugee families, P. R. Banerjee and his family also reached Pabna. It was because of Sri Sri Thakur's immense grace that Mr. Banerjee's family was saved. (*Ocean in a Teacup*)

(23). An account of Jatindra Lal Dutta

This is an incident at the time of the second world war. I was living in Burma for my work. One fine morning, the sudden news came that Sri Sri Thakur had called all members of Satsang in

Burma (present-day Myanmar) to return to India at the earliest. He didn't mince words, and his orders were clear. As a fellow Satsangi, this was of great concern to me as to why he gave such an order. The opportunity to earn a decent livelihood, access to healthcare, an abundance of food and shelter, all these things were available in Burma for us, and Sri Sri Thakur knew this. Hence, we were unable to understand the reason for the message.

I had already ended a long leave and rejoined work. I had no intention to return to India soon. One morning, I got a telegram from Ahmedabad about my elder brother, Prasanna Kumar Dutta (Joint Secretary, Satsang Ashram), who had been severely sick during his tour there. The day after, I received another telegram from the ashram stating that Sri Sri Thakur wanted me to shift Prasannada from Ahmedabad to Calcutta for treatment. For this purpose, I had to leave Burma. After two months of painful treatment in Calcutta, my brother lost his life. To pay for his treatment I had taken many loans and was in serious debt. To be able to return the loans, it was essential that I go back to Burma and work. So, I went to seek Sri Sri Thakur's permission to leave. He emphatically refused. It was a very distressing time for me mentally. Due to my long absence from work, even my salary had stopped. Under a lot of financial pressure, I pleaded with Thakur to permit me to leave for Burma. He refused permission yet again.

One day, I thought to myself, should I leave without informing anyone? However, the fear of some forthcoming disaster always preoccupied me. I was really caught between the devil and the deep sea, with no respite in sight. In such a state of despair, news that Japan has declared war, and had repeatedly bombed many major areas in Burma. Rangoon (present-day Yangon) has been decimated completely. The news was that it only took a moment for all wealth, life, and property to be smashed to dust. It was then that I came to realise why Thakur had ordered all Satsangis to return from Burma to India. However, the story doesn't end there.

In the city of Rangoon, people could hear *special* sirens minutes before the explosions went off. This was the signal for people to run into the nearest underground shelters to save themselves. One of the Satsangis, Rajkumar, later narrated how, in the thick of the battle and explosions, he could see Sri Sri Thakur's majestic hand shielding him and protecting his life. He narrated this divine sight to a fellow devotee, Sheelda. In the wrath of war, almost everything had been irretrievably destroyed; more than a thousand villages ceased to exist. And yet, Sheelda and Rajkumarda in what would be nothing short of a miracle, escaped unhurt. (*Ishta Manane*)

(24). *Sri Sri Thakur with the Clergyman*

During 1922-23, Reverend Fred Hawkyard was the director of the British Christian Mission at Pabna. One afternoon, two boys went to his apartment adjoining the Church and introduced themselves as students from Satsang Tapovan School, Hemayetpur. Bowing before him with folded hands, they said, "Sir, would you be so kind as to tell us the story of Jesus Christ?" The priest replied, "That is a very commendable request, but the story of Jesus is a long one and cannot be told all at once. Today I am very busy, come to the church here at 10 o'clock on Sunday morning and you will be given a lesson on Jesus. Tell me where you live and why you want to hear the story of Jesus?." The boys explained, "We live in Satsang Ashram. Thakur is our Guru and he loves Jesus Christ very dearly. Christmas is coming shortly, and we want to arrange a surprise for him on Jesus' birthday by telling him the whole story."

Rev. Hawkyard did not have a good opinion of Thakur and Satsang. He thought the organisation was a group of fanatics who concocted medicines that were supposed to have magical properties. However, he was impressed by the thought of the boys. He thought over the matter for some time and said, "Well, I do have an English one-act play for school children. Only last year we talked about doing a Bengali version, but somehow we never got around to it. If the English text is of any use to you, you are welcome to do it."

"Oh! That would be splendid!" The boys jumped to their feet. "Our teacher translates English very well! He will help us."

When Christmas came, the boys invited the clergyman to come and see the rehearsal. He agreed.

He found no trouble in locating Tapovan School once he arrived at Hemayetpur. When he reached the school gate, he was escorted respectfully to the rehearsal. After watching it, he was deeply moved. He found himself singing with the rest. Then he was taken to meet Thakur who was in the machine shop at that time. He cleaned his hands and received the Reverend with all earnestness. For more than an hour, they discussed theology. Hawkyard was amazed and strangely affected to hear a dhoti-clad Indian speak of Christ as the Son of God with a depth and feeling seldom encountered among Christians, and with a strong conviction, he was forced to admit, that was often lacking in his own carefully prepared sermons. When he took leave, Thakur invited him to return soon and suggested that he teach the children more about Christ whenever it was convenient for him. Sri Sri Thakur's mother, Manmohini Devi, extended the invitation to Mrs. Hawkyard. The clergyman left in a warm glow of friendly fellowship.

When the Reverend took his seat on the riverboat, he found by his side an elderly Muslim man with a long white beard. When he introduced himself, the co-passenger bowed his head in reverence and said, "I am Sayed Khaliluddin, moulvi of the Islamic community of Pabna." The moulvi, after knowing that his co-passenger had met Thakur a little while ago, said, "He has an amazing personality." Hawkyard replied, "A truly amazing man", and went on to add, "I would go so far as to say, Thakur is one of the few real Christians!"

The moulvi's eyes sparkled, and he said, "And I would say that He is one of the few Muhammedans. I wanted my son to become a true Muhammedan. He has been at Tapovan for four months and is doing very well. His health had always been delicate, but under Thakur's guidance it has greatly improved."

For the clergyman, this trip was only the beginning of a long and close friendship with Thakur, and the devotees of Satsang. Mrs. Hawkyard and her husband made regular weekly trips to Satsang and interacted with the children, teaching them to experience and honour all religions with a broad mind, Sri Sri Thakur's true mission. *(Ocean in a Teacup)*

(25.) Rescuing Chandranathda

This happened in 1943. Sri Sri Thakur was sitting by the embankment near river Padma in the ashram, surrounded by a group of devotees. Bimalendu Bikash Sarkar from Calcutta arrived at the ashram and paid obeisance to him. Sri Sri Thakur seemed worried and suddenly asked, "How has Chandranathda been?"

Chandranath was Bimalendu's brother-in-law. The latter replied, "He is always busy with his business, I haven't been able to keep in touch with him for the past couple of days. It was only when I arrived here that I got to know that he and his family had travelled to Kushtia, and from there had taken a ferry to reach Hemayetpur."

Sri Sri Thakur was restless that night, and kept asking different people about Chandranathda's whereabouts. As the darkness of the night cast its shadow upon the ashram, Sri Sri Thakur's restlessness increased manifold. All of a sudden, Sri Sri Thakur got up from his chair, put on his slippers, and set course towards the river. Walking across the sand banks of the river, he arrived at the edge. Many devotees followed him to that point; they carried lanterns, clothes, sticks, etc. The atmosphere was extremely tense. Sri Sri Thakur called upon Bankimda. According to his instructions, Bankimda and a few devotees took a boat, and travelled deep into the river, shouting: "Chandranathda, Chandranathda, Chandranathda!" They carried a gun and a few torches. Sri Sri Thakur kept standing on the shore, waiting for them to return. After a few hours, Bankimda returned with Chandranathda and his family.

On being asked, Chandranathda said, "While coming from Kushtia towards the Hemayetpur Ashram, the boatman had lost his way, and was heading in a different direction. As they moved forward, they descended into utter darkness. These routes around the Pabna River were infamous for robbery and murder. The whole family was anxious and chanted the *Satnam* given by Sri Sri Thakur all the time. Had Bankimda not called out to them at the right time, any mishap could have happened. It was for this reason that Sri Sri Thakur had asked Bankimda to carry a gun with him. (*Sri Sri Thakur Anukulchandra*[1])

(26). *The Divine Khichdi*

A devotee, Akshay Kumar Mukhopadhyay, from Calcutta visited the Hemayetpur Ashram every two months. In 1946, his younger son, Vishu, was severely stricken with typhoid. Despite the doctors' best efforts, their medicine did not work. His condition worsened day by day, and Akshay was considerably worried. One day, he suddenly remembered what Sri Sri Thakur had once told him, "If you are ever in need, please write to me." Akshayda immediately sent a postcard to Sri Sri Thakur explaining his son's condition. He did not discuss it at home. Two days later, after returning from work, his wife told him that their son (Vishu) had been blabbering in his sleep, "Thakur had come to our home, and we did not even offer him a seat." Akshayda did not pay much heed to this and went about his business. Later, Vishu talked in his sleep, this time with much more clarity and elaboration.

Vishu asked his father, "Did you write a letter to Sri Sri Thakur?" Akshayda was taken aback, and asked,"Why? Who told you?" Vishu replied, "Thakur had come. He gave me a very sweet orange to eat. He said you had written to him. He told me: When you recover, you must come to Deoghar. I will prepare the best khichdi (an Indian delicacy of rice, lentils, vegetables and spices cooked together on low heat) for you."

Vishu's health started showing very positive signs of recovery after this incident. After he had completely recovered, Akshayda visited Deoghar with his family. At the time of *Pranam*, Sri Sri Thakur pointed to Vishu and asked his father, "Wasn't he ill some time ago?" Akshayda replied, "Yes, he was. It is due to your grace that he is now safe." The night before their return, the entire family visited Ananda bazar (the dining space for all ashramites). An attendant there told them, "Please wait a little longer. On Thakur's instructions, a special khichdi is being prepared for you." Hearing this, Akshayda suddenly remembered Vishu's ramblings during his illness. Now he had no doubt that Thakur had indeed come to meet his son, given him a sweet orange and promised him khichdi. The next morning, the family went to take leave of Sri Sri Thakur, He again looked at the boy, and asked, "How was the khichdi last night? Did you enjoy it?" Vishu nodded with a shy smile. (*Sri Sri Thakur Anukulchandra*[1])

(27) Inheritance of Priceless Wealth

On 29 December 1941, on the eve of a conference, there was a huge gathering at the Hemayetpur Ashram. Devotees were keen to have a darshan of Sri Sri Thakur. A young man with a shaved head prostrated before him. Sri Sri Thakur remarked, "Why have you done this to your head?" The young man replied, "My father has passed away." Thakur inquired further,"What happened to him?" The man said, "He was suffering from high fever, cough, and other complications. We did everything within our means, but it wasn't enough to save him. My father's last moments with us were strange. That morning, he called upon me, and said, "Son, my time has come. I will have to leave this world today. At my passing, I want all of you not to cry, but sit by me and repeat the *Satnam*. I would like to depart while listening to it." He then wanted your (Thakur) picture to be kept in front of him. He said, "Looking at him, I can transcend from this world to the next."

In an apologetic tone, he told us, "I could not give you the great material pleasures of wealth or property. However, I am leaving you with my most priceless possession in this world, my Master, Sri Sri Thakur. Never forget my Thakur. Your first responsibility is that of a devotee, so do not neglect your practice of *Jajan, Jaajan,* and *Istavriti.*"

"After this, his condition deteriorated. We were with him when he breathed his last. We went on chanting the Holy Name as he had wished. He opened his eyes once or twice, and looked at your picture; he tried his best to repeat your name within, but had respiratory issues. Baba then suddenly screamed, 'Look, look, Sri Sri Thakur has come to take me in his golden chariot. How magnificent is my Guru's embodiment !!' He uttered, 'Dayal, Dayal, Dayal' and that was the end."

Sri Sri Thakur listened in silence, and said to the young man,- "Your father was a pure soul. Since he adhered to the Master all his life, at the time of his passing, he deserved to be united with the divine presence. His soul has now found its rightful place in the great beyond. *(Alochana Prasange,* Part II)

(28). *Homecoming*

Shyamacharan Mukherjee (popularly known as Gopalda) was returning to the ashram after spending a few days with his mother in Calcutta. Not wishing to interrupt the work of fellow ashramites, he had not informed them of his return. So there was no one to receive him at Ishwardi railway station, Pabna. It had been raining and the streets were wet and muddy. He sat on a bench on the platform to roll up his trousers and remove his shoes to walk to Satsang, Hemayetpur.

An elderly woman extended her palms to him, as if begging. When he took out some coins from his pocket, she closed them. Gopalda found she was not quite aware of her surroundings. He asked, "What is it, Ma? Are you in any trouble?" She cried, "My son died last week. He has been cremated, and gone forever from our lives." Gopalda got to his feet. The old lady's sari was wet. Holding her arm, he said, "You have been in the rain and look tired. Let me walk you to your home so you can rest." She replied, "There is no home. I could not pay the rent, so I left. My son died last week. No son, no home."

Gopalda took the old lady with him, traversing the four-mile-long muddy road to the ashram. The first thing he did was take her to Sri Sri Thakur. "She has no one. Her only son died last week." At the mention of her son, the woman was overcome with grief and could not speak. Thakur jumped up from the stool on which he was sitting and threw his arms around her. "Why do you weep, Ma? I am your son." He held her close until her sobbing stopped. "Go and bathe, then come back here. I need you." The old lady wiped her eyes and smiled. Gopalda was struck anew at how swiftly Thakur's touch healed the suffering. (*Ocean in a Teacup*)

(29). *Communicating with Souls Departed*

One morning, Nafarda (Nafarchandra Ghosh) was oil massaging Sri Sri Thakur and other devotees were around them. They were discussing the presence and movement of the departed souls in our world. As the atmosphere around this topic gathered momentum, Sri Sri Thakur said, "The souls of a number of Satsangis come to me." Nafarda, with enthusiasm, inquired, "Does Jatish's soul also come to you?" Thakur said, "Yes, he comes to me every day." Jatish Ghosh was one of Sri Sri Thakur's sincere workers and also one of Nafarda's close friends.

Nafarda requested that the next time Jatish comes to Sri Sri Thakur's presence, he wants to meet him. Sri Sri Thakur faintly smiled, and replied, "All right, when he visits me tomorrow, I will see to it that you meet him." The next morning around 8 a.m., Sri Sri Thakur shouted out loudly at the top of his voice, "Nafraa, Nafraa, Nafraa..!" Nafarda came running and saw an unbelievable sight—a cloud-shaped face in a gaseous state, and yet starkly resembling that of Jatishda was in the presence of Sri Sri Thakur. Nafarda was scared out of his wits. He ran to Thakur's feet, sat there, and kept shivering until the strange form disappeared. Sri Sri Thakur embraced Nafarda, and lovingly asked, "Why did you get scared? Since you didn't talk to Jatish, he got upset and left." (*Sri Sri Thakur Anukulchandra[1]*)

(30). His Master's Grace (Ramashankar Singh)

The 1930s was a tumultuous decade for India. Mahatma Gandhi's non-cooperation programme was growing into an ever-expanding mass movement. There were many who felt that this method was too slow; violence, both independent and organised, constantly flared up here and there. Terror and counter-terror seemed to be spreading all over.

On a cold January night in 1939, a man in saffron clothes arrived at the Hemayetpur Ashram; without informing anyone about his presence, he simply sat on the ground floor balcony of the ashram's guest house. Seventy yards or so from there was Sri Sri Thakur's residence. It was already late at night. Before going to bed, Sri Sri Thakur instructed his disciple, Bholanath Sarkar, "Go and check what is that faint sound outside? Is there someone around the guest house?" Bholanath saw the *sadhu* (monk) sitting outside the guest house smoking a *bidi*. The monk wanted to see Sri Sri Thakur at the earliest. Bholanath returned and informed Him. Sri Sri Thakur got up from bed and told Bholanath to call the monk.

He came to Sri Sri Thakur, and introduced himself as Ramashankar Singh and that he was involved in the freedom struggle against the British Empire and that there were several cases of violence against him. He was accused in a conspiracy case in an explosion in a train compartment. Though it was intended to kill several British officers in it, it also killed many innocent civilians. Now he was wanted dead or alive by the police; there was even a 20,000-rupee bounty on his head.

Sri Sri Thakur firmly asked, "Why have you come to me?" Ramashankar replied, "I do not want to participate in violent struggles or actions any more. After the train explosion, I realised, many innocent people lose their lives in such events. I am repenting of my actions, I have in the past concealed my identity, and lived in your Satsang Ashram at Kushtia for a month, but this burden is becoming unbearable now. I have talked to Pramathda, and have taken initiation (*Diksha*). I have heard many great things about you; now I have come to your feet, and need your shelter. I give you my word that I will never be involved in such activities henceforth." Sri Sri Thakur kept quiet for a while, and then replied, "Perhaps I can help you, but for that help to be of any meaning, it will require immense faith and courage from you." Ramashankar agreed and was willing to go to any extent believing Thakur. He confessed that after initiation, he had not followed any of its principles. Sri Sri Thakur asked him to abide by all that had been instructed. "You must offer *Istavriti* before sunrise to your Love Lord (*Ishta*). If you have no money, you can go and pluck a few flowers or leaves from the garden, and offer them as *Nibedan*. Ramashankar agreed, bowing his head with folded hands.

Thakur then instructed Ramashankar to surrender, and to confess any and every crime he had committed, to cooperate with the police and answer all their queries. He subsequently did as told. He was tried in court and sent to the Bihar state prison.

Sri Sri Thakur knew about Ramashankar's case, and discussed his prospects with many lawyers, finally, giving the responsibility of his release to Bholanath Sarkar. Bholanathda upon arriving at Pabna, met the DIG of the Criminal Investigation Department and told him the multi-faceted details of the case. After a subsequent investigation, it came to light that Ramashankar now was a reformed, civilised person. In due time, the court released Ramashankar on parole. Bholanathda travelled to Calcutta and informed about this development to Sri Sri Thakur in Hemayetpur. His reply was swift, and it read, "Dress him up like a prince on your way to the ashram." As ordered, Bholanathda bought some new clothes for Ramashankar, and presented his reformed self at Thakur's feet in Hemayetpur.

Ramashankar was escorted by Bholanathda to the Pabna Police once a month to ensure his good behaviour in civil society. After the fourth such consecutive visit, the law authorities were convinced of Ramashankar's reformation, and he was in due time completely acquitted of all charges, and released unconditionally. Under Sri Sri Thakur's supervision, Ramashankarda was trained in labour management and welfare and became an expert advisor on the subject. In 1951, Ramashankar visited London, France, and Vienna as a labour delegate from India, and his work was highly praised. (*Purushottam*)

(31). *The Bengal famine*

By 1940, the European war had gained momentum. When the rice crop in Satsang's farms was ready for harvesting, Thakur suggested that no contracts of sale were to be negotiated. All the rice should be stored for the ashram's use. He also advised devotees throughout Bengal who cultivated rice, not to sell but to store their new crop. A wave of controversy followed this advice. The European war skyrocketed the price of rice. Already, speculators were offering the peasants two or three times their former value. Devotees of Satsang saw a golden opportunity was slipping through their hands and pressured Thakur to let them consider selling at least part of their abundant crop. But Thakur was firm. Big granaries looking like giant beehives sprang up at Satsang.

The vision of untold wealth for the landlords and peasants of Bengal was short-lived. The new wealth disappeared faster than it came. By January 1942, Bengalis were selling furniture, jewellery, and even their children in order to eat. Faulty distribution and the inflated needs of war had brought famine to Bengal. Thousands of villagers migrated to Calcutta in the vain hope of finding food. Leaves were cooked and eaten. In the city, men fought with dogs, cats, and rats for the miserable contents of garbage cans. Each morning, carts of the Calcutta Municipal Corporation went about the grim business of gathering dead bodies from streets and doorways.

To the Satsang community in Hemayetpur, inhabitants from ten miles away came to join the daily free rice line. The storerooms that had seemed so extravagantly large a few months ago, were emptied one by one, but the supplies held out until the next crop was ready; no starvation death was reported from that area. (*Ocean in a Teacup*)

(32). A Rescue from Greed and Humiliation

In 1920, the sister-in-law of a business tycoon in Calcutta was severely ill for a long time. The gentleman was willing to pay 20,000 rupees to a doctor who could cure her. The value of 20,000 rupees back then is way more than several lakhs today.

Charumohan Chattopadhyay of Howrah had a friend named Satishchandra Joyardar, a famous doctor in Kushtia town adjacent to Pabna. Charumohan Babu assumed that since Dr. Joyardar was one of Sri Sri Thakur's close devotees, he could certainly cure the patient with Sri Sri Thakur's blessings. Charumohan was all set to receive the large amount, and share a part of it with his compatriot, Dr. Joyardar. Goaded by greed, Charumohanda visited Sri Sri Thakur in Hemayetpur before meeting the doctor. Hearing him, Thakur said, "You have not come here to genuinely help someone, your greed has guided you here. Had it been a selfless cause, I would have appreciated the effort. However, if Satishda is willing to give this a try, please feel free to take him along with you." Charumohanda now travelled from Hemayetpur to Kushtia, and requested Satishda to come with him. Dr. Joyardar responded thus, "After receiving this news, I sat for my meditation, and asked Sri Sri Thakur about the health of this patient. I had a premonition, "If you cannot save her, what is the point of going?" He told Charumohanda that he would consider going to Calcutta only after getting a go-ahead from Sri Sri Thakur. "You can go back to Calcutta for now." Charumohanda was upset, and left.

Nonetheless, when Dr. Joyardar did reach Hemayetpur to seek Thakur's permission, he did not get it. He communicated the same to Charumohanda. After a week, the patient passed away. Charumohanda's greed did not come to light, and Dr. Joyardar's reputation was saved. (*Sri Sri Thakur Anukulchandra*[1])

(33) A Rose-hued ray of Light, and the trickster lady monk

In 1927, Sri Sri Thakur was staying for some time at a devotee's farm house, overlooking the Ganges in Baranagar. On his way back to Hemayetpur, he travelled to Naihati to spend a few days with one of his close friends, Sashibhushan Chakravarty. It was there that he met a *sanyasini*, who said her name was Haridasi. Although her complexion was a little dark, she was beautiful and intelligent. As Thakur was preparing to leave, she insisted on accompanying him to the ashram. A close disciple, Dr. Satish Joyardar, was also present. Thakur suggested that if she would like to come to Hemayetpur, she must learn Homeopathy from him to cure women patients. "Only then she may join us." However, Haridasi stayed at Dr. Joyardar's place only for a day and came down to the ashram.

Initially, she showed a lot of devotion. Later on, she confessed to Thakur that in reality, she desired him. Sri Sri Thakur made it clear that he had always addressed her as 'mother', and that is the way he would like to see her in the future too. However, Haridasi simply couldn't control herself. Once, during the night, she forcibly tried to embrace Thakur; he swiftly pushed her away and even reprimanded her. She immediately fled the scene. Listening to the noise, many ashramites gathered. When they searched for her, she was found sitting near the Padma riverbed, pretending to meditate. Sri Sri Thakur warned against anyone humiliating or confronting her on this matter. Haridasi made three more similar attempts and failed every time. At no cost was she ready to leave the ashram. Two years passed.

In 1919, during the early summer of April, there was an

unusual storm and heavy rains were imminent. Sri Sri Thakur had gone near the Padma River late at night. Taking this as an opportunity, Haridasi once again and with more passion and fervour started forcing herself on Thakur. At that instant, a rose-hued ray of light emitted from Sri Sri Thakur's being. Terrified at such a magnanimous sight, Haridasi called out loudly to the people nearby. When a devotee, Durganath Sanyal, and several others arrived at the spot, what they saw completely astounded them. The halo around Thakur's body persisted for at least 10-15 minutes. Later, Sri Sri Thakur admitted that such an incident had indeed happened, but when asked about the reason, he said that he himself was not aware of the mystery of such an occurrence.

Nonetheless, after this event, Haridasi was never to be seen anywhere near the ashram. (*Manas Tirtha Parikrama*)

(34). Just surrender unto Me

Sometime in 1929, Sri Sri Thakur was staying in Kolkata. One evening, there was a gathering of several distinguished dignitaries, including Barrister J. N. Dutta, and his wife (Dutta Ma). When they were alone, Dutta Ma in an emotional tone said to Thakur, "You came in my dreams. I remember asking you, 'Are you my spiritual guide?' And you answered, "Yes." Sri Sri Thakur replied, "Ma, why are you attributing all this to me? I am an ordinary man." But Dutta Ma did not stop. She went on chanting *slokas* and *mantras* with intense devotion, without caring for her surroundings. Sri Sri Thakur without blinking kept looking at her with affection. It was now time for everyone to leave, but Dutta Ma was unwilling to abandon her spot. Her husband, the barrister, tried his best to pull her out of her trance and leave, but he failed. Sri Sri Thakur intervened in a casual demeanour, "Your husband is comparable to God, and listening to him is your duty. Please go home." Dutta Ma said she would leave, but on one condition. "I want you to promise me, whenever during my meditation, I wish to see you, you shall appear before me." Sri Sri

Thakur ignored this statement. Dutta Ma was still unwilling to leave Thakur's side. After a moment, Thakur made an effort to murmur something in her ear. Her joy after this rose out of bounds, and she left for home happily.

A week later, Dutta Ma was back in the presence of Sri Sri Thakur, this time without Justice Dutta. After *Pranam*, she confided to Sri Sri Thakur, "Today, while I was eating, you had come to see me, and chanted a *sloka* to me, the sheer power of it was enlightening. I could not fathom it fully. From whatever I remembered, I spontaneously asked my husband to make a note of it in his diary. But why did you leave so soon, without completing or explaining what you had said? I simply cannot leave your side today until you repeat that great *sloka* to me."

At that moment, Sri Sri Thakur was in no mood to explain it. What he did instead was to not directly utter the *sloka*, but smartly included it in a *bhakti* song he was already rendering. It goes: "sarva-dharmân parityajya mâm ekam sharaG am vraja aham tvâm sarva-papebhyo mokshayic hyâmi mâ shuchah" (*Gita*. 18/66). (Abandon all varieties of religion and just surrender unto Me. I shall deliver you from all sinful reactions; do not fear.) The moment Dutta Ma got the hang of the song, and could recognise the *sloka*, she almost jumped up in joy, and told everyone that this was indeed the *sloka* she had heard. (*Premer Thakur*)

(35). No Malice towards his Defamers

'*Shanibarer Chithi*' (Saturday Newsletter) is a weekly Bengali magazine published from Calcutta, a sort of yellow journal. As Sri Sri Thakur's popularity was on the rise, to improve its sales, the publication concocted stories tarnishing his image. (A detailed discussion on this is available in Part One of this book). In those days, a Satsangi, Radhikanath Saha, would go from door to door in Pabna to sell this magazine. One day, while Radhikanathda was going about his usual activity, one of the customers asked, "Radhika, aren't you an honest devotee of Sri Sri Thakur?

Sajanikanta Das (editor of the magazine) is maligning Thakur, and you are going around selling this magazine? You are certainly committing a sin." Radhika was completely aghast and shocked at hearing this. He immediately stopped selling the magazine, got on his cycle and travelled all the way from Pabna to Hemayetpur, and went straight to meet Sri Sri Thakur. Thakur, on seeing the exhausted Radhika, asked, "How have you been?" Radhika responded, "I have been okay, but I have committed a grave sin against you." Thakur asked further, "What is it?" Radhika said, "This magazine has been publishing slanderous and mischievous stories about you. I am an illiterate man, and unknowingly I have sold several copies. Have I done something unforgivable?" Sri Sri Thakur replied with a smile, "How many copies do you sell? How is the demand for it in the market?" Radhika told Thakur a figure and said that the magazine sold well.

Sri Sri Thakur said, "I would rather go on to say, Radhika, go get some more copies, start selling them with zest." Radhika was surprised, and replied, "You are maligned in public, and you are asking me to boost the sale of a magazine that is doing so?"

Sri Sri Thakur, with a flicker of contentment in his eyes, said, "Listen, Radhika. Be it in the form of a critique or appreciation, my name, purpose, and work is what is being propagated. What else could I ask for?" (*Pralay Majumdar*)

(Postscript: Spreading rumours about Thakur was started by a certain scandalous group, when the then elites of Calcutta, consisting of barristers, doctors, professors, etc., came in large numbers to meet Thakur, and soon became his disciples. Among them who travelled to Hemayetpur Ashram, were those who persuaded devotees to go back by telling fabricated stories about Thakur. Sri Sri Thakur, on coming to know of this, did not express even a shred of disappointment, and said, "They are making my work easier; those devotees that come to me despite their doubts, are only more sincere in their faith. It is people like these that I need, they are helping this process." Sri Sri Thakur never held any grudge against his critics).

(36). The Strange Experience of Kamalaksha Sarkar

Kamalaksha Sarkar served the British Imperial Army from 1913 to 1918. As the First World War was drawing to its end, about 500 soldiers of the British army were returning from Azerbaijan to Baghdad. By the time they reached the barren large deserts of Mesopotamia, their food and water had been exhausted. As a consequence, only seven members of the cavalry survived. They, exhausted by enduring hunger and thirst, stopped near an enormous ant hill in the hot sand under a scorching sun. and waited for death to end their misery. The Kurds, who carried goods between traders and markets across the desert, often used that route on their camels. At times, some of them looted unwary travellers, sometimes even killing them and burying their bodies in the vast expanse of the Mesopotamian desert. The weary soldiers saw a Kurd at a distance who tossed seven large carrots, and pointed towards where they would find water. Among the seven surviving soldiers was Kamalaksha Sarkar.

After the war, the British government felicitated Kamalakshada with promotion to officer in the Bombay cavalry. He did not join as his mother did not permit him. Once, when travelling by train, at Jamshedpur station, he heard Tata Group announcing they needed job-seekers for their company. He got off, went to their office and got a job. The daily working wage back then was 6 annas, with accommodation in the company quarters nearby.

Once, Madhavi Mohan Mukherjee, a Ritwik, had gone to Jamshedpur for an initiation program (diksha) of Satsang. Looking for a Bengali family, he found Kamalaksha Sarkar's quarters. It was late in the night, so not wanting to disturb anyone, waited in the veranda until dawn. Meanwhile, the Sarkar couple had a strange dream that night that they were accepting initiation from someone. As morning dawned, and they opened their door, they saw a gentleman dressed in chaste white waiting for them. They had a long conversation, and both husband and wife accepted Sri Sri Thakur's Diksha. They came to know thereafter that their destined Guru was Sri Sri Thakur Anukul Chandra Chakravarty, and that his ashram was at Pabna, Hemayetpur. Madhavi Mohan had come as a representative of Sri Sri Thakur and had Initiated them. After finishing his work, Madhavi Mohan took down the addresses of other people nearby known to the Sarkars, and left. While leaving, he advised the couple, in order to maintain the bond of initiation and like all initiates, must pay a visit to their Guru at the Hemayetpur Ashram as soon as possible.

The couple travelled to Hemayetpur the next morning. On seeing Sri Sri Thakur, Kamalaksha Sarkar was aghast. He exclaimed, "I have seen you somewhere before, Sir. When the seven of us lay in hopelessness in the Mesopotamian desert, dying of hunger, the Kurd who had helped us looked exactly like you. He had given us seven carrots, and pointed to where we would find water. He saved our lives. The only difference between you and him in appearance is perhaps that he had no moustache like you." Hearing this elaborate description by Kamalakshada, Sri Sri Thakur, as usual, replied with a hearty smile. (Swasti Sevak, 2013)

(37) As is the Food, so is the Form that eats it

Once a childhood friend of Sri Sri Thakur had invited him over for lunch, and had every intention to serve him mutton. He ensured that Sri Sri Thakur agreed to come. When the day finally arrived, the friend asked his wife to cook a good mutton curry. When it was done, his wife bolted the kitchen door from the outside, and went for a bath. Returning, she found a little black dog in the kitchen with its head buried in the pot sumptuously eating the mutton. The creaking of the door opening scared the dog and it jumped out through a hole in the wall of mud and bamboo shafts. Thakur's friend was utterly disappointed. Since a dog had almost finished everything, they could no longer serve any of it to Sri Sri Thakur. The wife prepared a simple plain curry with rice, as her husband advised, and both of them waited for Thakur, but he did not turn up. Tired of waiting, the couple ultimately took their food, and decided to ask Thakur during the evening session at the ashram why he had not kept his word.

Thakur replied, "I did come to your place. I never knew your wife was such a good cook, I enjoyed the mutton curry to my heart's content." The friend retorted, "Don't make up stories; you are lying." Thakur then showed the wound over his bare right shoulder, saying, "When I jumped through the hole in the kitchen wall into your backyard, the broken bamboo shaft brushed against my body. I never lie, you should know that." The friend was shocked, and responded, "As far as my wife told me, it was a black dog that ate the meat, and jumped through a hole in the wall. When did you come?" Sri Sri Thakur smiled, and said, "If you serve me a dog's food, being a human myself, how can I have it?" (Santosh Joarder, Kaloda)

(38). The Military, out of nowhere

By 1925-26, enmity against the Hemayetpur Satsang had intensified, so much so that it was on the verge of becoming communal. The reason was Sri Sri Thakur's decision to set up a bank by the Satsang Ashram, that would help poor, landless farmers and labourers obtain loans at extremely low interest. This naturally affected the exploitation by many landlords and moneylenders. Consequently, these people with power and influence started assaulting the ashramites. They sent thugs to intimidate people, hired men to harass the ashram women on the streets, and would barge into the ashram to heckle people; once, they even set a cottage on fire.

It was the monsoon season. Sri Sri Borma's nephew had passed away suddenly. The hired goons made sure that the body could not be consecrated to fire in the village cremation ground. As the funeral proceedings started, the people carrying the corpse were beaten; they had to bring the body back. A rumour was spread throughout the village that Muslims would enter the ashram that night and provoke riots in its precincts. The efforts of Mother Manmohini Devi by visiting the homes of some of the troublemakers to settle for peace were unsuccessful. That was a long night. Sri Sri Thakur and Anant Maharaj kept vigil throughout. A generator was used to flood the premises with light. There was an avalanche of fear and anxiety. The youth prepared for a violent clash. However, the orders from Sri Sri Thakur were clear; no one was to even hold a lathi (stick) in their hands. Late in the night, news reached the ashram that a gang of miscreants were approaching crying out 'Allah hu Akbar', Sri Sri Thakur stood bravely near the ashram gate to face the adversaries. At this moment, out of nowhere, a small platoon of the Gorkha regiment of the Indian Army arrived. Ten to twelve well-built soldiers with modern weapons approached quickly. They conveyed Sri Sri Thakur their salutations, and stood guard in front of him, awaiting his orders.

This information reached the attackers. Knowing that the military had arrived, the hooligans fled through the rice fields, slipping, falling, and somehow managing to escape. The soldiers secured the ashram perimeters. In the end, they reassured Sri Sri Thakur, gave him their greetings, and in no time vanished into the night's darkness. The residents of the ashram now breathed a sigh of relief.

Afterwards, the police with some of the native Muslims of the village arrived, and requested Sri Sri Thakur to perform the last rites of Borma's nephew in the village cremation ground. Sri Sri Thakur said, "Such an action would unnecessarily further incite cynicism and animosity in the village. The cremation shall take place within the ashram premises." Upon inquiring about the names and whereabouts of the attackers, Sri Sri Thakur replied, "Physical punishment can never reform individuals. My world is one of forgiveness and love."

It is a mystery till today, how and from where did the military come to Satsang Ashram's rescue that fateful night? When asked about the incident, Sri Sri Thakur kept quiet and looked towards the sky. (Pranar Thakur)

(39). Detachment, defined

In May 1924, when Sri Sri Thakur was staying in Calcutta, a renowned barrister of the Calcutta High Court, Chittaranjan Das, had accepted Thakur's Diksha. A devotee, Sushil Chandra Basu, was asked by Sri Sri Thakur to stay at Barrister Das' residence on his visits to Calcutta. On one of them, Chittaranjan Babu told Sushilda, "There is a plot of land of about 50 bighas (31 acres) near the Ballygunge Lake area under my jurisdiction. I could give it to Satsang if you can convince Thakur to set up an ashram there. It would be really beneficial to our cause. Calcutta is well connected by road, rail, and air to all parts of the country. Being in the centre of the city, the ashram would attract a lot of positive traction, many important and powerful people would become a part of it, their support and influence would be extended towards the ashram. Sri Sri Thakur's word can reach far and wide, and in no time a great foundation of Satsang will be laid in Calcutta ."

Sushilda almost jumped at the proposal. His imagination soared high, Satsang in a vast area of 31 acres, a Satsang village, cottage industries of all sorts, educational institutions, super speciality hospital with the best doctors of Calcutta, VIPs coming one after another, the siren of their pilot vehicles sounding in distant places. This is the Satsang of my dreams. Sushilda beat his hands to his thighs, like a victory clap in excitement. What a fantastic proposition! The idea goaded him so much that he could neither eat, nor sleep. He went off to Hemayetpur before schedule.

After hearing everything, Sri Sri Thakur coolly responded, "All your and Dasda's propositions sound correct and sensible. The ashram will truly grow and diversify in Calcutta. However, as a matter of moral principle, to have an ashram in a rural area, where there are obstacles at every step, where our work can benefit the most downtrodden of society, that is a challenge one must aspire for. Once you overcome such adversities in extremely hostile circumstances, no problem can ever be an impediment for you. It is for this reason I choose to stay here in Hemayetpur, rather than moving to the comfort of Calcutta." Sushilda responded, "Even if you do not want to set up an ashram there now, since Dasda is offering us more than 30 acres of land, we must at least accept it. In future, if nothing else, we can sell it and earn a substantial amount of money that we can put to good use."

Sri Sri Thakur, true to his style, said, "Since there is no plan to set up an ashram there, why should we accept the land now? Perhaps it can be used for some other purpose. When we need the land, we shall see to it." While writing Sri Sri Thakur's biography expressing his opinion on the matter, Sushilda wrote, "I had not seen such selflessness on display in any human being." Perhaps this is reminiscent of Thakur's eponymous words:

> Money is not yours, but Man,
> Earn Men, as much as you can.
> (Manas Tirtha Parikrama)

(40). Growing Merit through Love

Panchanan Sarkar was a double M.A. After initiation and contact with Thakur, he left Calcutta to permanently settle at Hemayetpur. On the insistence of Thakur, he took charge of Tapovan High School as the superintendent. One day, Sarkar came to Thakur; he looked flustered and anxious. Thakur heard him complaining, "I plead with you to relieve me of the school's responsibility." Sri Sri Thakur asked, "Why?" Panchananda continued, "Most of the students here are good for nothing. There is no point in putting effort or money into them; it is a waste of time. I don't want to be a party to it. Either you relieve me or allow me to drive away the undeserving students through an entrance examination."

Sri Sri Thakur looked at Panchananda with a lasting smile, and with the heavy voice of a guardian asked, "Tell me Panchananda, which clothes does the washerman take from your house, dirty or clean." Panchananda retorted, "What kind of a question is that? Why would the washerman take clean clothes?"

Sri Sri Thakur said in a voice filled with laughter, "I am telling you the same thing, Panchananda. You are a washerman. Your job is to clean the dirty elements. If you drive them away from the school, what sort of a washerman will you be?" Panchananda had a mercurial temperament with a high spirit. He immediately understood Thakur's hint, and with folded hands said, "Thakur, bless me to clean the dirty elements, and make them men of your expectations."

Time passed. The teacher came to Thakur with a morose face. Thakur asked, "Why are you looking so exhausted? What's the matter?" Sarkarda knelt before Thakur and said, "This time, if the school performs miserably in the entrance exam, don't blame me. Without students of merit I can't show good results." Thakur looked him in the face, "What's that? You talk about all the negatives. If a student lacks merit, grow it in him."

Sarkarda was surprised, "What are you talking about, Thakur? How can I develop merit in a dunce?" Thakur said, "Through love. You can grow merit through love." Panchananda replied, "You will tell all the impossible things on Earth. You show me how love can make a stupid person meritorious?" Thakur laughingly said, "Let the time come. I will show you." The discussion ended there.

Winter has arrived. One morning, a little away from the three-foot bamboo enclosure of Thakur's sitting area, a dog was suckling and feeding its pups. Thakur looked at them and sent for the argumentative teacher. As soon as Panchananda arrived, Thakur gestured towards the pups and said, "Take one of these to your house, and train it with etiquette." Panchananda could not understand the purpose behind this, but since it was a strict order from Thakur, he concurred. After three months, one morning, Panchananda, before going to the school, visited Thakur to offer his oblations. Thakur asked about the pup. Panchananda replied with elation, "It has grown now to a good size. When I call, it comes to me; when I order it to sit, it obeys, and goes away when I signal. It has come with me and is now sitting near the bamboo fence." Thakur was very happy and asked his teacher-disciple to call the puppy nearby. As soon as Panchananda called it by name, it ran towards him. Panchananda demonstrated the pup's learning before Thakur, his teaching acumen. At a distance, the mother, along with her three other grown-up pups, was loitering. Thakur in a cajoling voice asked Panchananda to call the other pups. Hearing the loud call, the mother dog along with her three pups retreated out of sight. Now Thakur explained to Panchananda, "See the difference. All the four are born of the same mother; one out of them you took and brought up with care and affection, teaching it behaviour. Is learned and obeyed. It obeys you because it loves you. Have you not made the wild animal a disciplined pup and infused merit in it?" Panchananda now got the answer to his complaint. (Premal Thakur)

(41). The communal riots of 1946, and Thakur's departure from Hemayetpur

The agitation for independence intensified during the war years as did the brutal British suppression. By 1945, the flames of religious hatred and polarisation had been fanned to deplorable heights. Many responsible leaders of the Indian National Congress and Muslim League charged the British government with maintaining paid agitators to keep the communal fire burning to further their divide-and-rule policy. Ugly rumours began to spread that the Muslim League in Calcutta had proclaimed 16 August 1946 as Direct Action Day, to overpower the Hindus and claim India as an Islamic state.

The areas around Pabna were predominantly Muslim, and it

only took one isolated incident to heighten tensions. Many Muslim devotees came to Sri Sri Thakur with a word of caution, "Our influence is waning in the region. Men from Calcutta are constantly coming to our villages and inciting the locals with rumours. Blind faith makes reason impossible."

Direct action leads to reaction, and then to reprisals. The disturbances spread from cities to villages, separating communities from one another along religious lines. When the military restored some semblance of law and order, it was learned that about one hundred and twenty five thousand people had lost their lives in this senseless fighting. Upon hearing this, Thakur broke down completely. This great tragedy had caused him immense pain, and changed his mind and vision. He called for Sushil Chandra Bose and told him, "We are no longer safe. Go to Deoghar immediately and rent the largest building that is available. Say nothing of this to anyone." After Sushilda took a big bungalow on rent at Rohini Road, he along with his family and a few devotees left Hemayetpur and reached Deoghar on 2 September 1946.

14

SOME OF HIS DIVINE TIDINGS—DEOGHAR ASHRAM

(42). Subduing the Ego of the disciple

The detractors of the Satsang movement became more and more belligerent as their numerous attempts to destabilise the organisation failed miserably. So, they found an easy way to distort the relationship between Thakur and the ever-growing population of his Muslim disciples.

A notorious Muslim gang leader of the area, who had attempted to murder a Satsang member, lodged a complaint with the police that Borda and Bankim, an ashramite, had apprehended him. A case was registered accordingly. Things looked pretty bad because the judicial officer at the time was a Muslim who disliked everything about Hindus. An elderly devotee, Bholanath, approached Ray Hauserman, staying at Calcutta, inquiring if he knew someone in the government who could help. Ray remembered a friend, Jack Hughes, the aide-de-camp (French for camp assistant) to the governor. Ray explained to him the mischievous efforts of vested interests to create confusion and disturbance at Satsang by initiating false cases against the ashramites. Jack was convinced and made arrangements for a government inquiry of the case. It was found that the allegation was concocted and false; it was dismissed eventually.

When the news reached the ashram, everybody praised Hauserman for his efforts. At Calcutta, Guru brothers came and thanked him for performing a miracle and that he would occupy the front line of Satsang. All the admiration certainly gave his ego a good boost. He thought Thakur would praise him sky high. He decided to go to Hemayetpur at the earliest. In his own language:

"The next weekend, I approached the ashram looking forward to a special greeting. Thakur was sitting on the porch with some disciples and I bowed to him. He immediately started talking to someone else there. I sat and waited for him to at least recognise me. He would look past me, beside me, around me, but never at me. The next morning it was the same thing, and the next evening as well. When I asked a direct question, he answered briefly and that was all. I left on Sunday with hardly a nod from him. Half way back to Calcutta, I thought of Thakur's strange behaviour, and analysed how I was mad after the credit for the little job I had done for Satsang had not been acknowledged by Thakur. The more the expectation multiplies, the faster the peace you seek disappears. Ultimately, you are left with clouds of disappointment; frustrated, helpless, and alone."

"In a later discussion with Thakur, he said, 'Growth in devotion resembles a jagged shape, like lightning. It goes up very high, then slides down, but not as far as before, and again it goes up higher than before, and down but not as low. Then, he added, this is true if you have a living 'Ideal' to keep you pointed in the right direction.'

"The dismissal of the criminal case was a helpful experience for me. Expectations and the insidious effects of praise are not easy to avoid and overcome. Thakur's major psychological surgery on me, has over the years helped me to control my ego and expectations." (Being and Becoming)

(43). Love Him, and all shall love you

Edmund Spencer and Ray Hauserman, at the end of the First World War, after their initiation by Thakur, cancelled their return to America on the completion of their tenure in American Field Service in India. Sri Sri Thakur wanted them to be true Christians by loving Christ immensely without any expectations. He arranged for a reading of the Bible by a group of devotees including the two Americans.

Spencer was reading out the Bible. In verse 17 of chapter 5 where Christ says, "I come to fulfil not to destroy", Thakur nodded enthusiastically and said, "I think the characteristics of all Prophets is to fulfil those of the previous ones." At the end of the chapter, Christ said, "You are to be perfect even as your Father in heaven is perfect." Hauserman looked up at Thakur and blurted out, "Is not this requirement for perfection unrealistic? It seems to me to be totally impossible." Thakur's reaction was immediate, "Can't you just love Him, because you love Him? Can't you serve Him just because it pleases you to serve Him? Do that. I tell you then, you will imbibe Him in every atom of your existence, automatically, wherever you are and whether you ask for it or not." His intense conviction wrapped in soft affection created a tremendous influence on Hauserman. He writes:

"Like a light going on, all at once I knew it was true. I suddenly found the capacity to love inside me. All the doubts and misery and insecurities dissolved. I was feeling so free, I could only smile and chuckle. It is so easy, I wanted to shout. Thakur looked at me and I felt a complete rapport between us at that moment. It was as if he was saying inside my head, 'Now you have got the key, don't lose it.'

"Floating in this new inner world, I felt I was drunk with the joy of this discovery. Thakur knew about it and commented, 'Ray looks like a child of nature.' This experience of joy stayed with me for more than a month."

Hauserman wrote, after the reading of the Bible was complete he boarded a train to Calcutta. The joy he felt had not yet left him. He decided to commit to loving Christ through Thakur, and see what happened. The experience in that train compartment in his own words:

"In a crowded third class compartment, squeezed on the seat beside us and on the floor was a group of Bengali villagers. Among them were two women with babies, one of whom would not stop crying. Impulsively, I reached out and picked the baby up, so that the crying would stop. I held the baby for a few minutes until it went to sleep, then handed it over to the mother. Later, I felt hungry, but before I could ask, someone offered me a few bananas. I got thirsty, and a stranger offered a cup of tea in my hand before I could speak. I only needed to glance at someone, and they would nod and smile respectfully. The four-and-a-half hour trip passed by like a dream."

Thakur's approach was deceptively simple. The common urge for life and growth is his basic message. This can be achieved by love without expectation, which he called Being and Becoming. (Being and Becoming)

(44). The Master saves

In 1946, H. S. Suhrawardy was the Chief Minister of undivided Bengal. John Barrow was the governor. Suhrawardy, though loudly and publicly supported and sympathised with the Hindus, the government's attitude was otherwise. Noakhali at that time was an inaccessible district in East Bengal and had about 80 per cent Muslim population. Spread over forty square miles, it was home to more than two-and-a-half million people living in villages divided by canals and streams, accessible only by small boats and ferries. In October, the government transferred all officers from Noakhali, and replaced them with a hundred new officers, all of whom were fanatically anti-Hindu Muslims. A week later, communications with Noakhali were interrupted. Stories began emerging from terrified Hindus who had escaped; news of murder, rape, forced conversions and kidnappings. Soon, newspapers were reporting the breakdown of civil law and the entrapment of Hindus in their own towns, forced to convert, or be killed. Finally after suffering great loss, public outcry forced the government to bring in the army.

More than 7,000 of Thakur's disciples lived in Noakhali. One of the most prominent among them was Kali Mitra, the Headmaster of the largest high school in the district. He was also a popular leader, respected by both Muslims and Hindus. Rumours of his death caused great concern among the guru brothers and Hindus of the district, as well as in the Satsang Ashram, Deoghar.

Late in October, to everyone's surprise, an unshaven and unkempt Kalida was welcomed joyfully at Boral Bungalow, Satsang Ashram, Deoghar. With tears in his eyes, he knelt before Thakur. Thakur said, "You have come. Go, take a bath, eat and rest. I will hear about everything later." That evening, Mitrada told his tale to Thakur, "On 16 October Abu Mia, one of my students, came to my home early in the morning and said, 'Master, you have to leave quickly. They have just announced a 25,000 rupee reward on your head! There is nobody to protect you now, so please run away.' But I could not believe that this was happening. I thanked the boy for the warning, and returned home. Suddenly that evening I heard your voice. It was as clear as I hear it now. You said 'Get out Kali. Get out now!'

"I ran immediately from the house and heard you say, 'Get into the paddy field and hide!' Within a few moments a gang came to the house; they broke down the door and set the house on fire after they looted it. Fortunately, I had sent my family a few days earlier to a relative's place out of Noakhali. However, I spent that night in the paddy field.

"Just before dawn, you woke me up and said 'Go to Hazrat Ali's house.' I went, and as soon as he saw me, he hid me under some straw. I stayed there the whole day. Then again you spoke to me saying to go to Abdul Aziz's house, where he hid me in the women's quarter. You literally took me by the hand and guided me out of danger. You saved my life."

Thakur overlooked the praise. He enquired gently, "What about the others?" Kalida replied, "I do not know, Thakur. I have to go back. Now of course the military is there, Gandhi is holding peace meetings, but we hear of Hindus being stabbed in the back by the very Muslims who swore to protect their Hindu brothers and sisters." (Being and Becoming)

(45). Uncanny way of relief

Within a short period of Thakur's arrival at Deoghar, a number of stories circulated around the town: respite from chronic diseases, gaining some lost cherished objects, or restoration of domestic tranquillity when one fulfilled Thakur's request. One of the strangest events concerned a West Bengal police officer, Dulal Nandi, who arrived in torn clothes, unshaven and with bloodshot eyes. He narrated a pathetic story of suffering, his wife dying of cancer, two of his sons killed in a railway accident, and his recently-married daughter losing her first child. He was also a facing suspension charge for a crime he had not committed. He came on the insistence of his daughter to receive Thakur's blessings. He had considered committing suicide several times.

Dulal fell at Thakur's feet, and without waiting for an introduction poured out his aching heart. At the end, he said, "It's all over, Thakur. I am through. Whether it is bad karma or some curse, it doesn't matter anymore. The only way left is to end the suffering for all of us." As if this tragic tale hadn't been spoken, Thakur said, "Do one thing for me. Do you know those iron safes jeweller's keep in their shop for gold and gemstones? Get one for me. It should be at least 18 inches square."

Dulal was stunned. Without bothering a farewell, he got up abruptly with a grim look on his face and headed for the tea shop. His daughter bowed and thanked Thakur, hurrying after her father. When she reached the tea shop, Dulal out of disgust reprimanded her, "This is your Thakur! I am dying and he asked me for a safe." The daughter however said quietly, "Dad, we should get it for him." Dulal almost snarled, "I am being prosecuted, probably going to lose my job; your brothers are dead, your mother is dying, your daughter is gone, and I am to find a safe somewhere? This is what you call Thakur's blessings." The girl's eyes held a fanatic desperation, "No matter what happens, Dad. Thakur is all we have got. Even if we all die doing it, let us get the safe for him." Some weeks later Dulal arrived with the safe, and was told by Thakur to give it to Borda for the office. He left grimly, like a prisoner facing a death sentence.

Two months later Dulal, his wife, daughter and son-in-law turned up at the ashram. Resplendent in a neatly pressed police uniform he bowed before Thakur. Seeing his happiness Thakur laughed, "Go, bathe and eat. I will hear the details later." It was a strange story. After giving Thakur the iron safe, the case against Dulal was dropped, his wife regained her appetite, in a spontaneous remission, the doctor explained that the tumour in his daughter's abdomen had shrunk in size, and that she was pregnant again. On top of it, Dulal was promoted. But how was the safe linked to these events?

Panditji, one of the several resident astrologers had a ready explanation, "Dulal had the planet Saturn retrograde, and his stars had encircled Mars and Rahu (one of the many indicators in Indian astrology) of great misfortune. The only antidote for that is to donate iron to a true Brahmin, and Thakur knew that."

When someone asked Thakur how he knew all this, he repeated one of his favourite sayings, "There are more things between heaven and earth, Horatio, than are dreamt of in your philosophy." (Being and Becoming)

(46). Unique definition of income and expenditure

In 1962, Sankardas Banerjee, the then Finance Minister of West Bengal, visited the Satsang Ashram. He was a great economist. He was quite impressed with the activities of the ashram, such as the Ananda Bazar (a free food, community kitchen), the publishing house, Rasaishana Mandir (an Ayurveda medicine manufacturing unit), and many other such institutions. But where does the money come from? While paying an obeisance to Thakur, he asked gently, "What is your income, Sir?" Thakur replied affectionately, "Man is my income." Banerjee thought to himself, how man could be somebody's income and then asked another question, "If man is your income, what is your expenditure?"

Thakur gave a smiling reply, "Love is my expenditure'" A finance wizard was taken aback altogether. He was introduced to a new definition of income and expenditure. (Nilu Joarder)

(47). Are you God?

American devotee Ray Hauserman's mother came to visit her son and stayed for quite some time with him in the ashram. One evening they were sitting before Thakur. She rose without preliminaries and asked, "Thakur, a great many of your followers claim that you are God. Now I want to know what you say you are?"

An elderly disciple rose at once to say, "I can explain this." But the lady cut him off rather rudely, "I have already heard what all of you had to say. Now I want to know what Thakur says!" Thakur's face glowed with a wide boyish smile. Obviously he enjoyed the American mother's determination to get the answer to such an awkward question. He continued, "Ma, if they call me God, will it make me more than what I am? And if they call me devil, will it make me any less? I am as you see me."

She nodded with satisfaction, and sat down. When she was to return, on the last day, she said, "He can't be God. No man can. But Thakur has loved God so deeply that he has gained many qualities of God. He has become Godlike."

*

A Philadelphia bachelor, who had spent most of his adult life squandering inherited wealth, came to meet Thakur in the late Forties. He complained of being empty, his life had become tasteless, and a succession of psychoanalysts had failed to relieve his condition. He came with the intention of staying for a few days but eventually spent several months there. On his return to America, at the Calcutta Airport, he confided to a friend, "You know this is the first time in my life I am not afraid; the first time I ever believe that love exists outside of a lot of fancy words and trumped up acrobatics."

*

A diplomat's wife returned to Washington DC and wrote to Thakur, "Everyone here is taking Melatonin (a tranquiliser). I am constantly advising them to go and see you, the living tranquiliser." (Answer To The Quest)

(48). The Significance of Istavriti (Spiritual Oblation)

One of the most important devotees of Satsang, Sri Sri Thakur's teacher during his medical college days, Dr. Sashibhushan Mitra, questioned him once, "Can an ordinary, worldly person sincerely do Istavriti regularly?" In response, Sri Sri Thakur reminded Dr. Mitra of an incident from his own life, "When due to one's own mistake, they lose their path in life, and are abandoned in the abyss of utter darkness with no visible way out, it is my responsibility then to guide them to light. For this to happen, people have to follow a certain path. I have reiterated this time and again, and people do not understand. The story: Once Dr. Sashibhushan went far from home to see a patient all by himself. He was in a territory he didn't recognise very well, and quite naturally, while returning, he lost his way; it was evening. He kept on walking in increasing darkness; there was no sign of any house or village where even a trace of light could be seen. The roads were not getting any better either. In this hour of trouble, he prayed to Sri Sri Thakur. He saw a man carrying a lantern coming towards Dr. Mitra; he had never seen or known the man earlier, and yet he proposed to help, saying he had known the doctor and his work. Even after a lot of insistence, the man didn't reveal his identity, and evaded the question saying it wasn't possible on the good doctor's part to remember him. He walked with him to the nearest home, where some light could be seen from a distance. As they approached close to , Sashibhushan turned back only to find that the man had disappeared.

Dr. Mitra now realised the importance of Istavriti. In times of danger and need, Spiritual Praxis is the only way out. (Satwati, May, 2019)

(49). Surviving a plane crash

In 1952, Kalipada Raha came to Deoghar to pay respects to his Master. He had been initiated around 10 years ago, and was now a Saha-Prati-Ritwik (SPR). He comes to visit Thakur in regular intervals, about three-four times a year. By profession, he was a teacher and a well-to-do person in Rangoon. This time he had booked his return ticket by air from Calcutta to Rangoon.

The day before his departure, he prostrated himself before Thakur to take leave.. When he started to speak, Thakur, ignoring his submission, blurted out, "Hey Kali, can you get me an Ikmik brand cooker? It is not available here in the local market. Fetch me my sweet child from Calcutta." Calcutta is at a distance of 6-8 hours by rail or road. Kalipadada took the earliest train, and brought the aluminium cooker. Upon his return, when he opened the box to show the piece, Thakur was sad, "What Kali? What small cooker have you brought? Is there no bigger size?" Kalipadada explained that the bigger size is double the price. Thakur was happy and said, "Keep the small one here, I want the bigger one." Though Kalipadada was a little perplexed, he smiled and submitted to his wishes, "Thakur, I will hurry to Calcutta and bring the bigger cooker." Next day, he brought the bigger cooker packed in a cardboard box and opened it before Thakur expecting appreciation, but he found the Guru morose again; Thakur said, "This is aluminium; Is this cooker available in any other metal?" Kalipadada said, "Yes Thakur, a brass cooker is also available." Thakur smiled happily and said, "Get me that one. It will last longer." Kalipadada was left with no other choice but to go to Calcutta again. He brought the brass cooker and immediately left to board the train to Calcutta to catch his flight. He had no time to eat, and had even forgotten to take his blood pressure medicines. When he reached the airport, at the reception, he was told that his flight had already left an hour earlier. His head started reeling, and his blood pressure shot up. He sensed as if the floor was moving under his feet. The desperation brought him a kind of loneliness akin to what some people feel at the time of death.

He felt in his pockets for his purse. There was only enough money to pay the taxi fare from Rangoon (now Yangon) airport to his residence. Suddenly a ray of hope appeared. He recollected that his uncle, a businessman, was in Calcutta. He took a taxi, and reached his uncle's place and stayed there the night. He borrowed 200 rupees from him to buy another ticket, and reached the airport the next day. At the ticket counter when he told his name, the lady stood up, looked at him through the partition glass and asked, "Are you Mr. K. P. Raha?" Kalipadada said, "Yes. What's the matter?" The lady said, "Have you not seen the morning newspaper?" The flight to Rangoon (20-seater) had crashed. There were 19 dead and K. P. Raha is missing. Where were you, sir?" She ran inside the office and informed that Raha had survived. Kalipadada was escorted to the office. He narrated the whole episode of the Ikmik cooker, and how he had missed the flight, and who really saved his life. Thereafter, he was given a free ticket to Rangoon. (Thakur Anukulchandra)

(50). The Benefits of Istavriti (Spiritual Oblation)

Once, during a long discussion, Sri Sri Thakur told Sushilda (Basu) the process is full of varied qualities. Its pursuance has no limits. Sushilda said, "I have heard in Borishal (now in Bangladesh), during the turbulent times of communal riots, how members and workers of the Satsang were rescued through Ishtavriti their commitment to Spiritual Praxis sounds nothing short of a great miracle. A lot of people from that side have reported that Thakur himself was present there, actively involved in all of their protection."

Hearing this, Sri Sri Thakur said, "One of Labanya Maa's sisters saw me in a dream a few days earlier. She claimed to have served me puffed rice and milk for breakfast. Being in a hurry, I exclaimed, "Give it to me quickly; I need to leave for Barisal immediately." He kept quiet for a while, and started again, "I am nobody. Everything happens according to the will of the Almighty. It was indeed His hand that perhaps helped me save so many lives of our Satsangi brothers and sisters."

It is important to note here that those who were saved had a lot of faith in Sri Sri Thakur's path of life. It is also correct to state that people in the past have benefitted physically and mentally through the offering of Istavriti. It activates almost all essential organs, the entire neurological network, and puts the mind's problem-solving faculties to action. In times of danger, these abilities come as a great aid. But only those who are sincere and rigorous in their practice can reap these benefits. (Alochana Prasange. Part 1)

(51). Compassion towards the Downtrodden

In the Boral Bungalow, Thakur usually stayed in a well-lit hall in which he ate, slept and conversed with visitors several hours a day. Devotees claim it was almost physically impossible to keep up with him. In his early sixties, he began his day at 6 a.m., talking for a couple of hours to devotees till the afternoon, followed by lunch and a short nap. He then continued to work unbroken until after midnight. A large group of attendants worked in various shifts of two hours. As hectic as the atmosphere around him was, few could last longer than Thakur. Inside the Boral Bungalow, a big crowd stayed, as they had no other place to go. A group of nearly 40 widows clustered around Thakur because they had no other home. Their families were either dead or they had driven them out, Thakur was their last resort. Some found work as cook, nurse or nanny. The more aggressive and shrewd made their way into one of the smaller jobs around Thakur. Many were also quarrelsome.

Towards the end of 1958, Thakur suffered from high blood pressure. To ensure an afternoon rest, guards were placed at the entrance to his room, but the problem was not from the outside. Ever-ongoing petty grudges and squabbles regularly surfaced, and the quarrelling parties came to Thakur for justice. These situations were called 'privates', the complainant and the defendant were face to face alone with Thakur. Both parties would shout at the top of their voices. When they were exhausted emotionally, Thakur would quietly suggest a solution that brought about an adjustment, however temporary. One of these emotional encounters or quarrels occurred one day when Thakur was suffering from high blood pressure.

Janardan Mukhopadhyay was a communist leader in West Bengal. After meeting Thakur, and a series of arguments that followed, he ultimately accepted Thakur as his guide and became a full-time worker. One afternoon, he heard shrill noises coming from Thakur's room. When he entered, one of the doctors came running to him, pleading, "They are going to kill him before our eyes. You have got to do something." When Janardan interfered in the quarrel, one of the women imperiously shouted at him, "Private talk. Go away!" Janardan rebuffed her, "Private talk? You can hear every word out in the street." It made the warring parties sitting on the floor, silent. The only sound was Thakur's heavy breathing and occasional groaning. Janardan continued, "I have one question for you: Just who do you think will give you shelter and food and clothes and listen to your nasty quarrels when Thakur is not here? I will tell you;, Nobody! You will be out on the street where you belong, where your families drove you because of your selfishness. None of us will think twice before getting rid of you."

The brutal truth was like a slap in their faces, and they disappeared through the back door. Peace returned. Thakur stirred, and looking affectionately at Janardan, remarked, "Did you ever look in the pit under the open latrine, and see the bugs that are swimming in the excreta?"

"Not often", Janardan admitted. Thakur, coughed, cleared his throat, and said in a low voice, "Well, I have come to take those bugs out of the filth, and teach them to stand and walk like human beings in this world. If you are unable to endure the stench, then you will not be able to stay with me."

That was the last time Janardan ever tried to interfere in the squabbling of the widows. It was a living education in the treatment of almost every kind of psychological aberration. It was apparent he needed them, and was getting some form of relief from such exhausting quarrelling sessions. (Being and Becoming)

(52). Potency of his Holy Name: Concept and Practice

Ocean in a Teacup, a short treatise on Sri Sri Thakur written by His American disciple, Ray Hauserman, was published by noted publishers Harper & Brothers of New York. Eugene Exman was the religion editor as well as Vice-President of that organisation. He was familiar with the heritage of India through his acquaintance with Aldous Huxley, Gerald Heard, and Swami Prabhanananda. He was so impressed reading the manuscript of Hauserman's book that he expressed his persisting anxiety to Hauserman, asking if he could be taken to meet Thakur. And so they arrived at Deoghar.

During the lengthy discussions on various subjects for seven days Exman asked: "What is the benefit of repeating this holy name?" Thakur replied, "The continuous repetition of a particular word acts upon our nervous system, stimulates our brain cells, and then those cells become sensitised to the idea of that word. Words such as Om, Hring and Cling articulate subtle vibrations present in Creation. Such sounds carry creative power and develop keenness of perception. The word, Radhaswami, also carries great power as a Holy Name. Our spiritual perceptions deepen and develop, and I do not think we can acquire this particular kind of sensitivity in any other way. It has curative power. At least in those cases where the vital organs have not been ruined, it can bring life back." Before returning to America, Eugene took initiation from Sri Sri Thakur.

When Exman returned to New York, he wrote a letter to Hauserman:

Dear Ray,

I am writing to inform you that I reached New York safely. I was having lunch with an old friend who works for the Time Magazine, when a woman at a nearby table suddenly collapsed and slid to the floor, unconscious. I immediately got up and

knelt down beside her. I could find no pulse and she appeared lifeless. I put my finger on her forehead and began repeating the Name I learnt from Thakur. After about five minutes had elapsed, she suddenly opened her eyes, looked at me and said, "Thank you. I am all right." She got up and resumed lunch with her companion. My friend looked at me strangely as did many onlookers. That is the story. Please do tell Thakur about this.
With affection,
Gene.
(Being and Becoming)

(53) From Hippie to Preceptor

In the 1970s, particularly in the earlier half of the decade, many youngsters of the West took to psychedelic drugs and marijuana. They claimed they were temporarily getting a glimpse of a powerful inner world with the help of drugs. For a number of these youngsters, the fleeting glimpse created a longing for more. They came to India for the easy availability of opium and marijuana, but few could get the proper guide to tell them that the psyche and spiritual world could be opened without debilitating drugs, through the valid practice of meditation. The inner world can be permanently accessible through meditation. So a slogan became popular: "Drugs can be a door to the opening of the inner world, but not the room."

Two French young men arrived at Satsang, Deoghar—Andrey Lewis and his friend. Lewis was dressed in purple pyjamas, bare body with a tattoo of Lord Shiva on the inside of his right arm. He was a hardcore member of the 'International Hippie Community'—restless, desperate, always searching.

As the days passed, Andrey's loyalty became more evident, and he took initiation. His mother fell ill, and he made several trips to France for her treatment. His tenacity, commitment, and devotion to cure his mother impressed the ashramites. Sri Sri Thakur rightly observed, "He is a good boy." In time, Andrey became a Ritwik, and worked in America spreading the message of Sri Sri Thakur. (Being and Becoming)

(54) Love Jesus for the sake of Jesus

In April 1958, Ray Hauserman's mother decided to come and stay with her son at the Deoghar Ashram for a few days. She was accompanied by an old friend, and an active worker with a Mussoorie Missionary group, Helen. It was three months before Sri Sri Thakur's birth anniversary in July. A jubilant atmosphere persisted in the Ashram with huge crowds pouring in every day. Hausermanda, his mother, and her friend, Helen, were having their afternoon tea in the veranda and asking each other some peculiar questions—from where are so many people coming; why are they coming; what do they seek; Does Thakur really have so much influence? At this point, Goswamida (Satishchandra Goswami) passed by. Seeing an opportunity, Hauserman insisted his mother put these questions to Goswamida, who he believed would give the accurate answers. Goswamida was around 90 years old, a towering veteran at Satsang. Upon listening to the query, Goswamida said, "The crowd is increasing manifold because Thakur's message to the people has been clear in the recent past. Which is, no matter if you are a Hindu, Muslim, Christian, Jain, Sikh, Buddhist, or even a Zoroastrian, you must, first and foremost, strengthen your faith in a spiritual guide, a medium that can carry your soul through to your own God's abode. Only then your journey here will have some meaning." Helen was swift to respond, "In order to love Jesus, we can go to the many missionaries, to the Church; what would be achieved by coming here?" By this time, Goswamida had gotten busy and left, and it was decided that this question should be directly put to Thakur.

After the evening prayer, Sri Sri Thakur was sitting in his parlour with a close-knit group of devotees. Helen put forth her question, "I know if I love Jesus sincerely, to the best of my ability, it makes me a good Christian. You say the same thing. In that case, why should I share such profound love with Prophets of other religions?" Thakur responded, "I do not make a qualitative distinction between the Prophets of various religions. Prophets are enlightened beings, carrying forth the message of the Divine, which, in its oneness, is a fundamentally pluralistic idea. Hence, it is contradictory to follow one Prophet or Guru, and be antagonistic towards another. Your love for Jesus will find a new meaning if it is to be conveyed to the Divine through a messenger who understands this fundamental tenet of Christianity." Thakur took a brief pause, and sang a song in English:

Do love Christ for the sake of Christ.

Think of all true prophets as Christ.

Follow and fulfil that one in whom Christ lives with meaning and mercy.

This I believe is the essence of Christianity for the world!

Completing the song, Sri Sri Thakur conceded that he was not very good at English; however, in order to pursue an idea, a certain enthusiastic mannerism is difficult to contain. Helen by now was not only convinced, but exclaimed in a loud tone, "Very beautiful, very beautiful. I got my answer." (Ocean In a Teacup).

(55) Means to go to Dayal Dham

It was evening, and Sri Sri Thakur was sitting in the sprawling parlour of the Deoghar Ashram. Shivdulali Ma sluggishly walking with her stick came to him. She had a close, long-lasting relationship with Thakur since the days of Hemayetpur Ashram. When, in 1946, Thakur shifted to Deoghar, Shiv Dulali Ma came with him; her accommodation was arranged in the same bungalow as that of Thakur. A fairly intelligent woman, she would prepare tasty dishes of Sri Sri Thakur's liking, and this brought her immense satisfaction. That day, she asked Thakur if she wanted to travel to Dayal Dham (Thakur's divine abode in the afterworld). Thakur inquired, "Why do you want to go there?" She replied,

"It is there where I want to be reunited with you after my death." Thakur had an interesting response to such a desire. "Would you be able to recognise me?" he asked. After living all these years by his side, the old lady did not have any doubts that she would not be able to do so. Thakur reminded her, "It is because we are alive, and I am bound to this body that you can recognise me here; however, after death, my soul wouldn't necessarily be so apparent to you as it is in this physical appearance; will you be able to identify me even then?" After a pause, he said again, "You should continue chanting the Guru's Name; perhaps then there can be a chance that you will recognise me."

Shiv Dulali Ma was happy, and left after conveying her gratitude. Manilal Chakravarty, who was nearby inquired, what must people draw from this lesson that Thakur had just granted to Shiv Dulali? Sri Sri Thakur uttered, "Har se lage raho bhai/ Banat banat ban jai. Koila se maila choddey jab aag karey prabesh' (Be sincere in your efforts, fulfilment arrives sooner or later. Even coal glows with the touch of fire.) (Smritir Mala)

(56). Mother is to be worshipped

In 1953, Sri Sri Thakur was sitting inside the dome-shaped tent in the Thakur Bungalow precincts. An American journalist, after concluding his travels in India, was talking to Thakur regarding his experiences. He mentioned how he had struggled to love his mother. He even went on to say that the mere sight of her filled him with rage. On his days away from home, the memory of his mother brought him sadness.

Sri Sri Thakur listened, and became morose. His jubilant face lost its shine and became pale. He was tense, and asserted himself immediately saying, "But I love my mother immensely. When I ponder upon the fact that she is no longer with me in this world, the world around me becomes darker, I begin to lose my convictions." Thakur's eyes were now filled with tears. Looking at him, the journalist too, became sentimental. Thakur went on,

"There is no doubt, my mother had beaten me up badly during my childhood, so many times without a reason. Yet, I loved her, simply because if not for her, I would not have this life on Earth." The American heaved a deep sigh, apologised and abruptly left.

The next morning after, he came to Sri Sri Thakur's quarters, knelt with eyes full of tears, and submitted, "My Lord, I have come to realise that I should love my mother. I must love her. Please teach me, Thakur, how I can do it?" Thakur was elated listening to this; his heart filled with joy. He responded in a loving tone, and said, "My boy, you can only learn to love her through the love that resides within you, one that you are yet to discover." (Jiban Dyuti)

(57) **Language not a barrier**

Sri Sri Thakur was in the parlour of Deoghar Ashram discussing with many tourists and devotees from abroad with Kestoda interpreting. One of them asked, 'The story of Adam and Eve in the Bible is beyond my understanding. If it were so, as the fathers in churches preach that Adam was the first man and Eve the first woman, then how come so many people across the world differ vastly in their appearance, their hair and eye colours vary, and their physical features are different. How is this possible?" In reply, Thakur argued, "I believe what we miss in the Bible's narration is the possibility that it may have been not one pair of Adam and Eve created by God in one part of the world. There might have been several such pairs created across the world. Hence, it stands to reason that the children of all these pairs scattered all over the globe, in accordance with their geographical and climatic conditions, and evolved in differing ways. Therefore, there are so many of us, different in our physical features, skin colour, and yet we are all children of God." Before Kestoda could translate this, the questioner replied, "No thank you, Mr. Bhattacharyya, I completely understood what Thakur said." On further probing by others, the foreign national fluently explained to people in

English what Thakur had just said in Bengali. Seeing everyone's shock and surprise at such an occurrence, people inquired, "Thakur, you must explain, was this possible?"

Sri Sri Thakur explained, "If there is a certain unity in the universal feelings of all experiences, a confluence in our emotions and language is no longer a barrier. For example, if both a Bengali mother and a British memsahib lose their sons, both of them would be inconsolable in their grief; the British woman would say, "Oh, my son! Where have you gone? I cannot live without you. Come back to me." The same would be uttered by the Bengali mother in her own language. If both of them meet each other, they would very well understand what the other is going through, no matter if they don't grasp each other's language. What unites us as human beings are the universal joys and sorrows that we all go through together. (Jiban Dyuti)

(58) Kiranda gets Padma Shri

In April 1964, on an evening, Sri Sri Thakur was sitting quietly in the parlour of Deoghar Ashram. The general manager of the Ichapur Rifle Factory, Kiran Chandra Banerjee, came to pay his respects to Thakur and, as always, Sri Sri Thakur was very happy to see him. This was at a time when foreign relations between India, on one hand, and Pakistan and China on the other were worsening. Kiranda requested Thakur to tell him how to manufacture strong and lightweight weapons in India itself. In those days, the weapons our soldiers were using at the border were cumbersome and heavy. The root of the problem was that the raw materials and steel we used to make our guns had to be imported, and the cost was quite high. If the persisting tensions broke into war, all our import options would close. If it became necessary to use raw material available in India, we would end up producing weapons that were heavy. Kiranda wanted Thakur to provide a solution.

Sri Sri Thakur suggested, "You must first search and collate all the existing raw materials available in different parts of India, a small amount may be imported from abroad. For example, mica is available in India. If you use an alloy along with it, you can run a test and see if the results are favourable. After thinking for a while he went on, "Aluminium being a lightweight element is extensively available in India. It may just be suitable to make guns. You must mix it with an alloy to give it some stability from within, and run a test. As you may know, aluminium is used to make corrugated tin sheets along with an appropriate mixture of alloys. I don't see why we can't come up with lightweight and efficient weapons." Kiranda despite having a vast range of innovative ideas was inspired, Thakur nodded with a smile. He invited Kiranda to the adjacent room, so they continued their discussion in confidence. They talked for another one hour, and as Kiranda was about to leave, one could see a sense of confidence on his face.

A few years later, under Kiranda's leadership, his factory was able to manufacture lightweight, automatic guns. For this achievement, he was awarded a Padma Shri by the Government of India. (Smritir Mala)

(59) Be Concentric

In October 1955, during the birth anniversary celebrations of Sri Sri Thakur, the Vice-Chancellor of Utkal University, Dr. Pranakrushna Parija, was invited to address the evening meeting at Deoghar Ashram. Dr. Parija was an eminent professor, and a renowned scientist. Prior to the meeting, he was taken to receive the blessings of Sri Sri Thakur. He asked him, "Parijada, have you ever seen a torch light?" Prof. Parija said, "Yes." Thakur continued, "If the batteries inside a torch light are kept in random order, will the light work?" Dr. Parija sensing Thakur's method of solving problems, said, "No, it would not. Only when the batteries are faced in tandem towards the direction of the bulb, can we have light." Sri Sri Thakur was very happy with the answer, and said, "Indeed, you are right. That is the principle. For unity to prevail in a family, the younger members must listen to their elders." Similarly, in our world, each country is a battery. Without empathy and understanding among each other, would peace ever be possible in the world?" Dr. Parija concurred, and said, "You are absolutely right. It is only when the entire world accepts one man and his principles as their Ideal will we see the end of violence and suffering in society." Listening to this, Sri Sri Thakur embraced Prof. Parija in sheer joy. Thakur reiterated, "This is precisely what I tell people. Only when people follow the singular path of a Master with their communion a society will be formed." The conversation lasted for many hours.

Thakur came up with another one of his anecdotes, "Tell me Parijada, have you ever gone out as a teenager to shop for groceries? How would you know the correct weight of your purchases?" Prof. Parija replied, "I have done so several times. On a weighing scale, you put weights on one side and the goods on the other. When both the pans are at a level and the hand of the scale points straight upwards, you know the quantity is correct." Sri Sri Thakur was elated, and reiterated, "Yes, indeed, Parijada. In the weighing scale of life, the big pan is always trembling, without the small hand balancing it. Can life prosper in such a situation? The small hand is like Ishta (the Master), one that is stable, patient, and steady. The problems we see in families, society, and between nations today are rooted in disintegration, as a result of decentring from an Ideal."

Dr. Parija nodded in agreement, and rose to address the meeting. (Amruta Kahani)

(60) The Wonders of Istavriti

A Santhal (an indigenous tribe in India) devotee came to the ashram, and prostrated himself before Sri Sri Thakur. He told the devotee not to fail doing Istavriti every day in the morning, as he and his family had taken initiation recently. The devotee replied, "Baba, what kind of Istavriti can a poor man like me offer? All I earn and produce is barely enough to make both ends meet." Thakur was quick to intervene, and said, "It is not a matter of money. To cook your food, you must be using firewood, isn't it? You must be dumping the ash near the kitchen. Everyday take a handful and offer it to your Guru, this shall be your Istavriti. You should also see to it that your family members do so as well." This filled the Santhal man with elation. He went home, and told his wife, "What if we don't have any money? We shall fulfil our Istavriti by offering to Thakur the ash outside the kitchen." So it started. They would wake up early in the morning, and take a handful of the discarded ash, and deposit it in a clean spot. A month passed by, and offered ash accumulated in a corner of the living room. The Santhal was worried about how to carry such a large quantity of ash by himself to the ashram? He went to Thakur and explained he had done everything as per his instructions, but could not manage to bring the ash to Him.

Sri Sri Thakur reassured him that he had done the right thing by not bringing it. He asked, "Do you have any open land near your home? The Santhal responded affirmatively. Sri Sri Thakur continued: "So do one thing; take the seeds of a colocasia plant (Indian vegetable), along with soil, manure, and the ash that you have accumulated in your living room as Ishtavriti, and bury them in that open land. I am giving you a hundred colocasia seeds; do as I say." He strictly followed Thakur's word, and in no time the seeds grew into a hundred colocasia plants. From them, he plucked the finest pieces and went to meet Sri Sri Thakur. Thakur was very happy to receive them. He lovingly inquired, "How have you been?" He replied he was good, and that he had followed what Thakur had said to the last detail. In his quintessential tone, Thakur said, "Those Colocasia vegetables are all mine, like all the ash that had accumulated in your house." The Santhal agreed, and said, "Indeed. Everything I have is yours, including my own self." "If that is the case", said Thakur, "then follow my next instruction as well. Whatever fresh produce you have now in your farm, go to the market and sell them. You do not need to give me your earnings. Rather start a business using that money, and what you earn from it, offer a part as an offering for your Istavriti." In a few years, the Santhal turned out to be a fairly successful businessman, and a part of his earnings have always been since used for Istavriti.(Dr. Prasenjit Biswas)

(61) Tolerating the accusation of Hypnosis

In 1958, during the celebration of Sri Sri Thakur's birthday, a renowned litterateur of West Bengal was to preside over the evening's public meeting. It was customary to bring the guests of honour to Thakur for an introduction and receive his blessings. Jnanendu Bikash Goswami (Secretary, Satsang) had escorted the honourable guest into the presence of Thakur. He was sitting facing east, and as soon as he saw the guest turned his face away. Goswami seated the guests on a chair near Thakur and introduced him, "Thakur, he is a great writer of West Bengal. He will be presiding over today's evening meeting." Thakur, facing the other side, said, "Very good. He has taken the pain to come down here. I am obliged." Goswami was feeling sorry for such behaviour from Thakur. Showing indifference towards an eminent personality of such stature was extremely unusual for him. Even when an ordinary person came, Thakur unfailingly looked at them, asked out about their welfare, food and stay in the ashram; but today, what a pity, he is not looking at this writer at all. He was also apprehensive that the guest might leave the ashram following such an insult. In any case, he requested the guest to get up and ask for Thakur's permission to escort him to the meeting pandal. Thakur gave a nod but never looked at him.

It is pertinent to mention here the guest had been cautioned by ill-informed friends and relatives, "Be careful. Don't look into the eyes of Thakur, otherwise you will never return home. His eyes are full of hypnotic power. Don't look at them." That evening, the writer's wife was standing at a distance observing everything.

Accompanying her husband to the stage, she whispered, "Did you ever look at Thakur's eyes?" The great writer with a triumphant voice replied, "Have you gone mad? I did as I was warned by our well-wishers, and completely avoided his gaze." The wife replied, "I too, never looked at him. What if he had hypnotised me!"

Jnanenduda was right behind them, and overheard this. He was numbed; he started perspiring. He could now realise how Sri Sri Thakur had already known about the couple's suspicions, and managed to tolerate them without letting anyone know. In his mind, he apologised to Sri Sri Thakur for misunderstanding him. Thakur's love attracts people, and accusers on the other hand propagate it as hypnotism. (Santosh Joarder, Kaloda)

(62) Divine Economy

In 1947, communal riots broke out in undivided Bengal causing thousands of deaths.. After the partition of the country, East Bengal went to Pakistan. A large section wanted to stay in India, and they came with only the clothes on their backs. They settled in Habra, a town specially constructed to house refugees. A young boy, Harinarayan Chakravarty, from a refugee family, arrived in Satsang ashram in the Sixties. He came on the recommendation of Ritwik Jatindas. His father, a school educator, had died recently. His mother, four sisters, older and younger brothers were under extreme financial pressure. Hari was an intelligent, bright-eyed teenager filled with enthusiasm. He met Ray Hauserman, the American disciple, and requested, "Can you somehow help me with a place to stay. I will manage the rest. Then I can complete my studies." Hauserman arranged for his lodging in the ashram, and free meals at the Ananda Bazar.

Three weeks later, Thakur called Hauserman and said, "Go to Calcutta and buy two pieces of Than Kapar (white cloth without borders that widows wore), and take them to Habra. Give them to Hari's mother, and convey my blessings. Ask her to bring her family here to Deoghar to live with you."

Not only was Hauserman surprised, but also frightened. His financial condition was poor and unstable. He was managing somehow, but supporting seven children and a widow was more than he could imagine. With fear written on his face he meekly asked Thakur, "Will they stay permanently?" Thakur gave a cryptic reply, "Yes, it will be helpful for both of you."

Hauserman brought the family from Habra and lodged them in his quarters. Raising resources for clothes, education, medical treatment, and food for a large family put him in high gear. It was an orthodox Brahmin family; their customs and traditions went back for generations and Hari's mother was determined to run the house accordingly. The kitchen became out of bounds. She would not allow anybody to enter and touch the food. She was rigid and uncompromising. She fasted many days a month; new moon, full moon, quarter moon and existed on a glass of water on those days. However, she always cooked food and fed the family and guests sumptuously. The children attended the local school. Their results were above average. Hauserman anxiety had now vanished. He discovered a greater patience and tolerance within himself.

Narrating this episode, Hauserman wrote, "Obligation for others does alter your perception, and the spontaneous willingness to sacrifice provides practical lessons to the theories of nurturing the environment preached by Ritwiks during their talks over the years. Thakur's 'Divine Economy' always seemed inexhaustible. Resources expanded according to the new needs and demand. There is no end to it." (Ocean in a Teacup)

(63) The Repentance of Gobarda

Devotee Gobar Majumdar along with his family stayed at the ashram for a few days, and was all set to leave after paying his respects to Sri Sri Thakur. After leaving His presence, the family found their footwear was missing. He furiously walked back to Sri

Sri Thakur, and shouted, "What sort of an ashram is this? All of the world's thieves and thugs have gathered here. I am telling you clearly, if any day I find out who the thief is, I won't think about who he is. I will break his head and bury him. ". He kept going on and on for some time.

Sri Sri Thakur listened to Gobarda's ranting patiently, and then asked, "Tell me, Gobar, where do you live?" Gobarda replied, "Don't you know I live in Calcutta!" Thakur went on, "Aren't there hospitals in Calcutta?" Gobarda was now beginning to lose his patience. "Don't you know there are hospitals in Calcutta. Many of them, each bigger than the other."

Thakur: "So why don't you go and find me a physically and mentally fit person from one of those big hospitals?"

Gobarda: "Why would one go to a hospital, if they were fit?"

Thakur quipped: "That is exactly my point, Gobar. It is only after great physical and mental troubles, after tolerating a lot of pain, and persisting with bad habits for years that one ends up in a hospital." He continued, "But do the doctors break their patients' heads, and bury them or do they console and reassure them, giving them hope for the future? Similarly, perfect human beings don't come to our ashram either, you know that very well."

Gobarda was silent now. Thakur calmly pulled a pillow from under his knees, and placed his hand over his thighs, looked at him and waited for an answer. Since Gobarda was speechless, Thakur explained in a calm tone, "The thief will steal, that is certain. It is you who has to be careful. Whenever there is a crowd, you will find thieves swarming around for a chance. There are so many kinds of thefts in this world, only a few come to our notice. What about those we miss? Who shall you exclude from your hit list? Eventually, everyone becomes a suspect. If you indeed break everyone's head open, who will you live with, whom can you trust? If I throw someone out of here today, tomorrow someone else may come who will repeat the same mistake? In this way can we really solve a problem? What do you think?"

Gobarda had got his lesson, he was almost in tears. Sri Sri Thakur consoled him and explained, "I am getting older by the day, I am not as fit as I used to be. I am counting on you people, it is your shoulder that I wish to hold onto and walk. If you do not attempt to reform people, and instead shout at me, what am I supposed to do? You must remember, it is through your (my disciples) actions that people will be able to reach me." Gobarda couldn't see Thakur in such a state, and blurted out, "I accept my mistake, Thakur. I will work on myself, and be the ideal disciple you want me to be. I can no longer see you in such pain." (Premal Thakur)

15. Appendix

Initiation (Diksha) and the practices of Jajan, Jaajan, Istavriti, Swastyayani and Sadachar

Devotee: What is the purpose of initiation (Diksha)?[1]

Sri Sri Thakur: Initiation is to impart spiritual knowledge. Now you would ask, what is spiritualism? The answer is simple. It is the method by which your inherent, distinctive existential trait is unfurled and grows. Diksha comes from the Sanskrit word 'Daksha', which means the procedure that makes you more efficient.

Devotee: How does efficiency improve?[2]

Sri Sri Thakur: One has to be attached to him, who is the most efficient. Irrespective of our different natures, we all want well-being. In every being, there is sat-chit-ananda; sat represents existence, chit is the supreme power, and ananda stands for bliss of attainment.

Narrator: Sri Sri Dada recollects an incident (16-04-2015): Sometime in 1965-66, one day I was sitting near Thakur. He looked at me and uttered something as if he could read my mind: "You know, earlier I had asked for the initiation of 4 crore people, but nobody took it seriously; we could not reach the target. I had to reduce the figure to one crore and fifty lakh, the minimum number of people that we must Initiate at any cost."

In all humility, I questioned: "Sir, What is the use of such mass initiation?" Sri Sri Thakur retorted: "The use or no use is my headache. It's not your job. Your job is to do what I say." Sri Sri Dada continued: "Thakur is a beggar of men. Nobody knows how many great personalities will blossom with his initiation. You and I can't fathom the dormant inherent talent in a man—he may be a scientist, a scholar, a versatile leader, or a sleeping poet; only initiation can hammer it out. It is our solemn duty to knock at every door, fish for very good men for him, so that they can grow to the best of their abilities.

Devotee: Who can initiate?[3]

Sri Sri Thakur: Only the knower of Brahma can initiate. A realised Master is needed to impart proper initiation.

The Devotee: After initiation, in how much time can I become efficient?[4]

Sri Sri Thakur: It's not easy to give you a time frame. In a tiny seed lies the prospect of a future banyan tree. It all depends on you, your adherence to the Ideal, and how fast you come out of a complex-prominent living. In astrology, there is a saying, 'When Jupiter is in the centre, no star can do any harm.

Devotee: How does it happen, Sir?[5]

Sri Sri Thakur: If you are fully attached to the Ideal, and completely occupied with Him, you are not shattered in difficult times, and neither do you express clownish happiness in prosperity. You learn balance of mind.

Devotee: I may be attached to Him, but how to know if the Master cares for me?[6]

Sri Sri Thakur: It is the other way around. It is futile to measure how much God loves you, but it is worthwhile to introspect how much you love Him. The Ideal is the living embodiment of God. Take initiation from Him, follow His ways, and learn from Him.

Devotee: What do you think of an initiation done by the family priest?[7]

Sri Sri Thakur: That is a mere formality. He invariably advises you to take the final initiation from the Ideal (Sadguru), if you can find him.

Devotee: If no such advice comes from the family priest, then what must one do?[8]

Sri Sri Thakur: In that case, you must rely on your destiny. If you are fortunate to find the Ideal, hold fast onto him. Repeat the Name he gives you. He is my father, your father, father to all. Love him. Arjuna trusted Sri Krishna as a friend. When Sri Krishna said to him, 'Love me and do what I tell you to do', Arjuna followed, and benefited from it. Only then he could comprehend the powers of Sri Krishna and said, "O dear! You are my Guru, I worship you. In ignorance, I may have grieved you by my words or actions, so forgive me." Unless you are attached to a true Master, real understanding is quite difficult. Real understanding comes through the initiation from a Master, only when you follow him steadfast.

Devotee: Can I change my Guru?[9]

Sri Sri Thakur: You can change gurus, but not the Ideal (Sadguru). Initiation from Him is unique. It energises the initiation taken from all the other gurus. Simply getting initiated is of little avail, unless you love the Ideal with your heart and soul, and follow the discipline imparted by Him.

Devotee: If I follow the discipline, will He assure protection for me against all ills and misfortune?[10]

Sri Sri Thakur: Of course. The Ideal will save you only when you are totally dedicated to Him. Did not Sri Krishna tell Arjuna, 'Always think of Me, become My devotees worship Me and offer obeisance to Me. Thus I shall be with you without fail. I promise you this because you are very dear to Me.'

"Manmana Bhava Mad Bhakto Madjaji Mam Namaskuru

Mamevaishyasi Satyam Te Pratijane Priyosi Me." (Gita 18/65)

This means to concentrate the mind on the form of the Master, as Arjuna did. The name 'Arjuna' constitutes the idea of 'arjan', meaning 'to earn or acquire.' You have to earn the Ideal by your devotion, only then you are protected. In English, there is a saying, 'Keep alive your good habits.' The word 'habit' implies the connotation, 'Have it.' So, receive the mercy of the Ideal with your pure devotion.

Devotee: How does the Ideal save us from bad times?[11]

Sri Sri Thakur: In life difficulties do come. They come to prepare us so that we can overcome them. When we overcome it, we are bolder and more efficient than before. Attachment to the

Ideal provides the courage to face difficulties, rather than lamenting on our misfortune. In this manner, our personality is shaped and adjusted. Thus, we acquire knowledge and wisdom.

Devotee: Ravana was the son of a great rishi. They say he was very knowledgeable, then why did he fail?[12]

Sri Sri Thakur: What preserves existence is truth, and what destroys it is evil. Ravana worshipped Lord Shiva, but he went on annexing the kingdoms of others; he had an evil eye on the wives of others; so much so he started deceiving his inner Shiva. He got what he deserved.

Devotee: Nowadays murder, rape and child abuse are on the rise. What is the way out, Sir?[13]

Sri Sri Thakur: Keep away from such perverted fellows. You may help them in their need, but maintain a distance. Perversions are of two kinds, damaged and distorted. It is very difficult to set right distorted perversions. However, when the aberration is of a damaged kind, he can be saved if he follows a true Master. St. Augustine, Rishi Valmiki, Bilwamangal could transform themselves in this manner.

Devotee: Through the Ideal's initiation, can we hope evildoers would change to truth-seekers like St. Augustine, and Rishi Valmiki?[14]

Sri Sri Thakur: Evildoers are always in a minority. They get an upper hand due to the callousness and aloofness of good people. Good people do not unite and integrate so easily. If they are organised, and try to resist what is against existence, they will definitely win. And those evildoers will wither away automatically. I have prescribed five simple disciplines—Jajan (self-upliftment), Jaajan (nurture of the environment), Istavriti (willing oblation), Swastyayani (pursuit of well-being) and Sadachar (healthy living) on the eve of Diksha. They will help in moulding a better human being, rest assured. It is not possible at the present moment to comprehend the far-reaching effects of these practices. Now is the time to sow the seeds. Worthy men will mushroom in due course.

Devotee: Apart from this, what else is to be done on the eve of initiation?[15]

Sri Sri Thakur: After taking initiation, you must visit the Ashram to pay your obeisance to the Ideal (Sadguru). Spiritual connection (Diksha) precedes physical connection (visit); it is more worthwhile. Initiation is compared to re-birth, therefore an initiate is called twice-born. From this point on, the journey of your wellbeing starts.

Devotee: Please explain what is wellbeing?[16]

Sri Sri Thakur: Among all the machines we come across, the human system (body and mind) is unique. It's a perfectly designed system consisting of different sub-systems. These subsystems of different organ systems work together in a complex, dynamic and efficient manner for perfect health. Dynamism is the characteristic of highly evolved human beings. If the being is kept alert, active and mercurial, one can comprehend the finer aspects of things. When deeper understanding gathers momentum in the mind, it forms an experience. By your experience, you immediately know the pros and cons of any situation. You are able to make appropriate decisions in life when needed, you gain the critical faculty of judgement. This is due to motor-sensory coordination. At times, a man knows what to do, but fails to do so due to the predominance of passion.

Devotee: How do we fail to act despite knowing the right thing?[17]

Sri Sri Thakur: Listen to this story. Miscreants were trying to kill a person. He left his house and rushed to a safe hiding place. On the way, he finds a country liquor store. He thought a small dose of alcohol would energise him to reach his destination faster. He sat down and started drinking one round after another, became dead drunk and lay there. The attackers found him, and he lost his life. The highest regard for your Master, and the practice of the five disciplines, can tame your passionate tendencies to a large extent, and you can be saved from many pitfalls.

Narrator: Sri Ramakrishna Paramahamsa Dev related a similar anecdote on lack of alertness. It was summer. A travelling open-air opera group had camped at the outskirts of a village. The show was scheduled to start late after dinner time. A man with a mattress on his shoulder started from his house, and saw the opera orchestra performing the prelude to draw spectators. He decided to relax until the play started. He stretched himself on the mattress, and went to sleep. He woke up when the play was about to conclude.

Devotee: If initiation is so beneficial, why do the wealthy and powerful not opt for it?[18]

Sri Sri Thakur: Goats, before they are taken to the butcher, graze on little patches of green grass and tender leaves on the way. They are unaware of the slaughter awaiting them. A fish lured by a bait, does not know it is hooked to death. A man seldom knows what is in store for him. A wrong-doer suppresses his conscience, and assumes he cannot be harmed. The fact is he will be caught sooner or later. However, his inner deterioration begins from the moment he commits the wrong. He starts dying internally, slowly but surely. Sitting on the hill top of wealth and power, he dwells a life of untold mental misery. So I say, 'There is no glory in being a king without a Centre (the Ideal), and there is no ignominy in a life full of hardships that is bound to a firm Centre. Think of Hanuman of the Tretaya Yuga, of Sudama in the Dwapara Yuga, and of Chanakya and Shivaji in recent history.

Devotee: What happens when a devotee does not follow the rules of discipline?[19]

Sri Sri Thakur: He will be marginally benefitted as he is attached to the Centre, but in times of distress and sorrow, he may realise his mistake, repent his negligence and return to the path of strict discipline.

Devotee: Why then do some initiates undergo untold suffering?[20]

Sri Sri Thakur: It means, all the accumulated suffering due to the wrongdoings of previous births are taking effect. If the man, in spite of these hardships, ardently adheres to the Ideal, he will be soon endowed with peace.

Devotee: When a person is initiated not by his own volition but by persuasion or compulsion, will he gain anything?[21]

Sri Sri Thakur: Sri Ramakrishna Paramahamsa Dev has said, 'A jaundice patient has no appetite, but he has to be fed forcibly to maintain his immunity against infection.'

Devotee: Do you mean to say that self-realisation does not come in any other manner except from devotion to the Ideal (Sadguru)?[22]

Sri Sri Thakur: Mathematically, it may come, but not in reality. A man devoted to his parents gains a lot of mental wealth, unaware. His thoughts, speech, action and behaviour will be altogether of a high order. Similarly, when you are attached to the Ideal, your personality is bound to be better. For your spiritual endeavour, this is the easiest way. I have experimented with a number of methods like concentrating on the moon, on a needle point, practising the Vedantic way of neti-neti, nothing appeared to me more poignant than pure love for the Ideal (Sadguru). In everything else I found a sort of blankness and frustration. So, if you find the Ideal, don't lose him at any cost and surrender to him. After his mortal departure, follow the preceptor (Acharya) who has been anointed by Him.

Devotee: But the technique introduced by the Ideal is available through printed books. Can't I learn it on my own? Why should I seek initiation?[23]

Sri Sri Thakur: Initiation transmits the impulses of the Ideal to you. Mere bookish knowledge can get you only haphazard intellectual perception. Due to the lack of impulses within us, we cannot feel the benefits through our senses. It is like the difference between reading a play, and seeing it enacted on a stage. So, I say, seek the perfect man and follow him without fail. He is the moving spirit of all religions. He alone can seal the holes of passions threatening the smooth sailing of the boat of life.

Devotee: What about listening to spiritual discourses and taking part in religious rites?[24]

Sri Sri Thakur: They help you to set right the outer anomalies in your character, but the revitalisation of your brain cells is not touched upon. Hence, your energy level doesn't grow, nor does your will or concentration. Mere listening can only provide you with the bare minimum.

Narrator: In the Bible, Jesus said to his Apostles, 'Do not think that I have come to bring peace upon Earth. I have come to bring not peace but the sword. For I have come to set a man against his father, a daughter against her mother, and a daughter-in-law against her mother-in-law; and one's enemies will be those of his household.' Matthew 10: 34-42; Luke 12:49-53)

Sri Sri Dada (Ritwik Conference, October 2015) in his address said, 'Enthrone the Ideal in yourself and proclaim, I am yours, I am yours, I am yours. None is mine but you. Whatever I have, father, mother, brother, sister, wife, children, they are all your merciful gifts to me. I know they will all leave me, or I shall leave them sooner or later. Life after life I belong to you and to you only. Proceed in this manner, you will get peace and life will be wholesome. You cannot have Him by taking to cunning. Who tries to get Him by adroitness is an imbecile. To get Him, one has to be simple minded. Do not try to judge what He asks you to do, but do it with sincerity and all your might, and that is final.'

R. K. Narayan, a well-known Indian writer in English, puts it succinctly, 'Wife, children, brothers, parents, and friends...we come together only to go apart again. It is one continuous movement. Either they move away from us, or we move away from them. The Law of life cannot be avoided. The law comes into operation, the moment we detach ourselves from our mother's womb. All struggles and miseries in life are due to our attempts to arrest this law, or get away from it or in allowing ourselves to be hurt by it. The fact must be recognized: a profound unmitigated loneliness is the only truth of life. All else is false. No sense in battling against the law of life. (The English Teacher)

Devotee: How to get peace in life?[25]

Sri Sri Thakur: You have to love the Ideal (Sadguru) earnestly for peace to be with you. Peace does not mean stasis, or withdrawal from action; rather, it is to accept both the good and the bad with equanimity. Be Ideal-centric, love and peace will flow from Him.

Narrator: Thomas A. Kempis said, 'To attain peace Jesus ordained: (1) Do the will of others rather than your own. (2) Always choose to possess less rather than more. (3) Always take the lowest place and see yourself as lesser than others. (4) Desire and pray always that God's will may be perfectly fulfilled in you. (Imitation of Christ)

The Five Principles
Jajan (Self-upliftment)

Devotee: How does initiation bring about self-improvement?[26]

Sri Sri Thakur: During initiation, one is told how to meditate, introspect, and analyse his actions. Thus, he comes to realise how to make life more meaningful. When it is done regularly, the act of remembering the Ideal during meditation, causes tremendous energy to flow into our being. Self-confidence improves, and our abilities grow. Broadly, this is Jajan.

Narrator: Sri Sri Thakur has said, "Be consecrated to the Ideal, dedicate yourself to the service of the Ideal with an ardent concentric urge, equip yourself with everything in all respects, spread in your atmosphere an existential glow; make your life an enlightening activity, and make everything that concerns you thoroughly consistent; thus, you shall achieve becoming. This is an attuned secret of Jajan." The thoughts of the Ideal and His wishes possess our Being, the satiation of such a fulfilling urge is called Jajan. (An Integral Philosophy of Life)

Sri Sri Thakur in Magnadicta:

'Do meditate mantra on thy Lord

>   dawn and night,
>   do repeat the holy Name
>   mentally and meaningfully
>   in all the movements of daily life,
>   do materialise the direction
>   of the Guru (Master) in due time
>   that is Tapas—
>   the way to achievement!' (Verse 68)

Devotee: What is the process of repeating the Holy Name?[27]

Sri Sri Thakur: Repetition of the Name is a mental activity. The Name and its embodiment are inseparable. The destination of the Name is to reach the resplendent embodiment. By repetition of the Name, the brain cells are excited and become sympathetic. This diminishes our sensual hunger. By doing so mentally, by thinking of it silently, while talking, walking, or while doing any other activity, we attain the ability to solve problems that arise in our individual and collective life.

Devotee: How does it happen?[28]

Sri Sri Thakur: The continuous repetition of a particular word acts upon our central nervous system and increases the elasticity of the brain cells. Whatever we see, feel, hear, or think creates an impression in our brain. These impressions interact with the surroundings, all of which are stored in different brain chambers. The impulse of the impression again depends on the state of our mind and body, so comes conception. We can understand the finer conceptions provided our body and mind are capable of receiving them. The more the sensitivity and power of reception of the brain cells, the finer is our vision. I believe proper meditation can excite the inner thrill, and expand one's consciousness. A thing that was beyond our grasp now becomes comprehensible. The induced mental stimulation that comes from repetition of the Name excites the brain cells, and subsequently, combustion takes place. The result is that those impressions stored in the cells are released and appear in the consciousness in different forms, colours, essences, sounds, and so on. It is also a fact that meditation generates heat in our system. In Sanskrit, it is called Tapasya (the heat process). (Answer to the Quest)

Sri Sri Thakur in Magnadicta:
> The psycho-physical moulding
> of objects and affairs
> to fulfil the interest of the Principal
> unfurling the faculty
> of perception and conception
> discretion and remembrance
> with shortening of the reaction time
> is the fundamental of concentration and meditation.
> (Verse 116)

Narrator: The observation of Sri Sri Thakur has been confirmed by research: "The human system is able to both receive and transmit vibrations that constitute consciousness. Our level of awareness corresponds to the degree in which we are able to receive, decode, and transmit the clusters of vibrations in the cosmic field. The clearer the channel to receive and decode, the clearer is the perception and the picture that we receive. In a crude sense, it is similar to how a receiver is able to tune into a broadcast. To use an analogy, on a television screen, our sense of the picture is clearer when we receive the signal more efficiently and accurately. (The Intelligence of the Cosmos)

In this regard, Mahatma Gandhi had said: 'The Mantram becomes one's staff of life and carries one through every ordeal. It is not empty repetition. For each repetition has a new meaning, carrying you nearer and nearer to God.' (Living Thoughts of Great People)

Devotee: There is a dichotomy in Vaishnava's saying:
> One million lives
> spent on repetition
> Still Srikrishna, beyond horizon;
> And one utterance of Name of Hari

can absolve so many sins
that are beyond commission.

Jesus also said:

'Use not vain repetition as the gentiles do ... '

Devotee: What does this signify?[29]

Sri Sri Thakur: That is true. Mechanical repetition of the Name, but no real love or devotion to Him, can never be fruitful. That is why it is said that a million years of repeating the Name cannot bring realisation in the real sense. Without devotion to the realised personality, it becomes a vain repetition of empty phrases, as Christ warned.

Narrator: Sri Sri Thakur on meditation: 'People meditate but do not know what meditation is. Sometimes concentration becomes fixation. Fixation benumbs and flabbergasts the brain. The inclination towards the Ideal, the adorable, following His dictates, to think of Him with fondness, a desire to establish Him within oneself and in one's environment are the basic facets of proper meditation. It has been said earlier that when meditation is effective, our character is strengthened. After meditation, it is advised that savasana (corpse posture) must be practised.

Chakra-sadhana: Sri Sri Thakur has introduced a unique method to stimulate the pineal gland situated at the root of the nose for secretion of melatonin. Western research has found that melatonin functions as a synchronizer of the biological clock, a powerful free-radical scavenger, and wide spectrum antioxidant, twice more effective than vitamins C and E. Research has supported the anti-aging properties of melatonin. It is useful in Alzheimer's disease, migraine, cluster headaches, and body weight control, etc.

In the Indian Yoga system, the pineal gland is known as Ajna-Chakra, Divya-Chakshu or Jnana-netra. It is the doorway through which one develops the power of the mind such as quick thinking, correct analysis, and sharp memory.

Devotee: What is the essence of prayer?[30]

Sri Sri Thakur: The essence of prayer is to achieve your goal through diligence. Diligence fulfils the prayer. Without an aptitude for work, prayer is lifeless, and with an inclination towards hard work you will achieve the goal even without verbal prayer.

Sri Sri Thakur in The Message:
> Prayer is to draw out
> the holy talent that lies within,
> by a pursuit of praise
> in a conscious plane
> that invigorates the heart
> and accelerates ability

with an illuminating hope. (vol. I, 279)

Satyanusaran: Pray to the Supreme Father, "Thy will is good; I do not know what will make me good. Let thy will be fulfilled in me." And be ready to accept it; joy will remain, and sorrow will not touch you. Be not the cause of another's grief, none will be the cause of your grief.

Jaajan (Nurturing the environment)

Devotee: What is Jaajan?[31]

Sri Sri Thakur: Jaajan, in essence, is to divinise your environment, and make it Ideal-oriented. It is a service to others. The interest of the Ideal is the welfare of the people at large. First of all, you have to be good at heart, coherent and compassionate. You must at all times be alert and agile to help people. Every man hankers to live and grow. The best way of living and growing is to be anchored to the Ideal. This vital message has to be spread everywhere. That is the best service you can render to society.

Devotee: But how does it help me?[32]

Sri Sri Thakur: When you are ready to serve others, not for the fulfilment of your personal wishes, but to please the Ideal, then all spheres of the brain get activated, knots and obsessions of petty selfish desires melt away. Your personality begins to speak volumes. People will come to you with their problems. Listen to them patiently, console them and solve their problems. They will never leave you. You need not go on bragging about your Guru like a parrot. Your own example is enough. Do not think of it as kindness to others, but a pious duty for the love of your Guru.

Devotee: Is it possible to transform our society in this manner?[33]

Sri Sri Thakur: Social transformation is possible only when there is individual transformation. They are indivisible like milk and butter. Unless you change, your effort to change society will be futile. Remember, it is most auspicious when everyone's welfare is maximised.

Devotee: How should I present the Ideal before others?[34]

Sri Sri Thakur: Never introduce the Ideal as God incarnate. People have funny and weird ideas about God. They find it difficult to digest the idea of a living man as God; rather you should put forth before them how I live, and how I want others to live. If you wish to take me upon your shoulder, and carry to the people, your character should be a towering example for them.

Sri Sri Thakur in Magnadicta for Ritwiks and Jajaks (preachers and propagators):

> Lo! Verily do I warn
> keep yourself always
> with righteousness
> keen, tactful and alert
> that you can cope with complexes
> with all their obsessions
> that hinder to impart
> the bliss of heaven
> and adjust the chaos
> into a cosmos
> with every sharpness in work and deed.   (Verse 206)

Devotee: But will they listen to me?[35]

Sri Sri Thakur: An ordinary man is guided by his complexes. He first thinks of his gain at the cost of others. In short, the present man is self-centred and shallow. However, happiness lies in expansion. Expansion of the mind comes when there is a fraternal feeling for others. So one has to be more Ideal-centred than self-centred. This message is to be spread most tactfully with perseverance and patience. You should not be argumentative, but rather sympathetic and appreciative of the problems of others.. They should find a genuine friend in you. The warmth in your speech and behaviour will result in such an intimacy that people begin to follow what you say out of their own interest, but do not impose any abrupt change even if it is beneficial for them. If you ask a person addicted to alcohol to leave it, he will not do so, but rather leave you. So, your persuasion should be tactful. You must first show to him in reality the benefit you have received in your life by following the Ideal: vox mundum expletori. Vox supreme del (the voice of the fulfiller of mankind is the voice of Supreme God. (Magnadicta 110)

Sri Sri Thakur in Magnadicta:
> Never attend anyone
> with an argumentative approach
> but tactful interesting talk
> with sympathetic hearing
> and due appreciation
> brings out blissful active support
> and embrace from the core of one's heart. (verse 217)

Devotee: How to approach a person of higher strata?[36]

Sri Sri Thakur: Strategy is most important in Jaajan. First, you have to study a person's mind. Don't get nervous, remember you are Ideal-centric, hence mentally superior to him. Do not approach anyone with lowliness. The need of every man, irrespective of his status, is the same, self-preservation and growth. So if he finds in your approach a clue to solve his problem, he will listen to you. But be careful not to irritate him with your speech or action.

Sri Sri Thakur in Magnadicta:
> Never be in clash

> with resourceful, intelligent and honourable
> but carry your purpose
> for the principle
> in so tactful and elating a manner
> that you may get
> good, friendly and active service
> which may bring
> self compliance to them and you. (Verse, 219)

Devotee: How to know that I am successful in my Jaajan?[37]

Sri Sri Thakur: You may convince someone, but he may not have developed the conviction to accept your Jaajan. Today he may be convinced, but tomorrow he will be overpowered with suspicion, and may avoid you. So first you must try to inculcate confidence in him, that the acceptance of the Ideal is for his own good. There is no room for hesitation or doubt to rise.

Devotee: How to behave with the obstinate and the unruly?[38]

Sri Sri Thakur: People who are highly egoistic and argumentative try to establish their superiority over others. When you meet such a person, the first rule is to overcome his perversion using tactics to win him over; otherwise your Jaajan will be declared meaningless and useless for him in nearby circles. So be careful. It is better to avoid them if necessary. That is why our scriptures prohibit spiritual discussion with obstinate persons.

Devotee: How to tackle people with demonic qualities?[39]

Sri Sri Thakur: If you talk to them about Lord Sri Krishna or the Ideal, they will move away from you. Better to tell them about their existence and growth, so that they become curious and listen to you. Sri Ramachandra adopted this method to bring demons under his control, and make them his staunch devotees.

Devotee: Even after a prolonged discussion, why does a man refuse to take initiation?[40]

Sri Sri Thakur: It means you have not touched the right chord. You have not been able to inspire his innate need for life. Your approach has been superficial. The tone of your Jaajan should be so gracious that the other person should feel 'yes, here is the clue for a better life.' He is motivated by a stern desire to live and grow in a fruitful manner by taking shelter in the Ideal. Do not forget that everything depends on your own sincerity to the Ideal. If you fail in Jaajan, introspect, and try to find out where the mistake lies.

Istavriti (Willing Oblation)
Devotee: What is Istavriti?[41]

Sri Sri Thakur: Istavriti is the expression of gratitude to the Ideal. The first material oblation to him in daily life, with the eagerness to feed him first from your daily income. It should be spontaneous and volitional. It is a devotional offering, which must be ardent and without any expectations. When you offer Istavriti, your ideal automatically appears in your inner vision; you accept his guidance with a sense of surrender. This practice, I believe, is the prime mover of existence.

Devotee: What do you mean by the prime mover of existence?[42]

Sri Sri Thakur: When you offer something materially every day to your Love-Lord, you experience joy, and there is a surge of energy in your being. An attitude to fulfil him is induced in you. It crystallises your personality in a constructive manner, and improves your surroundings for a better life. Thus you unite your being with the existence of others under the benevolent force of divine grace.

Devotee: How is it possible? Please explain.[43]

Sri Sri Thakur: Urge is the mother of evolution. However, an urge without action does not lead you anywhere. So when there is a deep urge, the motor-nerve system of your body puts you in action. Just see how deep is the urge of the mother to take care of her children, putting in several hours of labour every day for years together. Your offering of Istavriti in the face of all odds and difficulties of life immediately relates you to a higher consciousness. By the virtue of this consciousness, there is a spontaneous desire in you to rescue your neighbour from his difficulty. So Ideal is the Number One, you add yourself as a zero to that number, then go on adding zeros for the number of people you take care of. The value increases from one to ten, from ten to hundred, from hundred to a thousand, and so on. That is evolution.

Devotee: But is it not difficult to do it regularly every day?[44]

Sri Sri Thakur: If you do it with the same attitude as you have towards your daily food, then it is not difficult. Just start with it now, then plan on how to continue with it every day. Remember, the primary thing is not the amount of money, or the food you are offering, but the urge to love him and give to him. You cannot be happy without giving him, without feeding him. This urge makes you more able than before.

Narrator: In Hindu households, before people start their meal, they first offer food to the Lord, and only then eat it. In Christianity, it comes under offertory, and in Islam under zakat. The underlying principle in all religious disciplines is to sacrifice and give first to your Lord, and then to the needy to elevate your being.

In the Bhagavad Gita (3/12), Lord Krishna condemns those who enjoy things without offering them to the Lord, He calls them thieves, and enjoins (3/26): 'If one offers Me with love and devotion, only a leaf, a flower, a fruit or water, I will accept it delightfully.'

Similarly, in the Bible, it is said: 'He that sacrificeth unto any god, save unto the Lord only, he shall be utterly destroyed.' (Exodus: 22:20, King James Version)

Sri Sri Dada observed (Ritwik Conference 14-7-2019): 'Whoever takes initiation has to perform Jajan, Jaajan, and Istavriti regularly. While initiating others if you advise them to do it, but do not do so yourself, it is sheer deceit. When we bluff, we cannot be Thakur's men. My father (Sri Sri Borda) often used to say:

'You are for the Lord
Not for others'
You are for the Lord

And so for others.'

I love Thakur, he is everything to me. I must follow him to come up to his expectations. This should be the criterion of living for all of us.

Devotee: Does Istavriti help us in our bad times?[45]

Sri Sri Thakur: Istavriti has tremendous power. It makes your mind dynamic to visualise the obstacles ahead and surmount them. You get ready beforehand, and face them courageously. More courage, less fear.

Sri Sri Thakur continues, 'Nobody can understand my anxiety and concern for all of you. Turmoil pervades my mind. I want all of you to be healthy, without problems, and enjoy a long life. If you rely on me and follow my instructions, you will be saved a lot of calamities. But you do not do that, your whims and fancies take over. Even in that case, the practices of Jajan, Jaajan, and Istavriti will save you from a lot of distress.

Devotee: What are the other benefits of Istavriti?[46]

Sri Sri Thakur: Modern man is addicted to money. Money creates mischief when not handled properly. Money should be used for the welfare of the public. Only then it can be called divine spending. Greed often makes us miserly, and kills our desire to give: it is dangerous for the growth of society. When the first act of the day starts by your 'offering' to him, the attitude of giving grows within you without your knowledge. You do not refrain from sharing a portion of your wealth for the common good. That is why it is termed in Sanskrit as Samarpana yoga (ability to surrender).

Devotee: Is there any fixed amount of 'offering' for Istavriti?[47]

Sri Sri Thakur: No. As I said, money, or material oblations are not as important as your ardour to offer to your Love-Lord. However, it should be equivalent to the normal meal of a person.

Devotee: What if the offering is mechanical?[48]

Sri Sri Thakur: Once you start with Istavriti, even if it is mechanical in the beginning, the commitment soon follows;

continue the practice without a break. Istavriti is complete only when it reaches the Ideal.

Devotee: Can Istavriti be done by borrowing money?⁴⁹

Sri Sri Thakur: No, it must be from your own earnings. However, when there is a crisis like a natural calamity, war, or any other disaster that makes you an absolute pauper, a handful of water, sand, soil, a flower or a leaf—anything available, can be offered, But this exception is reserved only in extreme cases. If you are otherwise a spendthrift, but austere about Istavriti, it is a deception of the highest order, pure and simple.

Devotee: In some quarters, our system of Istavriti is ridiculed. What to do?⁵⁰

Sri Sri Thakur: I eat, I sleep, I ease, because they make me exist. In the same way, Istavriti makes your existence better. Have you ever come across a good-doer getting his due of appreciation? No, people always try to pull him down. So do not pay any heed to them; move ahead on the path of your Ideal, come what may.

Narrator: Sri Sri Thakur has advised to offer Istavriti before sunrise. After accumulating it for 30 days, the total amount should be handed over towards the care of the Ideal by depositing it in Satsang centres, or directly into the account of the Ashram via banking channels. As this amount is sacrosanct, it should not be used for any other purpose.

Devotee: The Hindus observe a period of abstention on the eve of a death or birth in their family. Can Istavriti be offered during this period?⁵¹

Sri Sri Thakur: It is better to offer it through somebody else, or it can be offered all together when the stipulated period of abstention is over.

Narrator: On 20 July 1946, Sri Sri Thakur told Kestoda (Krishna Prasanna): I dreamt about Istavriti. Let me narrate it to you, Istavriti is the concentration of materialised ability known as Saamarthi Yoga. Unless Istavriti is included in spiritual discipline,

Siddhi won't come. I got this new idea in a dream. Dreams at times convey some very vital truths. Spiritual practice should be entwined with willing oblation for the proper functioning of the motor-sensory nervous system. (Dinapanji, vol. I, and Istabhruti)

Swastyayani

Devotee: What is Swastyayani?[52]

Sri Sri Thakur: Swastyayani is a Sanskrit word meaning the method to stay well. It is a very powerful vow. If you follow it sincerely, it bestows many benefits. Swastyayani improves a man's character, habits, his behaviour and also his will power. It integrates your personality, and streamlines your knowledge.

The five principles of Swastyayani:

Consider your body to be an instrument to serve your Beloved Ideal. You shall proceed with the strictest observance of all the underlying principles for the well-being and stability of yourself, so that it may continue towards progress intact and with perfect endurance in every phase of calamity.

You shall have to manipulate and regulate your desires and necessities for a congenial fulfilment of your Ideal.

Simultaneously, with an urge of intelligent reasoning, you shall try to carefully activate into tangible reality whatever occurs to you to be the best.

You must be ever ready to elevate the being and becoming of your environment in all possible ways, considering it to be the interest of your own life.

By pursuing these, and by increasing your dexterity and diligence, you shall have to offer to your Ideal, as decently as possible, before taking your daily meals, 'bhojyas' or eatables sufficient for two meals, or in lieu of that, an equivalent amount of money or more or articles in exchange of which such amount may be obtained. Preserve them every day with care, and on the expiry of 30 days, you should remit an amount of rupees three for the maintenance of your Ideal from that accumulated fund. Before taking anything for yourself, keep the rest in your custody and preserve it in such a way that it may not be wasted under any circumstances. Only one-tenth of the annual accumulation of the preserved oblations for the Ideal may be utilised in case of absolute necessity but beware of its misuse. The accumulated amount can be used as capital for expansion of your industry, trade or any other profit-earning activity, but be careful as a businessman does not touch his capital even during loss. Similarly, the Swastyayani capital should be preserved, even under adverse circumstances. That is how you build your character by adhering to the principles enunciated by the Ideal. Your steadfastness becomes an example for others. The surroundings are inspired by looking at you, and will come to you on their own will. Swastyayani makes you an able and honest entrepreneur, a dynamic industrialist, and a reliable businessman.

You have to introspect whether you are following the five principles of Swastyayani properly in your daily life? If you persist with this principle with acute tenacity, you will see sufferings, disasters, penury and planetary evils declining gradually.

Narrator: Sri Sri Dada observed (Ritwik Conference 12-7-2015): the moment we take the pledge of Swastyayani, we undertake the responsibility of life and growth of our environment. If the environment does not flourish, individual goodness withers. Hence it should be our endeavour to spread the principles of Swastyayani along with initiation to as many people as possible.

Sadachar (Healthy living)

Devotee: What is Sadachar (healthy living)?[53]

Sri Sri Thakur: Following the do's and don'ts for physical and mental health is the basis of Sadachar. Stay clean, stay well. Two streams flow; the first is your immune system, i.e., to recognize and accept whatever is conducive for living, and reject what depreciates it, and the other is to avoid disease and, if affected, go for proper cure. Remember, prevention is better than cure. However, one should not be too much physique-conscious. Normal clean living is enough. When our thoughts and way of living become wayward, they pervert the mind. Mental perversion creates a distortion in our brain cells, leading to illness. Take care of your mind. Make it calm, make it creative by your attachment to the Ideal. You will avoid mental and physical problems to a great extent.

Devotee: How to develop a healthy mind?[54]

Sri Sri Thakur: First of all, regulate your breath. Regulated breathing cools the mind, helps longevity. Be conscious of your breathing by repeating the Name internally; concentrating on the Ideal, you develop a healthy mind.

Devotee: What should be our way of living?[55]

Sri Sri Thakur: Choose a place and climate suitable for yourself. Some people like a tropical climate, while others enjoy a cold climate. Decide your place of stay accordingly. Get up before sunrise, wash your face and splash some cold water on your eyes. It improves eyesight. Stare at greenery in a far distance, or simply gaze at the horizon. It enhances the area of your vision. Likewise, try to hear distant sounds, it alerts your ears and prevents deafness. Do not strain your physical capacity while working. Follow the principles of hygiene.

Devotee: What are the principles of hygiene?[56]

Sri Sri Thakur: Avoid using other's beds, pillows, towels, and clothes. Your hair, beard, and nails should be clean. Don't put your hand in your mouth or nose frequently. Your footwear should be washed or polished before you start out. Keep your lavatory clean. A lavatory used by many carries infection. Do not urinate here and there. Better sit down to pass urine and wash after that. Take a good oil massage before bath. Choose the water you like—tepid or cold.

Devotee: How does infection enter our body?[57]

Sri Sri Thakur: It enters by two ways; personal contact and polluted atmosphere. Maintain physical distance from those whose habits are unclean. A clean body is more prone to contagion than a relatively unclean one. So be careful. Do not invite disease by maintaining close contact just to please anyone. The most important is, of course, your food.

Devotee: Why is food so important, Sir?[58]

Sri Sri Thakur: Whatever you eat, the essence of it influences your body cells. You will act according to the impulses they produce. Animals and birds take only that food congenial to their digestive systems. Eat food that is easy to digest, and does not strain the system; health is important and taste is secondary. Don't go by commercial advertisements of so-called health boosters. Unless you digest food properly, it will not nourish your system and may cause gastroenteritis in the long run.

Devotee: It is understood that non-vegetarian food contains more protein than its vegetarian counterpart. What do you have to say about this, Sir?[59]

Sri Sri Thakur: Maybe, but non-vegetarian food like meat, fish, eggs, etc., create abnormal heat and excitement in our nerves and genital organs. Similar is the effect of onion and garlic. All of them cause abnormal sexual obsession. There is another aspect to it; when a bird or animal is butchered, the sudden encounter with death spurts unbearable horror that electrifies poison in all the body cells of the dying creature. When we eat the dead flesh, the fear phobia is transmitted in a subtle manner through our system. It makes us susceptible to anger and anxiety, depresses our mind and reduces our longevity. When protein is available in harmless vegetarian food, why should we opt for a harmful non-vegetarian diet merely for a little more protein. Even when you take a non-vegetarian diet, don't have it quite often, and use antidotes like curd, etc., to nullify the poison.

Devotee: Nowadays, people, particularly the younger generation, prefer non-veg food and alcohol. What to do?[60]

Sri Sri Thakur: This may be one of the many causes behind the rise of diabetes, blood pressure, nervous breakdown and suicides. Our ancestors divided food into three categories: wholesome ideal diet (sattvik) that purifies one's existence and gives strength, health and satisfaction; a passion-inducing regal diet (rajasik) that is bitter, salty, hot, and pungent. This diet creates distress, misery, and disease in the long run, and finally, stale and decomposed diet (tamasik), a diet that is anti-life hence compared with darkness.

Devotee: Which food should we consider wholesome?[61]

Sri Sri Thakur: I prefer Habisanna as it is very wholesome— rice, boiled cereal, sesame paste, raw banana, ghee, milk and plantains. This combination fulfils all deficiencies. Seasonal fruits should also be consumed. In my view, if man labours hard, repeats the Holy Name and is mentally peaceful, rice and dal alone can provide enough nourishment.

Devotee: What is your personal experience in this regard, Sir?[62]

Sri Sri Thakur: I ate fish; it created an unhealthy excitement in my brain and distracted my mind. Rice, dal, fruits and vegetables, milk, curd, and ghee are the best for harmless nourishment. In my opinion, food should be simple and easily digestible, there is no need to make a big paraphernalia out of it.

Narrator: In 18th-century France, people indulged in luxurious food. Montesquieu, the French philosopher, remarked satirically:

'Lunch kills half of Paris,

Supper the other half.'

The Devotee: Beef-eating is on the rise. What do you have to say on this?[63]

Sri Sri Thakur: It is odious. Hazrat Rasul never recommended eating beef; rather he has said the blood and flesh of animals can never be accepted by God, and beef is harmful to human health.

Devotee: What are the other important aspects of food?[64]

Sri Sri Thakur: Keep the kitchen and the utensils neat and clean. The nature and temperament of the cook is also important. It is subtly transmitted into the food they prepare. The dress of the cook should be fresh, he should use a mask when cooking. People who serve food should also follow hygiene and cleanliness.

In India, domestic cooks are generally Brahmins, but being a Brahmin is not enough unless they maintain good hygiene.

Devotee: What about taking food in hotels and restaurants?[65]

Sri Sri Thakur: I do not approve of it. However, wherever you take your food, the place of preparation, persons preparing and serving the food, the place of eating should be spick and span. In my opinion, food is best when self cooked.

Devotee: In Odisha, people generally take water-soaked rice. Is it good?[66]

Sri Sri Thakur: Yes. It contains a good amount of vitamin B and is very nutritious for health. The rice is to be kept in an earthen pot with one centimetre of water above it, and it should be covered with a thin cloth and kept overnight or at least 8-9 hours for fermentation.

Narrator: AIIMS Bhubaneswar conducted research on the efficacy of water-soaked rice and found that it increases immunity, cleans the lungs, helps digestion and cures malnutrition. It is very helpful for pregnant ladies. Courtesy Hemanta Pradhan (YouTube)

Devotee: What is your opinion about collective dining?[67]

Sri Sri Thakur: Better avoided. Even when you join, maintain a sufficient distance from one another so that the cough, sneezes, exhaled air, and sputum of the man beside you do not affect you.

Devotee: What about members of the family taking food together?[68]

Sri Sri Thakur: It's good. It brings harmony among the members. It is also wise that the same quality of food is shared with the domestic help.

Devotee: Man becomes old, and age makes him lonely and constricted. What to do about it, Sir?[69]

Sri Sri Thakur: Negate age. If you think you are old, you are old. Let age go on its own way, why should you bother about it? Always feel young and energetic. Keep yourself busy with constructive work. Old age is not a curse, it makes you wiser due to more experience over time.

Devotee: How to stop ageing?[70]

Sri Sri Thakur: After reaching a certain age, we feel we are not as capable as before, and do not nurture the nerves of the genetic system. We feel they are no longer necessary and useful. This brings about morbidity. You can retain youthfulness if you are conscious of making your genetic system active and strong.

Devotee: Why are we affected by disease?[71]

Sri Sri Thakur: Worry and anxiety are the source, supported by adverse circumstances. Disease starts from the mind and percolates to the body. Besides, some diseases are hereditary, and arise out of inherent deficiencies in birth. The hereditary diseases can be controlled by self-discipline and timely intake of proper medicine. Contagious diseases can be avoided by taking proper precautions, like keeping a distance from the affected person, avoiding used clothes, beds and utensils of the patient.

Narrator: The European philosopher, Spinoza (1632-1677), mentioned: 'Mind and body always work together because what occurs in them is a parallel set of events. Everything that happens in one is linked to something that happens in the other. Consciousness itself is the idea of the body. Emotions are the bodily equivalent of mental ideas. (Understanding Philosophy

Devotee: Sir, tell me in a nutshell how to become an achiever in life?[72]

Sri Sri Thakur: Take the habit of a creeper, entwine yourself around the tree of the Ideal. Exalt everyone with his tidings of life and growth, in word and deed. Always bring something for Him when you come to see Him. Whatever you do or wherever you go, repeat His Holy Name. Surely, surely I tell you, you will achieve anything you want for your good, as well as for the good of others.

Bibliography

English
(From Satsang Publishing House, Satsang, Deoghar, Jharkhand)
Satyanusaran
Magnadicta
The Message (Vol. I - IX)
Discourses on the Ideal - Kerry Brace
Integral Philosophy of Life - Prafulla Kumar Das
Sri Sri Thakur Anukulchandra & Satsang - Krishna Prasanna Bhattacharyya (author & publisher)
Ocean in A Teacup -R A Hauserman, Harper & Brothers, New York, USA
Being and Becoming -R A Hauserman, Satsang Church, Virginia Beach, Virginia, USA
Answer to the Quest -R A Hauserman, Bharatiya Vidya Bhawan, Chowpatty, Bombay
A Pilgrimage to Memory - Prafulla Kumar Das (author & publisher)
Prophets and Prophecies- Justice Prafulla Kumar Banerjee(author & publisher), Patna
Reaching the Peak - N P Tripathy, Nabalipi Prakash Dhaara, Bhubaneswar
Thakur Anukulchandra - Manilal Chakravarty(author & publisher)
Man, God and the Universe - I. K.Taimni, Quest Books, Theosophical Publishing House, Adyar
Rumi Quotes -Delhi Open Books, New Delhi
The Spirit of Indian Culture – Dr Vivek Bhattacharya, Metropolitan Co. Pvt Ltd, Netaji Subhash Chandra Marg, New Delhi.
The Tantric Way - Ajit Mukherjee and Madhu Khanna, New York Graphic Society Books, Little Brown Company, USA
Tao Te Ching- Lao Tzu, Dover Publication, Mineola, New York, USA
The Tao of Physics – Fritjof Capra, Bantam Books, New York
The Tibetan Book of the Undivided Universe - David Bohm, Shunyata Press

Gems from the Gospel of Sri Ramakrishna - Sri Ramakrishna Math, Mylapore, Chennai
Tales and Parables of Sri Ramakrishna - Sri Ramakrishna Math, Mylapore, Chennai
Life After Death - Swami Vivekananda, Sri Ramakrishna Math, Mylapore, Chennai
Upanishad in Daily Life - Sri Ramakrishna Math, Mylapore, Chennai
Hindu Scriptures - R. C. Zaehner, Rupa & Co., Calcutta-New Delhi
Wine of the Mystic - The Rubaiyat - Omar Khayyam, Sri Sri Paramahansa Yogananda - Macmillan India Ltd, Daryaganj, New Delhi
The Imitation of Christ - Thomas A Kempis, Penguin Books Ltd.,England
Living Thoughts of Great People - Eknath Easwaran, Jaico Publishing House, Bombay
Stories from Yoga Vasistha – Swami Sivananda, Sivananda Ashram, Rishikesh
Cosmic Cradle – Elizabeth M Carman & Neil J. Carman, Sunstar Publishing Ltd, USA
Understanding Philosophy – J K Feibleman, Jaico Publishing House, Bombay
The Brothers Karamazov - Fyodor DostoyevsKY, Rupa Publications, Daryaganj, New Delhi
Khalil Gibran Reader - Jaico Books, Bombay
Islamic Mysticism In India – Narendra Kr Singh, ATH Publishing Corporation, Ansari Road, Daryaganj, New Delhi
The English Teacher - R K Narayan, Indian Thought Publication, Chennai
The Intelligence of the Cosmos - Ervin Laszlo, Inner Traditions Bear & Company, Rochester, USA
From Sex to Superconsciousness - Osho, Osho Media International Pune, India
Stories Told by The Mother -Sri Aurobindo Ashram, Pondicherry
How to Win Friends and Influence People -Dale Carnegie, Pigeon Books, New Delhi

Americans who have been reincarnated - H N Banerjee, Macmillan Publishing Co., INC, New York

Socio-religious Reform Movements in British India -Kenneth W. Jones

Bengali

(From Satsang Publishing House, Satsang, Deoghar, Jharkhand)
Punya Punthi
Alochana Prasange - compiled by Prafulla Kumar Das
Chalar Sathi - (compiled by) Krishna Prasanna Bhattacharyya
Nana Prasange -(compiled by) Krishna Prasanna Bhattacharyya
Amiyavani -Aswini Kumar Biswas
Satwat Katha - Satsang Publication
Ishtamanane - Satsang Publication
Atmajaner Katha -Satsang Publication
Sri Sri Thakur Anukulchandra 1- Satish Chandra Joardar, Satsang Publishing House
Sri Sri Thakur Anukulchandra 2 - Braja Gopal Duttaroy
Manastirtha Parikrama - Sushil Chandra Bose (author and publisher)
Dinapanji - Krishna Prasanna Bhattacharyya(author and publisher)
Smriti-Tirthe -Prafulla Kumar Das(author and publisher)
Mahamanaber Sagar Teere - Kumarkrishna Bhattacharyya(author and publisher)
Amar Jibane Sri Sri Thakur - Panchanan Sarkar (author and publisher)
Jivandyuti - Dr. Rebati Mohan Biswas, Alpha Publishing House, Deoghar
Taanr Katha - Guru Prasanna Bhattacharyya(author and pub
Sri Sri Thakur Anukulchandra O Bideshi Brinda - Phanibhusan Roy & Sikha Roy(author and publisher)
Bhakta Valaya - Phanibhusan Roy & Sikha Roy (author and publisher)
Katakatha Manepare, Smritir Mala - Manilal Chakravarty(author and publisher)

Punya Prabahe - Richinandan Chakravarty(author and publisher)
Purushottam Prasanga - Sailendra Nath Bhattacharyya(author and publisher)
Diprakshi, Priya Param, Navabeda Vidhata - Debi Prasad Mukherjee(author and publisher)
Premer Thakur - Amulya Ratan Ray(author and publisher)
Premal Thakur - Pralay Majumder(author and publisher)

Hindi

Purushottam - Jagdish Narayan(Satsang Publishing House, Satsang, Deoghar, Jharkhand)

Odia

Sree Gita Govindam - Jayadeva , Sri Srimad Bhaktivedanta Narayana Gosvami Maharaja
Pranar Thakur - Nakul Charan Das(author and publisher)
Amruta Kahani -Bikash Ranjan Bhowmick(author and publisher)
Param Uddhata Sri Sri Thakur Anukulchandra -Saroj Kumar Mohanty(author and publisher)
Istavruti - Hrushikesh Acharya(author and publisher)
Manabbadi Santha Bhimabhoi - Dr Sadananda Agrawal
Mahakabi Bhartruhari Shatakam - Dr Braja Sundar Mishra

BLACK EAGLE BOOKS

www.blackeaglebooks.org
info@blackeaglebooks.org

Black Eagle Books, an independent publisher, was founded as a nonprofit organization in April, 2019. It is our mission to connect and engage the Indian diaspora and the world at large with the best of works of world literature published on a collaborative platform, with special emphasis on foregrounding Contemporary Classics and New Writing.